GOD, SCIENCE & THE SECRET DOCTRINE

The Zero Point Metaphysics
and Holographic Space
of H. P. Blavatsky

Christopher P. Holmes

ZERO POINT
Institute for Mystical and Spiritual Science
Box 700, 108 Clothier Street East,
Kemptville, Ontario, Canada K0G 1J0
zeropoint@bell.net
(613) 258-6258
Visit: www.zeropoint.ca

God, Science & The Secret Doctrine

The Zero Point Metaphysics and
Holographic Space of H.P. Blavatsky

©2010 by Zero Point Publications
All rights reserved. No part of this publication may be reproduced in any form without permission from the author. However, the reader is free to quote shorter passages in criticism, reviews or other writings. Inquiries are welcome.

Cover Illustration: *Interference*, Neel Shearer, 2001
Book Design & Layout: Groundhog Computing Services, groundhogcs@cogeco.ca
Original artwork and illustrations by Anita J. Mitra, Ontario, Canada and Zeljka Zupanic, Croatia, zeljka@zviz.net.
Set in Arno Pro with titles in Berkeley Retrospective SSi.

ISBN 978-0-9689435-6-4

"Deity ... is in every point of the Universe." (S.D.I, p. 114)

Dedicated to the Holy World Star Helena P. Blavatsky

ENQUIRER. Do you believe in God?

THEOSOPHIST. That depends what you mean by the term.

ENQUIRER. I mean the God of the Christians, the Father of Jesus, and the Creator: the Biblical God of Moses, in short.

THEOSOPHIST. In such a God we do not believe. We reject the idea of a personal, or an extra-cosmic and anthropomorphic God, who is but the gigantic shadow of man, and not of man at his best, either. The God of theology, we say -- and prove it -- is a bundle of contradictions and a logical impossibility. Therefore, we will have nothing to do with him. (Blavatsky, The Key to Theosophy, p. 61)

The Secret Doctrine ... admits a Logos or a collective "Creator" of the Universe; a Demi-urgos—in the sense implied when one speaks of an "Architect" as the "Creator" of an edifice, whereas that Architect has never touched one stone of it, but, while furnishing the plan, left all the manual labour to the masons; in our case the plan was furnished by the Ideation of the Universe, and the constructive labour was left to the Hosts of intelligent Powers and Forces. But that Demiurgos is no personal deity,—i.e., an imperfect extra-cosmic god,—but only the aggregate of the Dhyan-Chohans and the other forces. (Blavatsky, The Secret Doctrine, I, pp. 279-80)

TABLE OF CONTENTS

Foreword by Donna Brown
Preface

I
The Secret Doctrine, H.P. Blavatsky & The Stanzas of Dzyan

1. H. P. Blavatsky & The Secret Doctrine 2
2. Cosmic Evolution & The Seven Stanzas of Dzyan 10

II
Ancient Wisdom & Modern Science

1. The Problem of God's Contracting Universe: As posed by Dr Carl Sagan, Paul Davies & Stephen Hawking 16
2. The Accidental and Random Universe & Evolution 26
3. The Quasi-Religious Dimensions of Modern Physics 33
4. God as Mathematician, Geometrician and Designer 38

III
The Cosmogenesis & Metaphysics of The Secret Doctrine

1. ONE ABSOLUTE REALITY: The Fundamental Dogma of Occultism 44
2. Before all Time
   a. The Stanzas of Dzyan: 46
   b. The Days and Nights of Brahma 49
3. Primordial Principles
   a. The Absolute & the Theological Trinity 52
   b. The Seven-Skinned Eternal Parent Space 54
   c. The Ceaseless Breath & Seven Luminous Lords—the Dhyan Chohans 57
   d. Dualities of Creation 59
   e. Expanding and Contracting: Within-Without from the Heart 62
   f. Seven Primary and Secondary Creations 62
4. Light: "The Great Protean Magician"
   a. From the Stanzas of Dzyan 66
   b. Darkness Radiates Light 69

	c. The Physics & Metaphysics of Light	70
5.	The Six Pointed Star & the Seventh Central Point	74
6.	FOHAT: Cosmic Electricity & the Seven Messengers of Will	79
7.	Zero Point Dynamics & Metaphysics	
	a. Laya Centres: Zero Point Origins and Ends	84
	b. Zero Point Foundations	87
	c. Cosmic Differentiation	91
	d. Seven Laya Centres: Zero Point foundations for the Laws of Nature	96
	e. From SEVEN HOLY CIRCUMGYRATING BREATHS to Whirlwinds, & Fohat's Circular Errands	99
8.	The Invisible Sun, the Solar Logos & the Ethers of Space	
	a. The Visible & Invisible Sun	104
	b. The Sevenfold Logos, Seven Rays & Seven Rounds	107
9.	Issues of Science	
	a. On Magnetism, Gravity & Solar Origins	110
	b. The Existence & Non-Existence of Gravity	113
	c. The Permanency and Impermanency of Matter and Atoms	115
	d. The Akasa and Ethers	116
10.	Blavatsky's Holographic Space	120
11.	*The Secret Doctrine* & Modern Science	123

I V
The Cosmogenesis & Physics of Modern Science

1.	Creation *Ex Nihilo* & Vacuum Genesis: On Being and Nothingness, the Plenum and Void	131
2.	The Mysteries of Cosmic Origins and Ends	
	a. Everything Adds up to Nothing	136
	b. The Singularity, which Can and Cannot Happen	138
	c. Stephen Hawking & the Badly Behaved Points	140
	d. A Big Bang Happens	142
	e. The First Three Minutes & the Farcical Chain of Accidents	147
	f. The Fate of the Universe & the Search for Dark Matter and Dark Energy	153
	g. The Multiverse, Hyperspace & the Big Foam	162
3.	Zero Point Fields	167
4.	The Mysteries of Matter	
	a. Unifying the Laws of Nature into one God-like Superforce	172
	b. Sculpting the Void: Seven Hidden Compacted Dimensions in Hyperspace	176
	c. Superstrings & M-Theory as Ultimate Solutions	181

5. *"The Baffling Holism"*: Quantum Interconnectedness & Non-Local Reality
   a. The Deterministic Paradigm of Physics 186
   b. The E. P. R. Paradox 187
   c. The Belief in Local Effects 189
   d. Bell's Inequality & Non-Local Effects 190
6. David Bohm on Wholeness & the Implicate Orders
   a. The Basic Paradigm 197
   b. On Relativity & Quantum Theory 198
   c. Active Information, the Quantum Potential & Deep Reality 201
   d. Analogies: From Holographs to Atomic Memory 206
   e. The Fullness of Emptiness 208
   f. The Fundamental Holomovement 210
7. The Universe as a Hologram
   a. Information as Third Force 212
   b. A Tale of Entropies and Black Holes 213
   c. On Black Holes & Alternate Space Dimensions 217
   d. The Illusion of Gravity 219
8. The Akashic Field & Laszlo's *Integral Theory of Everything* 223

V
Pilgrimage of the Monads

1. Monads 228
2. From the Stanzas of Dzyan 233
3. Evolution & Human Nature 237
4. The Head Dogma and the Heart Doctrine 242

VI
The Zero Point Metaphysics & Holographic Space of *The Secret Doctrine*

1. The Basic Holographic Paradigm 252
2. Gods, Monads & Atoms 254
3. Spinergy and G-Force 260
4. The Physics of Anti-de Sitter Spacetime, the Law of Karma & the Dissolution of the Kosmos 266
5. The Holographic Mind/Brain in a Holographic Universe 269
6. Monads in Hyperspace 279
7. Zero Point Origins of Consciousness 287

Table of Contents

V I I
The Secret Doctrine: A Final Word

1. Intelligent Design: Deity in every Point 292
2. 1/137: Nature's Magical Constant
    a. David Peat on Synchronicity and the Plenum 302
    b. Enigmas of the Alpha Constant 306
    c. And so, How many Fundamental Forces? 310
3. A Final Word 312

Appendix I: THE STANZAS OF DZYAN

About the Author

Bibliography

Forward by Donna Brown

In 1888, Helena Blavatsky published her masterwork—*The Secret Doctrine*—on the genesis of the cosmos and the creation and evolution of humankind. It provided a radical paradigm for cosmic, planetary and human evolution that not only dwarfed past and popular scientific theory, but anticipated many of its most current and striking developments.

One of its aims was to contest and counter the mechanistic materialistic worldview of the seventeenth and eighteenth centuries. Blavatsky intended to show that Nature was not "a fortuitous concurrences of atoms" or the result of an accidental or random process, but evolved as a result of an intelligent and profoundly meaningful design. She encouraged a dialogue between esotericists and scientists, and advocated for "the Secret Teachings to be contrasted with the speculations of modern science." Blavatsky understood that it was only by "placing occult teachings side by side" with scientific theory that the origins and ultimate fate of the Kosmos could be revealed.

Over 100 years have passed since Blavatsky issued this call. "While a few scientists and authors are beginning to explore the connection between these wisdom teachings and modern developments in science," they have, as mystic scientist Dr. Christopher Holmes points out, "only begun to scratch the surface!" Blavatsky's great treasure is still relatively unknown even today. Its abstruseness and the fact that most scientists disapprove of mixing so called hard science and mathematics with occult and mystical thought have relegated its astonishing mysteries to the realm of religious speculation and the pseudo-scientific.

Holmes, however, has no such objections and has given himself over to Blavatsky's challenge entirely. He seems uniquely placed to relate ancient mystical knowledge to the newest ideas in physics and science. His background includes a doctorate in clinical and forensic psychology and an in-depth understanding of current scientific theory. Over thirty years of study and research have provided him with a wealth of knowledge and insight into the teachings of Helena Blavatsky, the Kabbalah, Judaism, Gurdjieff, and a wide-range of esoteric doctrine.

Holmes begins by relating how the strange and seemingly incomprehensible *Stanzas of Dzyan*—which serve as the basis of *The Secret Doctrine*—anticipated the newest concepts of Cosmological Physics and can be understood as representing "a profoundly alternative interpretation of the facts and theories of science itself." He offers a penetrating look at the cosmogenesis and metaphysics of The Secret Doctrine that is sure to interest all those who have tried to decipher its hidden mysteries.

One of the foundational themes inspiring Holmes' work is the concept of zero point—a source point or singularity—that, as Holmes points out, Blavatsky articulated a century before it came into common usage. She described these dimensionless points as "material points without extension...'the material out of which the Gods' and other invisible powers clothe themselves in bodies" and the single point (or laya point) in which the entire universe concentrates itself.

The author expounds upon this concept at length, noting that the zero point is "not exactly a thing in itself—so much as a condition, or a place at which certain processes occur." He goes on to give a fascinating account of how "the zero point hypotheses can be applied to the study of the macrocosm, the Universe or Kosmos, to quanta or elements, and to the study of the microcosm—the inner world of human consciousness and Self-existence." "Just as science conceives that the huge universe grew from an infinitesimal singularity out of a quantum vacuum, so also," as Holmes suggests, we "have such a hidden zero point or singularity source condition—a singular I within the Heart."

Drawing upon a wealth of scientific papers, books, and diagrams, Holmes explores accepted and cutting edge theories in science including those of Einstein, Steven Hawkings, and David Bohm, to name a few. The General Theory of Relativity, Quantum Theory, Bell's Theorem, the concept of Holism, and numerous other theories such as Superstring and M-Theory are explained in a concise and clear fashion. These same concepts are then aligned or contrasted with the Secret Teachings to reveal a supremely valid portrait of how the Universe works and was created. We learn from Holmes how Blavatsky's notion of the Seven-Skinned Eternal Parent can be linked with "what science now describes as seven dimensional hyperspace and with the newer M-theory and the Calabi Yau spaces that exist at every point underlying the four dimensional complex." And that Blavatsky's view of Space—a living Unity or plenum—can be linked to Bohm's view of space "as the container of the implicate and superimplicate orders."

While portions of this book are not easy going, Holmes plunges the reader into the deep places of the occult and the new frontiers of science to come up with a lucid and provocative book. It unseals many of the Secret Doctrines mysteries as it weaves the seeming opposites of spirit and science into a new synthesis. It is a must read for those wishing to understand the complex and seemingly impenetrable world of Helena Blavatsky alongside the newest ideas of quantum theory. Holmes has created something of his own tour de force in *God, Science and the Secret Doctrine*. His book is destined to serve as a guidebook for all those that follow.

Donna Brown
The Esoteric Quarterly, Spring 2009
www.esotericstudies.net/quarterly

Preface

H. P. Blavatsky's *The Secret Doctrine* was published in 1888 and is relatively unknown in modern times. As it happens in this strange universe, Blavatsky anticipated numerous modern concepts and theories in physics concerning the creation of the Universe, the mechanisms of the laws of nature and the holographic paradigm in the areas of physics and the psychology of consciousness. Her writing foreshadowed the enigmas faced within modern quantum physics and cosmology, especially as pertain to the 'uncertainty principle' and the 'baffling holism' of quantum theory, as well as current enigmas concerning the nature of Space, zero point fields and the quantum ether. Most importantly, Blavatsky articulated the concept of the zero point or singularity origin of the Cosmos and a profound alternative view of the root principles of creation–the nature of the Aether and higher Space dimensions—the Void and the Divine Plenum.

Blavatsky states: "... 'material points without extension'... are... the materials out of which the 'Gods' and other invisible powers clothe themselves in bodies...." I have attempted to grasp the profound meanings of this claim and relate this ancient mystical teaching to the newest ideas in physics and science, and to explorations of human consciousness. The zero point hypotheses can be applied to the study of the macrocosm, the Universe or Kosmos, to material quanta or elements, and to the study of the microcosm—the inner world of human consciousness and Self-existence.

I sincerely hope that this work helps others to penetrate the *secret doctrines* explored by H. P. Blavatsky—a Holy World Star, if ever there was one. Blavatsky's archaic metaphysics and divine wisdom teaching articulated over a century ago provide astonishing insights into the enigmas and theories of modern physics, cosmology and consciousness studies. *"The Secret Doctrine"* actually provides a complex model of 'Intelligent Design' through *"divine microintervention"* involving the dynamics of zero point centres in holographic Space.

Christopher P. Holmes Ph.D. (Psych)
Kemptville, Ontario, Canada, 2010

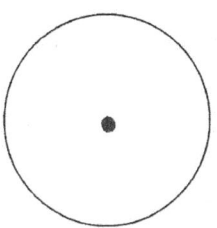

On Zero Point Dynamics
H. P. Blavatsky, *The Secret Doctrine*, 1888

An Archaic Manuscript ... is before the writer's eye. On the first page is an immaculate white disk within a dull black ground. On the following page, the same disk, but with a central point. The first ... Kosmos in Eternity, before the re-awakening of still slumbering Energy, the emanation of the Word ... The point in the hitherto immaculate Disk, Space and Eternity in Pralaya, denotes the dawn of differentiation. It is the Point in the Mundane Egg, the germ within the latter which will become the Universe, the ALL, the boundless, periodical Kosmos, this germ being latent and active, periodically by turns. The one circle is divine Unity, from which all proceeds, whither all returns. (*S. D. I.*, p. 1)

... "material points without extension" are Leibnitz's monads, and at the same time the materials out of which the 'Gods' and other invisible powers clothe themselves in bodies .... the entire universe concentrating itself, as it were, in a single point. (p. 489)

... all the so-called Forces of Nature, Electricity, Magnetism, Light, Heat, etc., etc., far from being modes of motion of material particles, are *in esse*, i.e., in their ultimate constitution, the differentiated aspects of that Universal Motion. ... When Fohat is said to produce "Seven Laya Centres," it means that for formative or creative purposes, the GREAT LAW (Theists may call it God) stops, or rather modifies its perpetual motion on seven invisible points within the area of the manifested Universe. *"The great Breath digs through Space seven holes into Laya to cause them to circumgyrate during Manvantara."* (Occult Catechism). We have said that Laya is what Science may call the Zero-point or line; the realm of absolute negativeness, or the one real absolute Force ... the neutral axis, not one of the many aspects, but its centre. ... "Seven Neutral Centres" then are produced by Fohat .... (pp. 147-8)

I
The Secret Doctrine, H. P. Blavatsky & the Stanzas of Dzyan

"... the occult side of Nature has never been approached by the science of modern civilization."

"... the Secret teachings ... must be contrasted with the speculations of modern science. Archaic axioms must be placed side by side with modern hypotheses and comparison left to the sagacious reader." (p. 480)

Blavatsky, *The Secret Doctrine*, 1888

1. H.P. Blavatsky & *The Secret Doctrine*

In 1888, Helena P. Blavatsky published *The Secret Doctrine: The synthesis of science, religion, and philosophy*. Manly Hall, an occult scholar, described Blavatsky's work as *"unquestionably the Magnus opus of the literature of the modern world."* *The Secret Doctrine* is a classic and authoritative work that has had a broad influence on the last century of western occultism. Blavatsky's teachings of *"Theosophy,"* *Theo* meaning God and *Sophia—wisdom,* are profound elaborations of the *"divine wisdom."* Theosophy articulates an ancient mystical knowledge and teaching about the divine and metaphysical nature of life.

The Secret Doctrine (1888) is a massive, almost incomprehensible document. It is composed of two volumes: the first, *Cosmogenesis,* deals with the "genesis" of the "cosmos" –the origin and creation of the universe. *Cosmogenesis* outlines the laws of cosmology, physics and metaphysics from an esoteric and occult perspective. Blavatsky made every effort in her work to represent the essence of the ancient mystical teachings about cosmogenesis and metaphysics, while contrasting these with the scientific theories of her day. Volume II, *Anthropogenesis,* deals with the creation (genesis) and evolution of humanity through various dimensions of existence and rounds (cycles) of life. *The Secret Doctrine* provides a sweeping view of the nature of life from the first moments of the awakening of the Kosmos to the final destiny of humankind and the Universe. In her *Magnus opus* of the literature of the modern world, occultist Blavatsky provides a tour of the cosmos substantially different from that of her contemporary scientists and science philosophers, and from that yet offered in the twenty first century.

Anyone who closely examines *The Secret Doctrine* must be impressed and perhaps overwhelmed by the author's erudition and knowledge. Madame Blavatsky draws material from many sources including ancient mystical and occult works, mythologies, religions, science and philosophy. Most importantly, *The Secret Doctrine* is based upon Stanzas from the *Book of Dzyan,* an ancient poetic text of Tibetan origin which apart from Blavatsky's writings seems largely unknown to modern scholarship. Blavatsky commented: *"The Book of Dzyan (or "Dzan") is utterly unknown to our Philologists, or at any rate was never heard of by them under its present name."* (p. xxii) The *Stanzas of Dzyan* are described as *"the heart of the sacred books of Kiu-ti,"* once known only to Tibetan mystics. Blavatsky describes a *"very old Book"* originally recorded in Senzar—the *"sacred sacerdotal tongue"* and derived from *"the words of the Divine Beings, who dictated it to the sons of Light, in Central Asia, at the very beginning of the 5th (our) race."* (p. xliii) Certainly, these are unusual claims and the origin of the Stanzas seems largely lost in antiquity. In fact, there are many things about *The Secret Doctrine* and the *Book of Dzyan* which are shrouded in mystery and enigma—as befits an individual as enigmatic and mysterious as H.P.B. herself.

Helena Petrovna Blavatsky was born in a Ukrainian town of Ekaterinoslav, Russia in the early morning of August 12, 1831 and died in May of 1891 in London, England. Through her extraordinary life, she travelled widely throughout the world—from the lands and pyramids of Egypt, the Caucasus and Middle East, to the mountains of Tibet and the lands of India, within Europe, as well as North, central and South America. She demonstrated psychical and unusual powers throughout her life and was involved in broad investigations of paranormal phenomena, particularly Spiritualism in America. Blavatsky was exposed to a wealth of the world's mystical, occult and spiritual practices, teachings and traditions. In addition, she was knowledgeable of the sciences of her day.

The *Theosophical Society* was officially founded in the United States on November 17, 1875. Blavatsky moved on to establish the Theosophical Society in India and within Europe. Today, her teachings are studied throughout the world by varied theosophical societies. Madame Blavatsky is regarded as the grandmother of modern western occultism, a unique synthesizer of the ancient wisdom teachings and a dramatic individualist who challenged the materialist and mechanistic science philosophy of the day, as well as social and religious conventions. Historically, her work introduced eastern mystical teachings to western audiences and she uncovered keys to numerous wisdom teachings of the early western traditions.

Madame Blavatsky claimed to have contact with Adepts or Masters of the Trans-Himalayan Brotherhood and to have partially acted as an *'amanuensis'* for her superiors in the occult hierarchy, who aided in her preparation of *The Secret Doctrine*. In modern terms, *amanuensis* might be labelled as 'channelling' but was described by H.P.B. as a form of psychological telepathy based on an electromagnetic connection existing between a Mahatma (a master) and his chelas (or students). Blavatsky also claimed to employ her trained spiritual perception and intuitive consciousness to draw from the *Akashic record*, the storehouse of knowledge and spiritual wisdom.

In Sylvia Cranston's biography, *The Extraordinary Life & Influence of Helena Blavatsky, Founder of the modern theosophical movement*, she quotes the prominent editor of an English newspaper, W. Stead, who wrote to Blavatsky in 1888 after receiving a copy of her work. His letter nicely captures the extraordinary character of Blavatsky and the remarkable nature of her Magnus opus—*The Secret Doctrine*.

> You are a very great woman and I do not think that anyone but yourself (either man or woman) could have written *The Secret Doctrine*, nor do I feel competent, from the depths of my ignorance, even to express

an opinion upon its extraordinary contents... I do not profess to understand you, for you inhabit space of more dimensions than I can even conceive, but I am not so great a fool as to be unable to see that you have a genius quite transcendent.... (Cranston, 1994, p. 361)

These comments provide a most appropriate perspective on this remarkable woman and this classic study of the ancient wisdom teachings. Blavatsky has also been appropriately labelled as *"the Sphinx of the nineteenth century"* and as *"among the modern world's trailblazing psychologists"* by sociologist T. Roszak. (Cranston, p. xxiii) Blavatsky attracted considerable attention and notoriety during her life and through the turn of the century after the publication of *The Secret Doctrine*. Admirers included those within the literary, artistic and scientific communities, as well as within broader society—those interested in a deeper spiritual understanding of life and the high ideals of the Theosophical Society. Some of the most well know admirers of Blavatsky included Albert Einstein, whose niece reported that he kept a copy of *The Secret Doctrine* on his desk; Robert Millikan and scientists associated with the Mount Wilson observatory; Elvis Presley, taken by Blavatsky's poetic account of the pilgrimage of souls—*The Voice of the Silence*; and Adolph Hitler, fascinated by occultism and racial history.

The Secret Doctrine provides keys to the original mystery teachings about the origin of the universe and the metaphysical nature of life and creation. We must take this so-called *"Magnus opus of the literature of modern world"* and consider the metaphysical and cosmological viewpoints espoused, while comparing the ancient wisdom teachings with the theories, facts and paradigm of modern science. No matter what the origin of the *Book of Dzyan*, or how *The Secret Doctrine* was produced, and despite the controversy surrounding Blavatsky as an individual, it is possible to examine the ideas, theories and claims of *The Secret Doctrine* in their own right as scientific hypotheses and theories. In fact, it is profoundly important to do so—insofar as *The Secret Doctrine* provides an intriguing perspective on many of the most profound questions confronting modern science. How does *The Secret Doctrine* completed in 1888 compare with the theories, data and paradigm of modern science a century later?

In the preface to *The Secret Doctrine*, Blavatsky explained three major aims of her work: The first was *"to show that Nature is not 'a fortuitous concurrence of atoms,' and to assign to man his rightful place in the scheme of the Universe...."* (p. viii) This aim expressed Blavatsky's desire to oppose the mechanistic and materialist science philosophy dominant in 19th century—a philosophy that regarded the origin of the universe and mankind as due to nothing more than fortuitous "accidents" which proceeded blindly through the laws governing material nature. Blavatsky characterized the *"holy creative Trinity"* of materialist science as that of *"Inert Matter, Senseless Force and Blind Chance."* (p. 505) This is the scientific paradigm still evident today in the writings of popular science writers—such as Drs. Sagan, Asimov and Hawking, Stenger and among the majority of physicists, natural scientists, psychologists and philosophers. In the modern view, the formation of life is an inherently random or accidental (fortuitous) process, and creation and evolution are regarded as having occurred within a godless Universe—devoid of spirit, demigods, spiritual intelligence or consciousness. The notions of randomness, uncertainty and accidental happenings are cornerstones of contemporary science philosophy.

In contrast, Blavatsky argues that there is nothing in nature which is truly random or fortuitous. Everything involves *creation by design* in a Universe full of meaning, life and interconnectedness. She quotes the poet Coleridge: "*Chance is but the pseudonym for God (or Nature), for those particular cases which He does not choose to subscribe openly with His sign manual.*" In Blavatsky's teachings, there is a hierarchy of creative intelligences who mathematically sculpt the void and whose influences are manifest as the laws of nature. She wrote: "*Nature geometrizes universally in all her manifestations... Nature correlates her geometrical forms, and later, also, her compound elements; and in which there is no place for accident or chance.*" (p. 97) Blavatsky provides keys to understanding a remarkable model of Intelligent Design inherent to the ancient wisdom traditions. Further, a human being is not simply a soul-less, biological organism, but has a profound deep connection into the grounds of being and thereby to the larger Cosmos.

The second aim of *The Secret Doctrine* was "*to rescue from degradation the archaic truths which are the basis of all religions; and to uncover, to some extent, the fundamental unity from which they all spring.*" Blavatsky explains that the ideas in *The Secret Doctrine* are not simply something which she has invented but which are scattered throughout eastern and western religions and mystery schools. The sacred scriptures of all times embody the same teachings, although "*hidden under glyph and symbol*" and unnoticed because of "*this veil.*" Blavatsky claims that the basic ideas of the secret doctrine are the essence of Hindu, Zoroastrian, Chaldean, Egyptian, Buddhist, Islamic, Judaic and Christian belief, all of which are said to have emerged from one original "*parent document.*" She writes: "*the Secret Wisdom was once the fountain head, the ever-flowing perennial source, at which were fed all its streamlets–the religions of all nations–from the first down to the last.*" (p. viii) The second aim of the S.D. is to "*rescue from degradation the archaic truths.*" In fact, these secret teachings have still eluded the mainstream of modern science, education and culture.

The third aim of *The Secret Doctrine* was to demonstrate that "*the occult side of Nature has never been approached by the Science of modern civilization.*" (p.viii) Unfortunately, a century later, this is largely still the case. Despite the fact that a few scientists and individuals search for the soul or explore mysticism and the new physics, scientists have hardly begun to scratch the surface of the ancient wisdom teachings. Indeed, scientists generally do not know of or understand the occult teachings. Beyond this pervasive ignorance, there is a more fundamental fear of mystical teachings, as mainstream scientists do not want to see their so-called *real science* mixed up with mystical nonsense, vague metaphysical speculations and superstitions. However, Blavatsky regarded scientists' attitudes towards mysticism as being indefensible. She bluntly accused them of being irrationally close-minded, noting that, "... in our days, Scientists are more self-opinionated and bigoted than even the clergy."(p. 509). At the start of the new millennium, this is still largely the case and contrary views are marginalized within science.

Madame Blavatsky did not regard science and occultism as incompatible. Rather, her view was that as science advanced, it *must* come to validate mystical teachings:

> There can be no possible conflict between the teachings of occult and so-called exact Science, where the conclusions of the latter are grounded on a substratum of unassailable fact. ... Science can, it is true, collect, classify, and generalize upon phenomena; but the occultist, arguing from admitted metaphysical data, declares that the daring explorer, who would probe the inmost secrets of Nature, must transcend the narrow limitations of sense, and transfer his consciousness into the region of noumena and the sphere of primal causes. To effect this, he must develop faculties which are absolutely dormant—save in a few rare and exceptional cases—in the constitution of the off-shots of our present Fifth Root-race in Europe and America. (pp. 477-8)

Blavatsky explains that when so-called "exact" science really achieves a correct understanding of the nature of life, it will confirm the claims of mystic seers who attained such dormant faculties and directly apprehend the underlying or innermost side of creation.

Blavatsky was aggressive in her attacks on the scientific opinion of her day, but not because of a disrespect for the aims of the scientists. Her concern was with the advancement of science and in *The Secret Doctrine*, she goes to great lengths to demonstrate the relationships between the ancient teachings and the prevalent scientific views. She notes:

> the Secret Teachings ... must be contrasted with the speculations of modern science, Archaic axioms must be placed side by side with modern hypotheses and comparisons left to the sagacious reader. (p. 480)

According to Blavatsky, the problem with the scientific theories is most simply that they are "wrong." Scientists deal only with the observable side of phenomena, rather than the underlying noumena, or causes–because they exclude consideration of the spiritual and metaphysical side of life. Eventually, this always leads to perplexities and unresolved issues:

> To make of Science an integral whole necessitates, indeed, the study of spiritual and psychic, as well as physical Nature. ... Without metaphysics, real science is inadmissible. (p. 588)

All science must ultimately lead to metaphysics and supernatural causes—because these exist!

In *God, Science & The Secret Doctrine*, we particularly examine the ancient wisdom in four major areas of inquiry, regarding: 1) cosmogenesis–the genesis or creation of the Universe; 2) the relationship of the laws of physics to ancient metaphysics–to explain the ultimate nature of matter, energy, time and space, and the mechanisms of the laws of nature; 3) evolution–which needs to be considered from a spiritual and metaphysical perspective, in addition to the biological; and 4) human consciousness–which originates out of deep metaphysical realities. According to an occult perspective, "*without metaphysics, real science is inadmissible*" (p. 588) and this applies to scientific study within each of these areas.

It is over a hundred years since the publication of *The Secret Doctrine* and there has been little change in the strict materialist perspective which dominates science philosophy. Many scientists, like Carl Sagan, imagine that believing in the spiritual nature of life, or in mysticism and ancient wisdom, involves believing in an old, long bearded man who sits up in heaven counting sparrows or talking to flowers. These scientists have no idea of the profound metaphysical philosophies embodied within the ancient wisdom teachings.

The Secret Doctrine does not contradict the *facts* of science. Rather, it is scientists' rigid adherence to a simplistic, mechanistic and materialist science philosophy which leads them to prejudge and mindlessly dismiss mystical claims of metaphysics and higher dimensions. Blavatsky noted in this regard:

> Occultism does not deny the certainty of the mechanical origin of the Universe; it only claims the absolute necessity of mechanicians of some sort behind those Elements (or *within*)—a dogma with us. ... It is easy for an astronomer ... to build a theory of the emergence of the universe out of chaos, by simply applying to it the principles of mechanics. But such a universe will always prove, with respect to its scientific human creator, a Frankenstein's monster; it will lead him into endless perplexities. The application of the mechanical laws only can never carry the speculator beyond the objective world: nor will it unveil to men the origin and final destiny of Kosmos. (1888, p. 594)

Normally, scientists simply close their eyes to these endless perplexities in science and psychology, instead of venturing into the unknown. However, essential ideas from *The Secret Doctrine* provide a remarkable alternative approach to interpreting the facts and theories of science itself, and to understanding additional contemporary scientific enigmas. Everything takes on new significance if the parts are considered in relationship to the whole and in relationship to underlying metaphysical causes. Mystical and spiritual teachings do provide all kinds of testable hypotheses, if we are ingenious enough to begin from first principles and draw out the implications and applications of such theories within different domains of scientific inquiry.

Most importantly, mystical studies entail self-study, the awakening of consciousness and the transformation of the human heart. In this way, the most advanced scientific methods require the individual process of psycho-spiritual transformation and include the scientist in the equation. Ordinary science is limited by the ordinary state of egoic consciousness and the commonly conditioned psychopathology of humankind. In contrast, mystical science includes the scientist him/herself in the equation and demands more, not less, from the seeker after truth. The key to the mysteries lies in understanding the nature of consciousness within oneself—by inner experience, sensation and taste. This might enable one to develop those *"faculties which are absolutely dormant—save in a few rare and exceptional cases—in the constitution of the off-shots of our present Fifth Root-race in Europe and America,"* as described by Blavatsky.

It is more than a hundred years since Blavatsky completed *The Secret Doctrine* and unfortunately, scientists are still far from having taken up her challenge of exploring the *"occult side of Nature."* Her comments from 1888 thus hold true today:

> Occultists believe they have a right to present their philosophy, however misunderstood and ostracised it may be at present. ... (the) failure of the scientists to discover the truth is entirely due to their materialism and contempt for transcendental sciences. (p. 600)

> Now that (scientists) have studied nature in the length, breadth, and thickness of her physical frame, it is time to remove the skeleton to the second plane and search within the unknown depths for the living and real entity, for its SUB-stance—the noumenon of evanescent matter. (p. 610)

H.P. Blavatsky did not expect *The Secret Doctrine* to be seriously studied by scientists and scholars in her day. In fact, she predicted:

> the rejection of these teachings "may be expected, and must be accepted beforehand. No one styling himself a "scholar," in whatever department of exact science, will be permitted to regard these teachings seriously. They will be derided and rejected *a priori* in this century; but only in this one. For in the twentieth century of our era scholars will begin to recognize that the *Secret Doctrine* has neither been invented nor

exaggerated, but, on the contrary, simply outlined.....(Introduction, p. xxxvii)

In 1888, Blavatsky's explanations of the creation of the Universe and of the laws of physics and metaphysics, offered a viewpoint totally incomprehensible in terms of what were the fashionable scientific viewpoints and theories. *The Secret Doctrine* was bound to be ignored and dismissed. As it happens however, in this strange universe, a century of scientific advances and the profound "new physics" and cosmology of twenty first century are beginning to vindicate Blavatsky's utterly awesome work on cosmic origins and ancient wisdom teachings. Ancient mystical maxims and modern scientific theories can be placed side by side to draw comparisons. When it comes to the ultimate questions of the origin of the Cosmos and the laws of nature, science and mysticism are not such a world apart. Science is beginning to arrive at those levels of reality spoken of by the mystics who penetrate the Heart and soul to the grounds of Being.

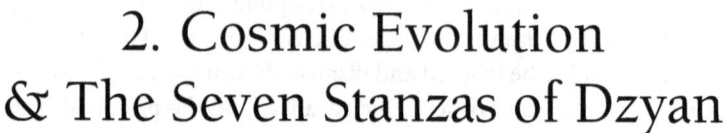

2. Cosmic Evolution & The Seven Stanzas of Dzyan

Modern physicist S. Hawking described Blavatsky's era:

nearly everyone in the 18th and 19th centuries believed that the Universe was essentially unchanging in time.... one could equally well believe that it had existed for ever or that it had been created in its present form a finite time ago. (1984)

Whereas scientific opinion of her day may have been so narrow in scope, Blavatsky provided a profoundly alternative vision of the nature of reality—grander in scope, complexity and subtleness than even the most advanced ideas in modern theoretical physics. In contrast to other people and scientists of her day, H.P. Blavatsky propound a view that the Universe emerged from a zero point or singularity condition, out of a seeming void and plenum—a seven dimensional hyperspace or 'Parent Space' with an underlying fundamental holomovement or 'Ceaseless Breath.' She explains how a Kosmos grows from a point source within-without to become a world but will eventually contract without-within back to a final zero point source—to return again into the sevenfold hyperspace of the Divine Mother. Blavatsky, in the 19th century, regarded our Kosmos as simply one such "wink in the Eye of Self-Existence" emerging from and dissolving back through zero point centres rooted into an underlying Ceaseless Breath within an Eternal Parent Space!

The second fundamental proposition of The Secret Doctrine, affirmed:

The Eternity of the Universe *in toto* as a boundless plane; periodically "the playground of numberless Universes incessantly manifesting and disappearing," called "the manifesting stars," and the "sparks of Eternity." The Eternity of the Pilgrim is like a wink in the Eye of Self-Existence. (p. 16)

Created universes, Sons or Winks in the Eye of Self-Existence, emerge from and dissolve into such zero point conditions in and out of an underlying void/plenum of the seven-skinned Eternal Parent Space.

In modern terms, the Eternal Parent Space of Blavatsky is the seven-dimensional hyperspace of the *quantum vacuum*—the quantum ether and zero point fields postulated within the most advanced models of physics (including Superstring and M-theory—the supposed 'Mother' of all theories). A modern physicist declares: *"All of physics is in the vacuum"* and this is exactly the viewpoint elaborated by Blavatsky. Blavatsky's explanations of the *causes of the laws of nature* are based upon an understanding of a seven dimensional hyperspace, the nature of Space as void and plenum, zero point centres within an underlying Electromagnetic Ocean, and the manner in which higher dimensional intelligences manifest within-without out of higher dimensional Space! Many of these ideas have now emerged within science itself, as will be demonstrated through these comparative studies.

No one in her era could have understood the full implications and applications of the wild claims and ideas Blavatsky presented to the world in *The Secret Doctrine*. However, the most profound 21st century physics, to distinguish it from twentieth century science dominated by Einstein and Heisenberg, is focused on exploring a deeper more fundamental substratum—as addressed by H.P.B. Scientists now explore the nature of nothingness, the basic enigmas of the quantum vacuum, the nature of higher dimensional Space at zero point levels, and the holographic principle in physics. These contemporary theories address the same issues explored within *The Secret Doctrine* a century earlier.

Of course, to understand and grasp it all, and how it could be so, and what it all means, is no easy task for the faint hearted. However, *The Secret Doctrine* deserves to be re-interpreted in the light of the newest physics and models of creation. It provided a basic holographic model of the Universe—a century before physicists arrived at such views. Blavatsky's Secret Doctrine has yet to be understood by modern science and it provides a profoundly alternative interpretation of the facts and theories of science itself.

* * *

The Seven *Stanzas of Dzyan* are replicated as an appendix to the text of *God, Science & The Secret Doctrine*. The Stanzas are reproduced from the standard modern Theosophical University Press edition of *The Secret Doctrine*, itself *"verbatim with the original edition."* (1888, 1970) The *Book of Dzyan* is an ancient poetic text of Tibetan origin, which apart from Blavatsky's writings seems unknown to modern scholarship.[1]

At the end of the seventh page of the Stanzas, you will find Blavatsky's original comments upon them. She writes:

---

[1] In the Theos-Talk Archives (October 1999), www.theosophy.com/theos-talk/ Grigor Ananikian, explained that Blavatsky's Asian and western Tibet/Bhutan/Kashmir contacts were with the Dzog chen order. It is suggested that the Stanzas originate from a "Central Asian Dzog chen root text that is used by the Kalmucks (with whom H.P.B. had early contact in the Caucasus) and Mongols. Also, that the Stanzas of Dzyan are of Dzog chen origin was stated by the Dalai Lama in 1992."

"Thus ends this portion of the archaic narrative, dark, confused, almost incomprehensible. An attempt will now be made to throw light into this darkness, to make sense out of this apparent NON-SENSE."

Indeed, Blavatsky presents the Stanzas and then takes 642 pages in Volume I, *Cosmogenesis*, to elaborate their meaning. She does this by drawing upon diverse esoteric teachings of both eastern and western traditions, symbols, myths and sacred number study; and by drawing comparisons with the science of her era.

The Stanzas actually depict the history of cosmic evolution—beginning *before* the point source origin of the universe. The root principles of creation are the higher dimensional seven-skinned *Eternal Parent Space* and an *Eternal Ceaseless Breath*. The Stanzas begin before the big bang when the world was empty and void, and the Spirit (Breath) moves across the face of the Waters (of Space). The Stanzas then depict the dynamic emergence of a cosmos, the dropping of a world egg, the emergence of the seven divine intelligences or Luminous Sons, and the unfurling of varied cosmic processes through different hierarchies of creation. These abstract causes and root principles *"phenomenalise in the form of the material Universe, by a process of conversion of metaphysics into physics, analogous to that by which steam can be condensed into water, and the water frozen into ice."* (p. 45) Blavatsky provides a remarkable account of how divine and spiritual intelligences within higher dimensions manifest through zero point dynamics to inform living beings and the laws of nature. Blavatsky states, *"metaphysical abstractions ... are the only conceivable cause of physical concretions."* (p. 45)[2]

Blavatsky's explanations of cosmogenesis and metaphysics are explored in Section III of *God, Science & The Secret Doctrine* with a progressive analysis of the Stanzas. Section IV then examines modern physics and cosmology while showing correspondences and differences between the two perspectives. Blavatsky's seemingly bizarre descriptions of metaphysical processes have anticipated many of the essential concepts of modern physics: vacuum genesis, singularity creation, 11 dimensional string theory and M-theory, quantum information theory and the holographic principle. Further, they shed a wholly different light on the enigmas of the "uncertainty principle" and the 'baffling holism' of quantum physics. 21st century science could arrive at an alternate understanding of this enigmatic uncertainty principle, as the key to its interpretation is hidden within *The Secret*

---

2   Book II of The Secret Doctrine, Anthropogenesis, provides a second set of Stanzas dealing with the evolution of life and humanity on earth, as well as within other rounds and through higher dimensions. Blavatsky criticized the evolutionary ideas of the day, noting: "neither Occultism nor Theosophy has ever supported the wild theories of the present Darwinists—least of all the descent of man from an ape." God willing, the author will develop book two of *God, Science & The Secret Doctrine* to explore the issues of evolution and the origins of humankind; again contrasting science and Blavatsky's wisdom tradition.

Doctrine and its teachings of the zero point centres. Blavatsky's perspectives on the mysteries of creation are ever more intelligible in light of the theories and findings of modern science.

I hope that as the reader grasps this work, then the awesome creation poetry of the *Stanzas of Dzyan* will become increasingly accessible. Whereas a cursory reading of the Stanzas alone might suggest *"apparent NON-SENSE,"* a careful study of the key concepts and meditation upon the Stanzas can allow us to grasp a profound ancient wisdom teaching as to the physics and metaphysics of creation.

The concluding portion of *God, Science & The Secret Doctrine* explores the origin and nature of human consciousness and self existence, in light of *The Secret Doctrine* and in the darkness of modern soul-less psychology. To this end, we compare the mystical 'Heart Doctrine' of Blavatsky to the common 'head doctrine' of modern psychology and science. Whereas the metaphysics and cosmology of Blavatsky are profoundly similar to 21st century physics, her psychology is a world apart from 20st century psychology!

Thus, we will discuss the nature of the 'I AM,' the plights of the Monads, the individual living beings, the 'winks in the Eye of Self-Existence.' Blavatsky's teachings allow us to apply a higher dimensional quantum information theory to understanding the Monadic essence existent within hyperspace dimensions, which by some hidden inner magic become "clothed in different bodies" based upon zero point 'laya centres.' Blavatsky offers a higher dimensional model of human existence within holographic Space, in comparison with which 20th century psychology looks puny and meagre indeed. Blavatsky states: *"The Mind is the great Slayer of the Real."*

Blavatsky explains that the *Stanzas of Dzyan* provide an *"abstract algebraic formula of... Evolution,"* which can be applied to *"all evolution."* There are *"seven terms of this abstract formula, related to the seven great stages of the evolutionary process, as described in the Puranas as the "Seven Creations," and in the Bible as the "Days" of Creation."* Of course, since man, as a microcosm of the macrocosm, embodies the Universe, the same abstract numerical and symbolic formulas can all be applied to understanding the zero point dynamics underlying the creation of the Universe and the emergence of the Monad. Studies of the physics and metaphysics of creation can then all be applied to understanding ourselves and the physics and metaphysics of our own hearts and consciousness. The Stanzas state:

"THE SONS EXPAND AND CONTRACT THROUGH THEIR OWN SELVES AND HEARTS; THEY EMBRACE INFINITUDE."
(III, 11)

At this point, to present a complete version of the Stanza might leave the reader bewildered, so we will examine aspects of Blavatsky's cosmological and metaphysical teachings which shed light on these enigmatic Stanzas and present the Stanzas in sections. The complete version of the Stanzas is in the Appendix and readers may want to read them before continuing with this exposition.

* * *

Thus, it is clear that, H.P. Blavatsky in 1888 certainly did not believe that the universe was always as it was or that it was created in its present form. Instead, she offered a model of cosmic creation and human existence which dwarfs the popular thought and science of the past century. *The Secret Doctrine* offers a profoundly alternative view of the nature of life, creation and the Universe. Studying the Stanzas with keys provided by Blavatsky's explanations and drawing relationships to modern science allows us to confirm Blavatsky's own predictions: *"For in the twentieth century of our era scholars will begin to recognize that the Secret Doctrine has neither been invented nor exaggerated, but, on the contrary, simply outlined...."* (p. xxxvii)

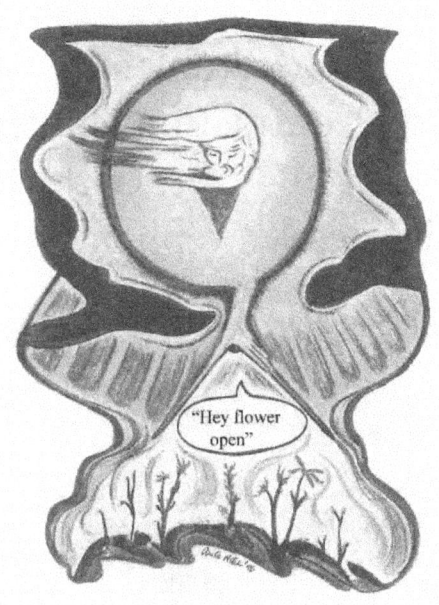

I I
Ancient Wisdom & Modern Science

"... to show that Nature is not "a fortuitous concurrence of atoms," and to assign to man his rightful place in the scheme of the Universe ... "
(S. D. I, p. viii)

"The application of the mechanical laws only can never carry the speculator beyond the objective world; nor will it unveil to men the origin and final destiny of Kosmos. ... Occultism does not deny the certainty of the mechanical origin of the Universe; it only claims the absolute necessity of mechanicians of some sort behind those Elements (or within)—a dogma with us." (S. D. I, p. 594)

Blavatsky, *The Secret Doctrine*, 1888

1. The Problem of God's Contracting Universe —As posed by Dr. Carl Sagan, Paul Davies & Stephen Hawking

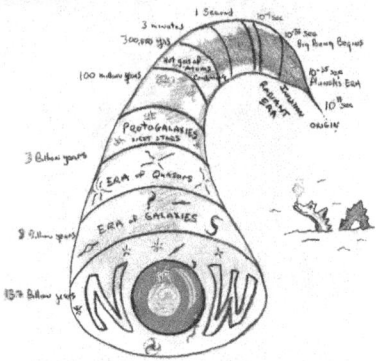

As we learn more and more about the universe, there seems less and less for God to do. Carl Sagan (1979, p. 268)

Modern science provides one set of answers to the mysteries of life. In the twentieth century, scientists have articulated an astonishing set of ideas about cosmic origins. The creation of the universe is now traced back to the first moments of existence estimated at some fifteen billion years ago. Physicists and astrophysicists describe the first instant of creation when the universe was 10^{-43} seconds old and less than a billion times smaller than the diameter of a proton in size, 10^{-33} cm! Such an infinitesimally small point source is called a singularity. Scientists propose that our vast universe had just such zero point or singularity origins.

Physicists are also seeking to unify the four fundamental laws of physics into one *"superforce," "superstring"* or holographic principle, which would have ruled creation at this first instant of creation before being divided into the various forces and particles of nature. Physicist Paul Davies labels this as the *'God like Superforce.'* Thus, scientists trace the universe back to what can be described as a zero point wherein all of the forces of nature are unified.

Beyond the singularity, physicists are concerned with the hidden dimensions of the quantum vacuum, the underlying source of all things. Space and the quantum vacuum are not really 'nothing' as appears to physical perception, but are full of particles, energies, forces and information. One modern physicist declares: *"The whole of physics is in the vacuum."* The quantum vacuum is both the void and the plenum, the nothingness and its potencies. At the beginning of time, all the quanta (particles) composing material reality manifested out of the seeming nothingness of the quantum vacuum—all through a process of symmetry breaking in higher space dimensions. Physicists label this modern creation scenario *'vacuum genesis'* and comment on its likeness to the *creation ex nihilo* of the mystical and Christian traditions.

From the first instant of creation to the world today, modern scientists have pieced together a fascinating, seemingly consistent and rational view of the origins and evolution of matter, the universe and solar system, the planets, biological life and ultimately humankind. There are theories about the origins of matter, the formation of stars, galaxies and solar systems, the origins of molecular substances and cells, and the neo-Darwinian evolution of plants, animals and human beings from lower life forms. Biologists, biochemists and medical researchers are busily unravelling the mysteries of genetics, the mechanisms of evolution and the dynamics of health and disease.

At the same time, neurologists and neuro-psychologists have explored that most complex and distinctive human organ—the brain, dissecting and mapping its structures and analysing its functions. The nature of intelligence and the capacities of thought and cognition have been subject to countless studies and experiment. In fact, philosophers, psychologists and sociologists seem to have probed every conceivable quirk and quark of the human psyche and its immensely complicated behavioural and emotional patterns.

In every department of the natural and social sciences, a massive literature, multiple theories and mini-theories and arrays of technologies have been accumulated—documenting the scientific advances made over the past century. The development of modern science is an amazing feat which contemporary science writers celebrate and praise lavishly. Clearly, modern science affords profound and penetrating insights into the nature of reality and the issues of origins. Imagine that, that the scientists trace the origin of the Universe to a point source singularity emerging out of a seeming nothingness!

Dr. Carl Sagan was a celebrated American astronomer and exo-biologist, science writer, television personality and host of the highly acclaimed *Cosmos* T.V. series. Over the past thirty years, Dr. Sagan was one of the most widely read of popular science writers to represent modern scientific ideas, facts and philosophy to the general public. In that role, Dr. Sagan romantically praised the advances of modern science and spoke eloquently on the topics of the nature and philosophy of science, the pseudo-sciences, religion, environmental and cultural issues.

In his writings, Dr. Sagan covered a wide spectrum of subjects ranging from the creation of the universe to the evolution of humankind; the nature of the brain and mind; explorations of alleged paranormal phenomena; environmental and political issues; and even a discussion of the *"God hypothesis."* In *Broca's Brain: Reflections on the Romance of Science*, Dr. Sagan considered the viability of religious teachings in view of science's spectacular advances. In a chapter, *A Sunday Sermon*, he ventured into areas where even angels might fear to tread to address 'the God hypothesis.'

In his sermon, Dr. Sagan argues that as science advances, we are able to explain natural phenomena without recourse to supernatural explanations. As an example, he considers the opening of a morning glory flower. He suggests that at one time, people used to believe that any such event was due to *"direct microintervention by the Deity."* Thus, in order for the flower to open, *"God had to say "Hey, flower, open."* Dr. Sagan then explains that scientists can now account for the opening of the morning glory because they understand phototropism and plant hormones and consequently, there is no need to refer to any sort of divine microintervention. Sagan then applies this same line of reasoning to the whole scheme of creation and evolution, and concludes: *"As we learn more and more about the universe, there seems less and less for God to do."* (1979, p. 286)

Dr. Sagan's comments pose what I call *"the problem of God's contracting universe."* Is it really correct to say that as science advances, there is less and less for God to do? Has science's progress really removed God from the entire skein of causality all the way back to the beginning—including the very first moment of creation? Carl Sagan expresses a sentiment common to most scientists: that science offers the only valid and comprehensive approach to understanding the nature of reality. Science involves submitting hypotheses to tests of empirical evidence, in terms of a specific set of rules and procedures, which allows one to falsify propositions. It represents a rational and objective body of knowledge, in dramatic contrast to religious teachings which Sagan portrays as only matters of dogma and belief. Dr. Sagan argues that the beauty and strength of the scientific method is that it has freed humans from the dogma and irrationality imposed by religious authority. In Sagan's view, the scrutiny of science exposes the subjectivity of religious insights and pronouncements like a 'candle in the dark.'

In this spirit, Sagan explains that scientists have come to regard all references to God as unnecessary. Sagan offers various examples of natural phenomena which were once believed to be caused by supernatural forces but which gradually 'yielded to scientific understanding.' He states that when Newton explained planetary motion in terms of the theory of gravitation, it was no longer necessary for the *"angels to push and pummel the planets,"* as suggested by Kepler with his *angelus rector* conducting the planets. Similarly, when the Marquis de Laplace offered a rational explanation of the origin of the solar system, then there was no need to invoke God to be involved in its creation. (1979, p. 286) Like most scientists, Sagan's concept of God is primarily that of a bearded patriarch.

Of course, Dr. Sagan's stories are entertaining but was he really serious about these scientific ideas disproving God? Who exactly is it that said angels had to push and pummel the planets, or that the existence of God is negated by a theory of gravity? Did Carl Sagan really believe that God takes time out from his busy schedule to tell the morning glories, *"Hey, flower, open"*?

Sagan's examples are most peculiar. His representation of a religious world view is a caricature; a straw man erected in order to push and pummel it with the formidable power of pseudo-scientific thought. By casting religious views in such simplistic terms, Dr. Sagan fixes the outcome of his debate between science and religion. Why would a theory about the origin of the solar system profoundly challenge the necessity of a God being involved in the origins of things? How do these modern theories, or scientific theories in general, bear upon the issue of whether God or Gods exist? Dr. Sagan confidently dismisses the possibility that spiritual or religious perspectives might offer any legitimate scientific hypotheses and he is simply asserting his belief that all religious and spiritual world views are inferior to science—the supposed epitome of rationality and objectivity.

In *The Mind of God*, Paul Davies, another popular science writer, presents a dialogue between an atheist and a theist, a scientist and a theologian, to illustrate arguments about the existence of God in light of scientific advance. Davies explains the current concept of *"the God of the gaps"* and discusses how God got *"squeezed out"* of science. Essentially, the thrust of the atheist's argument is the same as Dr. Sagan's—that as science advances, there is less and less for God to do—He gets squeezed out. Davies's atheist explains that science's capacity to do away with a God or gods now extends all the way back to the very questions of origins and interpretations of the meaning of the "big bang:"

> Atheist: At one time, gods were used as an explanation for all sorts of physical phenomenon, such as the wind and the rain and the motion of the planets. As science progressed, so supernatural agents were found to be superfluous as an explanation for natural events. Why do you insist on invoking God to explain the big bang?... Theists have always been tempted to seize on any process that science could not at the time explain and claim that God was still needed to explain it. Then, as science progressed, God got squeezed out. You should learn the lesson that this "God of the gaps" is an unreliable hypothesis. As time goes on, there are fewer and fewer gaps for him to inhabit. I personally see no problem in science explaining all natural phenomena, including the origin of life. I concede that the origin of the universe is a tougher nut to crack. But if, as it seems, we have now reached the stage where the only remaining gap is the big bang, it is highly unsatisfying to invoke the concept of a supernatural being who

has been displaced from all else, in the "last-ditch" capacity. (1992, pp. 58-9)

The problem of the *'God of the gaps'* is the same as the *'problem of God's contracting universe.'* As science advances, there are fewer "gaps" in scientific theory and less reason to regard the world as having "a creator" or to be the result of supernatural or metaphysical causes. The scientists assume that life can be explained most simply in terms of purely natural material processes. The theist's view that God might somehow be involved in the mysterious nature of the big bang and the emergence of a singularity is regarded as a last ditch effort to invoke a superfluous God hypothesis. This is a common attitude expressed by those scientists enthused with modern science and technology, who believe that they are close to solving the mysteries of origins.

In God and the New Physics, Paul Davies warns that even when we do find some gap in scientific theory, we should be most cautious about invoking supernatural agencies or forces as causes:

> What once seemed miraculous... perhaps requiring a supernatural input at the big bang, now seems explicable on ordinary physical grounds, in the light of improved scientific understanding. However astonishing and inexplicable a particular occurrence may be, we can never be absolutely sure that at some distant time in the future a natural phenomenon will not be discovered to explain it. (1983, p. 31)

Most scientists are of the opinion that there are few remaining gaps for God to inhabit, now that we are close to understanding the ultimate issues of universal origins.

The prominent physicist and cosmologist Stephen Hawking attempts to explain creation in such a way so as to avoid the God hypothesis. In his best seller, *A Brief History of Time* (1988), Professor Hawking puts forth the view that if scientists are successful in developing a unified theory of quantum gravity, then it would do away with the necessity of a big bang singularity. Hawking explains:

> all our theories of science are formulated on the assumption that space-time is smooth and nearly flat, so they break down at the big bang singularity, where the curvature of space-time is infinite.... predictability would break down at the big bang.... Many people do not like the idea that time has a beginning, probably because it smacked of divine intervention.... There were therefore a number of attempts to avoid the conclusion that there had been a big bang. (1988, pp. 46-7)

In Hawking's unified theory of quantum gravity, the mysterious singularity is simply *"smeared out"* according to the uncertainty principle of quantum theory. In this case, he argues, science will have arrived at a completely natural explanation of the origin of the universe and there is no need to invoke any metaphysical causes, or God, even in the beginning:

> the quantum theory of gravity has opened up a new possibility, in which there would be no boundary to space-time and so there would be no need to specify the behaviour at the boundary. There would be no singularities at which the laws of science broke down and no edge of space-time at which one would have to appeal to God or some new law to set the boundary conditions for space-time.... The universe would be completely self-contained and not affected by anything outside itself. It would neither be created nor destroyed. It would just BE. (p. 136)

Professor Hawking portrays himself as explaining away the big bang singularity in terms of natural laws, so that there is nothing left for God to do. He extends this line of reasoning back to the beginning of time in order to argue that we do not need mysticism, religion or God, now that we have science and his promises of a quantum gravity theory. In an interview, Hawking comments: *"We still believe that the universe should be logical and beautiful. We just dropped the word 'God.'"* (In Weber, 1986, p. 212)

Of course, heaven only knows why Dr. Hawking thinks that there is nothing "mystical" about a singularity—even if it is smeared out into the unity! Of course, Hawking does not consider any of the mystical teachings about zero point origins in his account of science, mysticism and religion. Most orthodox scientists hold pejorative views of religion and mysticism, regarding them as pseudo-scientific, irrational, superstitious, vague and misty belief systems. Charles Tart (1975) once commented that *"being a mystic is considered pathological by most... One of the most deprecating remarks you could make about a scientist's work is to say that it shows signs of being 'mystical.'"* (p. 111) This attitude is evident in Hawking's comments in an interview with Rene Weber (1986):

> I very much disapprove of mysticism.... I think it's a cop-out. If you find theoretical physics and mathematics too hard, you turn to mysticism. I think people who have this idea about mysticism in physics are people who really can't understand the mathematics. (p. 210)

Many scientists would agree with Hawking's contention, that those who turn to mysticism do so because they are incapable of meeting science's intellectual challenges. Thus, Heinz Pagels (1985a), in an otherwise marvelous book on the creation of the universe, quotes the physicist R. Feynman and draws similar conclusions:

> If you expected science to give all the answers to the wonderful questions about what we are, where we are going, what the meaning

of the universe is, and so on, then I think you could easily become disillusioned and look for some mystic answer. How a scientist can accept a mystic answer, I don't know. I can't believe the special stories that have been made up about our relationship to the universe at large because they seem to be too simple, too connected, too provincial. People ask me if science is true. I say no, we don't know what's true. We're trying to find out, and everything is possibly wrong." (Feynman, quoted p. 368) ... And where am I? I am in the present, this imperfect moment, trying to remain vulnerable to its intense specificity. There is no other time for me to be or place to go, no cosmic consciousness nor facile mysticism into which I can retreat. (p. 370)

In the views of Hawking and Feynmann, mysticism is nothing more than subjective fancy, the refuge of the intellectually challenged and emotionally self-indulgent—in contrast to the objective knowledge of science. Certainly, no one would look to mysticism for insights into the subtle dimensionality of creation or the mysteries of Space, or the issue of the origin of human consciousness.

However, it is readily apparent on reading Sagan, Pagels, Hawking and other popular science writers, who explore creation issues (i.e., Jastrow, Asimov, Davis, Gribbin, Trefil, Stenger), that these scientists are completely ignorant as to what esoteric religious and mystical teachings actually entail and how they compare to modern scientific theories. They confidently dismiss mysticism as nothing but vague pseudo-sciences, yet there is no academic or scholarly consideration of mystical or esoteric doctrines. In their eagerness to deny mysticism relevance or significance in the search for understanding, scientists betray their unmistakable ignorance of these subjects.

There is, however, one type of God that scientists are willing to admit. In his *Sunday Sermon*, Dr. Sagan comments that he is frequently asked after his lectures if he *"believes in God,"* and that his answer depends on what the word "God" is taken to mean. Like other scientists, Sagan is willing to accept the idea of God if we equate this concept with the sum of the natural laws of nature, but not if we identify God with some bearded patriarch sitting on a throne counting sparrows, or saying *"Hey, flower, open."* For Dr. Sagan, the God alternatives seem to be exclusively restricted to a choice between bearded patriarchs and natural laws. He is entirely unaware of the complex metaphysical models and systems which mystical and spiritual teachings put forth.

But clearly, a religious or spiritual person could hardly accept Sagan's identification of God as simply being a label for the sum of physical and natural laws. From a religious or mystical viewpoint, God transcends the laws of nature and is the source of these laws. This Divine Being is omnipresent (present everywhere as the source of all things), omnipotent (containing all potencies for creation and cosmic manifestation) and omniscient (all knowing). These attributes suggest that God is a form of Absolute Consciousness and Being which pervades and sustains creation, and yet is simultaneously transcendent, existing beyond the manifest Cosmos. Dr. Sagan may believe that he is appeasing devotional and religious sentiment but this God of material science—as the sum of natural laws—simply does not coincide with religious or mystical viewpoints.

Further, those who believe in God regard human beings as having a spiritual or soul nature, in addition to the life of the material body/brain. The "soul hypothesis" is a corollary of "the God hypothesis." God is said to be the source of the consciousness and life within the individual, the source of spirit and soul, and even a divine spark. From a religious and mystical viewpoint, all the laws of nature and of the psyche are ultimately of supernatural origin.

Despite his rather limited imagination on the subject of God, Carl Sagan is—excuse the expression—a brave and hearty soul. Thus, he offers some encouragement for the religiously-minded suggesting that:

> "... a questing, courageous and open mind seems to be the essential tool for narrowing the range of our collective ignorance on the subject of the existence of God." (1979, p. 311)

How true this is! The questions of the existence of God, spirit and soul, need to be approached with a questing, courageous and open mind, in order to overcome our ignorance about these important subjects. Unfortunately, scientists are not typically exposed to the esoteric side of religious and mystical teachings, and dismiss these possibilities without at all understanding what they entail.

Elsewhere, Dr. Sagan gets to the heart of the problem in his discussion of religion and science noting:

> it is a kindness neither to science nor religion to leave unchallenged inadequate arguments for the existence of God. Moreover, debates on such questions are good fun, and at the very least, hone the mind for useful work. Not much of this sort of disputation is in evidence today, perhaps because new arguments for the existence of God which can be understood at all are exceedingly rare. (1979, p. 130)

From a scientific perspective, traditional arguments for the existence of God are inadequate and superficial. They are untestable and cannot be falsified, and therefore are considered pseudo-scientific. Science meanwhile discovers natural laws and we might question how it would ever be possible to discover any God, demigods, divine beings or other supernatural forces manifesting in the phenomena of nature according to scientific principles. As Carl Sagan suggests, arguments for the existence of God which can be understood at all within a scientific perspective are exceedingly rare. The matter would seem to end here, with science and religion a world apart and irreconcilable.

Paul Davies' atheist elaborates these same arguments:

> Atheist: ... unless you (the theist) have other reasons to believe in God's existence, then merely proclaiming "God created the universe" is totally ad hoc. It is no explanation at all. ... One mystery (the origin of the universe) is explained only in terms of another (God). As a scientist I appeal to Occam's razor, which then dictates that the God hypothesis be rejected as an unnecessary complication. ... the bald statement that "God created the universe" fails to provide any real explanation unless it is accompanied by a detailed mechanism. One wants to know, for example, what properties to assign this God, and precisely how he goes about creating the universe, why the universe has the form it does, and so on. In short, unless you either provide evidence in some other way that such a God exists, or else give a detailed account of how he made the universe that even an atheist like me would regard as deeper, simpler, and more satisfying, I see no reason to believe in such a being. (1992, pp. 59-60)

God, Science & The Secret Doctrine is an attempt to take up the challenge posed by Drs. Sagan and Hawking and by Davies' atheist. The aim is to elaborate a model of how metaphysical and supernatural forces might indeed create and sustain material worlds and human consciousness, and to illustrate the applications of such a perspective. This is a model of "intelligent design" based upon the study of the esoteric metaphysics articulated within the authoritative work of H.P. Blavatsky, Kabbalah and other traditions. Otherwise, if we do not have a model of Intelligent Design, no further progress can be made in the theist-atheist debate. The theist will argue that nature shows evidence of intelligent design and the atheist will argue that it doesn't—that it is just all chance and randomness, and order inherent to material reality. A substantive God theory is needed which describes the mechanisms and dynamics of divine, spiritual and psychical forces, and how these are related to material processes—hence, simplifying the known, predicting new observations and allowing for empirical tests and verification. This is exactly what is inherent and hidden within *The Secret Doctrine*—a model of such metaphysical dynamics.

Of course, scientists also feel awe in the face of the mysterious nature of existence and do sometimes admit to their ignorance on the ultimate unknowns. Carl Sagan exemplifies this attitude and so, at times, does Stephen Hawking. In Shirley MacLaine's (1989) popular new age book *Going Within*, she recounted a rather unusual and paradoxical interaction with Dr. Hawking and his then wife, Jane:

> I don't remember who made the initial foray into the discussion of "truth beyond what is provable."... In any case, Jane (Mrs. Hawking) said she was often frustrated with Stephen and his scientific approach

to truth because she felt that there was an explanation for life that lay in the lap of the Gods and the heart.

"I don't like mysticism," Stephen said via his voice box computer. "But my wife and I don't always agree." He smiled at her and then at me. "But I need the heart because physics isn't everything."

He hesitated a moment and then said, "I need heart and physics, but I believe that when I die, I die, and it will be finished." (pp. 297-298)

Intuitively, Dr. Hawking feels that there might be something to the heart, something beyond his physics. On the other hand, with his mind and intelligence, Dr Hawking "believes" that when he dies, that's it. He will cease to be and there will be no simple retreat into mystical unity, God or heaven. He does not realize that his own favourite black hole physics, might apply to Self. Maybe he will prefer his nothingness for a while but eventually have time to review it all and ultimately to get it right or at least try again.

The Secret Doctrine proposed new arguments and theories concerning God and creation dynamics, which have never been understood by contemporary science or academic scholarship. This series is a serious scholarly attempt to take up these issues of metaphysics, science and religion, and to address the issues of God and the origins of both the Universe and human consciousness—in a new way, based upon the wisdom teachings of humankind.

Certainly, the God hypothesis and the soul hypothesis are not granted serious consideration by those who subscribe to Dr. Sagan's philosophical approach to universe, nor by adherents of Dr. Hawking's interpretations of quantum gravity theory. However, in the light of esoteric teachings, we can propose a physics with a heart and in fact penetrate to the heart of physics. The key to exploring the God hypothesis actually lies within the physics and metaphysics of the heart itself, the mysteries of zero points, holography and higher space dimensions.

Scientists simply do not understand what esoteric mystical teachings entail, particularly *The Secret Doctrine*, and how such ideas are related to scientific facts and theories. Consequently, when Dr. Sagan turns his careful thinking to spiritual realities and the existence of divinity, he ends up telling us about God talking to flowers, or angels pushing and pummelling the planets. In this rare book, I have attempted to *"modernize the God hypothesis,"* through a comparative study of modern psychology, physics and cosmology, with the ancient wisdom and secret doctrines. This is a worthwhile endeavour even if it is only *"to hone our minds for useful things."* At least it can be good fun as Dr. Sagan notes and even allow us to integrate physics and the heart for Dr. Hawking.

2. The Accidental and Random Universe & Evolution

The evidence for random universes is precisely zero.
Haisch (2006)

Scientists ascribe a peculiar role to accidental and random factors in the creation and design of the universe and the evolution of humankind. Whereas a religious view suggests that a divine Being or Intelligence created the world, life and human consciousness, scientists resort to *accident theory* to explain the mysteries. A critical analysis of twentieth century science with its materialist philosophy cannot avoid this puzzling feature—evident within Dr. Sagan's writings, as well as in numerous other popular accounts of creation, physics and evolution. Modern scientists regard many key creation and evolutionary processes as essentially the outcome of random or arbitrary processes, nothing more than fortunate and lucky coincidences within the stream of time which gave rise to human life on planet earth.

What happened in the beginning? The most recent scientific creation scenario is that of vacuum genesis and the emergence of the universe from a singularity point out of the quantum vacuum at the first instant of time. According to the uncertainty principle of quantum theory, the vacuum energy is continually fluctuating randomly, and on one occasion, this fluctuation *happened* to be strong enough to instigate the process of universal creation. Overbye (1983) depicts the creation scenario: *"(The Universe) ballooned accidentally out of the endless void of eternity... tiny bubbles of ordinary space appear randomly, and expand into separate bubble universes.... space-time itself can arise from random fluctuations in a primordial nothingness."* (1983, pp. 93 & 99) In this view, the first cause of creation is a *random* quantum event.

Astronomer Robert Jastrow, author of *God and the Astronomers* (1978) and *Genesis Revealed* (1979/1980), describes subsequent stages of the evolution of the universe. In reference to the formation of the stars and the solar system, he writes:

> These pockets of gas that evolve into stars are formed *by accident*, in the random motions of the clouds that surge and eddy through the Universe. (1977, p. 38)

> Nearly five billion years ago, in one of the spiral arms of the Milky Way Galaxy, a cloud of gaseous matter formed *by accident* out of the swirling tendrils of the primal mist. (1979, p. 38)

Jastrow attributes the evolution of the stars and solar system to accident and the force of gravity. He then moves on to the formation of the planets, where according to exact science:

> While the Sun was forming, smaller condensations appeared in the outer regions of the cloud. These condensations, appearing *by accident*, were also held together by gravity, as the Sun had been. The smaller knots of matter became the planets. (1980, p. 69)

Included among the accidentally formed planets was Earth. Jastrow continues:

> How our planet accumulated out of that halo of tiny, orbiting grains is one of the minor mysteries of science. Probably the accumulation resulted from random collisions occurring now and then between neighbouring particles in the course of their circling motion. (p. 42)

After evolving the stars, the solar system, the sun, planets and moon, and the earth—*all by accident* and the law of gravity—Jastrow moves on to describe the origins of life on earth through the theory of neo-Darwinian evolution:

> during the course of a billion years, every conceivable size and shape of molecule is created by random collisions.... (p. 47) Eventually, after countless millions of chance encounters, a molecule is formed that has the magical ability to produce copies of itself. (p. 48) Nature required several hundred million years of ceaseless, random experimentation to discover the chemical pathways to life on the earth.... (p. 51)... nature uses random accidents as the means of improving the design of living organisms. (p. 58)... accidental variations from one individual to another provide the raw ingredients for evolution. (1977, p. 6)

Not surprisingly, Carl Sagan was thoroughly enamoured with accident theory. In *The Dragons of Eden* (1977) and *Cosmos* (1980), he continually emphasized the randomness of evolutionary processes. Natural selection is the preferential survival of organisms which *by accident* are better adapted to their environment. Sagan explains: *"Biology is more like history than it is like physics; the accidents and errors and lucky happenstances of the past powerfully prefigure the present."* (1977, pp. 5-6) In regards to the most essential aspects of human beings, including consciousness, Sagan writes: *"all of these are, at least in part, the result of apparently minor accidents in our immensely long evolutionary history."* (1980, p. 282)

These passages represent the philosophical underpinning of a particular approach to science and the idea of evolution. Whereas the ancients attributed the origin and evolution of life to God, Yahweh, Lord Krishna, Divine Mind and Spiritual Intelligences, modern science suggests that the evolution of the universe and life on planet earth proceeded by random fluctuations and collisions, happenstance and circumstance, accidental mutations, stray cosmic rays, magical abilities, and *"a little bit of luck"*! And this accidental, random *stuff* is called scientific!

In *Shadows Of Forgotten Ancestors* (1992), Carl Sagan and Anne Druyan invoke the randomness feature of evolutionary theory to argue against the general concept of supernatural causes: *"It does not seem to be how a Deity intent on special creation would do it. The mutations have no plan, no direction behind them; their randomness seems chilling...."* (p. 84) In Sagan's view, consciousness itself is just another evolutionary feature which happened to evolve by chance, rather than being an intrinsic aspect of creation. Whenever so-called exact science reaches a certain limitation or boundary condition—that is, the limits of what it can plausibly explain—scientists reflexively and automatically invoke happenings, random processes and fortunate accidents as the supposed causal principles or agents.

Steven Weinberg, a well-known physicist and cosmologist, is the author of *The First Three Minutes* (1979), which chronicles the physics of the early universe. After providing a fascinating account of the origin and evolution of matter and energy in the early universe following the Big Bang, Dr. Weinberg concludes with these philosophical ruminations:

> It is almost irresistible for humans to believe that we have some special relation to the universe, that human life is not just a more-or-less farcical outcome of a chain of accidents reaching back to the first three minutes, but that we were somehow built in from the beginning.... But if there is no solace in the fruits of our research, there is at least some consolation in the research itself. Men and women are not content to comfort themselves with tales of gods and giants, or to confine their thoughts to the daily affairs of life; they also build telescopes and satellites and accelerators, and sit at their desks for endless hours working out the meaning of the data they gather. (pp. 143-4)

In Dr. Weinberg's view, to engage in *tales of gods and giants* or to feel that human life has some *"special relation to the universe"* is nothing more than a source of self-consolation and self deception. Such ideas, he believes, have nothing to do with the nature of reality discovered by science. Instead, he suggests that human life is more like a *"farcical outcome of a chain of accidents."* Humanity's saving grace consists of those scientists who struggle so valiantly to collect data and solve the mysteries of life and the universe—all while sitting at their desks. It seems quite evident to Drs. Weinberg, Jastrow, Sagan and Hawking, that there is less and less for God to do, now that we have real science with its accident theory.

Nevertheless, it certainly seems that scientists have merely substituted one unsubstantiated solution for another. The miracle of divine creation has been replaced by science's lucky happenstance, the random mutations of evolution and the uncertainties of quantum physics. However, as a theory or model, Dr. Sagan does not *prove* the accidental nature of any specific creation or evolutionary process. In fact, his claim is not even likely *falsifiable*. Traditionally, scientists have accepted the idea that, in order for a theory to be considered scientific, it should be capable of being falsified and hence subject to experimental testing, verification or disputation. In fact, accident theory itself cannot be disproved in terms of scientific criterion. Paradoxically, scientists criticize theologians for invoking a God of the gaps but then invoke their own accidental and random scheme to plug up the many gaps in evolutionary and physical theories.

There are numerous remarkable coincidences in modern science having to do with the manner in which the constants of nature are precisely fine-tuned to give rise to the structures of the physical universe and to life on planet earth. One of those life forms, human beings, then by chance, acquires the faculties of mind and intellect necessary to study the laws of science and creation and to question the origin and nature of their own consciousness and that of the whole universe. Surely there have been some remarkably fortunate occurrences!

In *The Mind of God* (1992), scientist Paul Davies discusses the interpretation of the many coincidences in science and life:

> The apparent "fine-tuning" of the laws of nature necessary if conscious life is to evolve in the universe then carries the clear implication that God has designed the universe so as to permit such life and consciousness to emerge. It would mean that our own existence in the universe formed a central part of God's plan. (p. 213)

The universe looks *as if* it unfolds according to some plan or blueprint—with certain essential conditions and laws initially set. In this case, the evolution of the universe and human consciousness have not been simply the result of a series of fortunate and arbitrary events, but are somehow "built in" from the beginning and derive from metaphysical dimensions. Davies explains:

> There is no doubt that many scientists are opposed temperamentally to any form of metaphysical, yet alone mystical arguments. They are scornful of the notion that there might exist a God, or even an impersonal creative principle or ground of being that would underpin reality and render its contingent aspects less starkly arbitrary. Personally, I do not share their scorn. ... We have cracked part of the cosmic code. Why this should be, just why *Homo sapiens* should carry the spark of rationality that provides the key to the universe, is a deep enigma. We, who are children of the universe—animated stardust—

can nevertheless reflect on the nature of that same universe.... How we have become linked into this cosmic dimension is a mystery. Yet the linkage cannot be denied. ... I cannot believe that our existence in this universe is a mere quirk of fate, an accident of history, an incidental blip in the great cosmic drama. ... Through conscious beings the universe has generated self-awareness. This can be no trivial detail, no minor by-product of mindless, purposeless forces. We are truly meant to be here. (pp. 231-232)

For the most part, scientists simply disregard the larger philosophical issues of science and focus on the reductionist program of explaining the mechanisms of particular life processes. Modern science is a *little bit science*, in the sense that the world is divided up into smaller and smaller and more varied bits. Scientists study these bits in all their different aspects but divorce them from understanding the underlying whole which sustains them. Perhaps evolutionary events are seen as random and arbitrary precisely because they are considered solely in terms of physical forces acting on blind matter. If the same events were studied in terms of a model which recognizes metaphysical forces, then the random and arbitrary properties might be revealed to be as illusory as the shadow play in Plato's cave.

Swami Prabhupada, a mystic sage, advised Dr. Benford, a physicist, to study the laws of nature but to understand them as manifestations of the Mind of God. Human consciousness and mind particularly need to be understood in this way—that is, as being rooted into the metaphysical nature of life. Maya is a world of illusion, not because it is unreal but because it does not contain its causes within itself. Anything in the material realm—whether a microbe, tree, cow, planet or a galaxy—is created and sustained by subtle, metaphysical dimensions and processes. The attempt to formulate a comprehensive explanation of the natural laws responsible for life, without referring to these metaphysical dimensions and their operative principles, is thus ultimately futile, as all things eventually lead back to the Divine Grounds of Being—to Lord Krishna, Brahman, the Tao, Void, God, or, what Blavatsky labels as simply THAT. From a mystical perspective, all manifest things embody deep inner forces, intelligences and laws. In this view, randomness is an illusion, which arises when bits are isolated and interpreted without reference to the whole.

We should not readily dismiss the intricacies of nature and creation by attributing them to random and accidental forces and thereby neglect to look for conscious design or higher intelligence, whatever that might be. H.P. Blavatsky provided the gems of wisdoms necessary for us to reinterpret many facts, theories and enigmas of modern science. Scientists should remain open to the possibility that order arises out of chaos, not accidentally and randomly, but as a consequence of underlying forces and laws, spiritual intelligences and even

Divine Beings, manifesting through zero point dynamics. Scientists seldom consider such ideas because they subscribe so unconsciously to a materialistic and reductionist philosophy with its denial of spirit and soul.

When it comes to the matter of attaining ultimate knowledge, Paul Davies is surprisingly open to the idea that a transformation of consciousness and the experience of mystical states might allow science to penetrate further into the cosmic mysteries. He concludes: *"It seems at least worth trying to construct a metaphysical theory that reduces some of the arbitrariness of the world. ... Possibly the mystical path ... (may) provide the only route beyond the limits to which science and philosophy can take us, the only possible path to the Ultimate."* (pp. 231-2) These comments are similar to those of Rene Weber, who suggests that mystics may ultimately be more scientific than the so-called objective scientists, because they include self-knowledge as *the key* to understanding the deeper nature of reality; thereby including themselves in the equations.

Mystical teachings maintain that the processes of creation and evolution embody metaphysical principles and dimensions underlying the material forms. The causes of things visible are invisible because they manifest from "within/without" from zero point sources rooted into an alternate interior Space. Maya, as the world illusion, arises as the mind apprehends only the surface appearances, studies everything in a dualistic way and fails to consider phenomena in relationship to underlying causes and dimensions. Materialist scientists regard any explanation which invokes divine intelligence as being superstitious, yet explanations of life and consciousness which invoke accidents, happenstance, random processes and a little bit of luck, are celebrated as being scientific! Blavatsky's critique of materialist science is as valid today as it was in 1888:

> That we owe the universe to the holy creative Trinity, called *Inert Matter*, *Senseless Form* and *Blind Chance*. Of the real essence and nature of any of these three, Science knows nothing, but this is a trifling detail. (p. 505)

H.P. Blavatsky presents a wholly alternative view of the role of random and accidental processes in the phenomena of nature. She writes:

> Nature geometrizes universally in all her manifestations. There is an inherent law—not only in the primordial, but also in the manifested matter of our phenomenal plane—by which Nature correlates her geometrical forms, and later, also, her compound elements; and in which there is no place for accident or chance. (p. 97)

She states that there is *"no place for accident or chance."* In fact, the first aim of The Secret Doctrine was *"to show that Nature is not "a fortuitous concurrence of atoms."*

How then could we look for God in the laws of nature or the study of the psyche and mind? We may not see angels pushing planets around or God talking to the morning glory plant, but might we find other more subtle forms of *"divine micro-intervention?"* Mystical and metaphysical ideas can indeed be brought into the domain of rational science and they do offer hypotheses which could be subject to scientific experimentation with the possibility of being falsified. *The Secret Doctrine* in fact allows for the reinterpretation of many other scientific facts and theories. When one thinks of it, what could be more irrational, pseudo-scientific and *ad hoc* than accident theory?

3. The Quasi-Religious Dimensions of Modern Physics

In *Pythagoras' Trousers: God, Physics, and the Gender Wars*, Margaret Wertheim provides a useful analysis of modern physics and she critically examines the physicists' obsession to find the ultimate *"Theory of Everything"* (or *TOE*) which would explain all the laws of physics within one grand theory. Why, she asks, do physicists assume the right to associate their endeavours with "God," the "mind of God," the 'God particle' and the like? Physicists assume the role of the "high priests" of science and associate God with their favourite particle, higher dimensional superstring or Theory of Everything. She writes:

> Stephen Hawking, Leon Lederman, and George Smoot—these are men at the heart of contemporary physics.... All these men have publicly associated the quest for a unified theory with God. In drawing an association with contemporary physics and God, they are not alone. Indeed, this kind of dialogue has become endemic among physicists—at least as far as their popular writing is concerned....
>
> But many physicists using the God drawcard are not engaged in serious theological or spiritual thinking. Following a millennia-old tradition that has associated mathematically based science with divinity, they simply assume it is legitimate to present their activities in a quasi-religious light. Despite the supposedly secular climate of twentieth-century science, some physicists are once again demanding that we see them as high priests, leading humanity "upward" toward transcendent, even divine knowledge of the world. (1997, pp. 221-222)

Stephen Hawking provides the most unusual paradoxes in his writings and philosophy. Most people—even many who have read *A Brief History of Time*—think that Hawking embodies a religious or spiritual attitude in his search for the ultimate quantum gravity theory. However, this is far from true and in interviews, Hawking readily dismisses the belief in God, afterlife, mysticism and the like—believing instead "in science" and 'natural laws' instead of 'supernatural laws.'

Wertheim examines the paradoxes of Hawking's public image and his inconsistent underlying attitude:

> TOE physicists themselves are associating a unified theory with God. The most famous in this camp is Stephen Hawking. In the introduction to Hawking's international best-seller *A Brief History of Time*, Carl Sagan alerts the reader that: "The word God fills these

pages. Hawking embarks on a quest to answer Einstein's famous question about whether God had any choice in creating the universe. Hawking is attempting, as he explicitly states, to understand the mind of God. The implication throughout his book is that a unified theory *transcends* space and time and somehow exists "beyond" the realm of material manifestation—a feat traditionally attributed to God alone.... (p. 217)

The immense success of *A Brief History of Time*—it has sold more than 5 million copies worldwide—and Hawking's personal success in the public arena, are, I believe, in part attributable to the quasi-religious tone in which he presents the enterprise of contemporary physics. Although his reference to "the mind of God" actually occurs at the every end of the book, it opens the film of the same name. As the filmmakers rightly recognized, in an age when many people are hungering for a rapprochement between the spiritual and the scientific, the concept of the physicist as high priest is immensely appealing. And, like Einstein, Hawking is very convincing in the role. He too has assumed an almost mystical aura, which in his case is compounded by the extreme disjunction between the power of his mind and the lameness of his body.... Hawking may be confined to a wheelchair, but his mind soars. Not even many physicists understand the concept of "imaginary time." He is a being seemingly poised at the junction of the human, the subhuman, and the superhuman—and many people long to believe that this disabled physicist might just take us to God.

Ironically, it is Hawking himself who has suggested that his relativistic-quantum cosmology might obviate the need for a "Creator." But he seems to want to have it both ways—at the same time pushing God out of the universe although invoking him as a constant subtext of his work. It is not at all clear from *A Brief History of Time* whether Hawking genuinely believes in a god, or whether he is just indulging in self-aggrandizement. Unlike Copernicus, Kepler, and Newton (and even Einstein in his own way), Hawking is not a serious theological thinker...Yet, whatever Hawking's true feelings about God, many people have come to see him as a scientific high priest, the inheritor of Einstein's mantle. (pp. 217-219)

The use of the words God, the mind of God, the God particle, and the God like Superforce are endemic to popular science writers and TOE theorists. However, the underlying attitude is usually that we no longer need God, now that we have modern physicists, as high priests, to answer the ultimate questions about cosmic origins.

Hawking is hoping to fill in the last "gap" in contemporary science, trying to exclude God from the universe by accounting for creation events in purely mathematical and physical terms, thereby explaining away the Big Bang singularity. Of course, to Hawking, there would be nothing "mystical" about singularities, quantum theory or the quantum vacuum. Carl Sagan similarly bandies about the name of God, admitting God only if we define "him" as the *sum of all the physical laws*, but not accepting any of the traditional attributes of God—that is, as an omniscient, omnipotent and omnipresent Being.

Scientists often regard science as the new religion and want to *metaphorically* see into the mind of God but they do not take to heart the deeper mysteries of what that quest might entail. Scientists leave themselves, their own consciousness and being, out of the equation. Furthermore, scientists simply do not realize the extent to which their own theories are beginning to vindicate mystical teachings—because of the pervasive lack of familiarity and appreciation of what such occult teachings entail.

Indeed, what is it that leads scientists to conclude that there is nothing 'mystical' about singularities, superstrings, the nothingness and plenum of the quantum vacuum, or other emerging ideas in physics? It is just as 'mystical' to have the singularity eventually smeared out, beyond the level of the zero point into imaginary time and the infinite, as for it to appear as a point source at all. Dr. Hawking does not even consider that such zero points, aethers, space and higher dimensions, the void and the plenum, have been the domain of occultists for hundreds and thousands of years. In fact, metaphysical expositions of creation bear profound relationships to modern theories.

Certainly, Dr. Hawking's logic or 'reasoning' in dismissing a Creator because of advancements in physics is quite irrational and a leap of faith on his behalf. His logic is about as rational as Dr. Sagan's, who states that there is less and less for God to do now that science can explain how the sun, phototropism and plant hormones cause the opening of morning glory flower. Now that we can explain these dynamics and other phenomena of nature in scientific terms, Dr. Sagan assumes we no longer have reason to invoke God, spirits and souls, as causal explanations. Dr. Sagan states that no one has seen God talking to the flowers, saying, *"hey, flower, open,"* and consequently, there is no reason to consider that God might *"micro-intervene"* in the laws of nature. Of course, Dr. Sagan himself did not know of Blavatsky's *Secret Doctrine* and her explanations of *how* the Gods and other invisible powers clothe themselves in bodies based upon zero point sources! Ironically, Blavatsky offers the ultimate model of "divine micro-intervention"—all through what Hawking labels as those *"badly behaved points!"*

We should be as sceptical of Dr. Hawking's interpretation of quantum gravity theory, as we are of Dr. Carl Sagan's assurance that: *"As we learn more and more about the universe, there seems less and less for God to do."* In fact, as we learn more and more, we find deeper and deeper enigmas and mysteries. In the same lecture in which he describes God's universe as contracting, Dr. Sagan does note, by the way, that there are many unresolved mysteries in science: " *What is the origin of the human species? Where did plants and animals come from? how did life arise? the Earth, the planets, the Sun, the stars? Does the universe have an origin, and if so, what?"* At the same time that Dr. Sagan is about to dismiss God as being irrelevant to understanding nature, he notes that all of the central questions concerning origins are not resolved! Thirty years after *Broca's Brain*, scientists still do not understand how life and human beings arose, how the earth, moon, planets and Sun were formed, nor the galaxies and super-galaxies, nor what is before the origin of the universe, nor many other issues in physics concerning all of the fundamental nature of matter and energy, time and space. The number and sheer complexity of the mysteries and enigmas confronting science are such that the question of the existence of God certainly does not hinge on whether or not the singularity can be smeared out—despite what Stephen Hawking suggests. Indeed, the existence of a singularity is not even inconsistent with religious and mystical perspectives but supportive of them, validating the mystical claims! Further, the advances in modern physics and cosmology, when properly understood substantiate many other of Blavatsky's claims and concepts.

In the 1970s and 80s, astronomer Robert Jastrow was comparing the big-bang scenario to the Genesis account of creation and noting certain similarities. All major religious and esoteric teachings depict creation as having occurred *once upon a time* and this basic idea was confirmed by the discovery of the big bang. Jastrow noted further how the idea—that God willed that there should be 'light"—made sense in terms of trying to depict early creation events, as energetic photons can create material particles. However, thirty years later, scientists have advanced from the big bang scenario to singularities, vacuum states and higher dimensions, we must consider how these concepts have also been articulated by occultist Blavatsky as within other esoteric teachings.

The search for unity itself arises out of the Judeo-Christian tradition of monotheism and the faith that all things are unified and part of one super-force or Divine Being. Although modern physicists associate their theories with the search for God, this is not usually accompanied by any serious spiritual search or informed mystical understanding. References to God and physics may help to sell books but they can obscure the basic mechanistic and materialist philosophy underlying scientific theories. Dr. Hawking feels that there might be something to the heart, something beyond his physics. On the other hand, with his mind and intelligence, Dr. Hawking "believes" that when he dies, that's it. He will cease to be and there will be no simple retreat into mystical unity, God or heaven—not even a black hole.

Madame Blavatsky (1888) noted that: *"the occult side of Nature has never been approached by the science of modern civilization."* Although Blavatsky wrote this over a hundred years ago, she would likely not change her attitude if she were familiar with the TOE theorists' speculative philosophizing about the mind of God, or Stephen Hawking's quantum gravity theory. Scientists are arriving at a knowledge of the profound depths of creation, but because they subscribe to a simplistic mechanistic outlook, they do not recognize or appreciate the mystical and metaphysical dimensions of their own theories. Blavatsky embodied the truly scientific attitude in her recommendation:

> The Secret teachings...must be contrasted with the speculations of modern science. Archaic axioms must be placed side by side with modern hypotheses and comparisons left to the sagacious reader. (*SD* I, p. 480)

4. God as Mathematician, Geometrician and Designer

In *Pythagoras' Trousers*, Wertheim traces the history of science and religion and demonstrates how entwined they have been. The roots of science are traced to the mystical teachings of Pythagoras, an Ionian philosopher who studied in the Egyptian mystery teachings, lived in Babylon and returned to Greece and Italy circa 600 BC. Pythagoras introduced mathematics to the Greeks, borrowing from the Egyptians and Babylonians. Wertheim outlines Pythagoras' essential ideas concerning the nature of numbers:

> Pythagoras saw the essence of reality in the immaterial magic of numbers. He believed the universe could be explained by the properties of numbers and the relations between them, a philosophy encapsulated in his famous dictum *"All is number."* (pp. 18-19)

> At the heart of Pythagorean thought were the whole numbers: 1, 2, 3, 4, 5, and so on. Pythagoras believed that numbers were divine and he equated them with the gods. The number 1 through 10, those of the *decade*, were said to be especially sacred. ... the deities had become abstract mathematical entities. The Pythagorean world picture was ... a metaphysical dance of numbers. ... Indeed might not number be the essence of form itself? ... The temporal numerical patterns apparent in the heavens and the spatial patterns made by numbers themselves convinced Pythagoras that all was indeed number, and that number was truly the essence of reality. (pp. 24-27)

In the earliest times, numbers were regarded as having mystical and magical properties. The esoteric mystical and occult literature is replete with sacred numerology, geometry, symbols, hieroglyphics, myths and so on, embodying such ancient teachings. Numbers do not simply follow each other in a linear way with each number simply being one more than the one before it. Instead, numbers are principles inherent within the metaphysical and physical nature of reality. Numbers, as symbols, depict the processes by which form is generated from formlessness.

Pythagorean thought was largely abandoned in the mainstream of religious science but has reemerged during different historic periods. In the twelfth century, the philosophy of Robert Grosseteste (1168-1253), the first medieval scientific thinker, embodied Pythagorean influences. Wertheim summarizes Grosseteste's metaphysics:

> In Grosseteste's metaphysics of light, we see the first full-blown expression of a mathematico-Christian cosmology, in which we may even recognize elements of the modern mathematical world picture. According to Grosseteste, the universe was generated from a point of primordial light—the divine illumination, or *lux*, of which visible light was said to be the physical manifestation. Now, because the definitive feature of light is that it propagates outward, like flares radiating from a candle, this original point immediately began to expand, forming the sphere of the universe. As the first emanation of God's power, Grosseteste believed that *lux* was ultimately the cause of all natural action in the universe. Indeed it was the primal force of the world. Man could not study the divine *lux* directly, but he could study its physical manifestation in light. Thus, Grosseteste believed light was the key to understanding the working of the natural world.... Grosseteste concluded that a mathematical understanding of light would serve as the model for understanding all natural influence, or what we would now call force.... this is close to what mathematical men believe today. In contemporary physicists' quest to understand the forces of nature, it is light that has generally served as the model. (pp. 49-50)

Grosseteste conceived of the Biblical Deity as a divine mathematician and viewed the mathematics and geometry inherent in nature as reflecting the same creative principles as inherent in the Mind or Being of God. His scientific work was in the study of optics, the refraction of light, rainbows and the like. In this view, creation emerged from a point of primordial light, the first point of cosmic manifestation. The underlying *lux*, or supernal light, is the metaphysical principle underlying creation.

Many pioneering figures in science's early years—such as Nicholas of Cusa, Copernicus, Kepler and Newton—evinced an avid interest in mystical teachings and doctrines. Nicholas of Cusa was a fifteen-century cardinal of the Catholic Church and regarded as the primary champion of mathematical science in his era. Wertheim summarizes Nicholas' views:

> In true medieval tradition, God was both the starting point and end goal of Cusa's metaphysical speculations. For him, the universe was the unfolding of forms already enfolded within God. Accordingly, to know the world was to know the unfolding of God, and the way to knowing was through *number*. Cusa believed that number was nothing less than the "image" of "God's mind"—thus to study mathematics was to study the mind of God. ... God and mathematics harmonized into a mystical theology that combined both prescriptions for spiritual transcendence and scope for a genuine mathematical science of nature. ... the primary purpose of mathematical study was to bring us ever closer to the undivided Oneness that is the source of all, in Cusa's words, that we may be "elevated in accordance with the powers of human intelligence" so we may come to see "the ever-blessed one and triune God." ... know God through numbers ... know nature through numbers. (pp. 56-57)

Nicholas's quest was to see into the mind of God, understanding both metaphysical and physical laws through numbers and to *"behold God's cosmic mathematical plan."* The mystical perspective regards creation as the unfolding of number patterns or forms already enfolded in God. The plenum contains all possible things in all possible states in an un-manifest or undifferentiated form. Creation occurs from within-without from zero point dimensions as divine principles are mathematically embodied in the generation of form out of formlessness.

In the seventeenth century, Kepler was *"the first true mathematical physicist"* and one of the *"great mathematical mystics of all time."* Again, we find the Pythagorean number philosophy:

> Kepler saw the world as the material embodiment of mathematical forms present within God before the act of Creation. "Why waste words?" he wrote. "Geometry existed before the Creation, is co-eternal with the mind of God, is God *himself*. ... geometry provided God with a model for the Creation." Thus, "where matter is, there is geometry." ....
>
> Just as geometry had provided God with the model for the Creation, Kepler believed that geometry was "implanted into man, together with God's own likeness." For Kepler ... "the human mind (was) a *simulacrum* of the divine mind," both being essentially geometrical. The implication was that man, as *mathematician*, was the true human

reflection of God: that it was through mathematical study of the world that we could truly participate in the divine. (Wertheim, p. 71)

According to *The Secret Doctrine*, a human being embodies the same numerological principles of enumeration or form-generation, as embodied in the dynamics of the creation of the larger universe.

In the seventeenth century Sir Isaac Newton established physics as the *"queen of the sciences."* Newton formulated the law of gravity and three laws of motion governing material objects. Newton's principles stood until Einstein's theories of relativity were formulated three hundred years latter. However, in addition to his 'legitimate science,' Newton left behind over *"a half million words on alchemy."* Newton held highly mystical views of space and its relationship to God. Wertheim explains:

> Newton's God did not oversee the maintenance of the world from some remote pinnacle; ... Newton's divine overlord was present throughout the material world. He achieved this omnipresence through the medium of space, which, for Newton, was nothing less than God's sensorium. By his omnipresence (mediated through space), God was all seeing, all-discerning, and finally, all ruling. In Newton's words: "He is eternal and infinite; omnipotent and omniscient; that is, his duration reaches from eternity to eternity; his presence from infinity to infinity; he governs all things, and knows all things that are or can be done." ... Most important, he argued that space must be *absolute* because it was synonymous with the presence of an absolute God. (p. 123)

"Space" is the medium of God's omnipresence and omniscience. Newton regarded himself as a restorer of the ancient wisdom which God had given to humankind and his ideas allowed for a synthesis of science and Christianity in his era. Historically, many scientists have held spiritual and/or mystical ideas about the nature of creation and its relationship to God.

Einstein's theories of relativity and the development of twentieth century quantum theory led to the discarding of several essential ancient ideas—such as those of Absolute Space and Time, and of the "aether", an immaterial something said to pervade all Space or to constitute Space itself. However, new concepts in physics—concerning hidden compacted space dimensions and/or hyperspace and the mysterious quantum vacuum with its zero point fields—provide new ways of understanding mystical concepts about creation physics and metaphysics, and concerning the nature of the Ether. Space provides the medium in which everything occurs. Newton describes Space as *"God's sensorium"*—a remarkable phrase!

From the turn of the last century, the development of modern science has led to an increasingly materialist philosophy of science and a divorce between religion and science. Scientists regard the laws of nature as inherent principles of matter and the idea of supernatural causes behind these laws has been dismissed. Materialist scientists reject a priori the idea that reality might be the embodiment of Divine Mind or Spiritual Intelligences, or that forms of such hidden sacred geometry are at work in the generation of form out of formlessness.

However, many of the seemingly bizarre concepts and claims of mysticism are in fact quite conceivable and understandable—in the light of the new concepts emerging within modern science. Unfortunately, physicists are simply speaking metaphorically about the mind of God and not seriously exploring such esoteric possibilities. Blavatsky took such comparative study of the wisdom teachings and the science of her day most seriously.

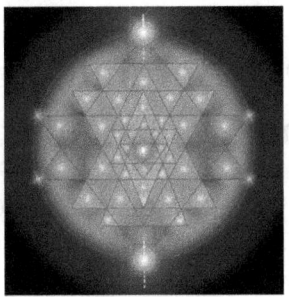

I I I
The Cosmogenesis & Metaphysics of *The Secret Doctrine*

"the Universe is contained in ovo in the first natural point...."
(Blavatsky, S. D. I, p. 118)

"Space is neither a "limitless void," nor a "conditioned fullness," but both ... Space is called in the esoteric symbolism "the Seven-Skinned Eternal Mother-Father.""" (S. D. I, pp. 8-9)

"... the majority of the eminent and learned materialists very often utter the greatest fallacies. Let us take the following case. Most of them reject actio in distans (one of the fundamental principles in the question of Aether or Akasa in Occultism), while ... there is no physical action, "which, on close examination, does not resolve itself into actio in distans.... """ (S.D., pp. 487-8)

"...for formative or creative purposes, the GREAT LAW (Theists may call it God) stops, or rather modifies its perpetual motion on seven invisible points within the area of the manifested Universe. "The great Breath digs through Space seven holes into Laya to cause them to circumgyrate during Manvantara." ... We have said that Laya is what Science may call the Zero-point ... " (S. D. I, pp. 147-8)

"Light is the great Protean magician and under the divine will of the architect, or rather the architects, the "Builders" (called One collectively), its multifarious, omnipotent waves give birth to every form; as well as to every living being. ... the sun ... is ... the lens, by which the rays of the primordial light become materialized, are concentrated upon our Solar System, and produce all correlation of forces." (S. D. I, p. 579)

1. One Absolute Reality
The Fundamental Dogma of Occultism

> There is but one indivisible and absolute Omniscience and Intelligence in the Universe, and this thrills throughout every atom and infinitesimal point of the whole finite Kosmos. (S. D. I, p. 277)

Modern science approaches an understanding of life and the universe from below, striving from the establishment of particulars to the formulation of universal principles. In contrast, mystical and occult teachings begin with the idea of the wholeness or unity of life and regard the particulars as differentiations of the Unity. Blavatsky states this *"first fundamental proposition"* of *The Secret Doctrine*:

> An Omnipresent, Eternal, Boundless, and Immutable PRINCIPLE on which all speculation is impossible, since it transcends the power of human conception... "unthinkable and unspeakable."... there is one absolute Reality which antecedes all manifested, conditioned, being. This Infinite and Eternal Cause... is the rootless root of "all that was, is or ever shall be." (S. D. I, p. 14)

Creation must be understood from above, with One undivided Absolute Reality as the root principle of all manifestation. Any manifest element, or quantum, ultimately resolves back in its innermost nature into the Unity of the Absolute. There are various statements and formulations of this principle through *The Secret Doctrine*:

> The first and Fundamental dogma of Occultism is Universal Unity (or Homogeneity).... (S. D. I, p. 58)

> If the student bears in mind that there is but One Universal Element, which is infinite, unborn, and undying, and that all the rest—as in the world of phenomena—are but so many various differentiated aspects and transformations of that One, from Cosmical down to microcosmical effects, from super-human down to human and sub-human beings, the totality, in short, of objective existence—then the first and chief difficulty will disappear and Occult Cosmology may be mastered. (S. D. I, p. 75)

> no manifested thing can be thought of except as a part of a larger whole: the total aggregate being the One manifested Universe that issues from the unmanifested or Absolute—called Non-Being or "No-Number," to distinguish it from Being or "the One Number." (S. D. I, pp. 87-8)

> The radical unity of the ultimate essence of each constituent part of compounds in Nature is the one fundamental law in Occult Science. (S. D. I)
>
> The fundamental Law, ... the central point from which all emerged, around and toward which all gravitates, and upon which is hung the philosophy of the rest, is the One homogeneous divine SUBSTANCE=PRINCIPLE, the one radical cause. ... It is latent in every atom in the Universe, and is the Universe itself. (S. D. I, pp. 272-3)

The Secret Doctrine begins with the Unity of creation and all phenomena are regarded as impermanent and illusory differentiations.

Whereas occultism or mystical/spiritual teachings begin with the One and derive the manifold from the One, science has worked in the opposite direction. It began with the many—the myriad of living forms and the manifest phenomena of nature and strives towards understanding the ultimate causes and universal principles. This is the direction that modern physics and cosmology has moved in tracing the universe back into a singularity condition and attempting to unify all the known laws of nature into one Theory of Everything, or *"god-life superforce"* (a phrase coined by Paul Davies in *God and the New Physics*, 1983). The wholeness of reality is also intrinsic to the theories of quantum physics itself, as all elements are part of one overall quantum system emerging from a singlet state.

In their efforts to unify the laws of nature and to understand the first moments of creation, scientists are arriving at the point where the mystics begin. Modern science and occult science are not incompatible but complement each other. We have to grasp the whole in order to understand the parts and understand the parts in order to approach the whole. The beginning, like the ending, is the unity or wholeness of creation within the Absolute. All mystical and spiritual teachings are founded on this fundamental postulate of the Unity of all things—in God, Brahman, the Absolute, the Deity, or within simply THAT.

Traditionally, God is described as omnipresent, omnipotent, omniscient—present everywhere, containing all potencies and all knowing. Thus, if God exists, then ultimately, as we penetrate to the heart of being, to the heart of matter, or to the heart of ourselves, or of Space, then we must arrive at the Unity, and there must be some unusual transitional levels in between. Any finite thing when traced far enough must merge again into the infinite. H.P.B. states most simply: *"The fundamental dogma of Occultism is Universal Unity."* (S. D. I, p. 58) Blavatsky also suggests that all physics pursued far enough must lead to metaphysics.

2. Before all Time

a. The *Stanzas of Dzyan*:

The first and second *Stanzas of Dzyan* depict the ultimate realities during the *Nights of Brahma* when the Universe has yet to be created. This is a pre-Big Bang era, when the Son (the relative space-time continuum of the manifest universe) has yet to be born out of the root principles of creation. During the Nights of Brahma, everything is absorbed in the DARKNESS and the ETERNAL NON-BEING—THE ONE BEING:

STANZA I

1. THE ETERNAL PARENT WRAPPED IN HER EVER INVISIBLE ROBES HAD SLUMBERED ONCE AGAIN FOR SEVEN ETERNITIES.

2. TIME WAS NOT, FOR IT LAY ASLEEP IN THE INFINITE BOSOM OF DURATION.

3. UNIVERSAL MIND WAS NOT, FOR THERE WERE NO AH-HI TO CONTAIN IT.

4. THE SEVEN WAYS TO BLISS WERE NOT. THE GREAT CAUSES OF MISERY WERE NOT, FOR THERE WAS NO ONE TO PRODUCE AND GET ENSNARED BY THEM.

5. DARKNESS ALONE FILLED THE BOUNDLESS ALL, FOR FATHER, MOTHER AND SON WERE ONCE MORE ONE, AND THE SON HAD NOT AWAKENED YET FOR THE NEW WHEEL, AND HIS PILGRIMAGE THEREON.

6. THE SEVEN SUBLIME LORDS AND THE SEVEN TRUTHS HAD CEASED TO BE, AND THE UNIVERSE, THE SON OF NECESSITY, WAS IMMERSED IN PARANISHPANNA, TO BE OUT-BREATHED BY THAT WHICH IS AND YET IS NOT. NAUGHT WAS.

7. THE CAUSES OF EXISTENCE HAD BEEN DONE AWAY WITH; THE VISIBLE THAT WAS, AND THE INVISIBLE THAT IS, RESTED IN ETERNAL NON-BEING—THE ONE BEING.

8. ALONE THE ONE FORM OF EXISTENCE STRETCHED BOUNDLESS, INFINITE, CAUSELESS, IN DREAMLESS SLEEP; AND LIFE PULSATED UNCONSCIOUS IN UNIVERSAL SPACE, THROUGHOUT THAT ALL-PRESENCE WHICH IS SENSED BY THE OPENED EYE OF THE DANGMA.

9. BUT WHERE WAS THE DANGMA WHEN THE ALAYA OF THE UNIVERSE WAS IN PARAMARTHA AND THE GREAT WHEEL WAS ANUPADAKA?

Stanza I mainly depicts the lack of differentiated existence: Time was not, universal mind was not, the Seven Lords were not, the Causes of Existence had been done away with, and so on. What was then? Naught was. Only the Absolute Non-Being which is Infinite Being—beyond the comprehension of the finite mind, existed. One Stanza describes everything as "RESTED IN ETERNAL NON-BEING—THE ONE BEING," most associated with Darkness. Blavatsky explains: *"Darkness, then, is the eternal matrix in which the sources of light appear and disappear."* (p. 41)

Stanza I depicts the Absolute and yet suggests differentiated aspects and forces latent within the Darkness of Non-Being. The *'Eternal Parent'* referred to in the first verse is the seven-skinned Eternal Parent Space—which for Blavatsky is the ultimate Aether of Space itself. In the terminology of modern physics, this is a seven dimensional hyperspace. The Stanzas also refer to the SEVEN SUBLIME LORDS, who are the divine intelligences latent in non-being and who are the ones who 'sculpt the void' during creation processes and manifest through the laws of nature. The Eternal Parent Space and Seven Lords serve as the root principles for material and spiritual creation, but remain undifferentiated and in Darkness.

STANZA II

1. ... WHERE WERE THE BUILDERS, THE LUMINOUS SONS OF MANVANTARIC DAWN? ... IN THE UNKNOWN DARKNESS IN THEIR AH-HI PARANISHPANNA, THE PRODUCERS OF FORM FROM NO-FORM—THE ROOT OF THE WORLD— THE DEVAMATRI AND SVÂBHÂVAT, RESTED IN THE

BLISS OF NON-BEING.

2. ... WHERE WAS SILENCE? WHERE THE EARS TO SENSE IT? NO, THERE WAS NEITHER SILENCE NOR SOUND; NAUGHT SAVE CEASELESS, ETERNAL BREATH, WHICH KNOWS ITSELF NOT.

3. THE HOUR HAD NOT YET STRUCK; THE RAY HAD NOT YET FLASHED INTO THE GERM; THE MATRIPADMA HAD NOT YET SWOLLEN.

4. HER HEART HAD NOT YET OPENED FOR THE ONE RAY TO ENTER, THENCE TO FALL, AS THREE INTO FOUR, INTO THE LAP OF MAYA.

5. THE SEVEN SONS WERE NOT YET BORN FROM THE WEB OF LIGHT, DARKNESS ALONE WAS FATHER-MOTHER, SVÂBHÂVAT, AND SVÂBHÂVAT WAS IN DARKNESS.

6. THESE TWO ARE THE GERM, AND THE GERM IS ONE. THE UNIVERSE WAS STILL CONCEALED IN THE DIVINE THOUGHT AND THE DIVINE BOSOM ...

The second Stanza continues to depict the pre-manifestation state. It also introduces the Ceaseless Eternal Breath existent within pre-existence: NAUGHT SAVE CEASELESS, ETERNAL BREATH, WHICH KNOWS ITSELF NOT. (II, 2) This is a fundamental movement, breath and activity within the Absolute and is the counterpart of the ETERNAL PARENT SPACE. Within *The Secret Doctrine*, the *Eternal Parent Space* and the *Eternal Ceaseless Breath* represent the Divine Mother and Divine Father principles, the roots of matter/space and spirit. These are both present within the Eternal NON-BEING. Verse I 8, states: "LIFE PULSATED UNCONSCIOUS IN UNIVERSAL SPACE."

Thus far, the Mother, Father and Son are undifferentiated, hence One, but latent in Non-Being. So also, the Builders of Form from Formlessness, the Seven Sublime Lords or Seven Luminous Sons are not manifest bur latent. Stanza II, 4 foreshadows what is to happen when creation occurs: HER HEART HAD NOT YET OPENED FOR THE ONE RAY TO ENTER, THENCE TO FALL, AS THREE INTO FOUR, INTO THE LAP OF MAYA." This suggests that creation is instigated with the penetration of a RAY (of light or of the logos) into the Heart of the Divine Mother, the Eternal Parent Space. The Eternal Non-Being, the Parent Space and the Ceaseless Breath thus produce a 'Son,' as the Three fall into Four, and the creation of the impermanent world of *maya*.

2b. The Days and Nights of Brahma

Whereas the first fundamental proposition of *The Secret Doctrine* postulates one Absolute or Deity which antedates manifest creation, the second fundamental proposition affirms:

> The Eternity of the Universe *in toto* as a boundless plane; periodically "the playground of numberless Universes incessantly manifesting and disappearing," called "the manifesting stars," and the "sparks of Eternity." "The Eternity of the Pilgrim" is like a wink of the Eye of Self-Existence. The appearance and disappearance of Worlds is like a regular tidal ebb of flux and reflux. (pp. 16-17)

Blavatsky explained a basic *"law of periodicity"* whereby all cosmic phenomena undergo periods of creation and dissolution, ebb and flow, activity and passivity, emergence and dissolution. Any created Son manifests out of the Absolute Being/Non-Being at the beginning of time and ultimately dissolves again back into Non-Being at the end of time. The *"Eternity of the Universe"* thus gives rise to innumerable *"Sons," "manifested Universes"* or *"Winks in the Eye of Self-Existence."* The whole of the present Universe is but one of the *"numberless Universes,"* all emerging as sparks of the Eternal. Between periods of cosmic manifestation, the *"dark mystery of Non-Being"* reigns and *"darkness filled the boundless All."* During the Nights of Brahma, *"the hosts of Dhyan Chohans, and all the existing Elements are at once merged into their original."* (pp. 372-3)

In accordance with Hindu mythology, the periods of cosmic manifestation are referred to as the *"Days of Brahma;"* while periods wherein the Universes are absorbed into the ultimate states of Non-Being are referred to as the *"Nights of Brahma."* These are also referred to as periods of *Manvantara* (cosmic manifestation) and *Pralaya* (cosmic dissolution):

> The esoteric doctrine teaches... that the one infinite and unknown Essence exists from all eternity, and in regular and harmonious successions is either passive or active.... these conditions are called the "Days" and the "Nights" of Brahma. The latter is either "awake" or "asleep." (S. D. I, pp. 3-4)

In modern terminology, Blavatsky's describes an infinite number of expanding and contracting universes or Kosmoses over Eternity:

> Upon inaugurating an active period, says the *Secret Doctrine*, an expansion of this Divine essence, from *within outwardly*, occurs in

obedience to eternal and immutable law, and the phenomenal or visible universe is the ultimate result of the long chain of cosmical forces thus progressively set in motion. In like manner, when the passive condition is resumed, a contraction of the Divine essence takes place, and the previous work of creation is gradually and progressively undone. The visible universe becomes disintegrated, its material dispersed; and "darkness," solitary and alone, broods once more over the face of the "deep. " To use a metaphor... an outbreathing of the "unknown essence" produces the world; and an inhalation causes it to disappear. *This process has been going on from all eternity, and our present universe is but one of an infinite series which had no beginning and will have no end.* (Blavatsky, Isis Unveiled, 1877, Vol. II, pp. 264-5,)

In 1877, Blavatsky was describing endless series of expanding and contracting universes emerging out of the root principle of the Divine Essence of the Absolute. These concepts predate the modern scientific hypotheses concerning the void/plenum of the quantum realm, hyperspace dimensions and oscillating periods of universal creation and dissolution, by over a century!

The two opening *Stanzas of Dzyan* depict the Nights of Brahma which are followed by the unfolding of the Cosmos from within/without—out of the Eternal Parent Space and the Ceaseless Breath. Creation involves the sequential differentiation of the seven luminous Lords and subsequently of seven fold elements and planes of existence. So also, *"... at the time of pralaya these seven successively re-enter into each other. The egg of Brahma is dissolved with its seven zones, seven oceans, seven regions, etc."* (S. D. I, p. 257) Blavatsky describes the dissolution of the Cosmos, explaining that *"Everything will have re-entered the Great Breath"* (p. 266) and further that, *"everything that exists is resolved into the primal element, to be remodelled at the end of that longer night."* (p. 371)

Blavatsky provides a model of an oscillating universe, wherein the Absolute periodically gives rise to innumerable manifested Cosmoses or Sons. Certainly, there are profound similarities between such views and those of modern cosmologists who now consider that the *"spacetime foam of the quantum vacuum"* might give rise to innumerable universes over time—just like such an 'Eternal Parent Space,' and that there might be oscillating universes which are influenced by earlier cycles. So also Blavatsky notes: *"Our Kosmos and Nature will run down only to reappear on a more perfect plane after every PRALAYA."* (S. D. I, p. 149)

Blavatsky further notes that such periods of activity and rest occur on different levels. So in addition to the Pralaya at the close of the Age of Brahma, there are is a Solar Pralaya at the end of a cycle within the solar system; and planetary pralaya at the end of each Globe period formed in cycles of seven rounds.

Blavatsky certainly knew that the earth had not existed forever and that it was not created in its present form. She described our current era as the Fourth of Seven Rounds of life within our Solar System and current humanity as the fifth of seven root races within the current round. Blavatsky envisioned a far more ancient history to our planet and solar system within the cosmic order than most scientists consider even today, and similar cycles of rest and activity occurring on different levels within the larger Kosmos.

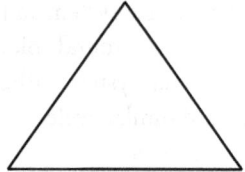

3. Primordial Principles

a. The Absolute & the Theological Trinity

The first fundamental proposition of *The Secret Doctrine* postulates the existence of the Absolute. The Absolute is identified with Absolute Being and Consciousness, and also with Absolute Non-Being and Unconsciousness. It is described as 'the void' to finite minds and as the 'divine plenum' (the container of all) to the mystically awakened. It is the Absolute Darkness and the Infinite Light. In paradoxical descriptions, Blavatsky elaborates upon the nature of the Absolute Being, which is Absolute Non-Being.

At times, Blavatsky refers simply to 'THAT'—that beyond any conception of human thought or understanding—the 'unspeakable' Omnipresent, Eternal, Absolute Reality which antecedes all manifested and conditioned being. This is the Infinite and Eternal Cause, the rootless root of all manifestation.

The Absolute Non-Being contains the potencies of life and creation in a latent state—in the fullness of the Divine Plenum:

> In the sense and perception of finite "Beings," THAT is Non-"being," in the sense that it is the one BE-NESS; for, in this ALL lies concealed its coeternal and coeval emanation or inherent radiation, which, upon becoming periodically Brahma (the male-female Potency) becomes or expands itself into the manifested Universe. (S. D. I, p. 7)

The Absolute exists at a substratum of existence beyond the level of material differentiation—beyond the level of quanta, wherein we encounter the limits of the Planckian units. The Absolute Being/Non-Being is the 'Eternal Matrix'—out of which sources of light or manifest creation appear and disappear.

Blavatsky explains the root principles underling the emergence of the Cosmos. She describes the Absolute firstly as being both the Absolute Being and Non-Being—the plenum and void. These concepts correspond to the Ayin and En Soph of the Kabbalist; and in the language of the modern physicists, it corresponds to the void and plenum of the quantum vacuum with its zero-point fields. The modern scientific idea of *vacuum genesis* is certainly consistent with Blavatsky's archaic teaching concerning the Nights of Brahma and that creation manifested out of a paradoxical void/plenum of the Absolute.

The One Omnipresent Life is periodic in its manifestation and this gives rise to the *Days and Nights of Brahma* (the Creator) and the pilgrimages (or incarnations) of the Son. *"The dark mystery of non-Being"* reigns during the state of *pralaya* between periods of cosmic manifestation (or *Manvantara*). Any created Cosmos emerges out of the Absolute Being/Non-Being at the beginning of time and resolves back into THAT at the end of time. However, the root principles of the Void/Plenum sustain always any existent Cosmos—any relative space/time complex.

The Absolute, the Absolute Being and Non-Being, is the ultimate essence. Blavatsky describes it as *"without any relation to manifested, finite Being."* (S. D. I, p. 15) In order to bring the notion of the Absolute into a discussion of metaphysics and cosmogenesis, it is depicted in terms of a basic *"metaphysical trinity."* The Absolute is taken as: i) "Be-ness," or THAT—which is unspeakable, and most identified with Darkness and Non-Being; ii) the *Ceaseless Eternal Breath* and iii) the *Eternal Parent Space*. Understanding this trinity is essential to understanding the *Stanzas of Dzyan* and how Blavatsky's ancient metaphysics are related to modern physics.

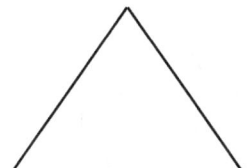

Eternal Parent Space   Ceaseless Eternal Breath

Blavatsky introduces the trinity of *"Be-ness, Abstract Space, and Abstract Motion:"*

> This "Be-ness" is symbolized...under two aspects. On the one hand, absolute abstract Space, representing bare subjectivity.... On the other, absolute Abstract Motion...symbolised by the term "The Great Breath".... Thus, then, the first fundamental axiom of the Secret Doctrine is this metaphysical One Absolute—BE-NESS—symbolised by finite intelligence as the theological Trinity. (p. 14)

At different points, various terms are used to depict the Abstract Space and Abstract Motion, the Mother and Father principles latent within the Absolute.

3b. The Seven-Skinned Eternal Parent Space

Abstract Space is the *Eternal Parent Space* which is contrasted with the non-eternal manifest spacetime complex of a created universe or Son. The Eternal Parent Space is an absolute Space, the source of innumerable sparks of self-existence that emerge out of Non-Being. In modern terminology, the Eternal Parent Space is a "hyperspace," "superspace" or the "big foam of the quantum vacuum" with its zero point fields. It is not manifest 'in' the external space/time dimensions as we ordinarily conceive of these, but rather it underlies and sustains them. The Eternal Parent Space is the mother principle and ultimate Aether. This is described in the first verse: "THE ETERNAL PARENT WRAPPED IN HER EVER INVISIBLE ROBES HAD SLUMBERED ONCE AGAIN FOR SEVEN ETERNITIES."

Blavatsky criticized the scientists of her day who regard Space as empty, void and lifeless, and not simultaneously the plenum and *living*. She explains: "*Space... viewed as a "Substantial Unity"—the "living Source of Life"—is as the "Unknown Causeless Cause," is the oldest dogma in Occultism, millenniums earlier than the Pater-Aether of the Greeks and Latins.*" (pp. 9-10)

> Space is neither a "limitless void," nor a "conditioned fullness," but both: being, on the plane of absolute abstraction, the ever-incognisable Deity, which is void only to finite minds, and on that of *mayavic* perception, the Plenum, the absolute Container of all that is, whether manifested or unmanifested: it is, therefore, that ABSOLUTE ALL. ... Space is called in the esoteric symbolism "the Seven-Skinned Eternal Mother-Father." It is composed from its undifferentiated to its differentiated surface of seven layers. (S. D. I, pp. 8-9)

In the cosmogenesis of *The Secret Doctrine*, a key to the mysteries of creation lies within the archaic teaching regarding the seven-skinned *Eternal Parent Space*. In this view, the entire phenomenal world is regarded as an outgrowth or unfolding of patterns of creation inherent within this root principle of the Divine Essence. The Eternal Parent Space is the ultimate Aether, or hyperspace dimension, which sustains physical reality. While modern physicists might wonder what patterns of existence might be pre-existent in non-existence, Blavatsky maintains that the sevenfoldness of all things is latent in the Eternal Parent Space and then embodied in all realms of Nature and creation. The Stanzas of Dzyan refer to the seven dimensional nature of creation: "THE SEVEN REGIONS ABOVE, AND THE SEVEN BELOW" (V, 2).

Blavatsky was highly critical of the scientific views of her era, particularly when it came to understanding *space*. She wrote: "*... Space is, in the sight of the* materialists, one boundless void in nature—blind, unintelligent, useless." (p. 587) Instead of regarding Space as an *"abyss of nothingness,"* the occultist regards it as a substantial living Entity—the *"real world,"* in contrast to the illusory world of visible causes and effects. Space is the Plenum—the Unity in which there is a connection and correlation of all matter and forces. Space is the container and body of the Universe with its seven principles.

Without this Aether of Space there would be no forces of nature, no elements, no creation:

> SPACE, which, in their ignorance and iconoclastic tendency to destroy every philosophic idea of old, the modern wiseacres have proclaimed "an abstract idea" and a *void*, is, in reality, the container and *the body of the Universe* with its seven principles. It is a body of limitless extent, whose PRINCIPLES, in Occult phraseology—each being in its turn a septenary—manifest in our phenomenal world only the grossest fabric of *their sub-divisions*.... Kabalistic teachings (show) this idea, e.g., the seven-headed Serpent of Space, called "the great Sea." (S. D. I, p. 342)

Space, to the scientists of Blavatsky's era, was a passive background within which three-dimensional atoms move about interacting only through local effects and external relationships. In contrast, Blavatsky's "SPACE" refers to the "real SPACE" of the "Eternal Parent Space" rather than the three dimensional space of the manifest phenomenal existence. Real SPACE is described as *a living Unity*, an apparent Void—to the finite mind or to physical perception—but the Divine Plenum, container of all, to the mystically awakened!

> The Waters of Life, or Chaos—the female principle in symbolism—are the vacuum (to our mental sight) in which lie the latent Spirit and Matter. (p. 64)

This SPACE is the ultimate AETHER—the root principle of manifestation within both the spiritual and material worlds. Whereas scientists of her day were arguing about the reality of the "ether," before dismissing the concept in the early part of the twentieth century, Blavatsky never wavered in her insistence of the primacy of the Aether. This Aether is the container and foundation for the laws of nature and all cosmic manifestations and is the Eternal Parent Space itself.

This concept of the Aether is dramatically different from the ether being proposed in her day by the scientists, although, ironically, it is more compatible with recent scientific concepts.

> The whole range of physical phenomena proceed from the *Primary* of Ether—Akasa, as dual natured Akasa proceeds from undifferentiated *Chaos*, so-called.... Modern Science may divide its hypothetically conceived ether in as many ways as it likes; the real Aether of Space

will remain as it is throughout. It has its seven principles, as all the rest of nature has, and where there was no Ether *there would be no sound*, as it is the vibrating sound-board in nature in all of its seven differentiations. This is the first mystery the Initiates of old have learned. (S. D. I, p. 536)

The Eternal Parent Space, the ultimate Aether, has seven skins, a nature inherent within the Divine Essence. When creation occurs, the "first born" are the seven Luminous Sons, seven Divine Intelligences, who create seven dimensional spiritual worlds and subsequently seven dimensional material worlds. Everything is sevenfold because this septenary nature is latent in the Divine Essence even before the initiation of the creative forces. It is a pattern of being, of existence, pre-existent in Non-Being—in the Aether of the Eternal Parent Space! Cosmic manifestation entails the unfolding of this inherent sevenfold nature within spiritual and material realms of creation.

Understanding this enigmatic doctrine is a key to understanding the mysteries of cosmology, physics and metaphysics—both modern and ancient. Blavatsky's explanations of the Seven Skinned Eternal Parent Space provide a remarkable and profound teaching of the ancient wisdom religions, most pertinent to the issues of modern science. Blavatsky writes:

> Everything in the metaphysical as in the physical Universe is septenary.... The evolution of life proceeds on these seven globes or bodies from the 1st to the 7th in Seven ROUNDS or Seven Cycles. (S. D. I., p. 158)

The opening *Stanzas of Dzyan* thus refer to the Seven Eternities, the Seven Ways to Bliss, the Seven Sublime Lords and the Seven Truths, and the Seven yet to be born from the Web of Light. In terms of the theological trinity, SPACE is the feminine principle—the Mother- principle, the roots of matter. It is equated with *"the Great Sea,"* the *"Chaos"* and with the *"Deep. "* In the *Book of Genesis*, before the beginning: *"Darkness was upon the face of the deep. And the Spirit of God moved upon the face of the waters."* The terms "the deep" and "the waters" refer to the SPACE, the ultimate Aether of the Eternal Parent Space:

> Number seven is quite as much insisted upon and emphasized ... in the *Book of Dzyan*. "The Great Water (the Deep or Chaos) is said to be *seven* cubits deep"—"cubits" standing here of course for divisions, zones, and principles. Therein, "in the great mother, all the Gods, and the *seven great ones* are born." (S. D. I, p. 674)

The primordial nothingness—the quantum void/plenum in its nature as the Eternal Parent Space—has an inherent seven-fold nature. This is profound teaching of the archaic wisdom traditions which anticipates the most startling and revolutionary ideas emerging within science in the twenty first century.

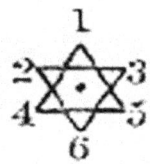# 3c. The Ceaseless Breath & Seven Luminous Lords—the Dhyan Chohans

> ... there are only seven Self-born primordial 'gods' emanated from the trinitarian ONE. (S. D. I, p. 203)

> ... the upper Sephirothal Triad emanates the lower seven Sephiroth —the seven Rays or Dhyan Chohans; (p. 130)

The counterpart to the Abstract Space is Abstract Motion, most frequently referred to as the Ceaseless Breath—a fundamental movement out of which all manifest movements proceed as modifications:

> one absolute attribute (is) eternal, ceaseless Motion, called in esoteric parlance the "Great Breath," which is the perpetual motion of the universe.... That which is motionless cannot be Divine. But then there is nothing in fact and reality absolutely motionless within the universal soul.... (S. D. I, p. 2)

In the *Stanzas of Dyzan*, before creation began, *"THERE WAS... NAUGHT SAVE CEASELESS ETERNAL BREATH, WHICH KNOWS ITSELF NOT"* (II, 2), and which *"PULSED UNCONSCIOUS IN UNIVERSAL SPACE."*

The Ceaseless Breath is the source of the Logos, which Blavatsky describes as a *"Seven-vowelled sign, the Breath crystallized into the Word."* Blavatsky describes this aspect of the Deity as *"an arcane, living (or moving) FIRE, and the eternal witnesses to this unseen Presence are Light, Heat, Moisture,"*—this trinity including, and being the cause of, every phenomenon in Nature." (pp. 2-3) The Ceaseless Breath is the cause of Light, Heat and Moisture and the laws of nature are claimed to be due to its sevenfold modification.

In the first Stanza of Dzyan, verse three states: UNIVERSAL MIND WAS NOT, FOR THERE WERE NO AH-HI TO CONTAIN IT. The AH-HI refer to the Dhyan Chohans:

> The AH-HI (Dhyan-Chohans) are the collective hosts of spiritual beings—the Angelic Hosts of Christianity, the Elohim and "Messengers" of the Jews—who are the vehicle for the manifestation of the divine or universal thought and will. They are the Intelligent Forces that give to and enact in Nature her "laws"... This hierarchy of spiritual Beings, through which the Universal Mind comes into action, is like an Army—a "Host," truly.... (p. 38)

The term Dhyan Chohans is used by Blavatsky in different contexts to refer to different sets of divine and spiritual beings and intelligences which sculpt the void, fashion and inform the phenomena of nature. The original Dhyan Chohans are the *"SEVEN SUBLIME LORDS"* or the *"SEVEN SONS"* latent within the Divine Essence before creation is initiated. During the Nights of Brahma, *"THE SEVEN SONS WERE NOT YET BORN FROM THE WEB OF LIGHT. DARKNESS ALONE WAS FATHER-MOTHER."* (Stanza II, 5)

When cosmic differentiation occurs, the Seven Luminous Lords are the first to emerge from within the matrix of Non-Being. They are described as *"emanating"* out of the triune Absolute. These Seven Lords are referred to by varied names throughout Blavatsky's writings and the esoteric literature. These are the Seven Divine Intelligences, the Seven Rays, the Seven Logi, the Elohim and the Seven Builders of form from formlessness. These Seven Luminous Intelligences inform from within/without the laws of nature and all cosmic manifestations within the diverse realms of creation. The manifested universe is informed by a hierarchy of such divine and spiritual intelligences, all serving to *"contain the Universal Mind,"* as Stanza I, 3 describes.

Stanza III, 4 then depicts the first instances of creation, when *"THE THREE FALL INTO THE FOUR. THE RADIANT ESSENCE BECOMES SEVEN INSIDE, SEVEN OUTSIDE."* The Seven inside are the Builders of form from formlessness, the Divine Intelligences that sculpt the void. Blavatsky describes the original differentiation of the SEVEN Sons depicted in Stanza IV:

> Stanza IV shows the differentiation of the "Germ" of the Universe into the septenary hierarchy of conscious Divine Powers, who are the active manifestations of the One Supreme Energy. They are the framers, shapers, and ultimately the creators of all the manifested Universe... they inform and guide it; they are the intelligent Beings who adjust and control evolution, embodying in themselves those manifestations of the ONE LAW, which we know as "The Laws of Nature."
>
> Generally, they are known as the Dhyan Chohans, though each of the various groups has its own designation in the Secret Doctrine.
>
> This stage of evolution is spoken of in Hindu mythology as the "Creation" of the Gods. (pp. 21-22)

The original Dhyan Chohans are described as the *"divine Flames"* and as the *"formless Fiery Breaths"* as they are variants on the Ceaseless Breath. The Ceaseless Breath is the source of the Logos, the *"Seven-vowelled sign, the Breath crystallized into the Word."*

A commentary on the Stanzas provided by Blavatsky notes:

> "It is through and from the radiations of the seven bodies of the seven orders of Dhyanis, that the seven discrete qualities (Elements), whose motion and harmonious Union produce the manifested Universe of Matter, are born." (Commentary) (S. D., p. 259)

The notion of the Eternal Ceaseless Breath is similar in modern science to the ceaseless activity inherent within the void/plenum of the quantum vacuum and the zero point fields. The quantum and sub-quantum domain are never still. Blavatsky's description of the Ceaseless Breath is also consistent with David Bohm's idea of the *"fundamental holomovement,"* out of which all manifest movements arise as *"modifications"* of the fundamental movement. For Blavatsky, all cosmic processes and the laws of nature are derivatives of the underlying Ceaseless Breath. However, scientists do not conceive that such activities might actually embody hierarchies of such divine and spiritual intelligences; even angels and archangels.

3d. The Dualities of Creation

Ultimately, the divine and metaphysical essence of creation exists as a unity and then as a Holy Trinity. However, when it comes to explaining cosmic manifestation, Blavatsky often talks of dualities—those of Spirit and Matter, the Father and Mother principles, pre-Cosmic ideation and pre-Cosmic substance, subjectivity and objectivity. In this case, the Eternal Ceaseless Breath is taken as the root of the active Spiritual, Father, pre-cosmic ideation Force; while the Eternal Parent Space is the root of the receptive, Material, Mother, pre-cosmic Substance principles:

> the Absolute is...that Essence which is out of all relation to conditioned existence .... But once that we pass in thought from this (to us) Absolute Negation, duality supervenes in the contrast of Spirit (or consciousness) and Matter, Subject and Object.
>
> Spirit (or Consciousness) and Matter are, however, to be regarded, not as independent realities, but as the two facets or aspects of the Absolute, which constitute the basis of conditioned Being whether subjective or objective.
>
> Considering this metaphysical triad as the Root from which precedes all manifestation, the great Breath assumes the character of precosmic Ideation. It is the *fons et origo* of force and of all individual consciousness, and supplies the guiding intelligence in the vast scheme of cosmic Evolution. On the other hand, precosmic root-substance is that aspect of the Absolute which underlies all the objective planes of Nature.

Just as pre-Cosmic Ideation is the root of all individual consciousness, so pre-Cosmic Substance is the substratum of matter in the various grades of its differentiation.

Hence it will be apparent that the contrast of these two aspects of the Absolute is essential to the existence of the "Manifested Universe." Apart from Cosmic Substance, Cosmic Ideation could not manifest as individual consciousness, since it is only through a vehicle of matter that consciousness wells up as "I am I." a physical basis being necessary to focus a ray of the Universal Mind at a certain stage of complexity. Again, apart from Cosmic Ideation, Cosmic Substance would remain an empty abstraction, and no emergence of consciousness could ensue.

The "Manifested Universe," therefore, is pervaded by duality, which is, as it were, the very essence of its EX-istence as "manifestation." (S. D. I, p. 15)

The Eternal Father and Mother are the male and female principles in root nature. These opposites are latent in the Absolute Non-Being/Being before creation and operate within all things on every plane of the universe during cosmic manifestation. Stanza II, 6 of Dzyan describes these principles as present and latent in the Darkness before creation: "THESE TWO ARE THE GERM, AND THE GERM IS ONE. THE UNIVERSE WAS STILL CONCEALED IN THE DIVINE THOUGHT AND THE DIVINE BOSOM." During the Nights of Brahma, the Father, Mother and Son are One and rest within the primal and eternal matrix of Darkness and Non-Being.

The Secret Doctrine provides a valuable perspective on the first two verses of the *Book of Genesis*, which elaborate similar themes.

> 1. In the beginning God created the heaven and the earth.
> 2. And the earth was without form, and void;
> and darkness was upon the face of the deep.
> And the Spirit of God moved upon the face of the waters.

Verse 1 states that God created the heaven and the earth—just as Blavatsky elaborates the creation in Spirit and Matter; a realm above and a realm below. Verse 2 depicts the pre-creation condition—the void and darkness of the Absolute, during the Nights of Brahma. The "Spirit of God moving upon the face of the waters" is equivalent to the Ceaseless Eternal Breath within the Eternal Parent Space—the great Sea, Chaos, seven cubits deep. *The Secret Doctrine* provides a framework for examining and understanding the profound insights within the first verses of the Book of *Genesis*. Further, Genesis depicts creation as requiring six days, with God resting on the seventh, suggesting the sevenfoldness inherent to nature and cycles of time and creation.

The symbol used by Blavatsky to depict the mysteries of creation is the *caduceus of Mercury*, the God of Wisdom. She quotes from an esoteric doctrine:

> *The trunk of the ASVATTHA (the tree of Life and Being, the ROD of the caduceus) grows and descends at every Beginning (every new manvantara) from the two dark wings of the Swan (HANSA) of Life. The two Serpents, the ever-living and its illusion (Spirit and matter) whose two heads grow from the one head between the wings, descend along the trunk, interlaced in their embrace. The two tails join on earth (the manifested Universe) into one, and this is the great illusion, O Lanoo!* (S. D. I, p. 549)

The caduceus of Mercury represents a trinity of forces as the two snakes intertwine around the central rod, which descends from the head of the Swan. In modern usage by the medical profession, the head of the Swan is replaced by a knob on the top of the central rod.

Blavatsky explains that this symbol also represents involution and evolution of a Cosmos out of its 'laya condition.' In fact, she refers to the caduceus as a "laya rod" and explains that it depicts:

> A *lemniscate* (figure eight) for the evolution downward, from Spirit into matter; another form of spiral, perhaps in its reinvolutionary path onward, from matter into Spirit, and the necessary gradual and final absorption into the laya state, that which Science calls in her own way "the point neutral as to electricity" etc., or the *zero* point. Such are the Occult facts and statement. They may be left with the greatest security and confidence to Science, to be justified some day. ... at the hour of Pralaya, the two aspects of the unknowable deity, "the Swan in darkness"—Prakriti and Purusha, nature or matter in all its forms and Spirit—no longer subsist but are (*absolutely*) dissolved.... (S. D. I, pp. 550-552)

The Caduceus can be used to represent the theological trinity and to depict the interaction of spirit and matter upon the varied planes of creation. Both differentiate out of a neutral zero point source at the beginning of time and dissipate into the zero point source at the end of time. All of this is depicted in this most mysterious and archaic symbol depicting the spiritual and material forces in creation.

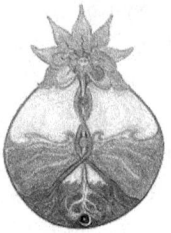

3e. Expanding and Contracting: Within-Without from the Heart

Stanza II, verse 4 describes what has to happen to end the Nights of Brahma and to initiate a new cycle of Manvantara: HER HEART HAD NOT YET OPENED FOR THE ONE RAY TO ENTER, THENCE TO FALL, AS THREE INTO FOUR, INTO THE LAP OF MAYA. Before creation unfolds, the heart of the Divine Mother has to open and be illuminated by a Ray of Light. The Kosmos then grows from this awakened laya centre.

> a centre of spiritual energy which is unborn and eternal and which exists in the bosom of Parabrahman at the time of Pralaya, and starts as a centre for conscious energy at the time of Cosmic activity. (p. 130)

The Secret Doctrine suggests that the primordial point of cosmic differentiation is within the bosom or heart space of the Divine Mother.

The creation and dissolution of any Kosmos then involves the expansion or contraction from the original laya centre:

> It proceeds from without inwardly, when it is everywhere, and from within outwardly, when it is nowhere.... It expands and contracts (exhalation and inhalation). When it expands the mother diffuses and scatters; when it contracts, the mother draws back and ingathers. This produces the periods of Evolution and Dissolution, Manwantara and Pralaya.... Hot breath is the Father ... Cool Breath is the Mother... (S. D. I, pp. 11-12)

When the universe is *"nowhere"*—i.e., at the moment of creation—it expands from within the Divine Essence or the Absolute outwardly to create planes of spiritual and material creation. The term Brahma translates as *"creator"* and is derived from the root *"brih,"* which means to expand or increase. During the inauguration of an active period of creation, Brahma (the male-female principle latent in the Absolute) expands within/without in a manner akin to the budding of a lotus.

The birth of the Universe is associated with the *"Breath of the Father,"* described as *"the Hot Breath."* The seven Breaths of the Seven Sons generate Light, which produces fire, heat and motion. The Cosmos is born in fire and expands when the Breath of the Father is upon it.

When the Universe is 'everywhere,' it is described as contracting from "without inward." This contraction is associated with the *"Cool Breath of the Mother,"* which gathers in the Sons (the material/spiritual worlds) back to the Divine Bosom. The Divine Mother is the Eternal Parent Space. At the end of time, the manifest universe is withdrawn back into the hyperspace dimensions of this root Space principle. The contraction of the universe is thus associated with the maternal (and material) principle but is not regarded as due to the effects of gravity, at least as gravity is commonly understood or misunderstood. Instead, the contraction of the universe is a motion induced within the Eternal Parent Space by a modification of the Eternal Ceaseless Breath.

The *"mother draws back and ingathers"*—to her Bosom or Heart. In a sense, the love of the Divine Mother holds creation together, a form of cosmic gravity, by which the Sons are eventually gathered back to her bosom or heart. Movement within hyperspace thus initiates the universal contraction, just as the Father's modification of the Ceaseless Breath serves to expand the Universe. The expansions and contractions of the Sons are associated with the heart in the Stanzas below.

> IT EXPANDS WHEN THE BREATH OF FIRE IS UPON IT; IT CONTRACTS WHEN THE BREATH OF THE MOTHER TOUCHES IT. THEN THE SONS DISSOCIATE AND SCATTER, TO RETURN INTO THEIR MOTHER'S BOSOM AT THE END OF THE GREAT DAY, AND RE-BECOME ONE WITH HER; WHEN IT IS COOLING, IT BECOMES RADIANT, AND THE SONS EXPAND AND CONTRACT THROUGH THEIR OWN SELVES AND HEARTS; THEY EMBRACE INFINITUDE. (Stanza III, Verse 11)

The primary zero point laya centre of a living being is within the heart—whether the heart of a Kosmos or of a human being.

Blavatsky describes highly energetic activity during the process of creation (like a big bang at incredibly high temperatures); while Matter or the material mother principle, related to gravity and the parent Space, "ingathers" the universe at the end of time. However, everything is rooted into the Divine Essence—from the beginning to the end of time and during all time. All things are guided from within/without as the ultimate causes of the laws of nature are governed by principles existent and pre-existent within the Divine Essence.

The Universe is worked and guided from within outwards. As above so it is below, as in heaven so on earth; and man—the microcosm and miniature copy of the macrocosm—is the living witness to this Universal Law and to the mode of its action. (S. D. I, p. 274)

Everything is guided and informed from within/without. The vital life forces and intelligence expand and contract through the Heart of Being—giving rise to the forces and cycles of the creation and dissolution of many Sons, Worlds or Winks in the Eye of Self-Existence.

3f. Seven Primary and Secondary Creations

According to esoteric teaching there are seven primary, and seven secondary "creations"; the former being the Forces *self-evolving* from the one *causeless* FORCE; the latter, showing the manifested Universe emanating from the already differentiated *divine* elements.... Occult Philosophy... never uses the term "creation," nor even that of "evolution," "with regard to *primary* 'Creation';" but calls all such *forces* "the *aspects* of the Causeless Force." (S. D. I, p. 446)

The Seven Luminous Lords are not 'created' as such, as they are preexistent during the Nights of Brahma, although undifferentiated in a laya state.

When creation occurs, higher spiritual worlds and lower material realms are formed.

"R. Yehudah began, it is written: 'Elohim said: Let there be a firmament, in the midst of the waters. ... At the time that the Holy ... created the world, He (they) created seven heavens Above. He created seven earths Below, seven seas, seven days, seven rivers, seven weeks, seven years, seven times ....(S. D. I, p. 447)

Primary Creation is called the *Creation of Light* (Spirit); and the *Secondary*—that of Darkness (matter). Both are found in *Genesis*.... The first is the emanation of the *self*-born gods (Elohim); the second of physical nature. (S. D. I, p. 450)

The Seven Sons "emanate" out of the Matrix of Non-Being and the Divine Intelligences then give rise to Spiritual Intelligences. The Seven Inside then inform the Seven outside.

Cosmic manifestation entails the unfolding or manifestation of this inherent seven-fold nature within successive spiritual and material dimensions.

"Everything in the metaphysical as in the physical Universe is septenary." (p. 158) The first-born are the Seven Luminous Sons, "THE PRODUCERS OF FORM FROM NO-FORM." (Stanza II, 1) and they serve to sculpt the void through sacred geometry, bringing forth Form out of Formlessness (Rupa out of Arupa).

> THUS WERE FORMED THE RUPA AND THE ARUPA: FROM ONE LIGHT SEVEN LIGHTS; FROM EACH OF THE SEVEN, SEVEN TIMES SEVEN LIGHTS. THE WHEELS WATCH THE RING.....(V, 6)

The multidimensional universe consists of a divine world of emanations, then creation in light and spirit, and then creation in darkness and matter—heaven and earth. The sevenfoldness is evident throughout as within the Eternal Parent Space before the emergence of the Kosmos. The Seven inside inform the Seven outside.

The term Dhyan Chohans is used to depict the sevenfold divine intelligences and powers and also to refer to the spiritual intelligences which are their progeny. *The Secret Doctrine* postulates a hierarchy or host of such intelligences:

> Esoteric doctrine teaches that the Dhyan Chohans are the collective aggregate of divine Intelligence or primordial mind, and that the first Manus—the seven "mind-born" Spiritual Intelligences—are identical with the former. (p. 452)

> The whole Kosmos is guided, controlled, and animated by almost endless series of Hierarchies of sentient Beings, each having a mission to perform, and who—whether we give to them one name or another, and call them Dhyan-Chohans or Angels—are "messengers" in the sense only that they are the agents of Karmic and Cosmic Laws. They vary infinitely in their respective degrees of consciousness and intelligence .... (pp. 274-275)

Whereas the plan of the Kosmos is a product of the Logos, the Dhyan-Chohans within their varied realms are the masons or builders who carry out the constructive labors. *The Secret Doctrine* maintains that there are indeed *"Hosts of intelligent Powers and Forces."*

4. LIGHT: "The Great Protean Magician"

Light is the first begotten, and the first emanation of the Supreme, and Light is Life, says the Evangelist and the Kabalist. Both are electricity— the life principle, the *anima mundi*, pervading the universe, the electric vivifier of all things. Light is the great Protean magician and under the divine will of the architect, or rather the architects, the "Builders" (called *One* collectively), its multifarious, omnipotent waves give birth to every form; as well as to every living being. From its swelling electric bosom, spring *matter* and *spirit*. Within its beams, lie the beginnings of all physical and chemical action, and of all cosmic and spiritual phenomena; it vitalizes and disorganizes; it gives life and produces death, and from its primordial point gradually emerged into existence the myriads of worlds, visible and invisible celestial bodies. It was at the ray of this First mother, one in three, that "God," according to Plato, lighted a fire which we now call the sun," and which is not the cause of either light or heat, but merely the focus, or, as we might say, the lens, by which the rays of the primordial light become materialized, are concentrated upon our Solar System, and produce all correlation of forces. (S. D. I, p. 579)

Light has a most mysterious nature and is not understood within modern science. Archaic mystical teachings and modern science both depict light as a fundamental primordial element responsible for the creation and materialization of cosmic phenomena. Blavatsky describes light as the *"great Protean magician,"* which embodies the Will of Builders and gives rise to all forms and living beings. She also describes a *"primordial point"* of such light, or *lux*, as that from which emerges a *"myriads of worlds."* A ray of this light is the fire and spirit of the sun and allows for *"all correlation of forces"* within the Solar System as *"its multifarious, omnipotent waves give birth to every form."* Light is *the great Protean magician* and the means by which the Builders or Architects create and sustain the Cosmos.

4a. From the *Stanzas of Dzyan*

The *Stanzas of Dzyan* provide varied references to Light which illustrate these themes. In the first stanza depicting the 'Night of Brahma,' Light is not mentioned, however Darkness is and it is regarded as a form of Absolute Light:

Stanza I: Verse 5: DARKNESS ALONE FILLED THE BOUNDLESS ALL

Stanza II: 1. ... WHERE WERE THE BUILDERS, THE LUMINOUS SONS OF MANVANTARIC DAWN? ... IN THE UNKNOWN DARKNESS ...

Darkness is depicted as the ultimate source, as in the Book of Genesis with its *"darkness upon the face of the deep."* The Luminous Sons are initially absorbed within the darkness.

Stanza II then depicts what occurs when creation is instigated: A 'ray' (of light or the divine Logos) will penetrate into the Germ within the Heart of the Divine Mother.

3. THE HOUR HAD NOT YET STRUCK; THE RAY HAD NOT YET FLASHED INTO THE GERM;

4. HER HEART HAD NOT YET OPENED FOR THE ONE RAY TO ENTER

5. THE SEVEN SONS WERE NOT YET BORN FROM THE WEB OF LIGHT, DARKNESS ALONE WAS FATHER-MOTHER

In Stanza II, the Luminous Sons remain in the Darkness, but this darkness is described also as paradoxically "THE WEB OF LIGHT." Stanza III then depicts the creation process:

Stanza III

3. DARKNESS RADIATES LIGHT, AND LIGHT DROPS ONE SOLITARY RAY INTO THE MOTHER DEEP. THE RAY SHOOTS THROUGH THE VIRGIN-EGG. THE RAY CAUSES THE ETERNAL EGG TO THRILL, AND DROP THE NON-ETERNAL GERM, WHICH CONDENSES INTO THE WORLD-EGG.

Blavatsky elaborates upon the nature and role of this solitary ray:

> "the Ray," differentiates the "Waters of Space"; ... "Chaos ceases, through the effulgence of the Ray of Primordial light, dissipating total darkness by the help of the great magic power of the WORD of the (Central) Sun." (p. 231)

The non-eternal Germ is the zero point emergence which then condenses into the 'world egg.'

4. THEN THE THREE FALL INTO THE FOUR. THE RADIANT ESSENCE BECOMES SEVEN INSIDE, SEVEN OUTSIDE.

5. THE ROOT REMAINS, THE LIGHT REMAINS, THE CURDS REMAIN ...

In Blavatsky's commentary on this last verse, she writes:

The "Light" is the same Omnipresent Spiritual Ray, which has entered and now fecundated the Divine Egg, and calls cosmic matter to begin its long series of differentiations. The curds are the first differentiation, and probably refer also to that cosmic matter which is supposed to be the origin of the "Milky Way"—the matter we know.... this matter...becomes, at the first reawakening of cosmic motion, scattered throughout Space; appearing...in cluster and lumps, like curds in thin mild. These are the seeds of the future worlds, the "Star-stuff." (S.D., p. 69)

6.... AND THE OCEAN WAS RADIANT LIGHT, WHICH WAS FIRE, AND HEAT, AND MOTION. DARKNESS VANISHED AND WAS NO MORE;

7.... THE RADIANT CHILD OF THE TWO, THE UNPARALLELED REFULGENT GLORY: BRIGHT SPACE SON OF DARK SPACE, WHICH EMERGES FROM THE DEPTHS OF THE GREAT DARK WATERS.... HE SHINES FORTH AS THE SON;...

8.... THE GERM IS THAT, AND THAT IS LIGHT, THE WHITE BRILLIANT SON OF THE DARK HIDDEN FATHER.

9. LIGHT IS COLD FLAME, AND FLAME IS FIRE, AND FIRE PRODUCES HEAT, WHICH YIELDS WATER: THE WATER OF LIFE IN THE GREAT MOTHER.

10. FATHER-MOTHER SPIN A WEB WHOSE UPPER END IS FASTENED TO SPIRIT—THE LIGHT OF THE ONE DARKNESS—AND THE LOWER ONE TO ITS SHADOWY END, MATTER;

This Stanza depicts the metaphysical processes of creation. A ray of light emanates from the darkness, penetrates into the Mother Deep and causes the emergence of the non-eternal germ which condenses into the world egg. Creation follows the pattern then of seven inside, seven outside. Stanza III has two references to the Light emerging out of the Darkness, describing the BRIGHT SPACE SON OF DARK SPACE and the WHITE BRILLIANT SON OF THE DARK HIDDEN FATHER. These are beautiful poetic descriptions.

Light is depicted as the primordial element which is 'cold flame' and then this generates fire, heat and water from its potencies. Stanza III concludes with the creation of a spiritual world above in light and a material world below, in matter.

Stanza IV

3. FROM THE EFFULGENCY OF LIGHT—THE RAY OF THE EVER-DARKNESS—SPRUNG IN SPACE THE RE-AWAKENED ENERGIES;

Stanza V

6. THUS WERE FORMED THE RUPA AND THE ARUPA: FROM ONE LIGHT SEVEN LIGHTS; FROM EACH OF THE SEVEN, SEVEN TIMES SEVEN LIGHTS. THE WHEELS WATCH THE RING....

Stanza VI

2. THE ONE RAY MULTIPLIES THE SMALLER RAYS. LIFE PRECEDES FORM, AND LIFE SURVIVES THE LAST ATOM OF FORM. THROUGH THE COUNTLESS RAYS PROCEEDS THE LIFE-RAY, THE ONE, LIKE A THREAD THROUGH MANY JEWELS.

Light or the "effulgence" of the primordial Light, or Logos, is the great protean magician giving rise to the many forms of life through generations of effects. Similarly, Verse 3 of the *Book of Genesis* states; *"God said, Let there be light, and there was light"* and this light is the structural essence of creation. The last verse of Stanza V, notes then: *"THUS WERE FORMED THE RUPA AND THE ARUPA: FROM ONE LIGHT SEVEN LIGHTS; FROM EACH OF THE SEVEN, SEVEN TIMES SEVEN LIGHTS."* The Rupa and the Arupa refer to the form-bound and formless realms—generated through the sevenfoldness of the original Light. In sum, the Stanzas and archaic philosophy assign a central role to Light as the great protean magician, the Ray with its *"multifarious, omnipotent waves,"* which *"give birth to every form; as well as to every living being."*

4b. Darkness Radiates Light

Fire and Water, or Father and Mother, may be taken...to mean the divine Ray and Chaos. "Chaos, from this union with Spirit obtaining sense, shone with pleasure, and thus produced the Protogonos (the first born light)," says a fragment of Hermes.... Darkness is the one true actuality, the basis and the root of light, without which the latter could never manifest itself, nor even exist. Light is matter, and DARKNESS pure Spirit. Darkness, in its radical, metaphysical basis, is subjective and absolute light; while the latter in all its seeming

> effulgence and glory, is merely a mass of shadows, as it can never be eternal, and is simply an illusion, or Maya. Even in the mind-baffling and science-harassing Genesis, light is created out of darkness "and darkness was upon the face of the deep"—and not vice versa. (S. D. I, p. 70)

Darkness is regarded as the Eternal element and the original light emanation is a reflection of its concealed nature as pure spirit. Hence, all of creation is regarded as a 'maya'—an impermanent illusion relative to the root principles within the Darkness.

Blavatsky has a unique view and interpretation of the role of Lucifer in this cosmic drama. She shuns the dogmas of the church and exoteric western belief, and provides an alternative perspective on the nature of Lucifer:

> *Demon est Deus inversus.* The devil is now called Darkness by the Church, whereas, in the Bible (see Job), he is called the "Son of God", the bright star of the early morning, Lucifer (see Isaiah). There is a whole philosophy of dogmatic craft in the reason why the first Archangel, who sprang from the depths of Chaos, was called Lux (Lucifer), the "Luminous Son of the Morning," or manvantaric Dawn. He was transformed by the Church into Lucifer or Satan, because he is higher and older than Jehovah, and had to be sacrificed to the new dogma. (pp. 70-71)

Blavatsky uses an interesting Latin phrase: *Demon est Deus inversus.* The Devil is God inverted. Blavatsky does not acknowledge an independent evil power in Lucifer, who is regarded instead as the 'luminous Son of the morning' or manvantaric dawn. Blavatsky notes elsewhere:

> Archaic philosophy, recognizing neither Good nor Evil as a fundamental or independent power, but starting from the Absolute ALL (Universal Perfection eternally), traced both (Good and Evil) through the course of natural evolution to pure Light condensing gradually into form, hence becoming Matter or Evil.... (S. D. I, p. 73)

Evil is that which is most removed from the light and truth of the Absolute. Blavatsky regarded the church as having distorted the ancient and esoteric role of both the darkness and of the role and nature of Lucifer.[1]

---

1   In Blavatsky's letters to her family in Russia, XI, she writes to her sister and comments upon the choice of the title 'Lucifer' for the Theosophical Society journal about to be published: *"We are about to found a magazine of our own,* Lucifer. *Don't allow yourself to be frightened: it is not the devil, into which the Catholics have falsified the name of the Morning Star, sacred to all the ancient world, of the 'bringer of light.' ... in St John's* Revelation *does it not say, 'I, Jesus, the morning star'? I wish people would take this to mind, at least. It is possible*

4c. The Physics & Metaphysics of Light

The advances of physics have not yet rendered light a mundane element or principle. Instead, the mysterious nature of light poses fundamental scientific questions about the nature of reality. Prominent physicist David Bohm (1986) explored the mysteries of light from a physical vantage point. Bohm notes that according to quantum field theories:

> Mass is a phenomenon of connecting light rays which go back and forth, sort of freezing them into a pattern. So matter, as it were, is condensed or frozen light. ... Therefore all matter is a condensation of light into patterns moving back and forth at average speeds which are less than the speed of light. ... when we come to light we are coming to the fundamental activity in which existence has its ground, or at least coming; close to it. ... Light is what enfolds all the universe ... Light in its generalized sense (not just ordinary light) is the means by which the entire universe unfolds into itself. ... It's energy and it's also information—content, form and structure. It's the potential of everything. ... light transcends the present structure of time and space and we will never understand it properly in that present structure. ... Light is the background which is all one but its information-content has the capacity for immense diversity. Light can carry information about the entire universe. The other point is that light, by interactions of different rays, (as field theory in physics is investigating today), can produce particles and all the diverse structures of matter. (pp. 45-8)

Religious and mystical teachings emphasize that creation involves the descent of supernal Light through higher dimensions of Space—which results in the formations and structures of spiritual and material reality. In the *Book of Genesis*, God says, *"Let there be light."* So also, in Kabbalah, a line of light descends from the Crown Sephiroth of Kether zigzagging down through the inward dimensions of the *Tree of Life* through prism effects and symmetry breaking, and this gives rise to the varied world orders of an increasing more dense material nature. Similarly, the Vedic tradition similarly speaks of the *'white radiance of Brahman'* as disrupting the three *gunas* or *modes of nature*, breaking the symmetries existing within the laya state and resulting in the creation of seven degrees of Maya or seven planes of existence. In these mystical traditions, light simply cannot be known in terms of the *"present structure of time and space,"* as Bohm describes.

Recall Wertheim's overview of Grosseteste's metaphysics which emphased how his "mathematico-Christian cosmology" was really quite compatible with

that the rebellious angel was called Lucifer before his fall, but after this transformation he must not be called so."

modern approaches in physics towards understanding the nature of light and to unifying the laws of nature. These formulations are most compatible with the secret doctrines of Blavatsky:

> the universe was generated from a point of primordial light–the divine illumination, or lux, of which visible light (is) the physical manifestation.... this original point immediately began to expand, forming the sphere of the universe. As the first emanation of God's power, ... lux was ultimately the cause of all natural action in the universe. Indeed it was the primal force of the world. ... Grosseteste concluded that a mathematical understanding of light would serve as the model for understanding all natural influence, or what we would now call force. ... In contemporary physicists' quest to understand the forces of nature, it is light that has generally served as the model. (1997, pp. 49-50)

In this view, the underlying *lux* or supernal light is the metaphysical principle underlying creation. The metaphysics of light entails the *lux* informing realms of spiritual and material creation from within/without. Furthermore, the dynamics and properties of light in the physical world reflect these same principles—as above, so below. Grosseteste conceived of the Biblical Deity as a divine mathematician and viewed the mathematics and geometry inherent in nature as reflecting the same creative principles inherent in the Mind or Being of God. All of these notions are in accord with the secret doctrines of Blavatsky.

Numerous mystical cosmologies depict light as the first manifestation of cosmic creation—emerging out of Darkness and Non-Being. In these views, all material, cosmic and spiritual realities are regarded as latent within the plenum and brought forth or revealed through the mysterious potential of light. Mystical teachings depict the processes of creation as entailing the 'freezing' of light: a condensation or crystallization of supernal light through a hierarchy of broken symmetries which precipitate dimensions of Being out of Non-Being. These concepts are in no way disproved or contradicted by modern physical theory but actually supported by them.

D. Bohm discusses the nature of light according to the 'special theory of relativity.' In this view, as an object approaches the speed of light, its:

> internal space and time change so that the clocks slow down relative to other speeds, and the distance is shortened. You would find that the two ends of the light ray would have no time between them and no distance, so they would represent immediate contact. ... In itself, when it (light) is self-referential, there's no time, no space, no speed. ... as you approach very high speeds your own internal time and distance become less, and therefore if you were at the speed of light you could

reach from one end of the universe to the other without changing your age at all.... existentially speaking or logically speaking, time originates out of the timeless. ... light transcends the present structure of time and space and we will never understand it properly in that present structure. (1986, pp. 44-6)

Light *"transcends the present structure of time and space"* and if we could travel at the speed of light, we could "reach from one end of the universe to the other." Light is clearly not simply a mundane phenomenon. It is unfortunate that Blavatsky could not draw from the work of Bohm and modern physicists, to elaborate or illustrate her teachings. Mystical teachings suggest that light indeed has a deep hidden and supernal nature, which transcends the level of understanding attained within modern science.

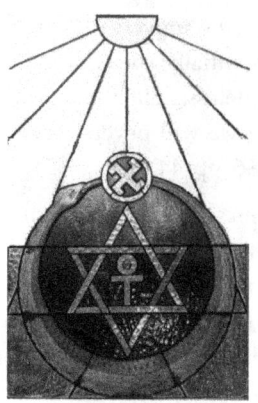

5. The Six Point Star & the Seventh Central Point

> the "Six-pointed Star" ... is the symbol, in almost every religion,
> of the *Logos* as the first emanation. ...
> The six-pointed Star refers to the six Forces or Powers
> of Nature, the six planes, principles, etc., etc.,
> all synthesized by the seventh, or the central point in the Star. ...
> In its Unity, primordial light is the seventh, or highest
> principle ... the light of the unmanifest Logos.
> But in its differentiation is becomes Fohat,
> or the "Seven Sons." The former is symbolized by the
> Central Point in the double-Triangle; the latter
> by the hexagon itself, or the "six limbs" of the Microprosopus ... .
> (S. D. I, pp. 215-6)

The symbol of the double triangle with a central point is of profound importance to occult studies and is especially emphasized within *The Secret Doctrine*. This symbol depicts the sacred geometry inherent to the Kosmos and the nature of the Dhyan Chohans (and Fohat). This symbol has an ancient history and is not only the Star of David or Seal of Solomon for Judaic-Christian occultists, but also the double triangle is a sign for Vishnu, the *Sri-Antara* of the Brahmins and the yogic symbol for the heart chakra.

This archaic symbol replicated below is copied from *The Secret Doctrine*. The figure has three aspects—a central point, an upward turn triangle representing fire and spirit, and a downward turned triangle representing the element water (or material creation). The central point represents the laya centre or the first point, the living entity and the Logos, while the triangles represent the inherent spiritual and material nature and forces manifested within the matrices of existence. Understanding this symbol is of profound significance, especially with the central point which is often excluded—as in the Rothschild red shield or on the flag of Israel, which are empty inside. The primary symbol of Theosophy is the Seal of Solomon with the Egyptian *ankh* in the centre to represent the 'living entity.'

The Theosophical Publishing House in London, England published a third volume of *The Secret Doctrine* in 1897. It is composed of selections of Blavatsky's extensive writing and notes which she apparently intended to include in a third volume. In a chapter on *"The Hexagon with the Central Point, or the Seventh Key,"* Blavatsky wrote:

> Pythagoras viewed the hexagon formed of two crossed triangles as the symbol of creation, and the Egyptians, as that of the union of fire and water (or of generation), the Essenes saw in it the Seal of Solomon, the Jews the Shield of David, the Hindus the Sign of Vishnu (to this day); and if even in Russia and Poland the double triangle is regarded as a powerful talisman—then so wide-spread a use argues that there is something in it. It stands to reason, indeed, that such an ancient and universally revered symbol should not be merely laid aside to be laughed at by those who know nothing of its virtues or real Occult significance. (p. 105)

Blavatsky quotes an occultist, from *Things Concealed*, depicting the Seal of Solomon with a central point: *"The seventh key is the hieroglyph of the sacred septenary, of royalty, of the priesthood (the Initiate), of triumph and true result by struggle. It is magic power in all its force, the true "Holy Kingdom." In the Hermetic Philosophy it is the quintessence resulting from the union of the two forces of the great Magic...."* Blavatsky then concludes: *"The force of this key is absolute in Magic. All religions have consecrated this sign in their rites."*

The Star of David with its central point is used by Blavatsky to depict the nature of the Seven Luminous Sons or the Dhyan Chohans:

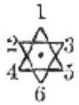

The "Sephiroth of Construction" are the six Dhyan Chohans, or Manus ... synthesized by the seventh "B'raisheeth (the First Emanation or *Logos*), and who are called, therefore, "the Builders of the Lower or physical Universe" all belong Below. These six whose essence is of the Seventh—are the *Upadhi*, the base or fundamental stone on which the objective Universe is built, the *noumenoi* of all things. Hence they are, at the same time, the Forces of nature, the Seven Angels of the

Presence, the sixth and seventh principles in man; the spirit-psycho-physical spheres of the Septenary chain.... (S. D. I, p. 375)

God is first One, then Three and then Seven. This is a basic principle of intelligent design elaborated within *The Secret Doctrine* and claimed to be inherent to all cosmic phenomena. These profound principles are all embodied within this symbol which has a unitary, triune and sevenfold nature. Just as white light can be divided by a three sided prism to yield a spectrum of colors, so also the nature of Deity is described as triune and sevenfold.

The seventh element has a distinct status as the essence, original or fulfillment of the other six elements. In terms of understanding light, a three sided prism is considered to divide the spectrum into seven colors—red, orange, yellow, green, blue, violet and indigo. However, more often the spectrum is considered to consist of six colors and violet and indigo are not differentiated. In this case, white light might be considered as the seventh color as it is a composite of the other six colors and includes them all. This significance ascribed to the 7th element relative to the other six is very significant. Certainly the point or ankh at the centre of the Star of David has special significance and position relative to the six angles and sides.

Different examples can be used to illustrate such a distinction between the six and the seventh element. For example, in the *Book of Genesis*, God creates the world in six days and then rests on the seventh, marking its distinctive nature as a completion or fulfillment of the six. In the *Tree of Life* of the Kabbalah, the Sephiroth of Tipheret is regarded as central to the seven Sephiroth below which emanate from the supernal triad. The sphere of Tipheret is associated with the Heart and with the Divine Mother in the sphere of Binah. As the seventh of the Sephiroth below the abyss in Kabbalah, Tipheret is on the central pillar directly below Keter and is the only Sephiroth below to have a direct path to all three supernal Sephiroth.

Another example of such a distinction between six of something and a seventh involves the nature of Space itself. Although in some native traditions, there are considered to be four primary directions of east, west, north and south, other traditions add the above and below as directions and the seventh direction is taken as within the human heart. The seventh direction in higher dimensional holographic physics is at the zero point or laya centre of the coordinate system. Blavatsky mentions the six directions of Space and how these are symbolized.

> By the "Six directions of Space" is here meant the "Double Triangle," the junction and blending together of pure Spirit and Matter, of the Arupa and the Rupa, of which the Triangles are a Symbol. (p. 118)

The *Secret Doctrine* offers a model of intelligent design in which God is stated to geometrize in all manifestations according to sacred numeric and geometric principles. Firstly, God, or the Deity, THAT or the Absolute, for Blavatsky, is One. This is the fundamental proposition of *The Secret Doctrine*. When metaphysical processes give birth to a 'Son' or 'Kosmos,' the first point of unfoldment represents the logos or living entity and it represent a new One, as a microcosm of the macrocosm. This One similarly manifests a triune and sevenfold nature and such patterns are reiterated through many generations of causes and effects. In this view, the Star of David embodies these sacred principles of design and might be represented by the number 1/137. The 1 in the numerator of this fraction indicates the Deity or the Absolute, or the fundamental Unity; while the 1 below indicates the emergent point or logos, which then is divided by three and yields seven. This number 1/137, more than any other number, embodies the Secret Doctrine's arcane wisdom teaching concerning creation physics and metaphysics.

The Dhyan Chohans are the first to emerge from the Chaos, Seven Luminous Sons, divine intelligences who sculpt the void. Through their generations, a hierarchy of spiritual intelligences, sentient beings, serve as masons, to guide and inform the laws of nature and the processes of Kosmic involution and evolution—as well as the Laws of Karma. The basic template for these metaphysical processes is depicted in the profound Star of David with its central zero point laya centre and these patterns of triune and sevenfold creation are reiterated through the dimensions of 'real Space,' the Aether, from the Heart of being.

Of all symbols, the Star of David with its central point or ankh best represents the metaphysical teaching of *The Secret Doctrine* and of Theosophy. Blavatsky ascribes great significance to this symbol as a key to understanding the mysteries:

> It is then only in this "light" (of consciousness) of mental and physical perception, that *practical* Occultism can throw this into visibility by geometrical figures; which, when closely studied, will yield not only a scientific explanation of the real, objective existence of the "Seven sons of the divine Sophia," which is this light of the Logos, but show by

means of other yet undiscovered keys that, with regards to Humanity, these "Seven Sons" and their numberless emanations, centres of energy personified, are an absolute necessity. Make away with them, and the mystery of Being and Mankind *will never be unriddled, not even closely approached.* (p. 430)

As above, so below: The sevenfold Star of David is used by Blavatsky to illustrate the nature of the first born Dhyan Chohans, Fohat and his Seven Sons, as well as the metaphysical forces and laws of nature surrounding the core of any emergent Son.

6. FOHAT: Cosmic Electricity & the Seven Messengers of Will

Within *The Secret Doctrine*, understanding the role and significance of Fohat is a key to understanding the mysteries of cosmogenesis and the relationship of the laws of physics to ancient metaphysics. Blavatsky writes:

> But just as the opposite poles of subject and object, spirit and matter, are but aspects of the One Unity in which they are synthesized, so, in the manifested Universe, there is "that" which links spirit to matter, subject to object.
>
> This something, at present unknown to Western speculation, is called by the occultists Fohat. It is the "bridge' by which the "Ideas" existing in the "Divine Thought" are impressed on Cosmic Substance as the "Laws of nature." Fohat is thus the dynamic energy of Cosmic Ideation; or, regarded from the other side, it is the intelligent medium, the guiding power of all manifestation, the "Thought Divine" transmitted and made manifest through the Dhyan Chohans, the Architects of the visible World. Thus from Spirit, or Cosmic Ideation, comes our consciousness; from Cosmic Substance the several vehicles in which that consciousness is individualised and attains to self—or reflective-consciousness; while Fohat, in its various manifestations, is the mysterious link between Mind and Matter, the animating principle electrifying every atom into life. (1888, p. 16)

Just as a human is described as having a body, soul and spirit, so also is the Cosmos. Fohat is that agent of spirit which ensouls the material body of the cosmos; *"the animating principle electrifying every atom into life."* Fohat is the *"dynamic energy of Cosmic Ideation"* and embodies the intelligence of the spiritual builders, or the Seven Luminous Sons within the medium of space.

V. 1 - THE PRIMORDIAL SEVEN, THE FIRST SEVEN BREATHS OF THE DRAGON OF WISDOM, PRODUCE IN THEIR TURN

FROM THEIR HOLY CIRCUMGYRATING BREATHS THE FIERY WHIRLWIND.

The PRIMORDIAL SEVEN each entails a modification of the fundamental Ceaseless Breath. These are the first born from the Darkness and Matrix of Non-Being. The Seven Breaths are 'circumgyrating,' indicating that they are vortices spinning around a centre. These in turn produce "the Fiery Whirlwind." FOHAT is the fiery whirlwind. Fohat links the seven primary realms of spiritual creation above to the seven realms of material nature below.

Whereas modern science has historically focused on the duality of matter and energy, Blavatsky depicts a trinity of forces—of Divine Thought and Cosmic Substance, and Fohat that bridges these worlds—the animating principle electrifying every atom or living being in life. *The Secret Doctrine* is thus consistent with the triune distinction made between matter, energy and intelligence as emerging in quantum information theory and the holographic paradigm. Science is beginning to recognize information as a 'third force' within the medium of space, in addition to the dual matter and energy.

Fohat is the energetic principle, the fundamental cosmic electromagnetism and it conveys the influence of divine and spiritual intelligences upon matter.

> Fohat runs the Manus' (or Dhyan-Chohans') errands, and causes the ideal prototypes to expand from within without—viz, to cross gradually, on a descending scale, all the planes from the noumenon to the lowest phenomenon, to bloom finally on the last into full objectivity—the acme of illusion, or the grossest matter. (p. 63)

> It is through Fohat that the ideas of the Universal Mind are impressed upon matter. Some faint idea of the nature of Fohat may be gathered from the appellation "Cosmic Electricity" sometimes applied to it; but to the commonly known properties of electricity must, in this case, be added others, including intelligence. (p. 85)

Modern scientists do not conceive that the laws and phenomena of Nature might embody a 'third force' of Divine Intelligence, although they conceive of 'information' as latent within the space of the quantum vacuum. According to Blavatsky, Fohat is the Messenger of the Primordial Sons of Light and Life, the Dhyan-Chohans, running their errands and impressing their divine thoughts and intelligence into the seven realms of material creation below.

Just as there are seven Luminous Sons or seven circumgyrating Breaths, and seven primordial matters latent in the Eternal Parent Space, Fohat is also sevenfold and described as having seven sons. Blavatsky writes:

> Fohat...is One and Seven, and on the Cosmic plane is behind all such manifestations as light, heat, sound, adhesion, etc., etc., and is the "spirit" of ELECTRICITY, which is the Life of the Universe. As

an abstraction, we call it the ONE LIFE; as an objective and evident Reality, we speak of a septenary scale of manifestation, which begins at the upper rung with the One Unknowable CAUSALITY, and ends as Omnipresent Mind and Life immanent in every atom of Matter. Thus, while science speaks of its evolution through brute matter, blind force and senseless motion, the Occultists point to *intelligent* LAW and *sentient* LIFE, and add that Fohat is the guiding Spirit of all this. ... the "Messenger of the primordial Sons of Life and Light." (p. 139)

Fohat is Cosmic Electricity—the energetic and vivifying principle linking Cosmic Spirit (the Intelligence principle) to Cosmic Matter (the Material principle). The Seven Luminous Sons act through the seven Fohats which convey their influences into the seven realms of creation. Blavatsky explains:

"Matter is the vehicle for the manifestation of soul on this plane of existence, and soul is the vehicle on a higher plane for the manifestation of spirit, and these three are a trinity synthesized by Life, which pervades them all." (S. D. I, p. 49)

Just as a human being has a three-fold nature—of body, soul and spirit, so also does the Universe or Kosmos.

Blavatsky elaborates upon the nature of Fohat and his seven Sons:

Fohat, the constructive Force of Cosmic Electricity...has *seven sons* who are *his brothers*; ... The Seven "Sons-brothers," however, represent and personify the seven forms of Cosmic magnetism called in *practical Occultism* the "Seven Radicals," whose co-operative and active progeny are, among other energies, Electricity, Magnetism, Sound, Light, Heat, Cohesion, etc. Occult Science defines all these as Super-sensuous effects in their hidden behavior, and as objective phenomena in the world of senses.... (p. 145)

The Sons of Fohat are the Messengers of the primordial Seven Sons of Light and Life, the Elohim or Seven Creators. Fohat is Cosmic Magnetism and Electricity in its varied forms—all variations of One force. Blavatsky's formulation of all the forces of nature as variations of one fundamental force represents exactly the type of unified theory that contemporary physicists regard as the Holy Grail of science.

Stanza V of the *Books of Dzyan* depicts the role of FOHAT and his SEVEN SONS, also referred to as the LIPIKA, and their roles in cosmic creation:

2. THEY MAKE OF HIM THE MESSENGER OF THEIR WILL. THE DZYU BECOME FOHAT, THE SWIFT SON OF THE DIVINE SONS WHOSE SONS ARE THE LIPIKA, RUNS CIRCULAR ERRANDS. FOHAT IS THE STEED AND THE THOUGHT IS

THE RIDER. HE PASSES LIKE LIGHTNING THROUGHT THE FIERTY CLOUDS; TAKES THREE, AND FIVE, AND SEVEN STRIDES THROUGH THE SEVEN REGIONS ABOVE, AND THE SEVEN BELOW. HE LIFTS HIS VOICE, AND CALLS THE INNUMERABLE SPARKS, AND JOINS THEM.

3. HE IS THEIR GUIDING SPIRIT AND LEADER. WHEN HE COMMENCES WORK, HE SEPARATES THE SPARKS OF THE LOWER KINGDOM THAT FLOAT AND THRILL WITH JOY IN THEIR RADIANT DWELLINGS, AND FORMS THERE-WITH THE GERMS OF WHEELS. HE PLACES THEM IN THE SIX DIRECTIONS OF SPACE, AND ONE IN THE MIDDLE—THE CENTRAL WHEEL.

4. FOHAT TRACES SPIRAL LINES TO UNITE THE SIXTH TO THE SEVENTH—THE CROWN; AN ARMY OF THE SONS OF LIGHT STANDS AT EACH ANGLE, AND THE LIPIKA IN THE MIDDLE WHEEL. THEY SAY: THIS IS GOOD, THE FIRST DIVINE WORLD IS READY, THE FIRST IS NOW THE SECOND. THEN THE "DIVINE ARUPA" REFLECTS ITSELF IN CHHAYA LOKA, THE FIRST GARMENT OF THE ANUPADAKA.

6. ... THUS WERE FORMED THE RUPA AND THE ARUPA: FROM ONE LIGHT SEVEN LIGHTS; FROM EACH OF THE SEVEN, SEVEN TIMES SEVEN LIGHTS. THE WHEELS WATCH THE RING....

Fohat is One and sevenfold, as are the Primordial Seven and the Aether of Space. Fohat forms the germs of wheels—with a central wheel surrounded by six additional wheels—illustrated by the "Seed of Life" symbol, essentially a variation on the Star of David.

> Fohat, running along the seven principles of AKASA, acts upon manifested substance or the One Element, ... and by differentiating into various centres of Energy, sets in motion the law of Cosmic Evolution, which, in obedience to the Ideation of the Universal Mind, brings into existence all the various states of being in the manifested Solar System.
>
> The Solar System, brought into existence by these agencies, consists of Seven Principles, like everything else within these centres. Such is the teaching of the trans-Himalayan Esotericism.... (S. D. I, p. 110)

Both the higher AKASA—the Aether of the Seven Skinned Eternal Parent Space and the lower Solar Ether are sevenfold.

As Blavatsky describes the role of Fohat, we can understand its relationship to ideas in modern science and philosophy. She explains:

> Fohat, then is the personal electric vital power, the transcendental binding Unity of all Cosmic Energies, on the unseen as on the manifested planes, the action of which resembles—on an immense scale—that of a living Force created by WILL ... Fohat is not only the living Symbol and Container of that Force, but is looked upon by the Occultists as an Entity—the forces he acts upon being cosmic, human and terrestrial, and exercising their influence on all those planes respectively. ... On the Cosmic, it is present in the constructive power that carries out, in the formation of things—from the planetary system down to the glow-worm and simple daisy—the plan in the mind of nature, or in the Divine Thought, with regard to the development and growth of that special thing. He is, metaphysically, the objectified thought of the gods; the "Word made flesh," ... the active force in Universal Life. (S. D. I, p. 111)

Fohat is *"metaphysically"* the *"objectified thought of the gods."*

In her model of intelligent design, Blavatsky does not consider a bearded patriarch sitting on a throne talking to the flowers, but she does speak of the *Elohim* or the Seven Luminous Sons, who first emerge from the matrix of Darkness and non-Being, the builders of form from formlessness. Fohat serves to convey the Will and intelligence manifest from the seven realms above (the realms of Divine Intelligence and Mind) to the seven below (the seven planes of spiritual and material manifestation). Fohat emerges at zero point levels as the living Force or electric vital power within any living breathing being or Cosmos.

> Each world has its Fohat, who is omnipresent in his own sphere of action. But there are as many Fohats as there are worlds, each varying in power and degree of manifestations. The individual Fohats make one Universal, Collective Fohat .... (p. 143)

Fohat is described as *"the transcendental binding Unity of all Cosmic Energies."* Fohat is also a source of gravitational influence established within higher dimensional Space of one's own heart holding it all together. Fohat serves to bind living cosmos together and convey the influences of higher dimensional dynamics into the manifest realm below. The Hearts of living beings are their LIFE centres, wherein we might find Deity, which is within *"every point of the universe."* Fohat is also the *"vital electric force that leaves the body at death"* (p. 673), whether a Kosmos or a Son.

7. Zero Point Dynamics & Metaphysics

a. Laya Centres: Zero Point Origins and Ends

> ... the Universe is contained in ovo in the first natural point.... (Blavatsky, S. D. I, p. 118)

The view of a universe emerging from a white hole singularity out of nothingness at the beginning of time and withdrawing into a black hole singularity at the end of time is perhaps the most beautiful and symmetrical model of creation that one might imagine. A cosmos emerges and dissolves back through point sources into nothingness. Number issues from no-number and eventually returns to it. *The Secret Doctrine* offered this perspective over a century before scientists considered such bizarre views and possibilities concerning the origin and ends of the universe. However, there are very significant differences between the perspectives of Blavatsky's occult science and the theories of modern times.

Firstly, modern scientists situate singularities only at the beginning of time and possibly at the end, but do not consider the possibility that they are *constant throughout* time. In contrast, *The Secret Doctrine* maintains that the singularity or zero point state and condition is present throughout the whole period of manifestation. Living cosmoses are *founded upon such zero point laya centres*— represented by the singularity. Higher dimensional intelligences *inform* material nature within/without through such laya centres.

In creation, differentiation occurs within/without from such inner LIFE centres and at the dissolution of a Kosmos, the LIFE principle withdraws from without/within to the neutral Laya centre. The Laya condition represents the 'eternal' or constant principle within the Living Cosmos, the essential LIFE.[2] This mysterious zero point centre persists throughout the life of any living cosmos and is not simply the Alpha and Omega points—although it may disappear from view somewhat in between as it is *veiled by nature*. Further, *The Secret Doctrine* suggests that all different *living Cosmoses* or Sons, on different orders of scale, have such zero point laya centres. These centres are the means by which lower dimensional physics, material and energetic systems and processes, are produced and informed by a higher dimensional metaphysics.

---

2 Blavatsky talks of a circle whose centre is everywhere and circumference nowhere; and also, of a circle whose centre is nowhere and circumference everywhere. Contemplating both forms of this mystical axiom allow us to conceive of the nature of the unusual zero point source.

Blavatsky describes the dissolution of the Cosmos *"at the hour of the Pralaya,"* as the informing principles withdraw into the neutral laya centre. She refers to a "path onward" from matter into Spirit and further,

> the necessary gradual and final reabsorption into the *laya* state, that which Science calls in her own way "the point neutral as to electricity" etc., or the *zero* point. Such are the Occult facts and statement. (p. 551)

Blavatsky provides this overview of the evolution of the Cosmos and its eventual dissolution:

> evolution ... may be thus formulated as an invariable law; a descent of Spirit into Matter, equivalent to an ascent in physical evolution; a reascent from the depths of materiality towards its *status quo ante*, with a corresponding dissipation of concrete form and substance up to the LAYA state, or what Science calls "the zero point," and beyond. (S. D. I, p. 620)

The Secret Doctrine thus postulates the dissolution of the universe into a Laya Centre at the end of time. The term Pralaya might be applied in reference to the Kosmos as a whole, to the existence of a Sun (a Solar Pralaya) or to a human being.

Life enters and exits a human being through the higher dimensional physics of the heart and at death, the consciousness and life principle withdraw into the subtle dimensions of the heart as the soul leaves the body (or rather the body is shed, like a piece of clothing.) Similarly, other cosmoses such as Galaxies, Suns and Planets, have such LIFE CENTRES—zero point foundations as judged from a material perspective, at the heart of their being. Further, just as when a human being dies, the body is left behind, so also, when a sun or planet or galaxy dies, the informing principles withdraw into the laya centre and the physical body is left behind. Thus, the *"refuse and sweat of the Mother"* scattered through the Kosmos, referred to in the *Stanzas of Dzyan,* are those substances which are the material by-products of previous generations or cycles of the Mother's labors.

Blavatsky describes the life principle as withdrawing from one body, tunneling through real Space or the Aether and re-emerging in another spacetime for another Round of life and existence. This is analogous to the modern descriptions in physics of movement through black holes or wormholes. Such processes occur on the level of a Solar Manvantara as the informing principles of the Sun and planets evolve through different bodies within different rounds of life within our solar system! Thus, zero point dynamics and processes allow the LIFE centre within to be constant through different 'rounds' and 'races,' cycles and webs, or the matrices of life. Blavatsky characterizes Suns and planets as being governed by these dynamics. Upon death, the life principle can 'tunnel' through the ethers and re-emerge in another cycle and spacetime in a progressive series of unfoldment. Just as a human being might live varied lives, so also does the LIFE element within a Kosmos, a Sun or a planet, or an Atom. It is the existence of such a higher dimensional holographic metaphysics at the heart of being that allows for such possibilities. As the *Stanzas of Dzyan* explain: "THE SONS EXPAND AND CONTRACT THROUGH THEIR OWN SELVES AND HEARTS...."

The claims of *The Secret Doctrine* are certainly worthy of scientific consideration, placing mystical axioms side by side with modern theories in order to re-interpret the theories and data of science. Although modern scientists conceive of zero point origins and ends for the Universe, they do not consider the continued existence of this singularity condition throughout a period of creation, nor do they regard other living beings as having such *'zero point foundations.'* For Blavatsky, the universe has a zero point laya centre, as does a galaxy, a Sun, and a human being. As it happens, astronomers do now conceive that galaxies can have such black holes and singularities at their centres but have yet to consider the Solar system in this light.[3] Scientists do not imagine that the Sun might have such a LIFE centre— the Invisible Sun described by H.P.B.

The zero point condition is the centre out of which a higher dimensional holographic physics produces the manifestations of life. Modern scientists regard all of the causes of life phenomena as resulting from random and fortuitous concurrence of matter and energy. They never entertain the possibility that life is the product of higher intelligences informing material creation within-without through zero point dynamics.

It is easy to misunderstand the nature of zero points—as they are likely to be viewed as existing within the four dimensional spacetime, like a spiritual spark 'in' the heart. In reality, the case is quite different. Dea, a physicist who is well versed in *The Secret Doctrine*, explains the remarkable view of 'space' implicit to Blavatsky's teachings:

> space-time is created by being squeezed out of a point.... a space-time structure (is created) out of a single point! With this interpretation of space-time, certain paradoxes of nonlocality which require superluminal speeds are no longer paradoxes. The reason is that everything is always connected because everything is really part of the same point....

It is very difficult to truly grasp these seemingly bizarre ideas as our ordinary understanding of everything is so upside down, mistaken and deluded. The zero point centre does not exist within the universe but rather everything exists surrounding the zero point laya centre! It is the centre which is everywhere

---

3 "Galaxies and other complex structures have grown from microscopic seeds—quantum fluctuations—that are stretched to cosmic size by a brief period of "inflation."" (Oskriker, Steinhardt, *Scientific American*, Jan., 2001)

and yet nowhere. All external reality is an illusory projection from such higher dimensional realities.

7b. Zero Point Foundations

> ... 'material points without extension' are ...
> the materials out of which the "Gods" and
> other invisible powers clothe themselves in bodies.
> (Blavatsky, S.D.I, p. 489)
>
> ... such a point of transition must certainly possess special
> and not readily discoverable properties. (p. 628)

Blavatsky labels a Cosmos as a *"Son,"* as a *"wink of the Eye of Self-Existence"* and as a *"spark of eternity."* Whether a Universe, a quantum or an individual divine spark, the laws of nature manifest in the material worlds are due to Divine and spiritual forces and intelligences emerging from within/without through zero point dynamics. The Gods and other invisible powers manifest their forces or influences through zero point dynamics within higher dimensional space—the foundations for all living cosmos. Any Cosmos, any Universe, any Monad (a divine or spiritual spark), any atom or quantum, is thus *"worked and guided from within outwards"* through the dynamics of zero point centres.

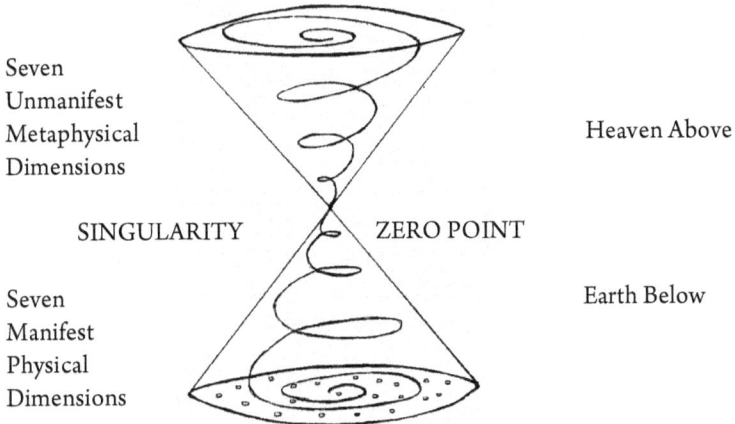

Seven
Unmanifest
Metaphysical
Dimensions

Heaven Above

SINGULARITY   ZERO POINT

Seven
Manifest
Physical
Dimensions

Earth Below

Blavatsky uses various terms to depict these invisible points—labeling them also as *"layu centers"* and *"laya centers."* The influences of divine or spiritual realms upon the physical realm emerge through these laya centres, which exist at or beyond the level of material differentiation.

A zero point is not exactly a 'thing' in itself—so much as a condition or a place at which certain processes occur. It is not simply a 'point particle' but a whole inner world where influences and forces emerge from deeper levels of being into physical manifestation. Blavatsky describes these unextended points beyond the level of physical differentiation as the true 'atoms,' or what we would now call the 'quanta' of physics. In 1888, scientists had no idea of such a point source origination of the universe or of atoms having such an interior nature as is now postulated. However, Blavatsky described such zero point sources, undifferentiated Laya Centres, as the basis for atoms, Sons and Cosmos!

Blavatsky describes these invisible zero points and how the nominal realm acts through such points to 'inform' natural phenomenon:

> A "neutral center" is, in one aspect, the limiting point of any given set of senses. Thus, imagine two consecutive planes of matter as already formed; each of these corresponding to an appropriate set of perceptive organs. We are forced to admit that between these two planes of matter an incessant circulation takes place; and if we follow the atoms and molecules of (say) the lower in their transformation upwards, these will come to a point where they pass altogether beyond the range of the faculties we are using on the lower plane. In fact, to us the matter of the lower plane there vanishes from our perception into nothing—or rather it passes on to the higher plane, and the state of matter corresponding to such a point of transition must certainly possess special and not readily discoverable properties. (S. D. I, pp. 147-8)

For Madame Blavatsky, at the heart of matter, at the heart of the Cosmos, or at the heart of the individual is a zero point laya center—a metaphysical foundation rooted within into the Eternal Parent Space, the Ceaseless Breath and the Infinity of the Absolute. The laws of nature, the intelligence and life principles which inform material reality emerge within/without from these metaphysical dimensions and zero point dynamics which sustain the physical realm.

Blavatsky explains that the views of the mystic philosopher Leibnitz represent *The Secret Doctrine* teaching of how a dimensionless point within material reality might extend inwardly into the infinity of a metaphysical realm:

> "Leibnitz... could not rest content in assuming that matter was composed of a finite number of very small parts. His mathematical mind forced him to carry out the argument *in infinitum*. And what became of the atoms then? They lost their extension and they retained only their property of resistance; they were the centres of force. They were reduced to mathematical points... but if their existence in space was nothing, *so much fuller was their inner life.* ... having reduced the geometrical extension of the atoms to nothing, Leibnitz endowed them with an infinite extension in the direction of their metaphysical

dimension. After having lost sight of them in the world of space, the mind has, as it were, to dive into a metaphysical world to find and grasp the real essence of what appears in space merely as a mathematical point. As a cone stands on its point, or a perpendicular straight line cuts a horizontal plane only in one mathematical point, but may extend infinitely in height and depth, so the essences *of things real* have only a punctual existence in this physical world of space; but have an infinite depth of inner life in the metaphysical world...."

This is the spirit, the very root of occult doctrine and thought. The "Spirit-Matter" and "Matter-Spirit" extend infinitely *in depth*, and like "the essence of things" of Leibnitz, our essence of things *real* is *at the seventh depth*; while the *unreal* and gross matter of Science and the external world, is at the lowest end of our perceptive senses. (S. D. I, Blavatsky quoting Mertz, p. 628)

In this view, any point within the relative time/space continuum extends inwardly into the metaphysical realm and ultimately into the Unity which pervades and sustains creation.

In order to understand the doctrine of zero points, we must realize that they are beyond the level of discrimination as afforded by the reach of the physical senses:

The chemist goes to the *laya* or zero-point of the plane of matter with which he deals, and then stops short.... But the full Initiate *knows* that the ring "Pass-Not" is neither locality, nor can it be measured by distance, but that it exists in the absoluteness of infinity. In this "Infinity"... there is neither height, breadth nor thickness, but all is fathomless profundity, reaching down from the physical to the "para-para-metaphysical." (S. D. I, p. 131)

What Blavatsky describes as the *zero point*, or the *Ring Pass Not*, is at the level of the Planckian units in physics where physical manifestation becomes apparent and measurement is possible.

The creation and dissolution of any Universe—whether a cosmos, or other living beings—originates from and resolves back into zero point laya centres. Blavatsky thus anticipated modern concepts of creation from a singularity and the idea that the universe itself could conceivably dissolve back into such a singularity at the end of time. Creation, or the descent of spirit into matter, involves the emergence from a zero point laya centre. Further, the forces of nature are generated by activities occurring within/without through the inner dynamics of such zero point centres. (In physics, these concepts anticipate modern ideas of the rolled up, compacted dimensions existing at every point underlying the four large spacetime dimensions and serving as the foundations for physical laws.)

Blavatsky's remarkable perspective provides profound insights into many enigmas and theories of modern science. In the light of her doctrine of the laya centres and zero point dynamics, we certainly might have anticipated the formulation of the 'uncertainty principle' within modern quantum physics. For if we trace any particle back far enough, trying to measure its attributes, we encounter what Blavatsky calls the *'ring pass not,'* where the quanta passes from one plane of perception into a higher dimensional realm—into a seemingly unfathomable and infinite realm. Any particle must thus 'vanish from perception' on a lower plane as we penetrate into its inner most nature.

And so, if we try to fully determine a particle's position and momentum simultaneously, it disappears into the infinite, because this is the realm from which it emerges. And, as Blavatsky notes, *"... the state of matter corresponding to such a point of transition must certainly possess special and not readily discoverable properties."* The uncertainty principle is the natural manifestation of this paradox of zero point sources possessing *"special and not readily discoverable properties."*

Blavatsky's profound archaic philosophy was elaborated over twenty years before the formulation of the quantum hypothesis and a century before modern views of creation of the Universe from a singularity. The 'naught points' or singularities of modern science are the 'rings pass not' described by Blavatsky. Further, her teachings are clearly consistent with modern concepts of the quantum vacuum as being paradoxically both void/plenum and the notion of "vacuum genesis" as elaborated in contemporary science. However, *The Secret Doctrine* provides a radically different perspective and interpretation of such modern concepts and theories.

In *The Secret Doctrine*, any cosmos is a "Son" with such a point source of unfoldment. Each Son is also described as a *"wink of the Eye of Self-Existence"* and a *"spark of eternity."* These descriptions apply equally to the existence of a macroscopic Universe and to material quanta. However, what is so utterly profound about Blavatsky's teaching, relative to modern science, is the idea also that there are similarly *'quanta of consciousness'*—zero point divine sparks or Monads established within the higher dimensional Heart Space of human beings!

Although modern science conceives of the zero point origins of quanta and cosmos, the idea that human consciousness might similarly have such mysterious zero point origins is never considered. However, everything is rooted within the One, whether a manifested cosmos, an individual monad or a unitary quantum. All living Cosmos expand and contract through such zero point sources established within their own Hearts. Everything in creation is informed in this way— within/without from zero points. This is truly an awesome ancient mystical teaching which bears profound relationships to emerging scientific viewpoints.

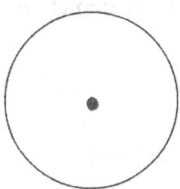

7c. Cosmic Differentiation

An Archaic Manuscript ... is before the writer's eye. On the first page is an immaculate white disk within a dull black ground. On the following page, the same disk, but with a central point. The first ... Kosmos in Eternity, before the re-awakening of still slumbering Energy, the emanation of the Word ... The point in the hitherto immaculate Disk, Space and Eternity in Pralaya, denotes the dawn of differentiation. It is the Point in the Mundane Egg, the germ within the latter which will become the Universe, the ALL, the boundless, periodical Kosmos, this germ being latent and active, periodically by turns. The one circle is divine Unity, from which all proceeds, whither all returns. (S. D. I, p. 1)

The Secret Doctrine depicts the Cosmos as emerging from a central point within a circle or disk—the Point in the Mundane Egg. The circle represents the divine Unity out of which the point emerges and into which it will eventually return.

Stanza 1 of the book of Dzyan depicts conditions during the Nights of Brahma, when "DARKNESS ALONE FILLED THE BOUNDLESS ALL," (I, 5) and, "THE CAUSES OF EXISTENCE HAD BEEN DONE AWAY WITH," and "RESTED IN ETERNAL NON-BEING—THE ONE BEING." (1, 7) In this case, "NAUGHT WAS," (1, 6)—there was no time, no universal Mind, no seven ways to bliss, no Seven Sublime Lords. The Father, Mother and Son were One. Prior to creation, "THE ETERNAL PARENT WRAPPED IN HER EVER INVISIBLE ROBES HAD SLUMBERED ONCE AGAIN FOR SEVEN ETERNITIES." (I,1)

Stanza II continues to describe the state of Existence prior to the process of cosmic creation and differentiation. The dual principles of the Father and Mother, Divine Thought and the Divine Bosom, are undifferentiated: *"These two are the germ, and this Germ is one."* (II, 6) The Ceaseless Eternal Breath is introduced as the counterpart to the Eternal Parent Space. The Stanza also mentions "THE BUILDERS, THE LUMINOUS SONS OF MANVANTARIC DAWN," (11, 1) who are absorbed in the Unknown Darkness: "THE SEVEN SONS WERE NOT YET BORN FROM THE WEB OF LIGHT." (II, 5)

Two verses of Stanza II then depict the processes that lead to cosmic differentiation.

> 3. THE HOUR HAD NOT YET STRUCK:
> THE RAY HAD NOT YET FLASHED INTO THE GERM;
> THE MATRIPADMA HAD NOT YET SWOLLEN.[4]
>
> 4. HER HEART HAD NOT YET OPENED FOR THE ONE RAY TO ENTER, HENCE TO FALL, AS THREE INTO FOUR, INTO THE LAP OF MAYA.

At the moment of creation, the Heart of the Mother will open and a 'RAY' will flash into the germ. The theological trinity of That (the Absolute Non-Being), the Eternal Parent Space and the Eternal Ceaseless Breath, then fall into four—as the Son or Cosmos is differentiated.[5] The term Maya refers to the illusory worlds of creation, which are impermanent relative to the world of the Absolute.

Stanza III then depicts the first instances of creation:

> 1. ... THE LAST VIBRATION OF THE SEVENTH ETERNITY THRILLS THROUGH INFINITUDE. THE MOTHER SWELLS, EXPANDING FROM WITHIN WITHOUT, LIKE THE BUD OF A LOTUS.
>
> 2. THE VIBRATION SWEEPS ALONG, TOUCHING WITH ITS SWIFT WING THE WHOLE UNIVERSE AND THE GERM THAT DWELLETH IN DARKNESS: THE DARKNESS THAT BREATHES OVER THE SLUMBERING WATERS OF LIFE ....
>
> 3. DARKNESS RADIATES LIGHT, AND LIGHT DROPS ONE SOLITARY RAY INTO THE MOTHER-DEEP. THE RAY SHOOTS THROUGH THE VIRGIN EGG. THE RAY CAUSES THE ETERNAL EGG TO THRILL, AND DROP THE NON-ETERNAL GERM, WHICH CONDENSES INTO THE WORLD-EGG.

One solitary Ray of light penetrates into the Mother Deep (the Eternal Parent Space) and this initiates the process of material creation. In Kabbalah, this line of light is the *kav*, drawn down from the En Soph Aur (the Limitless Light). Blavatsky elaborates:

> The solitary ray dropping into the mother deep may be taken as meaning Divine Thought or Intelligence, impregnating chaos. This,

---

4   Matripadma refers to the Mother Lotus.

5   In a similar way, the Kabbalist describes the conjunction of the supernal triad of Sephiroth as giving birth to Da'at, the Son, sent into exile in the worlds below.

however, occurs on the plane of metaphysical abstraction, or rather the plane whereon that which we call a metaphysical abstraction is a reality. (p. 64)

In modern science, the instigation of creation is described as the result of a 'random' quantum fluctuation within the vacuum, which disrupts the state of perfect symmetry and leads to the differentiation of the laws of nature. Such a 'ray of light' emanating out of the Absolute would indeed constitute such a 'quantum fluctuation,' although a law-conformable one and not simply a random or fortuitous event.

The Virgin Egg within the Eternal Parent Space then drops the *"Non-Eternal Germ,"* which condenses into a 'world egg.' Blavatsky explains:

> And just as the fecundation of an egg takes place before it is dropped; so the non-eternal periodic germ which becomes ... the mundane egg, contains in itself, when it emerges ... "the promise and potency of all the Universe. ... The simile of an egg also expresses the fact taught in Occultism that the primordial form of everything manifested, from atom to globe, from man to angel, is spheroidal, the sphere having been with all nations the emblem of eternity and infinity—a serpent swallowing its tail. ... The mystery of apparent self-generation and evolution through its own creative power repeating in miniature the process of Cosmic Evolution in the egg. (pp. 64-5)

In modern science, cosmologists have a similar concept concerning how the universe ballooned outwardly from its original singularity condition. Science writer, K. Cole depicts the modern creation scenario of the *"inflationary universe:"*

> Once upon a time (about twenty billion years ago), there was nothing—although not the kind of nothing we're used to today. To be specific, there was something (or nothing?) called a false vacuum ... packed to the brim with energy and even speckled with occasional particles. ... One day? eon? Millisecond? What do you call time before time began? a particularly large fluctuation jarred the false vacuum with such force that it began to disintegrate. Whoosh went the universe, inflating from a billionth the size of a proton to the size of a grapefruit in less than a millionth of a trillionth of a trillionth of a second. The time was now one trillionth of a trillionth (or so) of a second after the universe began. The universe has been expanding ever since ... All the particles and energies within it come from the energy of the false vacuum. ... The evolution of the universe explains the nature of our present vacuum; the nature of vacuums explains the evolution of the universe. ... In the end, says (physicist) Wilczek, "physics has totally turned around: now its accepted that most things

started out as nothing. Now we have to explain why certain things aren't nothing any more." (Cole, 1985, pp. 78-80)

Cole depicts a series of creation events very similar to those depicted by Blavatsky and the *Stanzas of Dzyan*.

Firstly, there is a primordial nothingness, a seeming void and mysterious plenum. Secondly, *"a large fluctuation"*—a random quantum fluctuation—jars the vacuum in the first instance of creation, which is similar to the Ray that penetrates into the Mother Deep. Thirdly, the universe emerges from a singularity point source, billions of times smaller than the size of a proton. Fourthly, the *'inflationary era'* lasts from 10^{-43} to 10^{-35} of a second, during which time this point inflates to something *"the size of a grapefruit."* In *The Secret Doctrine*, this is the dropping of the World Egg from the non-Eternal Germ. Finally, the Universe continues to expand since the first moments of creation. Madame Blavatsky depicted all of these creation events in 1888! Is it any wonder that she thought no one in her era would believe her?

This is the modern creation scenario: From nothingness, a random quantum fluctuation, a zero point or singularity, a sudden inflation and dropping of the world-egg, and then an expansion of the universe from within/without. This extraordinary and bizarre view of cosmic origins from modern science is really quite consistent with Blavatsky's archaic Secret Doctrine! Of course, physicists and cosmologists wonder where it will all end: in an eternally expanding universe or one which will eventually contract and perhaps return again to a singularity condition. This scenario is sometimes referred to as the 'big crunch,' a term coined to contrast this ending with the 'big bang' creation event. On this issue, *The Secret Doctrine* makes it clear that the life principle within living beings will eventually return through such zero point dynamics into the Eternal Parent Space, returning again to the Bosom of the Divine Mother.

The next stanza describes the next phase of cosmic evolution:

4. THEN THE THREE FALL INTO THE FOUR. THE RADIANT ESSENCE BECOMES SEVEN INSIDE, SEVEN OUTSIDE. THE LUMINOUS EGG, WHICH IN ITSELF IS THREE, CURDLES AND SPREADS IN MILK-WHITE CURDS THROUGHOUT THE DEPTHS OF THE MOTHER, THE ROOT THAT GROWS IN THE DEPTHS OF THE OCEAN OF LIFE.

The three—Be-ness, Abstract Motion and Abstract Space, fall into four. The fourth is the Son, the emerging Cosmos. The Radiant Essence becomes seven inside and seven outside—as both the metaphysical and the physical realms will embody the same inherent sevenfold nature. The Luminous Egg curdling and spreading through the Depths of the Mother involves the creation of the differentiated matters and energies out of the void/plenum throughout the expanding realms of creation. Blavatsky states such: *"The radiant essence curdled and spread throughout the depths"* of Space. *From an astronomical point of view this is easy of explanation: it is the "milky way," the world-stuff, or primordial matter in its first form. (p. 67)*

At this time in the Stanzas, the Ocean (of Space) *"WAS RADIANT LIGHT, WHICH WAS FIRE, AND HEAT, AND MOTION."* (III, 6) Certainly, such fire, heat and motion are consistent with modern views of a hot, energetic Big Bang creation event.

> III, 10. FATHER-MOTHER SPIN A WEB WHOSE UPPER END IS FASTENED TO SPIRIT—THE LIGHT OF THE ONE DARKNESS—AND THE LOWER ONE TO ITS SHADOWY END, MATTER; AND THIS WEB IS THE UNIVERSE SPUN OUT OF THE TWO SUBSTANCES MADE IN ONE, WHICH IS SVÂBHÂVAT.

The Father and Mother spin a web of spirit and matter which becomes the universe, forming the matrix of creation.

> III, 11. IT EXPANDS WHEN THE BREATH OF FIRE IS UPON IT; IT CONTRACTS WHEN THE BREATH OF THE MOTHER TOUCHES IT. THEN THE SONS DISSOCIATE AND SCATTER, TO RETURN INTO THEIR MOTHER'S BOSOM AT THE END OF THE GREAT DAY, AND RE-BECOME ONE WITH HER; WHEN IT IS COOLING, IT BECOMES RADIANT, AND THE SONS EXPAND AND CONTRACT THROUGH THEIR OWN SELVES AND HEARTS; THEY EMBRACE INFINITUDE.

Any Son or space-time universe expands and contracts through variations of the Eternal Ceaseless Breath. During creation, THE BREATH OF FIRE IS UPON IT, that of the Father-Brahma. The dissolution of the Universe back into Prayalaya will eventually occur after "THE BREATH OF THE MOTHER TOUCHES IT," and the life principle withdraws back into the neutral undifferentiated laya centre at the heart of being. In between, the Pilgrim or Son ventures into worlds spun of the web of spirit and matter through a seven-dimensional Maya.

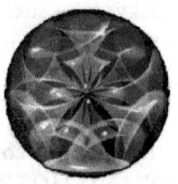

7d. Seven Laya Centres: Zero Point Foundations for the Laws of Nature

VI, 2. THE SWIFT AND RADIANT ONE PRODUCES THE SEVEN LAYA CENTRES... AND SEATS THE UNIVERSE ON THESE ETERNAL FOUNDATIONS.... (Stanza VI, 2)

The seven *Layu* centres are the seven Zero points, using the term Zero in the same sense that Chemists do, to indicate a point at which, in Esotericism, the scale of reckoning of differentiation begins. (S. D. I, pp. 138-9)

According to Blavatsky, the laws of nature manifest in the material worlds are due to divine and spiritual intelligences within super-sensuous states of being. These influences are conveyed by Fohat through zero point dynamics to manifest outwardly within the life of any 'Son'—whether that of a universe, a quantum or a human being. Blavatsky describes the influx of formative forces manifesting from within the higher spiritual and divine realms into the lower material realm as acting through *"holes dug in Space"*—*"invisible points"* or *"zero-points."* Fohat's influences emerge through the seven Laya (or Layu) Centres, those wheels and vortices are at zero point levels where material differentiation begins. It is this process which *"ends as Omnipresent Mind and Life (being) immanent in every atom of Matter."* (S. D. I, p. 139)

Blavatsky describes the seven inside as *"digging holes in Space"* to channel their intelligence/influences into the material realm. Thus, seven invisible zero points holes dug in space are established as a foundation for physical manifestation and the laws of nature:

all the so-called Forces of Nature, Electricity, Magnetism, Light, Heat, etc., etc., far from being modes of motion of material particles, are *in esse*, i.e., in their ultimate constitution, the differentiated aspects of that Universal Motion.... When Fohat is said to produce "Seven Laya Centres," it means that for formative or creative purposes, the GREAT LAW (Theists may call it God) stops, or rather modifies its perpetual motion on seven invisible points within the area of the manifested Universe. *"The great Breath digs through Space seven holes* into Laya to cause them to circumgyrate during Manvantara." (Occult Catechism). We have said that Laya is what Science may call the Zero-point or line; the realm of absolute negativeness, or the one real absolute Force ... the neutral axis, not one of the many aspects, but its centre. ... "Seven Neutral Centres," then are produced by Fohat .... (S. D. I, pp. 147-8)

In this view, the foundation for the laws of nature and of material quanta (and the foundation of human consciousness) are the invisible Laya Centres—which extend from physical dimensions into the underlying metaphysical realm of the Eternal Parent Space and the Ceaseless Breath. The Gods and other invisible powers "clothe" themselves in bodies based upon such zero point dynamics and holes dug in space, through which Fohat acting as an electromagnetic force links the intelligence above to the material realm below.

Although the Zero Point is sometimes described as being singular, at other times it is described as having this sevenfold differentiation. Like Fohat, it is One and Seven. It is from such mysterious zero point conditions that the differentiation of a Cosmos, a quantum or Monad begins. Modern scientist, Paul Davis (1984) described such a model of 11 dimensional theory in modern physics where 7 'compacted dimensions' are rolled up into elements at zero point levels. Davis explained, *"think of the extra dimensions as somehow inside the atom"* (p. 160). Remarkably, Blavatsky explained exactly this type of peculiar inner dimensionality to 'atoms,' quanta, Monads and cosmoses over a century ago, Accordingly, Blavatsky's model suggests that there is a complex metaphysics to reality at zero point levels.

> The "Imperishable Laya Centres" have a great importance, and their meaning must be fully understood if we would have a clear conception of the Archaic Cosmogony. (S. D. I)

Blavatsky maintained an unusual conception of the permanency and impermanency of matter. She states that matter is eternal—but only in its first undifferentiated condition—in *"the laya state."* Material quanta, Cosmoses, and Monads are differentiated from a 'laya state'—an apparent zero point source or condition. The material quanta, structures and organization come and go through different cycles of cosmic manifestation, but the laya centers are 'imperishable.'

The following diagram conveys the idea of the various forces underlying any material quantum as represented by the final product of the *Tree of Life* the lowest sphere referred to as *Malkuth* or the *Kingdom*. The quantum is a function of all of the forces which pass through the higher dimensions of the *Tree of Life* and which emerge from within the root principles of creation. Ultimately, everything is a derivative of the Theological Trinity of Be-ness, the Eternal Parent Space and the Ceaseless Breath. The Eternal Parent Space has an inherent sevenfoldness and hence produces seven pre-material protyles, or seven Ethers as modifications of the fundamental Akasa. The Ceaseless Breath is similarly differentiated into the Seven Luminous Sons—the Dhyan Chohans. The Seven Fohats mediate between the higher realms and the spheres below. These three—the Seven Protyles, the Seven Luminous Sons and the Seven Fohats—can be considered to form a 'metaphysical trinity,' as distinct from the 'theological trinity' above. In the *Tree of Life*, the metaphysical trinity forms a downward turned triangle below, in contrast to the upward turned triangle of the theological trinity above.

Other Stanzas depict the unfolding of the Seven Laya Centres in a sequential process. In terms of modern physics, this is called *'sequential symmetry breaking'* out of a state of 'perfect symmetry' hypothesized to exist before cosmic differentiation from the Akasa. This sequential symmetry breaking is depicted in the Stanzas:

VI, 2. THE SWIFT AND RADIANT ONE PRODUCES THE SEVEN LAYA CENTRES, AGAINST WHICH NONE WILL PREVAIL TO THE GREAT DAY "BE-WITH-US," AND SEATS THE UNIVERSE ON THESE ETERNAL FOUNDATIONS SURROUNDING TSIEN-TCHAN WITH THE ELEMENTARY GERMS.

3. OF THE SEVEN—FIRST ONE MANIFESTED, SIX CONCEALED, TWO MANIFESTED, FIVE CONCEALED; THREE MANIFESTED, FOUR CONCEALED; FOUR PRODUCED, THREE HIDDEN; FOUR AND ONE TSAN REVEALED, TWO AND ONE HALF CONCEALED; SIX TO BE MANIFESTED, ONE LAID ASIDE. LASTLY, SEVEN SMALL WHEELS REVOLVING; ONE GIVING BIRTH TO THE OTHER.

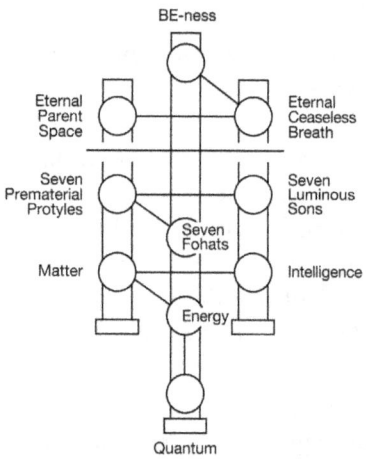

From the perspective of *The Secret Doctrine,* all of these higher level and primordial realms underlie material manifestation of a cosmos or quantum. Subsequently, any physics carried far enough has to lead to this ancient metaphysics. In contrast, the naive materialist science philosophy of the past century takes only the last sphere of the *Tree of Life* as 'reality:' the material realm governed by mechanistic laws and considers that there is no underlying metaphysics to such processes. In contrast, Blavatsky explained how all things are created, sustained and dissolved through zero-point dynamics rooted into higher dimensions and the primordial realms.

All the laws of physics are founded upon zero point foundations and these are the portals for higher dimensional influences. Further, these processes proceed on successive levels or planes of being, creating manifest reality within-without from zero points levels. H.P. Blavatsky certainly held a remarkable view of physics and the metaphysical processes underlying familiar reality.

The zero point teaching provides a highly valuable alternative perspective on the mysteries of creation, as well as on the newest theories of modern physics and cosmology. Blavatsky is suggesting that the true causes of phenomena in the outer world are founded upon these zero point sources—in a manner quite consistent with the newest models of higher compacted dimensions, zero point fields, black-hole information processes and holographic physics—as we shall see. The Gods and other invisible powers clothe themselves in bodies based on such zero point foundations, seven circumgyrating holes dug in space!

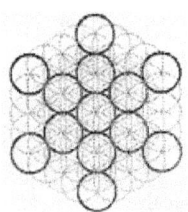

7e. From SEVEN HOLY CIRCUMGYRATING BREATHS to Whirlwinds and Fohat's Circular Errands

A certain *"spinergy,"* or 'spin energy' is inherent to the zero point foundations of a cosmos. This is attributable to the dynamics of the Eternal Ceaseless Breath and its seven modifications as conveyed through Fohat (or the seven Fohats). A circumgyrating motion is produced through the seven holes dug in Space. The Stanzas of Dzyan portray the Fiery Whirlwinds produced as modifications of the HOLY CIRCUMGYRATING BREATHS:

V, 1. THE PRIMORDIAL SEVEN, THE FIRST SEVEN BREATHS OF THE DRAGON OF WISDOM, PRODUCE IN THEIR TURN FROM THEIR HOLY CIRCUMGYRATING BREATHS THE FIERY WHIRLWIND.

2. THEY MAKE OF HIM THE MESSENGER OF THEIR WILL... FOHAT, THE SWIFT SON OF THE DIVINE SON WHOSE SONS ARE THE LIPIKA, RUNS CIRCULAR ERRANDS. FOHAT... PASSES LIKE LIGHTNING THROUGHT THE FIERY CLOUDS; TAKES THREE, AND FIVE, AND SEVEN STRIDES THROUGH THE SEVEN REGIONS ABOVE, AND THE SEVEN BELOW. HE LIFTS HIS VOICE, AND CALLS THE INNUMERABLE SPARKS, AND JOINS THEM.

3. ... HE SEPARATES THE SPARKS OF THE LOWER KINGDOM THAT FLOAT AND THRILL WITH JOY IN THEIR RADIANT DWELLINGS AND FORMS THERE-WITH THE GERMS OF WHEELS. HE PLACES THEM IN THE SIX DIRECTIONS OF SPACE, AND ONE IN THE MIDDLE—THE CENTRAL WHEEL.

The Eternal Ceaseless Breath, which is infinitely energetic, manifests as the Primordial Seven—the Seven HOLY CIRCUMGYRATING BREATHS. These breaths produce THE FIERY WHIRLWIND, the "MESSENGER OF THEIR WILL"—Fohat and his seven Sons, the *Lipika*. Fohat RUNS CIRCULAR ERRANDS and forms seven WHEELS in the six directions of space and one in the middle—as depicted by the *flower of life* symbol of ancient Egypt, with a central seventh point. Fohat conveys the influences of the Divine Intelligence from the SEVEN REGIONS ABOVE through to the SEVEN BELOW. Thus there are seven heavens and seven material worlds of varied subtleness and vibration, connected through the actions of the seven Fohats.

The *Stanza of Dzyan* depict the formation of the Laya Centres which serve as the foundations for the universe:

VI: 2. THE SWIFT AND RADIANT ONE PRODUCES THE SEVEN LAYA CENTRES... AND SEATS THE UNIVERSE ON THESE ETERNAL FOUNDATIONS SURROUNDING TSIEN-TCHAN WITH THE ELEMENTARY GERMS. 3. ... SEVEN SMALL WHEELS REVOLVING; ONE GIVING BIRTH TO THE OTHER. 4. ... FOHAT... MAKES BALLS OF FIRE, RUNS THROUGH THEM, AND ROUND THEM, INFUSING LIFE THEREINTO, THEN SETS THEM INTO MOTION; SOME ONE WAY, SOME THE OTHER WAY.

The laya centres, the eternal foundations for the Universe, are described as 'revolving' and 'set in motion' in different directions. Further, they are described as differentiating through sequential symmetry breaking, ONE GIVING BIRTH TO THE OTHER. Imagine such wheels within wheels, through different generations of causes and effects originating from a dynamic zero point centre established within the transcendental hyperspace of the Eternal Parent Space!

> "Wheels" … are the centres of force, around which primordial Cosmic matter expands, and, passing through all the six stages of consolidation, becomes spheroidal and ends by being transformed into globes or spheres. … This law of vertical movement in primordial matter, is one of the oldest conceptions of Greek philosophy, whose first historical Sages were nearly all Initiates of the Mysteries. The Greeks had it from the Egyptians, and the latter from the Chaldeans, who had been the pupils of Brahmins of the esoteric school. (pp. 116-7)

Madame Blavatsky offers modern science profound gems of insight into the possible mechanisms of Divine and Spiritual Intelligences in creating, maintaining and dissolving any finite holographic Cosmos. Instead of a bearded patriarch sitting on a throne telling the flowers to open for Carl Sagan, the Divine Workman carry out the Will of the Dhyan Chohans and spin their magic through the seven dynamic vortical action centres established within higher dimensional Space. Fohat, as the personified god or agent of DIVINE WILL, 'ensouls' the living cosmos through such sevenfold circumgyrating zero point centres. Such actions are then reiterated or multiplied through different generations.

> The one Cosmic atom becomes seven atoms on the plane of matter, and each is transformed into a centre of energy; that same atom becomes seven rays on the plane of spirit, and the seven creative forces of nature, radiating from the root-essence … The atoms emanated from the Central Point emanate in their turn new centres of energy, which, under the potential breath of *Fohat*, begin their work from within without, and multiply other minor centres. These, in the course of evolution and involution, form in their turn the roots or developing causes of new effects, from worlds and "man-bearing" globes, down to the genera, species, and classes of all the seven kingdoms (of which we know only four.) (p. 635)

This suggests that living beings have a complex inner multidimensional nature and that the influences of the vortical zero point dynamics are reiterated in a fractal way through higher dimensions to underlie the final material organization of the Cosmos.

Blavatsky suggests that indeed God does "micro-intervene" within the laws of nature and she proposes a concrete model of these dynamics. Further, this model is consistent with the holographic model of physics to be explored currently, which proposes that mini-black hole dynamics at zero point levels in an anti-de Sitter spacetime could embody and process vast amounts of information at incredible speeds. Holes dug in Space or mini-black holes can function as micro-processors. The activity of such dynamics and holes in space could create material-energetic processes on surrounding 'shells' of a holographic surface, which are essentially levels of the seven skinned Aether. Blavatsky actually suggests that living beings have such dynamical LIFE centres and existence is founded upon such higher dimensional zero point dynamics. We shall see currently that the theories of modern physics only add credence to such bizarre notions!

8. The Invisible Sun, the Solar Logos & the Ethers of Space

We must bravely face Science and declare, in the teeth of materialistic learning, of Idealism, Hylo-Idealism, Positivism and all-denying modern Psychology, that the true Occultist believes in "Lords of Light;" that he believes in a Sun, which, far from being simply "a lamp of day" moving in accordance with physical law, and far from being merely one of those Suns, which ... "are Sun-flowers of a higher light"—is, like milliards of other Suns, the dwelling or the vehicle of a god, and a host of gods. ...

The Sun is matter, and the Sun is Spirit. Our ancestors ... were ... wise enough in their generation to see in it the symbol of Divinity, and at the same time to sense within, concealed by the physical Symbol, the bright God of Spiritual and terrestrial Light. Such belief is now regarded as a superstition only by rank materialism, which denies Deity, Spirit, Soul, and admits no intelligence outside the mind of man. (p. 479)

Blavatsky's critique of science is as appropriate today to the mainstream of twenty-first century science as it was to the science of her day. Modern science denies Deity, Spirit and Soul, and is only beginning to admit 'intelligence outside the mind of man.' We still have a "an all-denying modern Psychology" and no serious particle or solar physicist would consider that there might be such *"Lords of Light"*—as actual sentient, intelligent and living beings within the Sun or Solar system. Of course, the materialist dismisses such possibilities as superstition and imagination and does not as consider them to pose serious hypotheses for science.

The scientific attitude of modern times is typified by Carl Sagan who declares that there is *"less and less for God to do"* now that we have modern science. We can explain the opening of the morning glory to the sun, not as due to a patriarch saying *'Hey, flower, open,'* but rather as due to physical laws concerning the sun's radiations and the plant processes of phototropism and photosynthesis. The Sun is not considered in science to involve any form of higher intelligence but simply to be a material mass in a state of combustion. The Sun is viewed in its material nature but not as having a spiritual nature. Similarly, Carl Sagan suggests that we no longer need Kepler's *angelus rector*, or angels, to conduct the planets and keep them in their course, because now we have a modern theory of gravity.

The Secret Doctrine provides a remarkable alternative view not only of the Sun, as a living being ruled by sentient beings, or *Lords of Light*, but further, Blavatsky challenges the very existence of Dr. Sagan's favorite gravity.

8a. The Visible & Invisible Sun

The Secret Doctrine actually suggests that there is some type of "material point without extension," an invisible spark or primordial atom, or seven holes dug in space, at the heart of the Sun. Similarly, such life centres are described within other living planetary and galactic bodies. It is through such dynamic point sources that higher Intelligences convey their influences through Fohat and his seven sons within the electromagnetic Ocean of Life of the solar system. Thus, the Sun is claimed to have such a zero point centre and to embody the Divine Intelligences of deeper realms beyond.

> The real substance of the concealed (Sun) is a nucleus of Mother substance. It is the heart and the matrix of all the living and existing Forces in our solar universe. (p. 290)

The Sun has an inner LIFE source derived from an *"invisible spark,"* *"primordial atom"* or *"nucleus of Mother Substance."* The Sun differentiates from a laya centre through the "Whirlwind," the initial motion, regulated and sustained by the Seven Breaths of the Dhyan-Chohans, who are then embodied within the solar Lords of Light. The Sun represents the Heart and the life principle within the Solar System:

> This "mystery," or the origin of the LIFE ESSENCE, Occultism locates in the same centre as the nucleus of *prima material* (for they are one) of our Solar system.
>
> *"The Sun is the heart of the Solar World (System) and its brain is hidden behind the (visible) Sun. From hence, sensation is radiated into every nerve centre of the great body, and the waves of the life-essence flow into each artery and vein. ... The planets are its limbs and pulses. ... "* (Commentary)

> Occult philosophy denies that the Sun is a globe in combustion, but defines it simply as a world, a glowing sphere, the *real* Sun being hidden behind, and the visible being only its reflection, its *shell*. ... the *visible* Sun only *a window cut into the real* Solar palace and presence,

which reflects, however, faithfully the interior work. (S. D. I, pp. 540-1)

The Sun is the *"heart of the Solar World"* and has a vital LIFE element—a *"nucleus of prima material."* Further, the physical Sun only reflects in matter the nature of the invisible Sun which is the source of its life and light.

Blavatsky elaborates upon the important correspondence between the heart and the sun:

> Thus, there is a regular circulation of the vital fluid throughout our system, of which the Sun is the heart—the same as the circulation of the blood in the human body—during the manvantaric solar period, or life; the Sun contracting as rhythmically at every return of it, as the human heart does. ... Astronomy knows of the fixed cycle of eleven years when the number of solar spots increases, which is due to the contraction of the Solar HEART. (p. 541)[6]

The Sun is a storehouse of Vital Force, *"the Noumenon of Electricity"* and *"from its mysterious, never-to-be-fathomed depths... issue those life currents which thrill through Space, as through the organisms of every living thing on Earth."* (p. 531) Further, Blavatsky explains: *"It is the Sun-fluids or Emanations that impart all motion and awaken all into life in the Solar System."* (p. 529)

Blavatsky describes the "Sons of Light" associated with the Sun:

> the "Sons of Light"... emanate from, and are self-generated in, that infinite Ocean of Light, whose one pole is pure *Spirit* lost in the absoluteness of Non-Being, and the other, the *matter* in which it condenses, crystallizing into a more and more gross type as it descends into manifestation. (S. D. I, p. 481)

Blavatsky describes the Sun as the Life-Giver of the physical world and the *"Concealed Spiritual Sun"* as the light and life giver of the spiritual and psychic realms. She explains:

> It is the 'Spirit of Light,' the first born of the Eternal pure Element, whose energy (or emanation) is stored in the Sun, the great Life-Giver of the physical world, as the hidden Concealed Spiritual Sun is the Light-and Life-Giver of the Spiritual and Psychic Realms. (S. D. I, p. 481)

In *Isis Unveiled* (1877), Blavatsky drew from varied traditions to illustrate the secret doctrines as they pertain to the nature of the Sun and the invisible Sun:

> The ancient sun-worshippers regarded the Great Spirit as a nature-god, identical with nature, and the sun as the deity, "in whom the Lord

---

6   Modern science recognizes a 22 year cycle in solar sun spot activity and has since Blavatsky's day.

of life dwells." ... "The sun is the source of the souls and of *all life.*" Agni, the "Divine Fire," the deity of the Hindu, is the sun, for the fire and sun are the same. Ormazd is light, the Sun-God, or the Life-giver. In the Hindu philosophy, "The souls issue from the soul of the world, and return to it as sparks to the fire." But, in another place, it is said that *"The Sun is the soul of all things*; all has proceeded out of it, and will return to it," which shows that the sun is meant allegorically here, and refers to the *central,* invisible sun, GOD, whose first manifestation was Sephira, the Emanation of En-Soph—Light, in short. ...

none of the ancients, the sun-worshippers included, regarded our visible sun otherwise than as an emblem of their metaphysical invisible central sun-god. Moreover, they did *not* believe what our modern science teaches us, namely, that light and heat proceed from *our* sun, and that it is this planet which imparts all life to our visible nature. "His radiance is undecaying," says the *Rig-Veda,* "the intensely—shining, all-pervading, unceasing, undecaying rays of Agni desist not, neither night nor day." This evidently related to the spiritual, central sun, whose rays are all-pervading and unceasing, the eternal and boundless life-giver. He the *Point;* the centre (which is everywhere) of the circle (which is nowhere), the ethereal, spiritual fire, the soul and spirit of the all-pervading, mysterious ether; the despair and puzzle of the materialist, who will some day find that that which causes the numberless cosmic forces to manifest themselves in eternal correlation is but a divine electricity, or rather *galvanism,* and that the sun is but one of the myriad magnets disseminated through space.... (p. 270)

The "Central Spiritual Sun" is depicted as a *"Point"* and as the source of an *"ethereal spiritual fire,"* which becomes the *"soul and spirit of the all-pervading, mysterious ether."*

Within *The Secret Doctrine*, it is not only the Sun which has such a concealed nature and laya centre but also other cosmic bodies with *"self-moving"* orbs. Blavatsky explains:

our Esoteric Doctrine ... teaches that it is this original, primordial *prima material,* divine and intelligent, the direct emanation of the Universal Mind—the ... divine light emanating from the *Logos*—which formed the nuclei of all the "self-moving" orbs in Kosmos. It is the informing, ever-present moving-power and life-principle, the vital soul of the suns, moons, planets, and even of our Earth. (p. 602)

Blavatsky describes Suns as differentiating from laya centres or primordial atoms during a *"manvantaric solar period:"*

Centres of Force at first, the invisible sparks of primordial atoms differentiate into molecules, and become Suns—passing gradually into objectivity—gaseous, radiant, cosmic, the one "Whirlwind" (or motion) finally giving the impulse to the form, and the initial motion, regulated and sustained by the never-resting Breaths—the Dhyan-Chohans. (S. D. I, p. 103)

Although there is an organizing and vital LIFE centre within the heart of any Sun, as within all living beings, Suns also accrue matter from their environment and the ethers during their formation:

> Having evolved from Cosmic Space, ... the Sun ... drew into the depths of its mass all the Cosmic vitality he could, ... after which he began feeding on "The Mother's refuse and sweat"; in other words, on those portions of Ether (the "breath of the Universal Soul") of the existence and constitution of which science is as yet absolutely ignorant. (S. D. I, p. 102)

The Sun differentiates from a vital LIFE CENTRE and embodies higher dimensional intelligences, light and breath—yet it draws on matters from its environment and the ethers during its growth and evolution. The Sun "feeds" upon the *"Mother's refuse and sweat,"* which are matters within the nebula as formed from previous worlds. The Sun also draws upon the Ethers from the *"breath of the Universal Soul."*

8b. The Sevenfold Logos, Seven Rays & Seven Rounds

> The first, or the purely *Formless* and *invisible* Fire concealed in the Central Spiritual Sun, is spoken of as "triple" (metaphysically); while the Fire of the manifested Kosmos is Septenary, throughout both the Universe and our Solar System. (p. 87)

> seven distinct rays radiate from the 'Central Spiritual Sun,' *all adepts and Dhyan Chohans are divisible into seven classes,* each of which is guided and controlled, and overshadowed by *one of the seven forms* of manifestations of the divine Wisdom. (p. 574)

The Sun's subtle emanations and radiations permeate the sevenfold solar ether, while originating from the sevenfold supra-solar Aether (or Akasha): Seven inside, seven outside. According to *The Secret Doctrine*, the laws of nature manifest in our world depend upon intelligent forces within unseen space—the solar ether and the higher Aether, the Akasa. There are various levels to the Aether of Cosmic Space:

> The totality of the Seven Rays spread through the Solar system constitute, so to say, the physical *Upadhi* (basis) of the *Ether of Science*; in which Upadhi, light, heat, electricity, etc., etc.,—the forces of orthodox science—correlate to produce their terrestrial effects. As psychic and spiritual effects, they emanate from, and have their origin in, the supra-solar Upadhi, in the ether of the Occultist—or Akasa. (p. 515)

Just as the Logos and the solar Ether are sevenfold, so are the 'globes' and 'rounds' of creation, life and evolution created within the Solar system. Blavatsky explains that a *chain* of existence, both involution and evolution, involves seven globes and seven rounds of life, each with seven races and seven sub-races. Everything in the physical and metaphysical worlds follows the same basic patterns of cosmic creation and design re-iterated through multiple dimensions of existence.

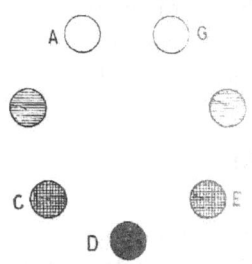

The first rounds of existence are within higher dimensional space and not made manifest within the physical realm as we understand it. Globe D, the fourth in this chain, is said to be our own and is the most physical of the entire chain. This is suggested by Stanza VI of Dzyan: 7. MAKE THY CALCULATIONS, LANOO, IF THOU WOULDEST LEARN THE CORRECT AGE OF THY SMALL WHEEL. ITS FOURTH SPOKE IS OUR MOTHER. There is an *involution* or *devolution* from Globe A to B, C and D and then a subsequent evolution from Globe D, to E, F and G. The processes of involution and evolution occur also within each Globe on multiple levels, cycles within cycles.

Blavatsky explains how between different rounds, the life principle within the living suns or planets or self-moving cosmic bodies, withdraws into its laya centre and can then re-emerge through space-time into a subsequent round to animate a new Sun or planet. This is a form of reincarnation occurring within the lives of *self-moving* bodies, animated and directed by the logos of the concealed Spiritual Sun. The following illustration from *The Secret Doctrine* depicts

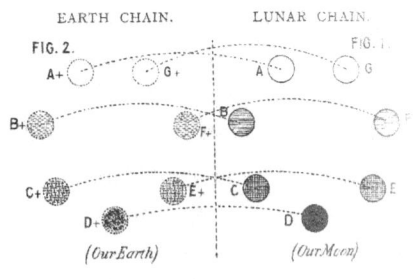

such transitional processes from our predecessor, the Lunar Chain, to the current Earth Chain.

These remarkable concepts are explained by Blavatsky:

> The Seven Beings in the Sun are the Seven Holy Ones, Self-born from the inherent power in the matrix of Mother substance. It is they who send the Seven Principle Forces, called rays, which at the beginning of Pralaya will enter into seven new Suns for the next Manvantara. (p. 290)

When a Sun or planet dies, the animating principle is said to withdraw into its undifferentiated laya condition and subsequently it is 'reborn' after a Night of Brahma. A Sun undergoes a period of Solar Manvantara followed by one of Solar Pralaya or dissolution.

> Heat (the Breath), attraction and repulsion—the three great factors of Motion—are the conditions under which all the members of all this primitive family are born, developed and die, to be reborn after a "Night of Brahma," during which eternal matter relapses periodically into its primary undifferentiated state. ... (S. D. I, p. 103)

These cycles proceed on many different levels within the lives of living beings.

The nature of the Sun has to be understood as having a psychic and spiritual nature in addition to its physical nature. The Lords of Light within the Sun emanate throughout the septenary ethers of Cosmic Space. The Sun is the Light and Life Giver embodying the Logos and its influences pervade the solar system on psychic and spiritual levels as the *"Soul and Spirit of Cosmic Space."* Of course, modern science has yet to conceive of the Sun as having such a zero point LIFE centre, rooted into an invisible Sun beyond. In order to understand the mysteries of the Sun, we must grasp the mysteries of the zero point laya centres and the nature of deep Space (or the ethers) within the cosmic Ocean of Life.

> To make of Science an integral whole necessitates, indeed, the study of spiritual and psychic, as well as physical Nature.... The duty of the Occultist lies with the *Soul and Spirit* of Cosmic Space, not merely with its illusive appearance and behavior. That of official physical science is to analyze and study its *shell* .... (S. D. I, pp. 588-9)

9. Issues of Science

a. Magnetism, Gravity & Solar Origins

> Gravitation is the sole cause, the acting God,
> and matter is its prophet, said the men of science
> only a few years ago. (Blavatsky, S. D. I, p. 492)

Blavatsky did not regard 'gravity' as being due simply to an attractive force between material particles because of their *mass property*, but rather to be one of the sevenfold variations of *Fohat*—the fundamental cosmic electricity. Gravity involves a variant of electromagnetic influences propagated through the soul and spirit of cosmic space:

> attraction or gravitation should be given up in favor of the Sun being a huge magnet... that acts on the planets as attraction is now supposed to do.... That such magnetism exists in nature, is as certain as that gravitation does not; not at any rate, in the way in which it is taught by Science.... It would, very likely, require one more conversant with science than is the writer, to combat with any success some of the now prevailing ideas about gravitation and other similar "solutions" of Cosmic Mysteries. (pp. 497 & 499)

As early as 1877 in *Isis Unveiled,* Blavatsky objected to the scientific view of gravity as the key force underlying the formation of the Solar system:

> there is no *gravitation* in the Newtonian sense, but only magnetic attraction and repulsion; and that it is by their magnetism that the planets of the solar system have their motions regulated in their respective orbits by the still more powerful magnetism of the sun, not by their weight or gravitation. (I, p. 271)

In *The Secret Doctrine,* Blavatsky challenged Laplace's nebular theory of the formation of the Solar System current in her day and which remains the mainstream view in modern times. In the Laplace's model, gravity is regarded as the effective agent of the formation of the sun and planets. A modern science text describes the *"origin of the sun and the earth:"*

> there was a huge cloud of very cold and rarefied gas and dust.... called the *parent nebula,* or the *parent globule.*... that parent nebula began slowly to shrink as a result of its own gravitational force. The grains of dust and molecules of gas were attracted to each other by gravitation.... gravitation took

only around 10 million years to form an adult Sun from the parent cloud ... The remains of the parent nebula formed the planets around their shining Sun. The large shapeless lumps of nebula circling the young Sun were molded by their self-gravitation into spherical shapes—planets. (Kleczek, Jakes, 1985, pp. 152-3)

This formulation, a hundred years after *The Secret Doctrine*, is based upon the Laplace theory discussed by Blavatsky:

Laplace thought that, consequent on the condensation of the atoms of the primeval nebula, according to the "Law" of gravity, the now gaseous, or perhaps, partially liquid mass, acquired a rotary motion. As the velocity of this rotation increased, it assumed the form of a thin disc; (S. D. I, p. 592)

Blavatsky discussed the different rotations of the planets, retrograde motion and other factors, not explicable in terms of the Laplace model—which issues remain unresolved in modern science. Blavatsky ascribes the rotation of the planets not as due to gravitation and random events, but to the fact that such cosmic bodies are ruled through laya centre dynamics and embody the Fiery Whirlwind. Thus, they are "self-moving" and there is a solar logo which binds together the solar system as the intelligence underlying the involution and evolution of substances and beings within that solar system.

Blavatsky explains that Stanza IV, verse 5 of the book of Dzyan refers to our Sun: *"THEN COME THE "SONS," THE SEVEN FIGHTERS, THE ONE, THE EIGHTH LEFT OUT, AND "HIS BREATH WHICH IS THE LIGHT-MAKER."* The seven fighters are the seven planets, while the eight is "the sun, the light-maker." The Sun, *Surya* in the Vedas, is described:

"Himself only a reflection of the Central Spiritual Sun ... as "the Eye of the World" (our planetary world). ... he is depicted as drawn by seven horses, and by one horse with seven heads former referring to his seven planets, the latter to their one common origin from the One Cosmic Element. This "One Element" is called figuratively "FIRE." (pp. 100-1)

Blavatsky contrasts this teaching with the theory of Laplace:

The Occult Doctrine rejects the hypothesis born of the Nebular Theory, that the (seven) great planets have evolved from the Sun's central mass.... The first condensation of Cosmic matter of course took place around a central nucleus, its parent Sun; but our sun, it is taught, merely detached itself earlier than all the others, as the rotating mass contracted, and is their elder, bigger brother therefore, not their father. (p. 101)

Blavatsky expresses the same teaching elsewhere, noting that *"the Sun and planets are only co-uterine brothers, having the same nebular origin, only in a different mode from that postulated by modern astronomy."* (p. 589)

In *The Secret Doctrine*, the Sun and other self-moving or rotating cosmic bodies have dynamic laya centres, and their formation is not due to gravity and the presence of mass, but rather due to the Dhyan Chohans operative within that sphere, as embodying Mind and Intelligence, and the magnetic attraction that these centres exert through the ethers of Space. Blavatsky writes:

> Whence the substance that clothes them—the apparent organism they evolve around their centres? The Formless ("Arupa") Radiations, existing in the harmony of the Universal Will... unite together an infinitude of monads—each a mirror of its own Universe—and thus individualize for the time being an independent mind, omniscient and universal; and by the same process of magnetic aggregation they create for themselves objective, visible bodies, out of the interstellar atoms. (p. 632-633)

The Sun embodies Seven Luminous Lords, as the Earth does its seven Pritis or Intelligences, as do other cosmic bodies—each has its own Logos or Intelligence in harmony with the Universal Will and these Intelligences, through Fohat, create bodies for themselves through magnetic influences propagated through the ethers of Space. Such emerging centres of force also feed off the refuse and sweat (or matters) created through earlier rounds of "the Mother's labors."

The nature of 'gravity' is the most important moot point here, as Blavatsky denies the usual concept of 'gravity' and instead views it as a variation of dynamics within the electromagnetic Ocean of Life. Gravity involves the sevenfold modification of Fohat, the Cosmic electricity, which vivifies and brings life into the body of the universe. Blavatsky states: *"Occultists... see in gravity only sympathy and antipathy, or attraction and repulsion, caused by physical polarity on our terrestrial plane, and by spiritual causes outside of its influence..."* (p. 513)

In modern science, 'gravity' is the predominant force used to explain not only the formation of the solar system but also larger scale structures within the Universe—such as galaxies and super-galactic clusters. Nevertheless, scientists are dumbfounded when it comes to finding the dark matter missing according to their models of gravity. Blavatsky's perspective suggests that solar formation and planetary rotation are related to the existence of dynamic centres within these cosmic bodies, which emerge from within without and which impart rotation to the masses as modifications of the Whirlwind and the Central Spiritual Sun.[7] In

---

7   Blavatsky's views of gravity are more similar to newer scientific views that both gravity and inertia involve the interaction of material particles with the surrounding fields of virtual particles within the zero point electromagnetic ocean of the quantum vacuum. In fact, new concepts within science are making her archaic teaching more conceivable

The Secret Doctrine, it is the divine light emanating from the Logos which forms the nuclei of all the self-moving orbs in the Kosmos. This is the informing moving power and life principle, the vital soul life of the Sun and planets.

Blavatsky condemns the small mindedness and bigotry of scientists who so readily dismiss such ancient mystical teachings. Blavatsky notes: *"... modern Cosmology and Astronomy now repudiate anything like research into the mysteries of being. The result is what might be expected; complete failure and inextricable contradictions in the thousand and one varieties of so-called scientific theories...."* (S. D. I, p. 589)

9b. The Non-Existence of Gravity

The Secret Doctrine postulates the dissolution of the universe into a Laya Centre or neutral zero point centre at the end of time. However, in Blavatsky's view, such a cosmic collapse or withdrawal would not be due to the effects of gravity on material nature.

> There will be, as there ever were in time and eternity, periodical dissolutions of the manifested Universe, but (a) a partial *pralaya* after every "Day of Brahma"; and (b) an Universal pralaya—the MAHA-PRALAYA—only after the lapse of every Brahma age. But the scientific causes for such dissolution, as brought forward by exact Science, have nothing to do with the true causes. (S. D. I, p. 552)

According to modern scientific theories, it would be the effects of 'gravity' which could bring about such a phase of contraction and ultimately *close* the universe, if there is enough mass in the universe for gravity to act upon. Scientists thus search for varied forms of 'dark matter' to close the universe through the effects of gravity. Scientists also search for dark matter to hold together the galaxies, for according to the law of gravity, there has to be much more mass present in the galaxy for it to maintain its form.

Scientists conceive of the possibility of the universe collapsing back into black holes and ultimately disappearing into a dreaded singularity. This 'big crunch' scenario contrasts with the 'big bang' scenario at the beginning of time. Blavatsky actually predicted such a scenario of Cosmoses and atoms emerging from and dissolving into such zero point Laya centres—white holes and black holes at the beginning and end of time. This was a century before modern science had any such a bizarre concept of our cosmic origins and ends.

Physicists are currently searching for the 'dark matter' which might close the universe through the effects of gravity. Thus far, there is not nearly enough visible physical matter to set in motion such a phase of universal contraction.

---

rather than less. However, science is still far from exploring her concepts of zero point or primordial elements within living beings, particularly the Sun.

Scientists now also postulate 'dark energy' to supplement 'dark matter' in order to explain the fact that the rate of expansion of the universe appears to be increasing. This dark energy remains as elusive as the dark matter.

However, Blavatsky denies the existence of gravity as it is commonly understood (or misunderstood) even in modern times. Instead, gravity is a variant of the electromagnetic force with its seven variants conveyed by Fohat and due to the electromagnetic influences of the sun, earth, moon and planets as propagated through the Aether of Space:

> Thus the Occultists are not alone in their beliefs. Nor are they so foolish, after all, in rejecting even the "gravity" of modern Science along with other *physical* laws, and in accepting instead *attraction* and *repulsion*. They see, moreover, in these two opposite Forces only the two *aspects* of the universal unit, called "MANIFESTING MIND"; in which aspects, Occultism, through its great Seers, perceives an innumerable Host of operative Beings; Cosmic Dhyan-Chohans, Entities, whose essence, in its dual nature, is the Cause of all terrestrial phenomena. For that essence is co-substantial with the universal Electric Ocean, which is LIFE.... (S. D. I, p. 604)

These explanations suggest that it is the presence of the "Manifesting Mind" conveyed through Fohat and operative at zero point levels within a universal Electric Ocean, which accounts for the phenomena attributed to the mysterious force of gravity.

In *Isis Unveiled*, Blavatsky wrote:

> By the radiant light of the universal magnetic ocean, whose electric waves bind the cosmos together, and in their ceaseless motion penetrate every atom and molecule of the boundless creation, the disciples... intuitively perceive the alpha and omega of the great mystery. Alone, the study of this agent, which is the divine breath, can unlock the secrets of psychology and physiology, of cosmical and spiritual phenomena. (*I*, p. 282)

Blavatsky explains that the true causes of gravity arise from *"the divine breath"*—and its modifications. These metaphysical processes involve the underlying *"universal magnetic ocean,"* whose *"electric waves bind the cosmos together."* The manifest phenomena of universal expansion or contraction are the outward and impermanent effects of the "Manifesting Mind" operative from zero point levels.

In relation to the fate of the Universe, it is clear that *The Secret Doctrine* suggests that the withdrawal or dissolution of the Universe is due not simply to the presence of 'matter' but involves causes produced within hyperspace by *the modification of the divine breath*. Recall the Stanza of Dzyan: "IT EXPANDS WHEN

THE BREATH OF FIRE IS UPON IT; IT CONTRACTS WHEN THE BREATH OF THE MOTHER TOUCHES IT." (III, 11) Blavatsky explains:

> It is attraction and repulsion, but not as understood by modern physics and according to the law of gravity; but in harmony with *the laws of Manvantaric motion*.... These laws are immutable; but the motion of all the bodies, which motion is diverse and alters with every minor *Kalpa*—is regulated by the *Movers*, the Intelligences within the Cosmic Soul. Are we so very wrong in believing all this? (pp. 529-530)

Blavatsky's views on the nature and non-existence of gravity are similar to new ideas emerging in physics concerning how gravitational effects could be based on electromagnetic zero point fields latent within the quantum vacuum—that is, within the ether of space itself. In this view, mass and inertia could be the result of electrodynamics within the quantum ether of the zero point fields which surround material particles. Inertia, or the resistance to movement, is due to the electromagnetic interaction of material particles with their own fields of virtual particles and the zero point flux fields in which they are embedded. Blavatsky's depiction of the "universal Electric Ocean" is quite compatible with such recent views of the zero point fields within the quantum physics as the possible source of gravity and inertia. Scientific views of the quantum vacuum as a form of quantum ether and hyperspace filled with 'zero point fields' and holographic information fields, is most similar to what Blavatsky described as the *"universal Electric Ocean."*[8]

9c. The Permanency and Impermanency of Matter and Atoms

> "MATTER IS ETERNAL, becoming atomic (its aspect) only periodically." (S. D. I, p. 552)

> "Matter is eternal," says the Esoteric Doctrine. But the matter the Occultists conceive of in its *laya*, or *zero state*, is not the matter of modern science; ... when the adept or alchemist adds that, though matter is eternal, for it is PRADHANA ('original base'), yet atoms *are born at every new manvantara*, or reconstruction of the universe, it is no such contradiction as a materialist, who believes in nothing beyond the atom, might think. There is a difference between *manifested* and *unmanifested* matter.... (S. D. I, p. 545)

---

8   The whole trend in modern physics is to regard all the physical laws as variations of one underlying "God like Superforce," in the terms of physicist Paul Davies. The Holy Grail of science involves this effort to unify gravity with the other three primordial principles in physics. Blavatsky similarly regarded all the laws of physics as variations of one underlying force—the Eternal Ceaseless Breath with its sevenfold modifications.

Blavatsky presented a remarkable viewpoint in 1888. The real Atoms, she maintained, are elements beyond the zero point level—existing prior to physical differentiation. These Laya Centres are the neutral or zero point centres, as perceived from a materialist perpective. The elements in the undifferentiated laya (sleeping) state are Eternal, while the material atoms or quanta are impermanent external manifestations of the underlying zero point centres and dynamics.

The true Atoms differentiate from the Laya condition at the beginning of each new Manvantara, or age, to manifest as a Kosmos or a quanta. At the end of time, the life principle within a living Kosmos or Son resolves back into the laya state with the dissolution or ingathering of the cosmos. Atoms are eternal in the laya or zero point condition, prior to differentiation, but all material matter is impermanent and will ultimately return to such a laya centre. This is a remarkable alternative concept of the nature of cosmoses, quanta and atoms.

Blavatsky describes the dissolution of the Cosmos *"at the hour of the Pralaya"* as the informing principles withdraw into the neutral laya centre. She refers to a "path onward" from matter into Spirit and further:

> "... the necessary gradual and final reabsorption into the *laya* state, that which Science calls in her own way "the point neutral as to electricity" etc., or the *zero* point. Such are the Occult facts and statement." (S. D. I, p. 551)

Blavatsky gives another similar overview of the evolution of the Cosmos and its eventual dissolution:

> evolution ... may be thus formulated as an invariable law; a descent of Spirit into Matter, equivalent to an ascent in physical evolution; a re-ascent from the depths of materiality towards its *status quo ante*, with a corresponding dissipation of concrete form and substance up to the LAYA state, or what Science calls "the zero point," and beyond. (S. D. I, p. 620)

Matter is thus Eternal, but real matter—in its laya state. Blavatsky provides quite an alternative perspective on this issue of science, as she does of many others.

9d. The *Akasa* and Ethers

The subject of the Aether is extremely subtle and complex and Blavatsky approaches it from varied angles using different terms and explanations. The term ether is most commonly used to refer to a fifth element, the original out of which emerge fire, water, air and earth. The ultimate Aether is the Eternal Parent Space referred to in allegory as the *Great Sea* or the *Chaos*.

The Cosmogenesis & Metaphysics of The Secret Doctrine

"Chaos"... contained in itself all the Elements in their rudimentary, undifferentiated State. They made of Ether, the fifth element, the synthesis of the other four; for the Aether of the Greek philosophers is not its dregs—of which indeed they knew more than science does now—which are rightly enough supposed to act as an agent for many forces that manifest on Earth. Their Aether was the *Akasa* of the Hindus; the Ether accepted in physics is but one of its subdivisions, on our plane,—the *Astral Light* of the Kabalists with all its *evil* as well as good effects.

Blavatsky distinguishes between the ultimate Aether or *Akasa* and the lower levels of such ethers, such as the sevenfold solar ether, which includes the *astral light* of the Kabbalist. However, Blavatsky's critical comments on science's limited conception of the ethers are not as applicable in the twenty first century as they were in her day; as physicists now regard the quantum vacuum itself with its zero point fields and information fields to be a *quantum ether* and to be based upon activities within higher dimensional space.

At the same time, Blavatsky's mystical conception of the upper Aether is still beyond those offered within materialist philosophies of science:

"What is the primordial Chaos but Aether?" it is asked in "ISIS UNVEILED." Not the *modern* Ether; not such as is recognized now, but such as *was* known to the ancient philosophers long before the time of Moses; but Aether, with all its mysterious and occult properties, containing in itself the germs of universal creation. *Upper* Aether or Akasa, is the celestial virgin and mother of every existing form and being, from whose bosom, as soon as "incubated" by the Divine Spirit, are called into existence Matter and Life, Force and Action. Aether is the Aditi of the Hindus, and it is Akasa. Electricity, magnetism, heat, light, and chemical action are so little understood even now that fresh facts are constantly widening the range of our knowledge. Who knows where ends the power of this protean giant—Aether; or whence it's mysterious origin? Who, we mean, that denies the spirit that works in it, and evolves out of it all visible forms? (p. 332)

Blavatsky describes the upper Aether or Akasa as *"containing in itself the germs of universal creation"*—the mother of all form and beings. This Upper Aether or *Akasa* is the *"celestial virgin"* and is *"incubated"* by Divine Spirit, or the Ray of life which penetrates into the heart of the Divine Mother. Spirit then manifests through the Akasa or Aether. Thus if we consider Space, it is not simply the ether or substratum of seven material skins, but Space is pervaded by the Spiritual Intelligences of the Dhyan Chohans and all the sentient beings which produce the laws of nature, energizing and materializing forms and living beings.

Blavatsky uses the term *Akasa* to refer to the ultimate Aether. This term is from the Vedas and refers to the 'emanations of Mulaprakriti,' or of root nature. The Vedas distinguish Purusha and Prakriti, Spirit and Matter, and regard Prakriti having one undifferentiated state 'Mulaprakriti' and seven differentiated forms (consistent with *The Secret Doctrine* and Kabbalah). Blavatsky notes: *"Prakriti in its primary state is Akasa,"* says a Vedantin scholar.... *It is, as said, the noumenon of the seven-fold differentiated Prakriti."* (p. 256)

Blavatsky was most critical of the science of her day for their view of Space as empty and void and as a passive background for the motions of atoms. Instead, Space is a living entity and its inherent properties allow for the unity and correlation of all manifest phenomena. The Akasa provides the medium ultimately for that Omniscience which thrills throughout every finite point of the universe, as H.P.B. describes.

> Official Science *knows nothing to this day of the constitution of ether*.... neither as akasa nor as the one sacred Aether of the Greeks, is it to be found in any of the states of matter known to modern physics. It is MATTER on quite another plane of perception and being .... the majority of the eminent and learned materialists very often utter the greatest fallacies. Let us take the following case. Most of them reject *actio in distans* (one of the fundamental principles in the question of Aether or Akasa in Occultism), while ... there is no physical action, "which, on close examination, does not resolve itself into *actio in distans*...." (S. D., pp. 487-8)

It is the presence of the Aether or Akasa which enables all *"actio in distans,"* or *non-local effects* and *quantum entanglement*. Ultimately, everything is entangled within the lower ethers and within the ultimate Akasa of Space. Whereas modern physicists have argued over the existence of 'action at a distance' and its role in everyday life, Blavatsky states that ultimately, all actions involve non-local influences and everything is correlated and unified within deep space.

> "Space is a substantial though (apparently) an absolutely unknowable living Entity." ... Space is the real world, while our world is an artificial one. It is the One Unity throughout its infinitude; in its bottomless depths as on it illusory surface; a surface studded with countless phenomenal Universes, systems and mirage-like worlds.... in the real world, which is a Unity of Forces, there is "a connection of all matter in the *plenum*".... (p. 615)

According to *The Secret Doctrine*, the whole range of physical phenomena and the laws of nature proceeds from the *Primary* of the Ether—Akasa. Furthermore, all things are interconnected and effects correlated through the Akasa:

A'kasa, the radiation of Mulaprakriti connected as the World-Soul is with all natural phenomena, known or unknown to science. ... Whatever the views of physical Science upon the subject, Occult Science has been teaching for ages that A'kasa—of which Ether is the grossest form ... is cosmically, a radiant, cool, diathermanous plastic matter, creative in its physical nature, correlative in its grossest aspects and portions, immutable in its higher principles. ... called the Sub-Root; and in conjunction with radiant heat, it recalls "dead worlds to life." In its higher aspect it is the Soul of the World; in its lower—the DESTROYER. (Blavatsky, 1888, pp. 10 & 13)

All things are ensouled through the Akasa and when the life forces withdraw from a material form or volume of space, it serves as the destroyer. As Newton described, *Space is God's sensorium* and Space enables the correlation of all forces and the workings of the laws of nature. In Blavatsky's view, understanding the nature of the Aether of Space is one of the keys to the ancient wisdom teachings and to understanding ancient metaphysics and modern physics.

10. Blavatsky's Holographic Space

> There is but one indivisible and absolute Omniscience and Intelligence in the Universe, and this thrills throughout every atom and infinitesimal point of the whole finite Kosmos which hath no bounds, and which people call SPACE, considered independently of anything in it. (S.D I, p. 277)

Blavatsky offers a profound alternative viewpoint relative to that of materialist science and common thought regarding the nature and mysteries of Space. If there is one Omniscience thrilling throughout every infinitesimal point of the whole finite Kosmos, then there are interior dimensions of existence wherein all manifest forces and phenomena are correlated and interrelated—within vast underlying information fields.[9] However, these information fields are invisible to us as human beings who imagine that we move about within an empty external four-dimensional spacetime complex composed only of matter and energy. For Blavatsky, the seemingly solid material world is illusory, an outgrowth of the causes at zero point levels while the forces of nature emerge within without from higher dimensional realms. In her radical view, the external spacetime complex is quite illusory and there are many worlds interpenetrating and sustaining our own space!

Blavatsky provides this remarkable passage discussing the presence of other worlds within the same Space as ourselves:

> The Secret Doctrine—postulating that conditioned or limited space (location) has no real being except in this world of illusion, or, in other words, in our perceptive faculties—teaches that every one of the higher, as of the lower worlds, is interblended with our own objective world; that millions of things and beings are, in point of localization, around and *in* us, as we are around, with, and in them; it is not metaphysical figure of speech, but a sober fact in Nature, however incomprehensible to our senses.
>
> But one has to understand the phraseology of Occultism before criticizing what it asserts. For example, the Doctrine refuses (as Science does, in one sense) to use the words "above" and "below,"

---

9   In fact, quantum theory itself suggests such a vast web of interrelationship within higher dimensional phase space. Quanta, which have emerged from a singularity condition, maintain a wave entanglement and the whole universe may be traced back to just such a singularity emerging out of the perfect symmetry of the void/plenum of pre-existence. Thus, quantum theory offers one way of understanding how there is an underlying unified information field which grows with the evolution of the universe.

"higher" and "lower," in reference to *invisible* spheres, as being without meaning.... Hence, when "*other* worlds" are mentioned—whether better or worse, more spiritual or still more material, though both invisible—the Occultist does not locate *these spheres* either *outside* or *inside* our Earth, as the theologians and the poets do; for their location is nowhere in the space *known* to, and conceived by, the profane. They are, as it were, blended with our world—interpenetrating it and interpenetrated by it. .... Although as invisible as if they were millions of miles beyond our solar system, they are yet with us, near us, *within* our own world, as objective and material to their respective inhabitants as ours is to us.... The inhabitants of these (worlds)... may be, for all we know, or feel, passing *through* and *around* us as if through empty space, their very habitations and countries being interblended with ours, though not disturbing our vision, because we have not yet the faculties necessary for discerning them.

... the men of science ... labor under the absurd impression that in the whole Kosmos, or at any rate in our own atmosphere, there are no other conscious, intelligent beings, save ourselves.... while Science sternly rejects even the possibility of there being such (to us, generally) invisible creatures, Society, while believing in it all *secretly*, is made to deride the idea openly....

Nevertheless, such invisible worlds do exist. Inhabited as thickly as our own is, they are scattered throughout apparent Space in immense number; some far more material than our own world, others gradually etherealizing until they become formless and are as "Breaths." That our physical eye does not see them, is no reason to disbelieve in them; physicists can see neither their ether, atoms, nor "modes of motion," or Forces. Yet they accept and teach them. (S. D. I, pp. 604-6)

This is a remarkable conception of the nature of Space—compatible with holographic and quantum information theory in modern physics. Space is not empty. Ordinary four-dimensional spacetime is an outward projection from within higher dimensions of real Space and emerges from zero point levels. Living beings have such deep roots in higher and real Space. Further, there are all kinds of other intelligences, worlds, dimensions and beings within the same space as ourselves although invisible to our perceptive faculties. This is analogous to how a scientist can produce multiple holographic images on a holographic plate by shifting the angle of the projecting light sources.

Blavatsky explains that there is a correlation of all forces within the plenum or through the *Akasa* and that everything is ultimately a part of the whole. The Omniscience is an information field about the whole present throughout every finite point of the universe! Blavatsky has provided a remarkable description of the possibilities of life in the holographic plenum of Deep Space. It is immensely difficult to fathom the depths of these occult views. How could millions of things, beings and worlds, be around us, and in us, sustaining and interpenetrating our worlds? To understand these possibilities and mystical doctrines requires a radical transformation in our consciousness and in our understanding of all the basic concepts of science: time, space, matter, energy, fullness and emptiness, myself and "I."

Blavatsky certainly provides a wild view of the holographic universe wherein a whole hierarchy of intelligences is implicated within any element—any living Kosmos. Further, she describes how such a higher dimensional metaphysics produces a lower four dimensional physics as well as a law conformable cosmic order. She notes in regards to the abstruse and abstract teachings of *The Secret Doctrine*:

> These abstractions become more and more concrete as they approach our plane of existence, until they phenomenalise in the form of the material Universe, by process of conversion of metaphysics into physics, analogous to that by which steam can be condensed into water, and the water frozen into ice. (p. 45)

Apparent material realities are projected out of the holographic dynamics of higher dimensional Space, illusory manifestations of nominal realms which underlie and sustain them—realities which Veil the true nature of Deity.

11. *The Secret Doctrine* & Modern Science

H.P. Blavatsky's remarkable teachings provide a revealing and unique perspective on theories and enigmas in modern physics, astronomy and cosmology.

In reference to cosmology, Blavatsky's *Secret Doctrine* has anticipated modern views of *vacuum genesis*, wherein the quantum vacuum is characterized as a seeming void and plenum; and the emergence of the Universe from a point source singularity. Further, *The Secret Doctrine* proposes that the Universe will eventually contract and return again to a zero point laya centre. This hypothesis is consistent with modern science, although scientists are still searching for the 'dark matter' which could so close the universe due to the god of material science—gravity, leading to such a universal contraction. Further, just as Blavatsky describes the innumerable universes emerging out of the root principles of creation, so also modern cosmologists now conceive that the 'big foam' of the quantum vacuum likely gives rise to an infinite number of Universes over time and that our universe is just one of these.

In reference to the issues of modern physics, Blavatsky's archaic doctrines could have led one to anticipate the paradoxes of the uncertainty principle which is the foundation for quantum theory. If we trace any atom or quantum back to its inner most nature, it must pass from the finite realm into an infinite realm from which it emerged. Thus, as we seek the origins and nature of matter or forces, we arrive at certain limits or the *Rings-pass-not*, at which the processes of physical differentiation begin and we can penetrate no further. A material element, or quantum, will disappear from view from the perspective of the lower plane.

Blavatsky's unusual teachings would certainly have led us to expect the "baffling holism" of quantum theory, its prediction of non-local effects, and all kinds of problems with infinities in the equations of quantum field theory. As we carry our investigations into nature back far enough into primal causes and origins, then the finite does pass over into the infinite—as all of life is ultimately of one undivided infinite whole. Further, somehow, between the finite and infinite are the zero point conditions or laya centers.

However, in comparing Blavatsky's views with modern science, I would argue that the most significant idea which she advances, which is still foreign to modern science, is the idea that *living beings* actually have such zero point centres by which these Gods and other invisible powers in higher dimensional Space and through the ethers, cloth themselves through zero point centres and dynamics. As noted by Jack Dea of the Department of Chemistry at Arizona State University, this implies a radically alternative model of the nature of Space and the construction of reality. It is easy to mistake the concept of zero point centres as these points are likely to be viewed as existing within the four dimensional space-time continuum. In fact, the external space-time complex or matrix is really founded upon or surrounding the zero point laya centre. J. Dea explains Blavatsky's unusual views:

> a space-time can be seen as a devise the point uses to distinguish between states. Space-time is infinite because the original point has infinite degrees of freedom. One way of looking at this process is that space-time came into existence by being squeezed out of a point. However in this of being squeezed out, space-time acquires characteristics different from its original pure energy states. Thus, from very simple properties, we have created a space-time structure out of a single point! With this interpretation of space-time certain paradoxes of nonlocality which require super-luminal speeds are no longer paradoxes. The reason is that everything is always connected because everything is really part of the same point. (1984, p. 91)

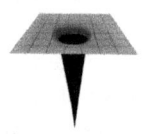

It is very difficult to truly grasp the ideas presented here, because our ordinary understanding of everything is so upside down, mistaken and deluded. The zero point centre does not exist within four-dimensional spacetime, but rather everything manifest exists within or surrounding, or based upon such zero point laya centres. These dynamics are propagated within-without through higher dimensional spaces through hierarchies of living beings. The Zero Point centres are not to be located in external space, which is an illusory projection of dynamics manifesting within without from zero point levels out of higher dimensional Real Space.

The zero point dynamics of living being is so significant, as they occur within real Space, in which there is a correlation of all forces through the Aether and further there is an Omniscience which 'thrills' throughout every such point. Jack Dea, as a scientists, had these profound reflections on the significance of *The Secret Doctrine* teachings:

> A scientist of the 1980's can adopt one of two basic attitudes towards the contents given out by H.P. Blavatsky's *The Secret Doctrine* (SD). The first attitude consists of disbelief. It assumes that the SD is the product of an overactive imagination and that no more time should be wasted in checking its claims. The second attitude consists of openness and a willingness to examine the claims of the SD in light of the best available knowledge. ... I studied the Secret Doctrine with both an open and yet critical mind. ... The writer must admit surprise at the similarity of description given by modern science and by the SD ... of space, time, matter, forces, and fields. ... In fact, before the

advent of quantum mechanics and field theory, the ideas of space as presented in the SD would have been considered nonsense. ... the SD claims that space has extensions beside the three dimensions. Such is also the approach taken by modern theoreticians working on unified field theory. ... The ultimate aim of physics, it has been said, is to unify. To unify all the forces in nature into one grand equation is the dream of the physicists. The aim of *The Secret Doctrine* is also to unify: to show that legends and traditions around the globe have common origins; and to show that all existence on this objective plane are derivative of a metaphysical plane. In this search for unification both modern science and the Secret Doctrine meet at a common point: the vacuum state of physics and the Laya point of the Secret Doctrine. (1984, pp. 86-94)

It is impossible within this work to address all of the profound relationships existing between Blavatsky's teachings and modern physical theories. Dea discusses supergravity theory, modern concepts of superspace, ideas concerning symmetry breaking, the derivation of forces from the vacuum state and much more. In fact, Blavatsky's ideas constitute an intriguing alternative perspective on many of the theories and paradoxes of modern science, and further *The Secret Doctrine* provides alternate scientific interpretations and hypotheses, especially that living beings have such zero point layer centres and such higher dimensional origins.

Blavatsky's archaic doctrines are beautifully illustrated by modern physical and cosmological theories, as we will see throughout the upcoming review of science. Scientists have penetrated into the void/plenum and hyperspace in their attempts to unify the physical laws and to understand the creation of the Universe. They have arrived at singularities, the quantum vacuum, a seven dimensional hyperspace, and a hierarchy of broken symmetries which generate form from formlessness, matter from nothingness—the forces that sculpt the void. Blavatsky explained such concepts over a century ago. Of course, Blavatsky expected the rejection of such concepts in her time, but predicted that *"in the twentieth century of our era scholars will begin to realize that The Secret Doctrine has neither been invented or exaggerated, but, on the contrary, simply outlined."*

Although in areas, *The Secret Doctrine* has anticipated modern physical and cosmological theories, there are other areas in which *The Secret Doctrine* challenges the formulations of modern science—in fact in every area. Blavatsky listed some of the issues in her day, which continue to plague modern theories:

> The so-called Forces, with Light and Electricity heading them, and the constitution of the Solar orb must be carefully examined; as also Gravitation and the Nebular Theories. The Nature of Ether and of other Elements must be discussed; thus contrasting scientific with

other Occult teachings, while revealing some of the hitherto secret tenets of the latter. (Blavatsky, 1888, p. 299)

Blavatsky offers a unique view of each of these issues. With regards to understanding Forces, Light and Electricity, she maintains that the causes of manifest phenomena lie within the super-sensuous or nominal realms which underlie and sustain these. Further, she maintained that these laws involve the sevenfold modification of a fundamental spiritual principle which occurs within a seven-dimensional Ether; and that there are actually existent beings and intelligences manifest in the phenomena of nature, particularly in the life of the Sun but also within the life of other self-moving bodies.

The *Dhyan-Chohans* or Lords of Light are embodied within the Sun, as a manifestation from the Sun's nucleus of primal matter or laya centre, rooted into the Invisible Sun behind. These forces emerge through the broken symmetries of a higher dimension hexagonal form embodying the Star of David with a central point. The errands of these Spiritual Intelligences or Beings are carried out through Fohat and his seven Sons, as variations on the fundamental Cosmic Electricity. These influences are propagated through the seven fold solar ethers and serve to enliven or ensoul living beings, and to produce the phenomena and laws of nature.

Of course, modern scientists would disdain such a mystical perspective on their own favorite Cosmos, where they are the demigods discovering the God particle of the Higg's boson, or eliminating God through smearing out the big bang singularity, and other such nonsense. The so-called real scientists, deny soul and spirit within the Cosmos, and instead prefer their God of Gravity, and their holy Trinity, as characterized by Blavatsky, *"That we owe the universe to the holy creative Trinity, called Inert Matter, Senseless Form and Blind Chance."* (p. 505)

Blavatsky is arguing that there is a whole higher dimensional physics underling and sustaining our laws of nature:

> Men of science may term them Force or Forces generated by matter, or "modes of its motion," if they will; Occultism sees in the effects "Elemental" (forces), and, in the direct causes producing them, intelligent DIVINE Workmen. ... Electricity, light, heat, etc., have been aptly termed the "Ghost or Shadow of Matter in Motion," i.e., supersensuous states of matter whose effects only we are able to cognize. (S. D. I, pp. 145-146)

> Science only errs in believing that, because it has detected in vibratory waves the *proximate* cause of these phenomena, it has, therefore, revealed ALL that lies beyond the threshold of Sense. It merely traces the sequence of phenomena on a plane of effects, illusory projections from the region that Occultism has long since penetrated. ... we must seek for the ultimate causes of light, heat, etc., etc., in MATTER

existing in *super-sensuous* states—states, however, as fully objective to the spiritual eye of man, as a horse or a tree is to the ordinary mortal. Such states can be perceived by the SEER or the Adept during the hours of trance, under the *Sushumna rav*—the first of the Seven Mystic rays of the Sun. (p. 515)

The Secret Doctrine does indeed offer a mystical view of the Kosmos with Intelligences and Beings, in hierarchies, carrying out the larger divine plan of manifesting Mind, throughout the diverse realms of nature. In this view, the laws of nature do not 'just happen' to be the way they are, but rather are the manifestations of divine principles of creation—particularly the laws of three and seven propagated within/without through different interior dimensions of existence in a law conformable way, with a hierarchy of masons, builders and such. Further, Blavatsky denies gravitation as due simply to blind material mass to be the causative agent within the formation of the solar system, as within larger universal dynamics. Instead, the Sun and planets embody zero point dynamics while their emanations and radiations permeate the ethers of the solar system, or of their respective realms:

> the planets are not merely spheres, twinkling in Space, and made to shine for no purpose, but the domains of various beings with whom the profane are so far unacquainted; nevertheless, having a mysterious, unbroken, and powerful connection with men and globes. Every heavenly body is the temple of a god, and these gods themselves are the temples of God, the Unknown "*Not* Spirit." There is nothing profane in the Universe.... (p. 578)

> the spiritual, central sun (is)...the *Point*; the centre (which is everywhere) of the circle (which is nowhere), the ethereal, spiritual fire, the soul and spirit of the all-pervading, mysterious ether; the despair and puzzle of the materialist, who will someday find that that which causes the numberless cosmic forces to manifest themselves in eternal correlation is but a divine electricity, or rather *galvanism*, and that the sun is but one of the myriad magnets disseminated through space—a reflection.... (p. 270)

Certainly, Blavatsky offers a profound view of the nature of reality and the patterns of intelligent design claimed to underlie the phenomena of life—the Builders or living Intelligences who fashion it all through the Akasa and zero point dynamics.

Blavatsky regarded the Sun and other self-moving bodies to indeed to be guided by such sevenfold intelligences, to have laya centres and to emanate and radiate through the Solar ethers to ensoul and enliven life within the solar system, and to assume different roles in different rounds of life and creation. The effects of the Sun and the Solar Logos occur not simply on the material plane but also on the psychical and spiritual. Without such causative elements, Blavatsky claimed that science would face endless enigmas in understanding our solar origins. Blavatsky predicted:

> astronomers...despair of the possibility of ever accounting for rotation, gravitation, and the origin of any mechanical physical laws—unless these *Intelligences* be admitted by Science. (p. 601)

Over a century after Blavatsky, the number of physicists and cosmologists who conceive of immaterial *Intelligences* or Builders within the Solar system could likely be counted on one hand. Further, such possibilities are never considered even in arguments for intelligent design—to propose that such actual living beings exist within the hierarchies of existence. Of course, there are still all kinds of enigmas in science about the Solar origins, issues of the planets, their rotation and composition, the nature of gravity and the unifications of the laws of physics in higher dimensions, the naughty singularities, the origins of life, the mysteries of evolution, the peculiarities of the mysterious ether, and the origins of consciousness, BUT, and of course this is a big but, no scientist is about to postulate invisible entities and intelligences to fill in the gaps in contemporary scientific theorizing. Now the modern world has so-called *real scientists*, who spend long hours at their desks, who look through telescopes and particle accelerators, and who understand mathematics and equations. The high priests of neo-materialism and soul less psychology and science, assume that we no longer need God now that we have promissory science riddled with enigmas.

Although physical theories are highly advanced and converging on the truths of *The Secret Doctrine*, modern scientists persist in attributing the circumstances of life to random and accidental processes and 'blind matter.' Scientists still *"wrench the formation of Kosmos and its living Forces from Spirit"* and do not conceive how Gods or other invisible powers might *"micro-intervene"* in the laws of nature or in the emergence of Life or human consciousness.

Unlike modern so-called creationists or Intelligent Design advocates, Blavatsky not only suggests that some Unfathomable Life source or God, manifesting through the Dhyan Chohans, the builders or masons, gives rise to life, but further, she articulates a scientific model of the physics and metaphysics necessary to explain mechanisms of this process! As she states, *"material points without extension,"* or zero points, are the material out of which the Gods and other invisible powers clothe themselves in bodies. This teaching offers a profound model of higher dimensional existence and the principles of mystical creation. It was unfortunate that in Blavatsky's day, the sciences of chemistry and cosmology provided no possible basis upon which to comprehend or evaluate her bizarre teachings. Fortunately, this is no longer true.

The Cosmogenesis & Metaphysics of The Secret Doctrine

Scientists should take up Blavatsky's challenges to modern science and explore the depths of occult wisdom. The materialistic conception of blind matter moving about in empty four-dimensional space is no longer valid even within the domain of established science. The concepts of zero point laya centres, the seven-skinned Eternal Parent Space, the void/plenum, the mysterious nature of light, are the stuff of the newest concepts of science and of the ancient wisdom. We turn next to review theories and paradoxes in modern science in more detail—all of which bear upon our attempts to critically evaluate the validity of *The Secret Doctrine*. We must take up the challenge to scientists posed by Madame Blavatsky:

> *the Secret teachings ... must be contrasted with the speculations of modern science. Archaic axioms must be placed side by side with modern hypotheses and comparison left to the sagacious reader.* (S. D. I, p. 480)

In fact, the deeper we go into science or into the mysteries then the more the wisdom teachings of *The Secret Doctrine* become apparent.

Blavatsky considered that scientific advance would bring humankind closer to her archaic teachings. She argued:

> There can be no possible conflict between the teachings of occult and so-called exact Science, where the conclusions of the latter are grounded on a substratum of unassailable fact. It is only when its more ardent exponents, over-stepping the limits of observed phenomena in order to penetrate into the arcane of Being, attempt to wrench the formation of Kosmos and its *living* Forces from Spirit, and attribute all to blind matter, that the Occultists claim the right to dispute and call in question their theories. (S. D. I, p. 477)

Blavatsky has provided a model for the existence of God that Dr. Sagan could have used to hone his mind. Perhaps God does not have to say to the morning glory, *"Hey, flower, open,"* but instead, micro-intervenes in the laws of nature through a hierarchy of divine, spiritual and psychical beings which manifest its Will and inherent Logos, all sustained through the Aethers of Space.

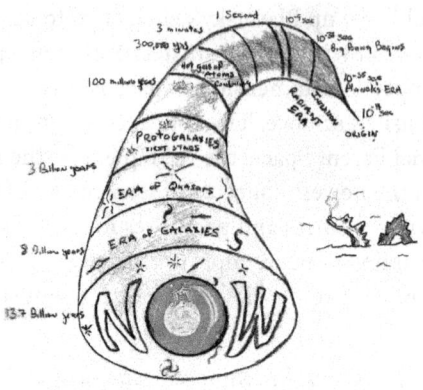

IV
The Cosmogenesis & Physics of Modern Science

> *Extrapolating all the way back to the beginning,*
> *the universe would appear to have begun as a point....*
> — physicist B. Greene, 1999 -

> *... the old idea of the vacuum—that it is empty space, nothingness—*
> *has also changed.... it is not empty; it is a plenum.... the view of the*
> *new physics suggests, "The vacuum is all of physics."... the universe*
> *itself sprang into existence out of nothingness—a gigantic vacuum*
> *fluctuation which we know today as the big bang.... creation ex nihilo—a*
> *creation out of nothing. The entire universe could be a representation*
> *of nothingness—the vacuum.... What doesn't exist, nothingness or the*
> *vacuum, is a kind of joke by the "eternal Maker of enigmas."*
> —physicist H. Pagels, 1985 —

> *... reality must be non-local.... no local model (of reality) can explain the*
> *quantum facts.*
> —physicist N. Herbert, 1987 -

> *Seven hidden dimensions of the universe... have been proposed in a theory*
> *that seeks to unify the forces of nature.... (the seven hidden dimensions)*
> *can be pictured as a small, compact structure such as a sphere that is*
> *associated with every point in space and every moment in time.*
> —physicists Freedman & Nieuwenhuizen, 1985 -

1. Creation Ex Nihilo & Vacuum Genesis
On Being and Nothingness, the Plenum and Void

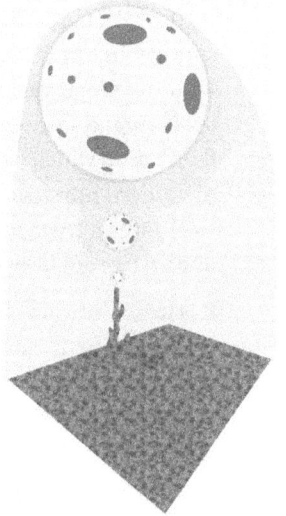

The scientific creation scenario is that of *"vacuum genesis:"* the creation of the universe out of the seeming nothingness of the quantum vacuum. This profound idea in modern physics and cosmology is completely in accord with the *creation ex nihilo* of religious and mystical teachings, and with Blavatsky's teachings within *The Secret Doctrine*. In the language of the mystics, before all time, the universe was *'without form'* and *'void,'* and *"darkness was upon the face of the deep."* (Genesis 1) In the language of science, before time, there existed only the quantum vacuum—a realm of seeming non-being, which serves as the root principle of the manifest universe.

Modern physicists have developed profound ideas about the nature of the quantum vacuum, the primordial nothingness. In *The Cosmic Code*, Heinz Pagels (1985a) provides elegant descriptions of the quantum vacuum as a void and plenum. In a chapter entitled *Being and Nothingness*, he explains:

> the old idea of the vacuum—that it is empty space, nothingness—has also changed. ... it is not empty; it is a plenum. The vacuum, empty space, actually consists of particles and antiparticles being spontaneously created and annihilated. All the quanta that physicists have discovered or ever will discover are being created and destroyed in the Armageddon that is the vacuum. ... Space looks empty only because this great creation and destruction of all the quanta takes place over such short times and distances. Over long distances the vacuum appears placid and smooth—like the ocean which appears quite smooth when we fly high above it in a jet plane. But at the surface of the ocean, close up to it in a small boat, the sea can be high and fluctuating with great waves. Similarly, the vacuum fluctuates with the creation and destruction of quanta if we look closely at it. ... at even smaller distances the vacuum would be revealed as a churning sea of all the quanta. ... the view of the new physics suggests, "The vacuum is all of physics." Everything that ever existed or can exist is already potentially

there in the nothingness of space. Physicists came to this remarkable view of the vacuum by way of a deeper understanding of Heisenberg's uncertainly principle and the existence of antiparticles. ... The vacuum randomly fluctuates between being and nothingness.

there are waves on the vacuum sea corresponding to very conceivable quantum, even those we have not yet discovered. All of physics—everything we hope to know—is waiting in the vacuum to be discovered. ... We might think of the vacuum as the lattice of springs with no spring vibrating—the absence of real particles. ... The vacuum is filled with the vibrations of very possible quantum. ... Maybe the universe itself sprang into existence out of nothingness—a gigantic vacuum fluctuation which we know today as the big bang. Remarkably, the laws of modern physics allow for this possibility. ... Aquinas ... thought the world was a *creation ex nihilo*—a creation out of nothing. The entire universe could be a representation of nothingness—the vacuum.

It is ironic how physics turned out in this century. The nineteenth and early twentieth century was characterized by a materialist outlook which maintained a sharp distinction between what actually was in the world and what wasn't. Today that distinction still exists, but its meaning has altered. What doesn't exist, nothingness or the vacuum, is a kind of joke by the "eternal Maker of enigmas." Theoretical and experimental physicists are now studying nothing at all—the vacuum. But that nothingness contains all of being. (pp. 243-7)

The study of the structure and nature of the quantum vacuum is at the very forefront of modern scientific inquiry. A physicist comments: *"All of physics is in the vacuum."* Consequently, scientists must penetrate into the heart of the quantum vacuum in order to resolve the fundamental mysteries posed within modern physics and cosmology by *"the eternal Maker of enigmas."*

This illustration depicts the quantum vacuum as envisioned by John Archibald Wheeler in 1957. As one examines the vacuum on smaller regions of space, it becomes increasingly chaotic—a churning sea of sub-manifest potentials. At the first level depicted, 10^{-12} centimeters around the level of atomic nuclei, space looks very smooth—like an ocean seen from an airplane overhead. At the second level of 10^{-30} centimeters, a certain roughness in geometry appears. At the third level of 10^{-33} centimeters, at the scale of Planck's

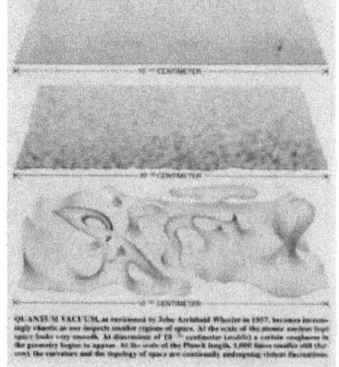

Source: Scientific American

length, the curvature and topology of space continually undergo violently energetic fluctuations.

Scientists and science writers describe the creation of the universe as resulting from a *"random quantum fluctuation"* within the quantum vacuum. Why random? Because the quantum vacuum is always fluctuating randomly at Planckian levels and on one occasion, this fluctuation 'happened' to be strong enough that it instigated the processes of creation:

> All of these (modern scientific) views of creation have one thing in common: they envision the universe coming into being as a quantum fluctuation, a random event; once the event has occurred, the laws of physics take over and our present universe develops. ... It may well be, then, in the words of physicist Edward Tryon, that "our universe is simply one of those things that happens from time to time." (Trefil, *The Moment of Creation*, 1983, p. 208)
>
> the universe itself may be nothing more than the result of a random fluctuation in quantum fields. (Morris, *The Nature of Reality*, 1987, p. 165)
>
> It ballooned accidentally out of the endless void of eternity, from a stillness so deep that there was no "there" or "then," only possibility. For one golden instant all creation was a harmony of energy and matter ruled by a single godlike force. ... The Universes sprouted from tiny seeds of the evolving chaos, grew and went their lonely ways. ... the universe is a false vacuum dense with energy that has been inflating forever; tiny bubbles of ordinary space appear randomly, and expand into separate bubble universes. ... in the yet to be discovered theory of quantum gravity, space-time itself can arise from random fluctuations in a primordial nothingness. This requires the universe itself to be, in some sense, nothing. (Overbye, 1983)

Modern cosmologists maintain that our universe might be only one of many to randomly emerge out of the primordial nothingness. The quantum vacuum is also labeled as a *space-time foam*, a *superspace* or *hyperspace dimension*. On an ultramicroscopic scale, the quantum vacuum has a foam-like structure due to its continual random fluctuations. This quantum foam is a form of hyperspace relative to the created four-dimensional spacetime universes that emerge out of this root substance. This hyperspace space is a form of Eternal Parent Space, a Big Foam of quantum space/time fluctuations—a void and plenum.

The idea of the "ether" dismissed within the mainstream of physics in the early part of twentieth century is emerging again in science—in the guise of the quantum vacuum (and the spacetime foam)—a hyperspace of hidden dimensions and zero point fields. All of manifest creation, the quanta of physics, the laws of nature and the patterns of cosmic design, are latent within a primordial Aetheric substance before they become manifest.

All of being is rooted in non-being. K. Cole notes: *"the evolution of the universe explains the nature of our present vacuum; the nature of vacuums explains the evolution of the Universe."* Could a logic or design exist in the void, in the nothingness of the plenum, even before existence? This is the essential question which scientists now struggling to understand. Heinz Pagels, in *Perfect Symmetry*, explains:

> The nothingness "before" the creation of the universe is the most complete void that we can imagine—no space, time or matter existed. It is a world without place, without duration or eternity, without number—it is what the mathematicians call "the empty set." Yet this unthinkable void converts itself into the plenum of existence—a necessary consequence of physical laws. Where are these laws written into that void? What "tells" the void that it is pregnant with a possible universe? It would seem that even the void is subject to law, a logic that exists prior to space and time. (1985, p. 347)

The quantum vacuum is the source of all being and has a hidden structure and dimensionality. When the creation of a universe occurs, the laws of nature latent in the root principles unfold from within/without as the un-manifest gives birth to the manifest. This is analogous to how a seed might contain the designs and logic of a plant, a tree, an animal or a human being, within itself—in a singlet state or singularity condition. So also, seeds of creation appear 'randomly' within the big foam and expand from within/without giving birth to manifest Cosmoses.

In order to understand the universe, we have to penetrate back into pre-existence and consider what might have existed before creation manifested. This sounds like a Zen koan: What patterns of existence might be pre-existent in non-existence? Blavatsky's archaic teachings actually provide an answer to this question: There is a fundamental Eternal Ceaseless Breath within a Seven Skinned Eternal Parent Space, and when creation occurs, this produces "Seven inside, seven outside." Blavatsky's archaic explanations of Space, as being paradoxically the void and plenum and as having a higher dimensional nature, are most directly applicable to the interpretation of modern theories. Of course, we must wonder what scientific evidence scientists have for their *"random quantum fluctuation"* —their primary *'fortuitous event.'* Further, we might wonder why we should prefer scientists' *fortuitous event* to Blavatsky's mystical account of a "ray" of supernal LIGHT penetrating into the Mother Deep.

2. The Mysteries of Cosmic Origins

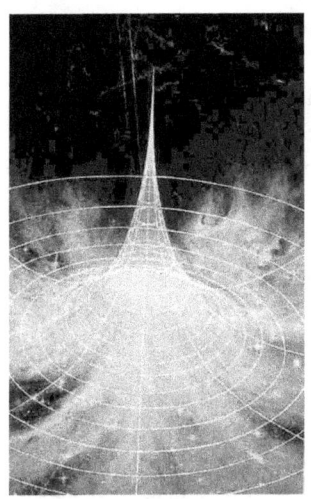

In the standard big bang theory, the universe begins with a point of zero volume and infinite density and temperature—a mathematical impossibility known as a singularity. *Origins*, 1985

The creation scenario of modern science offers a bizarre, seemingly incomprehensible model of cosmic origins. If modern theories are correct, then the whole of the currently vast universe emerged within/without from an infinitesimally small point source out of the *nothingness/plenum* of the quantum vacuum. The mythic dimensions of modern science bear profound relationships to the mystical dimensions of the ancient wisdom teachings.

Modern scientists date the so-called *big bang*, the original cosmic explosion that initiated the creation of the universe, to approximately 12 to 20 billion years ago. A recent estimate of the origin of the universe is 13.7 billion years (Laszlo, 2006). Evidence of the big bang comes from two primary sources: i) the current expanding state of the universe suggested by the red shift in the light spectrums of distant galaxies caused by their movement away from us—the Doppler effect; and ii) the residual background cosmic radiation detected by radio-astronomers—as an after-glow of the initial cosmic fireball. Scientists in the 1950s extrapolated backwards in time from the current expanding state of the universe to trace its origin to a 'big bang' creation event, where all the matters and energies were concentrated into one massive exploding super-sun like body.

In 1965, Steven Weinberg published a popular book *The First Three Minutes* depicting the astrophysical processes occurring during the first three minutes of the big bang. Weinberg stated that *"one-hundredth of a second (is) the earliest time about which we can speak with any confidence...*. (p. 2) At that time, the universe was about a hundred million degrees centigrade and the primary ingredients were electrons, positrons, neutrinos and photons. In addition, there were smaller numbers of heavier particles—protons and neutrons—all being created and destroyed within a sort of primordial cosmic soup.

However, during the last decades of the twentieth century, scientists penetrated even further back into the origins of spacetime and traced the big bang explosion back into a first instant of creation from a point source—a singularity condition. This first point is where the universe emerged at the level of the

'Planckian units'—at which measurement becomes possible according to the uncertainty principle.

At a singularity, the laws of physics and the distinctions of space and time, energy and matter, break down and everything appears to pass into infinity (and/or into nothingness). Physicists have arrived at complex enigmas while trying to understand singularities and their origins within the quantum vacuum. Space is not empty but mysteriously full. One scientist explains that: "*All of physics is in the vacuum*" —an opinion shared with the Kabbalists and occultist Blavatsky.

2a. Everything Adds up to Nothing

How could a universe of such immensity as our own emerge from a singular point or from nothing? As much as the idea may initially seem unreasonable, we can imagine the matter and energy of the universe returning again to a point source and a pre-big bang state with different energies and forces cancelling each other out, so that *it all adds up to zero*. As bizarre as this scenario may seem, this is exactly what modern astrophysics and cosmology have concluded in recent years.

According to the Laws of the Conservation, mass and energy can be converted into each other but the overall quantities must be conserved—in addition to other quantities, such as spin. However, if we imagine all of the matter/energy of the universe returning at the beginning of time into a primordial state, then different forces and elements might cancel each other out without violating the laws of conservation. Positive electrical charges would be cancelled by negative electrical charges; quantum spin properties of right and left spinning charges might cancel each other; and anti-matter could cancel out additional matters.

The idea of creation out of nothing in modern science is sometimes attributed to the physicist, Edward Tryon, who in 1973 had a vision:

> "I had a vision of a flash of universe appearing from nothing, appearing as a result of the laws of physics. I felt a chill of awe and exhilaration like I have not felt before or since."

Of course, Dr. Tryon would probably not describe his vision as a mystical experience—although one might well wonder whether he indeed should.

Whereas the idea of the cancelling out of positive and negative charges, spin components, matter and anti-matter, and so on, were established, Dr. Tryon extended this idea to consider the effects of gravity and gravitational collapse. Tryon reasoned that gravity or spacetime curvature can be taken as a negative force capable of cancelling out the positive energies contained in the residual matter and energy which remained after other components had been cancelled out. Ultimately then, the universe might *all add up to zero*. In a popular science article, Strauss (1985) explained:

Prof. Tryon reasoned that if something could be found which negates the amount of energy in the universe in the same way that a negative electric charge cancels a positive one, then the total energy balance might be described as a kind of nothingness. To rephrase it, the universe adds up to zero. ... the cancelling source might be the potential energy locked up in the pull of gravity. For various reasons, the energy connected with gravity is typified by physicists as a negative energy. While the ability of potential gravity to create a zero-sum effect in the universe was not proven then (or now), the idea of a universe which essentially cancelled itself out is pregnant with suggestions of how it came into being. ... a number of physicists ... have been attempting to describe the mathematics of the probability of the universe springing out of nothingness. ... *"I believe it won't be very long now—perhaps measured in decades—until people have a relatively complete theory of how the universe grew out of nothing,"* says Columbia University physicist Heinz Pagels. *"And then they can spend the next 300 years arguing over interpretations of that."* (1985)

Adding up all the matter and energy, as a +1, to the negative potential of gravity (-1), magically produces a zero-sum.[1] Imagine the universe running backwards in time, returning to a singularity point from which it had originally emerged and disappearing into the (apparent) nothingness of the quantum vacuum!

In modern science, a current issue concerns whether or not there is enough matter and energy in the universe to slow down its current expansion and to set into motion a phase of universal contraction. In the mainstream of science, it is considered that it would be the presence of matter and the principle of 'gravity' which could potentially close the universe. Historically, scientists have tended to assume that the universe would be closed as this most satisfies the search for ultimate unity and symmetry. Hence scientists search for the missing matter which could eventually set gravitational collapse into motion. In 1998, the experimental confirmation of the idea that neutrinos can indeed have mass was hailed as one such discovery which could tip the scales towards the eventual closure of the universe. Neutrinos are the most abundant know particles in the universe. There are however other possibilities and theories.

One possible scenario for the fate of the universe is that it will eventually begin an era of universal contraction. This would entail the accumulation of denser and denser black holes eventually collapsing into a final dreaded singularity—the Omega Point of infinite spacetime curvature at the end of time. This scenario is sometimes called the *"big crunch"* to contrast it with the *"big bang"*

---

[1] In this case, everything adds us to nothing—as suggested by Aleister Crowley's simple magical formula of the universe: $+1 + (-1) = 0$, or $+n + (-n) = 0$. (Holmes, *The Heart Doctrine*, 2010)

creation event. This is the *omega point*—as omega is the final letter of the Greek alphabet. If the universe is closed, then it began with a white hole singularity and will end in a black hole singularity—all between the Alpha and the Omega points. Expanding within/without from a singularity at the beginning of time, the universe could eventually contract without/within to a singularity at the end of time. It all might add up to nothing at the beginning of time and once again at the end of time. Such concepts are perfectly in accord with Blavatsky, who describes the first point of cosmic differentiation and follows evolution through to the final dissolution into the zero-point laya centres at the end of time.

The root principles of creation and dissolution are within the strange quantum vacuum: the apparent nothingness and plenum, which underlies and sustains the universe. The universe, the One, or 1, emerged from the nothingness/plenum, the zero, 0, the infinite root principle of creation.

2b. The Singularity, which Can and Cannot Happen

There are two major cornerstones of modern cosmology and physics: the general theory of relativity describing the law of gravity in terms of the curvature of four-dimensional spacetime; and quantum theory describing the four known laws of nature in terms of 'quantum field theories' (particle/wave, matter/energy theories). The universe is composed of matter and energy within time and space. These are the four basic elements of modern science. All four—matter, energy, time and space—originate at the big bang singularity and would dissolve again at the Omega point.

Modern big bang cosmology is based on Einstein's general theory of relativity, in which mathematically, there is nothing preventing a singularity condition where the measure of spacetime curvature passes to infinity. As spacetime curvature passes to infinity, the dimension of the universe diminishes to an infinitely minute point. The general theory of relativity allows for and predicts such unusual singularities.

However, the prediction of a singularity is inconsistent with the basic principle of quantum physics—the *uncertainty principle*. Einstein's general theory is 'classical' in that it does not incorporate the uncertainty principle. In classical physics, particles were thought to have a definite position and momentum at any point in time. Heisenberg developed the "uncertainty principle" in the late 1920s and it states that one cannot determine both the position and momentum of a particle to an arbitrary degree of accuracy. Instead, the more closely one measures the position, the greater the uncertainty about the momentum and vice

The Cosmogenesis & Physics of Modern Science

versa. Heisenberg compared the uncertainty principle to the man and women in a weather-house, where *"if one comes out, the other goes in."*[2]

The uncertainty principle specifies that the product in the measurement of the position and momentum of a quantum must always be equal to or greater than Planck's constant, called h. 'h' has a small but positive value (6.63×10^{-27} erg seconds) and this factor is a measure of discreteness in quantum processes. If $h = 0$, then the position and momentum of a quantum could both be known simultaneously to any degree of accuracy. The uncertainty relationship is depicted by the formula $\Delta p \times \Delta m \geq h$. If the value of either Δp or Δm approaches 0, meaning that either the position or momentum is completely determined, then the other property mathematically passes to infinity. And so, the general theory of relativity which describes the law of gravity predicts singularities, whereas quantum theory forbids them.

The time and dimensions of the big bang singularity are arrived at through quantum theory because the measurements of science become meaningless and undefined at the level of the singularity, or at what Blavatsky would call a 'Ring-pass-not.' In quantum physics, the basic Planck unit of measurement of distance, or extension, beyond which we cannot measure according to the uncertainty principle, is *10^{-33} centimetres*. This is the boundary of the singularity beyond which the scientist cannot penetrate through measurement. This 10^{-33} centimetres is inconceivably minute, billions of times smaller than the diameter of a proton. The point of creation of the Kosmos arises at this level where material differentiation begins from out of the void, with these limits as imposed by the uncertainty principle.

Scientists also ascribe to this point emergence a Planck measurement of time, *10^{-43} seconds*, which is the time required for light to travel the Planck distance. This is the fundamental unit of the measurement of time. The big bang singularity is thus a hypothetical point of emergence of universal creation at the level of the Planck units. This singularity is 10^{-33} cm in diameter at 10^{-43} seconds into creation. This is an inconceivably minute point emerging at an inconceivable brief first instant of time. This is where the unfolding of the infinite begins from within/without at essentially a zero point level. This is a bizarre and beautiful conception of the emergence of the universe from within the depths of the Deep—the point to which scientific theorizing and study has brought modern inquiries into universal origins!

---

2   A weather-house refers to small toy like weather device of European origin, perhaps novelties today. These usually stand under a foot in height and are constructed of wood, with male and female figures on a rotating axle with a small house behind them. If the measurement of the air's humidity is high, the female figure emerges from the small house and the male figure moves into the house; if the humidity is low, then the man emerges and the female retreats. The female is supposed to forecast rain and the male sunshine. As one figure emerges, the other moves into the framework of the house.

2c. Stephen Hawking & the Badly Behaved Points

> Hawking hopes that there may not be a Big Bang, no "edge" to the universe that can be singled out and pointed to as the initial starting point (the singularity). His resistance derives from the fact that he believes an edge entails a God—at least a causal principle that functions like a definite starting point. (Weber, 1986, p. 205)

In his best seller, *A Brief History of Time* (1988), the prominent physicist and cosmologist Stephen Hawking attempted to explain creation in such a way as to avoid *the God hypothesis*. Professor Hawking suggested that if scientists were successful in developing a unified theory of 'quantum gravity,' then it would do away with the necessity of a big bang singularity. The singularity is interpreted as a last remaining "gap" in science's explanatory framework, where religious and superstitious folk still invoke the idea of God or a Creator.

The problem for scientists, as Hawking explains, is that:

> all our theories of science are formulated on the assumption that space-time is smooth and nearly flat, so they break down at the big bang singularity, where the curvature of space-time is infinite. ... predictability would break down at the big bang. ... Many people do not like the idea that time has a beginning, probably because it smacks of divine intervention. ... There were therefore a number of attempts to avoid the conclusion that there had been a big bang. (1988, pp. 46-7)

In Hawking's unified theory of quantum gravity, the mysterious singularity would be "smeared out" according to the uncertainty principle of quantum theory. In this case, he argues, science will have arrived at a completely natural explanation of the origin of the universe and there will be no need to invoke any metaphysical causes, or God to account for the beginning. Heaven forbid that a singularity *"smack of Divine intervention."*

> "So long as the universe had a beginning, we could suppose it had a creator. But if the universe is really completely self-contained, having no boundary or edge, it would have neither beginning nor end: it would simply be. What place, then, for a creator?" (Hawking, 1988, pp. 140-1)

Professor Hawking strives to discover a *wave equation* for the universe consistent with quantum theory which could avoid any big-bang singularities by eliminating *"such badly behaved points."* (1988, p. 133) Hawking thus describes quanta in terms of the *"sum over history"* approach of physicist R. Feynman, where all possible paths of a quantum in *"imaginary time"* are added together to represent the quantum—instead of describing it as a point particle. (Essentially, the sum over history represents the plenum condition of all possibilities.) Hawking notes that, in this case:

> In real time, the universe has a beginning and an end at singularities that form a boundary to space-time and at which the laws of science break down. But in imaginary time, there are no singularities or boundaries. So maybe what we call imaginary time is really more basic.... (p. 139)

According to Hawking's philosophical musings, dissolving the singularities into imaginary time and dimensions would somehow mean that the universe would not require *"an undefined boundary condition,"* represented by the singularity. Dr. Hawking (1984) considers the philosophical implications of how quantum gravity theory could resolve the singularity enigmas:

> There would be no singularities at which the laws of science broke down and no edge of space-time at which one would have to appeal to God or some new law to set the boundary conditions for space-time. One could say: "The boundary condition of the universe is that it has no boundary." The universe would be completely self-contained and not affected by anything outside itself. It would neither be created nor destroyed. It would just BE. (p. 136)

Dr. Hawking's arguments for why we no longer need a Creator if we can smear out the singularity are really quite peculiar. Even if one smears out the naughty singularity, it still represents a boundary condition—what Blavatsky calls a 'ring-pass-not' or a portal between different levels of reality. Dr. Hawking's logic in dismissing God is his leap of faith—faith in his own intellect and the powers of rational science. In an interview, Hawking comments: *"We still believe that the universe should be logical and beautiful. We just dropped the word 'God.'"* (Weber, 1986, p. 212)

Of course, Hawking is not familiar with the fact that *The Secret Doctrine* deals with exactly such ideas and dynamics—concerning the point source origin and ends of the cosmos. Further, the notion of the quantum as being composed of *"all possible paths"* in imaginary time is related to what Blavatsky describes as the plenum of Space—the metaphysical realm underlying and sustaining all things and containing all possibilities in the Aether. Dr. Hawking's solution to the singularity problem is really no solution to the question of God's existence, although he imagines it to be and dresses up his views to represent so-called 'real science.'

Most scientists expect the singularity mysteries to be resolved with future developments in the unification of the laws of physics. Pagels (1985b) illustrated the common scientific attitude towards such enigmas:

on the basis of past experience, such singularities in the mathematical descriptions of physical entities simply reflect an incomplete physical understanding. The appearance of mathematical singularities in the description of nature is really a challenge to physicists to devise a better mathematical description based on deeper physical laws that avoid the singularity. The singularity at the origin of the universe implied by some models should be seen as a challenge, not a veil of ignorance behind which we may not look. (p. 244)

Materialist scientists resent what is labelled *"singularity mysticism"*—the idea that there is anything 'mystical' about zero point singularities rooted into the plenum. Of course, the claim that there is nothing mystical about such points is purely a philosophical leap of faith on the part of the materialist scientist. Generally, scientists are ignorant of those esoteric occult and mystical teachings which do provide doctrines relevant to such issues.

Before all time: a primordial nothingness and then a point, a naught point, a zero-point source of unfoldment emerging out of the infinity of the void/plenum and imaginary time! Of course, to so-called "real scientists," none of this implies anything mystical or supernatural although it surely still does indeed *"smack of Divine micro-intervention."* It is most noteworthy that Blavatsky depicted the zero point origins and ends of the Kosmos over a century before modern scientists.

2d. A Big Bang Happens

Ten or twenty billion years ago, something happened—the Big Bang, the event that began our Universe. Why it happened is the greatest mystery we know. That it happened is reasonably clear. (Carl Sagan, *Cosmos*, 1980)

Scientific ideas concerning cosmology, physics and astronomy have undergone profound changes over the past century or so, since Blavatsky's period in the second half of the 1800s. By the 1980s, the *"standard model of the big bang"* had been formulated based upon two foundations—Einstein's general theory of relativity, dealing with the law of gravity and the curvature of the 4-dimensional space-time continuum; and quantum field theories, which explain the "laws of nature" in terms of the transformations of matter and energy, particles and waves—within time and space. The Big Bang event marks the origin of these elements. A fifth element, the ether, was dismissed within the mainstream of science for most of the 20th century. However, physicists now declare: *"All of physics is in the vacuum"*— and physicist Paul Davis talks of the mysterious quantum vacuum as just such a *'quantum ether.'* 21st century physics promises *much ado about nothing*, as one author quips.[3]

---

3   For Blavatsky, the ether is Space itself—the higher Aether, the Seven-Skinned Eternal Parent Space. There is also a lower ether within the Solar System related to the

Einstein's (1916) General Theory of Relativity is one cornerstone of modern cosmology and provides a framework for understanding one of the four fundamental laws of physics—that of gravity. The effects of gravity include such things as the falling on an apple to the ground, the movement of the planets within the solar system and the cohesion of the galaxies. Material masses exert a gravitational pull upon each other which is inversely proportional to the distances between the masses. Gravity and electromagnetism were the two fundamental laws of physics recognized within science at the turn of the previous century because their effects are observable in every day visual experience of the world. (The remaining two forces in modern science, the 'strong' and 'weak forces,' involve phenomena at atomic and sub-atomic levels and were formulated later within the twentieth century.)

Since Galileo, it had been assumed within science that all bodies, regardless of mass, follow the same trajectory (path) in a gravitational field; i.e., they fall towards the local *'centre of gravity.'* Einstein reasoned then that the spacetime continuum itself might be regarded as having an intrinsic curvature which dictated the path of objects. He developed varied equations to specify the curvature of four-dimensional spacetime in terms of the distribution of matter and energy within spacetime. Matter/energy itself curved the space-time continuum and gravity was explained in terms of the geometric curvature of a 4-dimensional spacetime continuum.

Einstein's theory was based in part upon mathematical models developed in the late 19th century involving non-Euclidian geometry. Euclidian geometry is the geometry of supposed common sense, considering space as three dimensional and flat, such that any point within three-dimensional space can be defined in terms of three perpendicular axes (the x, y and z axis). Euclidian space does not seem to be anything in itself, as having any kind of curvature or feature, but is considered simply an empty backdrop against which things happen. In the non-Euclidian geometry used by Einstein, a 4-dimensional curvature is produced within space-time by the presence of matter/energy. The relationship between these is expressed in very complex mathematical formulas, where twenty functions of the co-ordinates of a point in spacetime are required to specify the curvature at that point. Ten of these functions correspond to a portion of the curvature which propagates freely in the form of gravitation waves or 'ripples of curvature;' and the remaining ten functions are determined by the mass, energy, momentum, angular momentum and internal stresses in the matter, as well as by Newton's gravitational constant, G. (DeWitt, 1983, p. 114) Einstein's equations provided the conceptual framework required for modern cosmology and the development of the *'standard model of the big bang.'*

---

light of the Sun with its seven rays of influence—as the Soul and Spirit of the solar space. Blavatsky talks of such 'astral light.' In physics, the ether, or 'quantum ether' is that of the quantum vacuum with its zero point fields and higher dimensions.

However, when it came to applying the general theory of relativity to analyzing the overall structure of the universe, Einstein like other scientists of his day assumed that the universe was static or unchanging in time. According then to the general theory of relativity, if matter and energy curved space-time, then this implied that all the matter in the universe should be attracted together and should be collapsing due to gravitational effects. In order to solve this problem, Einstein added a *'cosmological constant'* to his formulations, hypothesized to act as a repulsive force between particles at great distances, hence balancing the gravitational attraction and allowing for a static unchanging universe.

Einstein's later described his addition of the cosmological constant to his formulations of space/time as his *"greatest blunder,"* one of the most historic 'missed opportunities' within science. If the constant had not been added, Einstein might have predicted patterns of expansion or contraction within the larger universe instead of a static one. However, it was not until the 1920s that empirical data led astronomers to develop the still accepted model of the expanding universe.

In the period from 1912 to 1924, the American astronomer V. Slipher studied the light emitted by over eighty galaxies and determined that in most instances the light was shifted towards the red end of the spectrum. Scientists were familiar with the Doppler effect whereby the frequency of sound waves emitted by a moving object are shortened when that object is moving towards an observer and lengthened when the object is moving away from the observer. The simplest interpretation of the Slipher's red shift is that the galaxies are moving away from us and the wavelength of the light emitted is similarly drawn out or shifted into the longer red wavelengths. During the 1920s, the astronomer Edwin Hubble demonstrated that the more distant the galaxy, then the more its light is red-shifted, implying that it is receding from us at a greater velocity.

In 1927, the Belgian astronomer G. Lemaitre combined the principles of relativity with the idea of the expanding Universe and extrapolated into the distant past to predict what had happened 'in the beginning.' Lemaitre is regarded as the father of the big-bang theory, although he did not introduce the term. Lemaitre theorized that if the universe is now expanding, then at some point in the past, all the matter and energy of the universe must have been squeezed into one huge mass which he called the *'cosmic egg'* or *'primeval atom.'* Lemaitre argued that this cosmic egg must have been unstable and exploded. The super-atom was thought to have broken down into very massive atoms and then further into smaller and smaller, more stable atoms such as we find today.

The astronomer George Gamow adopted such a *'big bang theory'* but presented a different scenario of the first moments of creation.[4] At time zero, Gamow envisioned a mass of extremely condensed neutrons, termed *'ylem,'* a

---

4   Hoyle, Gold and Bondi proposed an alternative 'steady state model' of the universe. Hoyle, an atheist, espoused the same resistance to the idea of a beginning as that of Stephen Hawking; he disliked the idea of a beginning to the universe because it implied

Latin term for the substance out of which matter is formed. In 1948, Gamow, Herman and Alpher suggested that at the moment of creation, the neutronium cosmic egg disintegrated through a violent explosion into separate neutrons, some of which further broke down into protons and electrons. The incredibly high temperatures during the first moments of creation were thought to have allowed for protons and neutrons to be fused into stable atomic nuclei. In this view, the simplest atoms were formed first and should be more common than the heavier, complex atoms.

Gamow et al. reasoned that most of the heavier elements were also synthesized during the big bang but this turned out to be incorrect. In modern views, it is held that only hydrogen, hydrogen isotopes, helium and a small amount of light atomic nuclei were formed in the first minutes of creation. Heavier elements were created much latter in cosmic history in the interiors of stars or through supernova explosions. Understanding the abundance of various elements in the universe is one way scientists have of understanding what processes occurred during different periods of cosmic history.

And so, the idea emerged in modern science that the universe was created at some point in time through the explosion of a cosmic egg or cosmic fireball. The big bang involved incredibly high temperatures and pressure. Estimates of the age of the universe used to be about 5 to 7 billion years, while more modern estimates are in the range of 10 to 20 billion years ago. A most recent estimate reported on the *CoasttoCoastAm* radio show in 2008 and offered by Laszlo (2006) is that of 13.7 billion years.

The explosion of the big bang was not like the kinds of explosions that occur within space and time. Instead, the spacetime continuum itself was created at the moment of the big bang. The universe did not expand into a pre-existing space but actually served to create the expanding space-time continuum itself. In this case, any observer, no matter what his position in the universe, would seem to be at the centre—as all the galaxies are moving away from each other. The analogy most frequently used to illustrate this is the inflation of a balloon with many different points on its surface. As the balloon expands, the space-time between all of the points expands and there is no true centre (on the surface) from which the expansion can be measured—at least on the surface. The centre is in a sense everywhere but nowhere.

In 1948, Alpher and Herman predicted that heat radiation from the big bang must still exist as a low temperature radiation pervading the universe. Any hot body, at it cools, emits electromagnetic radiation, whose wavelength will increase as the body cools. Based on theoretical considerations, Alpher and Herman predicted: *"The temperature in the universe at the present time is found to be about 5 degrees K."* In 1965, Penzias and Wison were attempting to measure

---

the idea of a Creator. Hoyle is credited with having coined the term 'big bang' and using it on a BBC radio program "The Nature of Things."

the radio waves emitted by our galaxy and to their surprise they discovered a sizable amount of background radiation at 7.35 centimetres in the microwave spectrum. Further, this *"cosmic background radiation"* was independent of direction and time, which meant that its origin could not be from within our galaxy. This wavelength of radiation corresponds to a temperature of 3.5 degrees above absolute zero. This pervasive background radiation is now taken as a residue of the incredibly high temperatures of the big bang. Since 1965, this thermal radiation has been measured by radio astronomers at over a dozen wavelengths ranging from 73.5 centimetres to 0.33 centimetres, all of which are consistent with a Planckian distribution (used to describe 'black body radiation.') This cosmic background radiation is a remnant of the intense temperatures existent during the first minutes of creation.

The evidences for the expanding universe and Einstein's general theory of relativity are the basic foundations for contemporary views of the big bang and the expanding universe. However, in modern times, scientists consider that there also may be many universes in a 'multiverse,' with any number of spacetimes complexes arising out of the void-plenum of the quantum vacuum. These worlds emerge from point sources, undergo a rapid inflationary era (as in the dropping of the world egg), and then continue to grow as expanding universes and possibly contracting again into singularities at the end of time. The modern range of viewpoints is far more diverse than within the past centuries of science.

Certainly, Blavatsky was far ahead of her the science of her era in suggesting an expanding Kosmos emerging out of hyperspace (the Eternal Parent Space) from a point source and ultimately contracting again to be reabsorbed at the end of time into such a zero point laya centre! These basic concepts of *The Secret Doctrine* make such sense given the most recent theories of the physicists. Other aspects of the *Stanzas of Dzyan* are further consistent with modern descriptions of the early Cosmos. Blavatsky's archaic account begins with the penetration of a Ray of Light into the Mother Deep and the dropping of the "WORLD EGG."

> 4. THEN THE THREE FALL INTO THE FOUR. THE RADIANT ESSENCE BECOMES SEVEN INSIDE, SEVEN OUTSIDE. THE LUMINOUS EGG, WHICH IN ITSELF IS THREE, CURDLES AND SPREADS IN MILK-WHITE CURDS THROUGHOUT THE DEPTHS OF MOTHER, THE ROOT THAT GROWS IN THE DEPTHS OF THE OCEAN OF LIFE.

> 6. ...AND THE OCEAN WAS RADIANT LIGHT, WHICH WAS FIRE, AND HEAT, AND MOTION. DARKNESS VANISHED AND WAS NO MORE; IT DISAPPEARED IN ITS OWN ESSENCE, THE BODY OF FIRE AND WATER, OR FATHER AND MOTHER.

9. LIGHT IS COLD FLAME, AND FLAME IS FIRE, AND FIRE PRODUCES HEAT, WHICH YIELDS WATER: THE WATER OF LIFE IN THE GREAT MOTHER.

11. IT EXPANDS WHEN THE BREATH OF FIRE IS UPON IT; IT CONTRACTS WHEN THE BREATH OF THE MOTHER TOUCHES IT. THEN THE SONS DISSOCIATE AND SCATTER, TO RETURN INTO THEIR MOTHER'S BOSOM AT THE END OF THE GREAT DAY, AND RE-BECOME ONE WITH HER;

Blavatsky depicted the birth of the Kosmos in terms of "LIGHT" producing *"FIRE, AND HEAT, AND MOTION"* —as an expanding space-time Son emerges out of the Eternal Parent Space. Further, the Stanzas state that, "LIGHT IS COLD FLAME" and this light produces fire, then heat, which yields water (material matters). As the great protean magician, primordial light gives birth to fire, heat and motion—all consistent with the concept of a hot 'big bang' origin and of all matters and energies being produced out of a Divine Lux.

As Carl Sagan suggests, *"ten or twenty billion years ago, something happened,"* but of course, the matter of interpreting scientific facts is not nearly as clear or simple as one might imagine. Blavatsky's writing suggests that although something did happen to create the universe, the nature of what exactly happened involves forces and principles quite different from those that science understands. Blavatsky predicted a highly energetic creation event—in radiant light, which produces fire and heat and motion, and material products spreading like curds throughout the spaces of the expanding universe.

2e. The First Three Minutes & the Farcical Chain of Accidents

> ... human life is ... just a more-or-less farcical outcome of a chain of accidents reaching back to the first three minute ... .
> —S. Weinberg (1979)

In 1979, Steven Weinberg published a popular scientific account of the early universe, *The First Three Minutes*. Dr. Weinberg described the processes occurring during the Big Bang from the first $1/100^{th}$ of a second through the first three minutes of creation. We will review Dr. Weinberg's "standard model of the big bang" and then consider his philosophical musings on the meaning of it all.

At $1/100^{th}$ of a second into creation, after the inflationary era and the dropping of the world egg, Weinberg estimated the temperature of the big bang at 100,000 million degrees Centigrade (10^{11} degrees)—so hot that the nuclei of atoms could not be held together. Instead, the matter in this explosion consisted only of elementary particles—such as electrons, positrons, neutrinos, light (photons) and a much smaller amount of heavy particles, protons and neutrons. The number of photons per nuclear particles (protons, neutrons) is estimated at 100 million to 1. Light was the primary constituent of the universe and as Weinberg notes: *"... it is always possible to create any kind of particle-antiparticle pairs in collisions of pairs of photons."* (p. 76)

Weinberg describes the processes occurring during these early instances of creation:

> These particles—electrons, positrons, neutrinos, photons—were continually being created out of pure energy and then after short lives being annihilated again. Their number (was) fixed by a balance between the processes of creation and annihilation. (p. 4)

Weinberg estimated the density of the hot cosmic soup at four thousand million times that of water.

This standard model of the big bang is based partly upon Einstein's famous equation of $E=mc^2$. Before Einstein, in Blavatsky's era, scientists regarded mass and energy as distinct properties, each described by its own conservation law (the conservation of mass and the conservation of energy). In 1905, Einstein published a short paper on the "special theory of relativity" which implied that energy and mass might be converted into each other according to the formula of $E=mc^2$. Since c^2 is an extraordinarily large number, this equation suggests that fantastically large amounts of energy are bound up within material particles. Because of the incredible temperatures of the early universe, photons were able to produce material quanta, or alternatively, material particles would collide and annihilate each other while converting their mass back into radiant energy. Light, the great protean magician for Blavatsky, can give rise to many substances and forms.

After 13.82 seconds, the fireball's temperature had dropped to 3,000 million degrees, below the 'threshold temperature' for the creation of electrons and positrons out of the radiation energy. Positrons and electrons thus begin to rapidly disappear in mutual annihilation. The energy produced by this annihilation momentarily slows down the cooling of the universe.

The first steps in the nucleo-synthesis of atomic nuclei commence during these moments, through the collision of particles which form heavy hydrogen (composed of a proton and neutron), called deuterium H^2. In turn, a collision with another proton or neutron can produce the heaviest hydrogen isotope of tritium, H^3, which might collide with another proton to form Helium. The simplest atomic nuclei build up out of basic nucleons in this way. At 13.82 seconds, the nuclei of the basic isotopes of deuterium, H^2 and tritium H^3 are forming—but only momentarily. Because the universe is expanding so rapidly, the isotope nuclei form in momentary two-particle interactions and are then torn apart.

The Cosmogenesis & Physics of Modern Science

By the end of the first half hour of creation, the process of nucleo-synthesis is complete. Approximately 23% of the material particles left over are in the form of helium and the remainder is hydrogen. Most of the electrons and positrons had been annihilated, except for an excess of electrons to balance the charge of the protons. Stable atoms (with nuclei and orbiting electrons) have yet to form. Most of the energy of the early universe still consists of photons (69%) and neutrinos/anti-neutrinos (31%). Material particles comprise under 1% of the universe.

After the first half hour, the temperature of the universe continues to drop while the expansion continues. Weinberg identifies the period 700,000 years later as the next significant *phase change*. At that time, the temperature had dropped enough for stable atoms (hydrogen and helium) to capture and hold electrons—and thus form primary atoms. When the free electrons are trapped in atoms, then the universe becomes transparent to radiation. Thus, the universe shifts from a *'radiation dominated era'* to a *'matter dominated era.'* The temperature was 3000 degrees. The radiation of photons, neutrinos and anti-neutrinos can now escape, leaving the material particles behind, which are beginning to form huge gas clouds, as precursors to the formation of galaxies.

In the first three minutes, the universe was certainly intensely hot, energetic and dense—a fireball filled with light and elementary particles continually being created and destroyed within a sea of pure energy. Of course, aspects of this view of the early universe are also consistent with Blavatsky's. She wrote:

> Archaic philosophy ... starts from the Absolute All, (and) traced ... the course of natural evolution to pure Light condensing gradually into form, hence becoming Matter.

In the *Stanzas of Dzyan*, one verse suggests processes similar to those depicted by Weinberg. The luminous egg, the world egg, is described—as first becoming "SEVEN INSIDE, SEVEN OUTSIDE," and then it "CURDLES AND SPREADS IN MILK-WHITE CURDS THOUGHOUT THE DEPTH OF THE MOTHER... (III, 4). When milk curdles, material mass forms or condenses out of a liquid (the Waters of Space, or the ethers), just as material particles form out of the pure energy or light within the quantum vacuum.

Another verse, III-9, reads: "LIGHT IS COLD FLAME, AND FLAME IS FIRE, AND FIRE PRODUCES HEAT, WHICH YEILDS WATER, THE WATER OF LIFE IN THE GREAT MOTHER." LIGHT is actually produced by the Ceaseless Breath, and it produces COLD FLAME, then FIRE, then HEAT, which produces WATER. WATER is equivalent here to material and spiritual matters. Two verses later, the Stanzas suggest: "WHEN IT IS COOLING, IT BECOMES RADIANT," which is similar to Weinberg's description of how the universe only becomes radiant after cooling.

In two tables at the end of his book, Dr. Weinberg summarizes the elementary particles and radiations involved in the creation scenario of *The First Three Minutes*. The first table of elementary particles depicts *seven major particles* in *three classes*. These include photons, three leptons (or light particles) and three hadrons (heavy particles). Each of the hadron and lepton families have three generations of particles at different energetic levels. Further, there are seven particles within the lepton family and eight in the hadron family. The concept of the triune and sevenfold nature of reality can readily be applied as a model of these quanta, their families and generations.

One. *Properties of Some Elementary Particles*

	Particle	Symbol	Rest energy (million electron volts)	Threshold temperature (thousand million degrees K)	Effective number of species	Mean life (seconds)
Leptons	Photon	γ	0	0	$1 \times 2 \times 1 = 2$	stable
	Neutrinos	$\nu_e, \bar{\nu}_e$	0	0	$2 \times 1 \times 7/8 = 7/4$	stable
		$\nu_\mu, \bar{\nu}_\mu$	0	0	$2 \times 1 \times 7/8 = 7/4$	stable
	Electron	e^-, e^+	0.5110	5.930	$2 \times 2 \times 7/8 = 7/2$	stable
	Muon	μ^-, μ^+	105.66	1226.2	$2 \times 2 \times 7/8 = 7/2$	2.197×10^{-6}
Hadrons	Pi mesons	π^0	134.96	1566.2	$1 \times 1 \times 1 = 1$	0.8×10^{-16}
		π^+, π^-	139.57	1619.7	$2 \times 1 \times 1 = 2$	2.60×10^{-8}
	Proton	$p, \bar{p}$	938.26	10,888	$2 \times 2 \times 7/8 = 7/2$	stable
	Neutron	$n, \bar{n}$	939.55	10,903	$2 \times 2 \times 7/8 = 7/2$	920

In his second chart on radiation, Dr. Weinberg breaks the electromagnetic spectrum down—again into seven frequency ranges. How does this contradict the ancient occult idea of the seven rays of light emitted by the Solar Logos?

Two. *Properties of Some Kinds of Radiation*

	Wavelength (centimeters)	Photon energy (electron volts)	Black-body temperature (degrees Kelvin)
Radio (up to VHF)	>10	<0.00001	<0.03
Microwave	0.01 to 10	0.00001 to 0.01	0.03 to 30
Infrared	0.0001 to 0.01	0.01 to 1	30 to 3,000
Visible	2×10^{-5} to 10^{-4}	1 to 6	3,000 to 15,000
Ultraviolet	10^{-7} to 2×10^{-5}	6 to 1,000	15,000 to 3,000,000
X ray	10^{-9} to 10^{-7}	1,000 to 100,000	3×10^6 to 3×10^8
γ ray	$<10^{-9}$	>100,000	$>3 \times 10^8$

In Weinberg's diagrams, the triune and sevenfoldness of nature is evident in the particle families and their generations, and in the different forms of radiation.[5,6] In a similar way, the familiar material world is composed of three basic elements of protons, electrons and neutrons, composing atoms on seven levels of

---

5   Light has a triune nature with both an electric and magnetic aspect and it propagates along the Pointyng vector.

6   In more recent times, photons have come to be regarded as one of a class of 'gluons' or mediating particles. Each force of nature has particular 'gluons' which conveys the influences of that field—including photons carrying the electromagnetic force, gluons carrying the strong force, vector bosons mediating the weak force, and gravitons conveying the influences of gravity as 'ripples of curvature.'

The Cosmogenesis & Physics of Modern Science

the periodic tables of chemistry. Similar triune and sevenfold (or octave) patterns are evident in basic particle families, forms of radiations and in material atomic nature.

The following image is referred to as the *Hun Nab Ka*. It is from the book *The Holy Science* by contemporary investigator Uwe Rollie of Mexico. It illustrates the triune nature of light above, the radiation from that source and the materialization of levels of particles within two matrices—represented by musical notes and then numbers—as if particles or quanta.

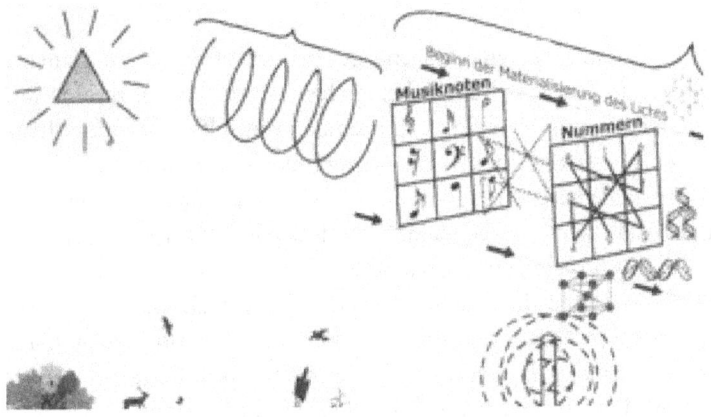

Illustration: From " Holy Science," Uwe Rolli, Merida, Mexico.

Scientific and mystical descriptions are not so far apart in some respects. However, when it comes time for Dr. Weinberg to sum up his work on creation, we certainly find a very different evaluation of creation than that offered by Blavatsky. After providing a fascinating view into the physics of the early universe, Dr. Weinberg concludes his exposition with these philosophical ruminations:

> It is irresistible for humans to believe that we have some special relation to the universe, that human life is not just a more-or-less farcical outcome of a chain of accidents reaching back to the first three minutes, but that we were somehow built in from the beginning. As I write this I happen to be over Wyoming en route home from San Francisco to Boston. Below, the earth looks very soft and comfortable—fluffy clouds here and there, snow turning pink as the sun sets, roads stretching straight across the country from one town to another. It is very hard to realize that this all is just a tiny part of an overwhelmingly hostile universe. It is even harder to realize that this present universe has evolved from an unspeakable unfamiliar early condition, and faces a future extinction of endless cold or intolerable heat. The more the universe seems comprehensible, the more it also seems pointless.

But if there is no solace in the fruits of our research, there is at least some consolation in the research itself. Men and women are not content to comfort themselves with tales of gods and giants, or to confine their thoughts to the daily affairs of life; they also build telescopes and satellites and accelerators, and sit at their desks for endless hours working out the meaning of the data they gather. The effort to understand the universe is one of the very few things that lifts human life a little above the level of farce, and gives it some of the grace of tragedy. (1979, pp. 143-4)

In Dr. Weinberg's view, to engage in tales of gods and giants, as does Blavatsky, or to feel that human beings have some *"special relation to the universe"* are simply due to self-aggrandizement and self consolation. Instead, Dr. Weinberg suggests that human life is more like *"a farcical outcome of a chain of accidents reaching back to the first three minutes."* Of course, if it were not for our telescopes and scientists who sit at their desks, like Dr. Weinberg, then indeed our lives in this hostile universe would be tragic.

Blavatsky stated that the first aim in *The Secret Doctrine* was *"to show that Nature is not 'a fortuitous concurrence of atoms,' and to assign to man his rightful place in the scheme of the Universe."* This aim expressed Blavatsky's desire to oppose the mechanistic and materialist science philosophy dominant in 1888—a philosophy that regarded the origin of the universe and appearance of mankind as being due to the blind working out of natural laws governing material nature. This is the scientific paradigm still evident today in the writings of popular science writers—such as Drs. Sagan, Weinberg, Asimov and Hawking, as among most other physicists, natural scientists, psychologists and philosophers.

There are stark differences between the accidental and farcical universe of Dr. Weinberg and popular science and the occult teachings of the ages and the religious metaphysicians. However, the nature of these similarities and differences are not readily appreciated. It is not the facts and theories of science which belie mystical teachings or *The Secret Doctrine*, but instead, it is the *philosophical interpretations* of the facts and theories of science. Modern scientists regard the processes of creation and evolution as inherently random and accidental, the results of happenstance and good fortune. In contrast, *The Secret Doctrine* portrays a universe full of significance, meaning and interrelationship—all embodying the laws of three and seven throughout the phenomena of Nature, right back to the beginning.

In fact, many major discoveries within modern science yield credence to what the mystics and occultists have long maintained about the patterns inherent in nature. Of course, we should not be comforted with tales of Gods and giants, as Dr. Weinberg notes, but then again, we should not be persuaded by the notion of a *"farcical chain of accidents,"* nor by the philosophical musings reached by those dedicated and brave scientists sitting at desks.

2f. The Fate of the Universe & The Search for Dark Matter and Dark Energy

Modern science views the universe as originating from a point source at Planckian levels of 10^{-33} centimetres, out of the void/plenum of the quantum vacuum, ballooning into a *'world egg,'* the size of a grapefruit—as described by one scientist, and then expanding from within/without ever since. Blavatsky similarly described a first zero point source of differentiation, out of the void/plenum of the Absolute (the Ceaseless Eternal Breath within the Eternal Parent Space), the dropping of the world-egg and the expansion of the universe from within-without when the 'Breath of the Father' is upon it.

Whereas Blavatsky's teachings are similar to modern scientific concepts of creation, her views differ dramatically from those of modern science as concerns the fate of the universe. Although, there is no current agreement within science as to what will eventually happen and different scenarios are considered, at the present time, the predominant scientific viewpoint is that the universe will expand forever—as its rate of expansion has recently been discovered to be increasing. In contrast, *The Secret Doctrine* clearly predicts that the Kosmos will eventually resolve from without-within at the end of time through zero point dynamics—to be reabsorbed into the root principles of creation for *Seven Nights of Brahma*. A cosmos contracts when the Breath of the Mother touches it. Thus, at the end of time, the Divine Mother, through a modification of the Ceaseless Eternal Breath, will ingather the Sons or Kosmos. It is *'as if'* gravity is love and the love of the Divine Mother pervades the Aether of Space and holds it all together. Eventually, She ingathers the Sons at the end of time. Of course, scientists imagine that it is their favourite 'gravity' and material mass that holds it all together, if at all, and they would arbitrarily dismiss such mystical and occult concepts. However, Blavatsky's teachings allow us to approach the wisdom of science with a sceptical attitude and inquiring mind. Mystical axioms must be placed side by side with modern hypotheses as much as this is possible.

We will consider the issue of the fate of the universe from the perspective of the science of the 1980s and the related search for *'dark matter,'* and then examine the newer 21st century cosmological model—which has led to the search for *'dark energy.'* Scientists acknowledge that the vast majority of the universe is invisible to us in one form or another, which *is* certainly consistent with *The Secret Doctrine* —although only if understood in a different way than that conceived of within the mainstream of contemporary thought.

In the 1980s, the critical question for astronomers and cosmologists was whether or not there is enough mass in the universe, such that the *'law of gravity'* will eventually slow down and reverse the expansion of the universe and set in motion a period of universal contraction. The issue of the fate of the universe was defined in terms of *the curvature and geometry of space*. If the universe as a whole is 'open,' with a negative hyperbolic curvature, then it will expand forever—in which case, space and time will be infinite. Alternatively, if the universe has a positive curvature and is 'closed,' then it will eventually collapse. In this case, time and space will be finite and the Universe could end in the *"big crunch."* The big crunch would involve the contraction of the material universe into massive black holes and eventually into a singularity.

In modern cosmology, the *'omega value'* is a density parameter defined in terms of the relationship between the actual density of the universe and the critical density required for gravitational collapse. 'Omega' is the last letter of the Greek alphabet and its value thus specifies the fate of the universe. If omega is less than 1, the universe does not contain enough matter to slow down the current expansion, and we live in an open universe which will expand forever. If omega is greater than 1, the universe will be closed. [7]

		OPEN	CRITICAL	CLOSED
FUTURE OF THE UNIVERSE		PERPETUAL EXPANSION	PERPETUAL EXPANSION	EVENTUAL COLLAPSE
DENSITY PARAMETAR Ω	$\dfrac{\text{ACTUAL DENSITY}}{\text{CRITICAL DENSITY}}$	$\Omega < 1$	$\Omega = 1$	$\Omega > 1$
DECELERATION PARAMETAR q_0	DECELERATION $\dfrac{\text{DISTANCE}}{(\text{VELOCITY})^2}$	$q_0 < \dfrac{1}{2}$	$q_0 = \dfrac{1}{2}$	$q_0 > \dfrac{1}{2}$
GEOMETRY OF SPACE		HYPERBOLIC (NEGATIVE CURVATURE)	FLAT (ZERO CURVATURE)	SPHERICAL (POSITIVE CURVATURE)

In the 1980s, the evidence suggested that we live in an open universe. Estimates of the mass of stars, the number of stars in galaxies and the numbers of galaxies in an average volume of space, yielded an omega value of only about 5% of the critical density. There was also evidence of non-luminous matter in gal-

---

7   In the 1980s, various arguments allowed researchers to place limits on the possible range of the omega value. Weinberg (1979) suggested that the critical density is *"5×10^{-30} grams per cubic centimetre, or about three hydrogen atoms per thousand litres of space."* Pagels (1985) estimated the omega value as *"10^{-29} grams per cubic centimetre—approximately ten hydrogen atoms per cubic meter."* These are incredibly small amounts of matter per volume of space and they highlight how scientists, for the most part, regarded the vast spaces of the universe as 'empty.'

axies and surrounding them, detected by the gravitational influences on the stars in galaxies—estimated at two times that of luminous galactic matter and accounting for another 10% of the matter required to reach an omega value of 1. Thirdly, the gravitational motion of galaxies within galactic superclusters suggested another source of non-luminous matter, perhaps up to 5% of the matter required to close the universe—in the form of cold rocks, burned out stars, clouds of gas, and maybe black holes (Dicus et al., *Scientific American*, 1983).

Astronomers still search for the additional mass required to close the universe—perhaps in neutrinos, the most abundant elements in the universe. In 1995, physicists at the Los Alamos National Laboratory announced experimental evidence that the 'electron-neutrino' has a tiny mass—estimated at one-millionth the weight of an electron. Other scientists have proposed other forms of 'dark matter'—including such as entities called WIMP's, for "weakly interacting massive particles," or "sparticles" in supersymmetry theory, or MACHOS, for "massive astrophysical compact hallo objects." Another possible candidate for dark matter is the high-mass subatomic vibrations predicted by superstring theory. (Kaku, 1987)

The search for 'dark matter' is not only an issue as concerns the fate of the universe, but it bears also upon the scientific understanding of the formation of galaxies and their rotations. In the 1930s, the astronomer Fritz Zwicky analyzed the rate of rotation of the Coma cluster of galaxies attempting to calculate the mass necessary to bind this cluster of galaxies. The mass required was approximately twenty times that observed. Zwicky postulated that there had to be a form of *"dunkle Materia,"* dark matter, whose gravitational pull held the galaxies together rather than allowing them to be torn apart by their rotary motion. In 1973, Ostriker and Pebbles at Princeton demonstrated that the gravitational pull of stars was not enough to hold the galaxies together and they suggested that galaxies might be surrounded by massive invisible halos—constituting approximately 90% of the mass of the galaxy. Further, studies of the Andromeda galaxy by Rubin demonstrated that the velocity of the gases nearer the centre of the galaxy or towards its periphery was a constant. The expectation had been that the gases would rotate more slowly as one moved towards the periphery of the galaxy, but this was not so. Kaku (1987) notes: *"The constancy of velocity of a rotating galaxy was now a universal fact of galactic physics. Dark matter was here to stay."* (p. 149)

The search for dark matter is necessary to explain the structure and dynamics of galaxies and super-galactic clusters, as well as to determine the fate of the universe. However, this search is premised on the view that gravity and material mass are the primary formative forces binding galaxies together and possibly the universe.

Illustration: *Scientific American*, Feb. 2007, *The Cosmic Grip of Dark Energy,* Conselice. Both dark matter and dark energy are postulated as forces serving to bind the galaxies together. The hands in the diagrams are intended to convey the concept of such a force binding the galaxies and are not Carl Sagan's *"angels sent to push and pummel the planets."* Recall that Dr. Sagan explained that we did not need angels anymore because a theory of gravity provided a 'natural' explanation.

In a *Scientific American* article, "The Future of the Universe," Dicus noted: *"... the question of closure has not yet been settled on experimental or observational grounds, (hence) both the open and closed possibilities need to be considered in any speculations about the distant future."* In 2010, this is still the case, as advances in modern physics suggest other dynamics may be involved in understanding the nature of gravity and in determining the ultimate fate of the universe.

Dicus et al. (1983) outlined a number of the transitions which an 'open' universe would undergo in this purely mechanistic, materialist view of universal dissolution. The cosmos runs down over endless time into increasing states of disorder or entropy. Firstly, within 10^{14} years after the big bang, the stars run out of fuel for nuclear fusion, having converted their hydrogen and helium into carbon and heavier elements until the 'iron limit' is reached. Our sun is estimated to live another 10 billion years and the last stars are estimated to stop shining when the universe is about 10,000 times its current age. Secondly, stars lose their planets through encounters with other stars in 10^{17} years. Thirdly, stellar encounters transfer kinetic energy between stars, leading some stars to be more closely bound to the galactic core, while others are ejected out of the galaxy—a phenomena referred to as 'galactic evaporation.' The galaxies gradually collapse then into super dense black holes—after about 10^{18} years.

The next two stages involve the postulated 'proton decay.' Those stars which escape from galactic collapse by evaporation will be warmed by the decay of protons, which will prolong their life. The decay of protons in intergalactic gas clouds will tend to thin out the gas while creating positrons, which may be annihilated in collisions with electrons. These developments are played out by the time the universe is 10^{32} years old. At this point, the universe is composed of a rarefied positron-electron gas, photons and neutrinos, and continually losing energy as the universe expands and super massive black holes are formed.

The last stage outlined by Dicus is the decay of the black holes: a quantum mechanical effect due to the uncertainty principle as postulated by S. Hawking. Thus, particles in black holes *'tunnel through the energy barrier'* to escape the region of the black holes as Hawking's Radiation. In this scenario, *"all black holes must eventually disappear, or evaporate"* within 10^{100} years. After this, the universe continues to expand as photons lose more energy, and the positrons and electrons are increasingly thinned out.

This whole scenario of the open universe brings to mind the lines from poet T. S. Elliot: *"This is the way the world ends. This is the way the world ends. Not with a bang but a whimper."* The open universe fizzles out over eons of time, tending always to increased entropy or disorder whereby all life is extinguished.

In the 'closed' universe scenario, the universe reaches a critical point when the expansion turns over to contraction. The wavelengths of the photons begin to contract and their energies increase. For this reason, the universe runs hotter as it contracts. As the photons gain energy, they will heat up the dead stars, causing them to burn rapidly, explode or evaporate. Denser and denser black holes form in areas of gravitational collapse. As the density of matter increases, the black holes become larger and larger, coalescing with other black holes. The black holes approach states of infinite density creating the dreaded singularities predicted by the general theory of relativity. Eventually, the "big crunch" scenario suggests that: *"All the black holes finally coalesce into one large black hole that is coextensive with the Universe."* (Dicus, 1983, p. 99)

A last scenario is that of an 'oscillating' or 'rebounding' universe. In this case, it is suggested that some 'unknown mechanism' might cause the universe to "bounce" back again, before or after the singularity is reached, and to begin another cycle of expansion and contraction. Some models of the oscillating universe suggest that the extra energy gained by the photons through the contraction might be conserved through the bounce, such that with each successive cycle, the universe would be larger than in the previously cycle.

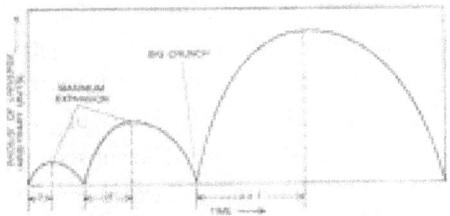

Scientific American, 1983

Blavatsky had a similar concept of oscillating universes, occurring through seven 'rounds' of existence, each with seven sub-rounds, seven races and seven root races, through the seven Days of Brahma.

In a recent *Scientific American* article, Conselice (2007) provides a modern estimate of the "dark matter" in the universe—as making *"up 85% of all matter."* Twenty years after Dicus (1983), scientists are still unable to specify the nature of the dark matter estimated to constitute 85% of the gravitational mass of the universe. The dark matter is missing both in terms of deciding the fate of the universe as concerns its expansion or contraction, and as required to bind the galaxies and galactic clusters together.

From the perspective of *The Secret Doctrine*, the enigmas of 'dark matter' arise because of scientists' misconceptions about the nature of gravity and galactic evolution. Further, scientists fail to conceive that such cosmic entities as galaxies might themselves have 'zero point centres' and that the influences of these dynamic centres are propagated through the complex seven fold ethers throughout the Space of a Cosmos. Blavatsky explains that there is a correlation of all forces within the Aether of Space—the plenum—and that gravity is result of electromagnetic fluxes within the underlying Ocean of Life. In such a case, there is no such missing 'dark matter' required to hold everything together—at least, not of the kind that scientists conceive with their mistaken materialist view of the nature of gravity. Unfortunately, two wrongs do not make a right and so a mistaken concept of gravity paired with a mistaken search for dark matter, does not solve the enigmas posed by astronomical observations. Scientists have yet to consider how a living Cosmos and cosmic bodies are not simply *"gravitationally bound objects,"* but rather are entities with dynamic zero point LIFE centres at the heart of their being. The influences of these dynamic centres permeate the sevenfold ethers of the space of any Cosmos, informing and sustaining the whole, and holding it all together.[8]

In the twenty first century, investigation into the fate of the universe has begun to undergo another radical shift. New evidence suggests that the universe's rate of expansion is actually increasing—for which there is no explanation in terms of the earlier 'standard model' based the force of gravity and the presence of matter, visible or dark, within the universe. Scientists now postulate a form of 'dark energy' hypothesized to be hurrying the expansion of the universe and also influencing the shape and spacing of galaxies. In the newest scenario, the vast majority of the universe is still hidden from us.

---

8   However, at the same time, the term 'dark matter' is not necessarily inconsistent with how we might try to understand *The Secret Doctrine* and it implications for the interpretation of scientific data and theories. However, it must be understood that from the perspective of the S.D., there is nothing which is purely 'material' as such, just as there is no 'gravity' as it is historically understood.

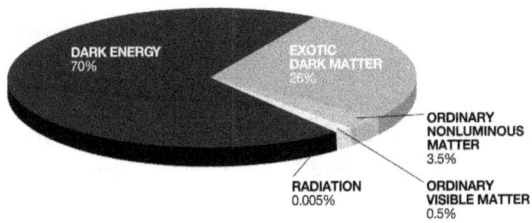

This proposed 'dark energy' is a revitalized version of Einstein's rejected 'cosmological constant' (Conselice, *Scientific American*, February 2007). It acts to stretch the very fabric of space. Dark energy is described as evenly distributed through the universe and its density is estimated at *"about 10^{-26} kilogram per cubic meter, equivalent to a handful of hydrogen atoms."* (Conselice, p. 35) The amount of such 'dark energy' in the solar system is roughly equivalent to the mass of a small asteroid. However, such a small amount of such dark energy within the expanses of the universe acts to increase its expansion rate and to play a role in shaping other galactic structures. Ostriker and Steinhardt (2001) described this dark energy as *"a nearly uniform haze that permeates space."*

This dark energy has also been labelled as the *"quintessence"*—in reference to the ancient Greek philosophy suggesting the existence of such 'a fifth element.' This is described also as a *"dynamic quantum field, not unlike an electric and magnetic field, that gravitationally repels."* (p. 47) The force of this dark energy is a form of anti-gravity possessing an unusual property of "negative pressure." Einstein's had postulated a version of this energy, the 'cosmological constant,' to exist within space even in the absence of matter or radiation and to oppose the force of gravity.[9]

In regards to the fate of the universe, Krauss (1999) explains that the former issue of whether or not there was enough mass and energy in the universe to close it, has been superseded by consideration of the dark energy or the "quintessence." Because the cosmological constant represents a fixed density of dark energy in space, in the long run, matter cannot compete in terms of slowing

---

9   The dark energy, or negative pressure, is associated with the quantum vacuum. However, a major problem is that physicists' calculations of the vacuum energy are *"120 orders of magnitude larger than the dark energy that cosmologists are postulating."* (Cowan, 2001) Such an enormous vacuum density would cause an exponential expansion of the universe and rip apart the electrostatic and nuclear bonds holding atoms and molecules together. Scientists have a hard time 'exorcising' such infinities from the equations of science to reach the 'finite results' observed within the world.

universal expansion—as any doubling in the universe's radius dilutes its density eightfold.

> In an expanding universe the energy density associated with a cosmological constant must win out. If the constant has a positive value, it generates a long—range repulsive force in space, and the universe will continue to expand even if the total energy density in matter and in space exceeds the critical value. ... Even this new prediction for eternal expansion assumes that the constant is indeed constant.... If in fact the energy density of empty space does vary with time, the fate of the universe will depend on how it does so. And there may be a precedent for such changes—namely, the inflationary expansion in the primordial universe, one that may eventually come to an end.

In the following diagram, the predictions for the universe based on the 'cosmological constant' or 'pure matter' both lead to an ever expanding universe; while the quintessence model allows for the possibility for the eventual contraction of the Universe (the line that branches on the chart). Krauss suggests that if there is some mechanism involving a shift in *"the energy density of empty space,"* then it is still conceivable that the universe might eventually contract again.

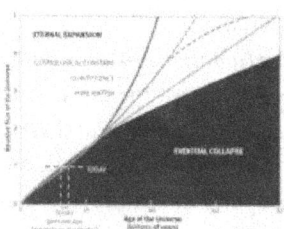

Source: *Scientific American,* Jan. 2001, Ostriker & Steinhardts, *The Quintessential Universe.*

The materialist science philosophy leads only to solar, cosmic and individual death and dissolution. Conselice (2007) provides this view of the eventual fate of the universe according to so-called 'exact science:'

> Some models predict that if dark energy becomes ever more dominant over time, it will rip apart gravitationally bound objects, such as galaxy clusters and galaxies. Ultimately, planet Earth will be stripped from the sun and shredded, along with all objects on it. Even atoms will be destroyed. Dark energy, once cast in the shadows of matter, will have exacted its final revenge. (p. 41)

This is the way the world ends, not with a bang but with a whimper. Everything eventually dies out and there is no life principle which could hold it all together. This purely materialist view of creation is what Blavatsky described as a *"Frankenstein monster,"* bound to lead to endless perplexities and enigmas concerning the ethers of Space and the nature of life.

In the terms of *The Secret Doctrine*, whereas the inflation or expansion of the universe involved the *Breath of the Father*, it would be the *Breath of the Mother*, a similar but complimentary process, which brings about a phase of universal contraction. What such a 'Breath of the Mother' entails, in terms of science, cannot be understood as simply involving the presence of 'dark matter' and the force of 'gravity.' Instead, it involves a 'modification' of the Ceaseless Breath and the sevenfold electromagnetic fluxes propagated through the ethers of space. Newer ideas in modern physics—on Superstring theory and M-theory, models of higher spatial dimensions and the holographic principle—actually suggest alternative perspectives on the issue of the fate of the universe that are more consistent with Blavatsky's archaic teachings.

Scientists struggle to find the dark matter and dark energy required to prop up their theoretical house of cards, based upon a fanciful notion of 'gravity' as the primary force of cosmic organization. The Frankenstein monster of science cosmology treats the whole of life as simply a 'material' thing—and excludes the possibilities of metaphysical dimensions and forces. Cosmoses are not considered to have any inner LIFE centres—the means by which the Gods and invisible powers 'clothe themselves in bodies.' Perhaps the fates of Cosmoses depends upon the existence of such zero point laya centres at the hearts of beings—Suns, Galaxies and the Universe, and somehow the magic of such dimensions serve to hold it all together through the ethers of space and the sevenfold modifications of the fundamental Divine Electro-Magnetic Life of the Ceaseless Breath.

To understand Blavatsky's teachings and their relationship to modern concepts is no simple task but study of *The Secret Doctrine* certainly enables us to ask alternative questions and offer alternative interpretations of the facts and theories of science itself. It is remarkable that Blavatsky's teachings have anticipated the essential issues and enigmas in contemporary cosmology and physics, while providing a metaphysical theoretical framework which radically reconstructs our understanding of the origins, nature and ends of the cosmos.

God, Science & The Secret Doctrine

2g. The Multiverse, Hyperspace & the Big Foam

Throughout the history of science, humankind has repeatedly been displaced from the centre of the universe. The Copernican revolution dispelled the illusion that the earth was at the centre and instead suggested that it and the other planets of the solar system revolved around the sun. Later scientific advance proved that the sun is not the centre of the universe with the stars fixed in the heavens around it. Instead, the sun is simply one of billions of stars in the Milky Way galaxy, itself one of billions of galaxies in the universe. In the outer world, the earth has no privileged position within the cosmic order but is like a grain of sand on a beach or a drop of water within an immense cosmic ocean.

New creation scenarios are again usurping human egocentrism. Whereas we might have considered ours to be the only universe, now it is apparent that there might be innumerable universes throughout the Eternities of the Infinite. In modern speculative physics and cosmology, theorists postulate varied possibilities for both 'multiverses' and 'parallel universes.' The new physics of nothingness suggest that space could indeed be full of various other worlds.

According to *Wikipedia*:

> A multiverse (or meta-universe) is the hypothetical set of multiple possible universes (including our universe) that together comprise all of physical reality. The different universes within a multiverse are called parallel universes. The structure of the multiverse, the nature of each universe within it and the relationship between the various constituent universes, depend on the specific multiverse hypothesis considered. Multiverses have been hypothesized in cosmology, physics, philosophy, theology, and fiction, particularly in science fiction and fantasy.... In these contexts, parallel universes are also called "alternate universes," "quantum universes," "parallel worlds," or "alternate realities." The possibility of many universes raises various scientific, philosophical, and theological questions.

On an ultramicroscopic scale, at Planckian levels and beyond, the vacuum is described as having foam like structure due to its continual random fluctuations. The vacuum is never still at zero point levels—like the Ceaseless Breath. This big quantum space/time foam is a form of hyperspace (or 'parent space') when considered in relationship to four dimensional spacetime universes which emerge out of the root principles. When creation occurs, a universe emerges from a singularity condition, inflates like a bubble or the 'dropping of a world egg,' and continues on cycles of expansion and contraction. The pattern of creation from point source and the inflation to a seed condition might be repeated through various levels of higher dimensional space, as bubbles appear within bubbles, within bubbles, as illustrated above.

Physicist Michio Kaku in *Astronomy* magazine, (May, 1996) compares the seething quantum vacuum to boiling water and presents this image of the Multiverse:

> The simplest analogy is boiling water, which is a quantum effect. Tiny bubbles constantly form in the water and then expand very rapidly. If we treat the universe like a bubble, then we see that our universe coexists with a sea of other bubbles. Our universe, then, may be nothing but a quantum bubble, the result of a quantum fluctuation in an infinite ocean frothing with universes. In this infinite ocean, called the multiverse, the vacuum is continually spawning new universes. In this picture, big bangs constantly take place, each representing a quantum fluctuation in the vacuum. (p. 34)

Wikepedia provides another basic description of the multiverse:

> The formation of our universe from a "bubble" of a multiverse was proposed by Andre Linde and fits well with the widely accepted theory of cosmic inflation. ... The bubble universe concept involves creation of universes from the quantum foam of a "parent universe." On very small scales, the foam is frothing due to energy fluctuations. These fluctuations may create tiny bubbles and wormholes. If the energy fluctuation is not very large, a tiny bubble universe may form, experience some expansion like an inflating balloon, and then contract and disappear from existence. However, if the energy fluctuation is greater than a particular critical value, a tiny bubble universe forms from the parent universe, experiences long-term expansion, and allows matter and large-scale galactic structures to form. (2007)

The authors use the term "parent universe" in a manner quite analogous to Blavatsky's description of the Eternal Parent Space.

The concept of a multiverse has been proposed to explain why our universe is so fine-tuned for conscious life as we experience it. If there were a large number (possibly infinite) of different universes, some of these would possess the physical laws (and fundamental constants) suitable for stars, planets and life to arise and exist. The *anthropic principle* is applied within science to conclude that we could only consciously exist in those universes which were finely-tuned for our conscious existence. The probability might be extremely small that there is life in most of the multiverses, where variations of the fundamental constants of nature may have led to the quick dissolution of emerging cosmoses. Scientists regard humankind as thus fortunate indeed to be in a such a verse of the multiverse, which happened by fortuitous circumstance, to have the right conditions for the random processes of creation and evolution.

In 1888, Madame Blavatsky described possibilities comparable to the modern concepts of such a Multiverse. A central tenet of *The Secret Doctrine* affirmed:

> "The Eternity of the Universe in toto as a boundless plane; periodically "the playground of numberless Universes incessantly manifesting and disappearing," called "the manifesting stars," and the "sparks of Eternity." "The Eternity of the Pilgrim" is like a wink of the Eye of Self-Existence. The appearance and disappearance of Worlds is like a regular tidal ebb of flux and reflux." (pp. 16-17)

Blavatsky described such an *"Eternity of the Universe"* giving rise to innumerable *"Sons,"* manifested cosmoses, or such *"Winks in the Eye of Self-Existence."* The whole of the present Universe is but one of the *"numberless Universes."*[10]

The concept of 'parallel universes' is also explored by theoretical physicists from varied backgrounds—in quantum theory, string theory and M theory. Quantum approaches to parallel worlds include Hugh Everett's many-worlds interpretation (MWI) of quantum theory, Richard Feynman's multiple histories interpretation and H. Dieter Zeh's many-minds interpretation. These approaches are characterized in *Wikepedia*:

> In most formulations, all the constituent universes are structurally identical to each other and though they have the same physical laws and values for the fundamental constants, they may exist in different states. The constituent universes are furthermore non-communicating, in the sense that no information can pass between them. The state of the entire multiverse is related to the states of the constituent universes by quantum superposition, and is described by a single universal wavefunction.

All of these proposals suggest that Space is full of the possible states of quanta and might be bifurcating into different parallel worlds at every moment.

In string theory, it has been proposed that different universes might exist for each of the large ensembles of solutions generated within 11 dimensional string theory. In the more recent M-theory, universes are viewed as possibly cre-

---

10 The earliest known records describing a multiverse are found in ancient Hindu cosmology, in texts such as the Puranas. They expressed the idea of an infinite number of universes, each with its own gods, inhabitants and planets, and an infinite cycle of births, deaths and rebirths of a universe, with each cycle lasting 8.4 billion years. The belief is that the number of universes is infinite. (Wikepedia).

ated by "collisions between membranes in an 11-dimensional space." Unlike the universes in the "quantum multiverse," the multiverses of string theory and M theory can even have different laws of physics. In general, the notion of parallel universes arises out of the concept of the infinite variability within Space, such that it is capable of supporting all these simultaneous interpenetrating worlds within worlds—as suggested by the phrase 'quantum superposition.'

In *Wikepedia*, the editors summarize the primary objections to modern views of multiverses and parallel universes, noting:

> Critics claim that these theories lack empirical correlation and testability, and without hard physical evidence are unfalsifiable; outside the methodology of scientific investigation to confirm or disprove; and therefore more mathematically theoretical and metaphysical than scientific in nature.

Views of parallel worlds and multiverses arise out of theoretical mathematics and speculations based on the study of the peculiar quantum vacuum. However, for the critics to argue that such theories are *"more 'metaphysical' than scientific,"* illustrates the simplistic dualism of sceptical pseudo-science and it generates a confusion of tongues. To be 'metaphysical' is posed as being contrary to being 'scientific'—a false duality. There can be a metaphysical approach to science or a scientific approach to metaphysics. In fact, according to Blavatsky, any physics taken far enough will lead to metaphysics, exactly because such indeed does exist. In fact, this is illustrated by the newest models of physics which we will be exploring within the next chapters, where the old physics of matter and energy within time and space is now regarded as the outward manifestation of a higher seven dimensional physics! Modern physics itself has led to such a higher dimensional metaphysics, just as Madame Blavatsky predicted and described.

Another depiction of 'parallel worlds' is provided by Blavatsky's description of Space. Recall portions of this description of Blavatsky's 'holographic Space.'

> "... The Secret Doctrine ... teaches that ... millions of things and beings are, in point of localization, around and *in* us, as we are around, with, and in them; it is not metaphysical figure of speech, but a sober fact in Nature, however incomprehensible to our senses. ... "*other worlds*" ... are ... blended with our world—interpenetrating it and interpenetrated by it. ... Nevertheless, such invisible worlds do exist. Inhabited as thickly as our own is, they are scattered throughout apparent Space in immense number; some far more material than our own world, others gradually etherealizing until they become formless and are as "Breaths." That our physical eye does not see them, is no reason to disbelieve in them; physicists can see neither their ether,

atoms, nor "modes of motion," or Forces. Yet they accept and teach them." (S. D. I, pp 604-6)

This suggests the existence of multiple worlds, planes of existence, beings and locations, all superimposed within the same space as our own—although invisible to us. Such bizarre and profound claims are beginning to be more intelligible given the speculative theories of the modern scientists—exploring the infinite variability of Space, multiverses and parallel worlds! There are various Multiverse and parallel universe scenarios offered within modern science, although it is little known how this might all relate to our human existence. In fact, *The Secret Doctrine* provides many clues perhaps as to how we might understand such invisible worlds interpenetrating our own, in such superimposed patterns within our very own Space.

3. Zero Point Fields

Quantum physics predicts the existence of an underlying sea of zero-point energy at every point in the universe ... referred to as the electromagnetic quantum vacuum since it is the lowest state of otherwise empty space. This energy is so enormous that most physicists believe that even though zero-point energy seems to be an inescapable consequence of elementary quantum theory, it cannot be physically real, and so is subtracted away in calculations. From this perspective, the ordinary world of matter and energy is like a foam atop the quantum vacuum sea. (www.calphysics.org)

The emerging *new physics* offers profound revisions of the basic concepts in science concerning the nature of space, the quantum vacuum, the zero point fields, the nature of mass and gravity. Of course, most scientists researching such possibilities would dismiss the idea that there is anything mystical about such subjects or that their studies of the *new physics* have anything to do with the study of consciousness, life and the nature of Self. However, the newest concepts in physics concerning the zero point fields illustrate and substantiate the ancient wisdom teachings about the nature of the underlying realm of Space.

The zero point field is a ground state field of energy, which constantly interacts with all subatomic matters. It is called the zero point field because fluctuations in the field are evident even at a temperature of absolute zero, when all matter has been removed. Fluctuations of the zero point field drive the motion of subatomic particles. It may be likened to the Ceaseless Eternal Breath within the Eternal Parent Space (or as an underlying *holomovement* within the ether of the quantum vacuum in Dr. David Bohm's theory of wholeness and the implicate order.)

Particles continually interact with the underlying zero point field and these interactions are mediated by *virtual particles*. Virtual particles appear out of quantum vacuum, combining and annihilating each other in the briefest instances of time (approximately 10^{-23} seconds depending upon the mass of the particles). All matter is supported and sustained by activity from within the underlying zero point field. The zero point field is a repository of numerous fields and ground energy states for the different forces in nature and all the virtual particles which mediate these forces. Thus, the zero point field is a *plenum*—defined by McTaggart (2002) as *"a background substructure filled with things."* (p. 22)

The dynamics of the zero point fields are now regarded as providing answers to many of the most intriguing enigmas of modern physics—such as the uncertainty principle, the wave/particle duality and the manner in which infinities continually pop up in the mathematics of quantum theory. All of the fluctuations and motions of particles involve dynamics within the zero point field, which is itself composed of diverse subfields.

The idea of the zero point field is derived from one of quantum physics' central tenets: Heisenberg's "uncertainty principle." The uncertainty principle states that certain pairs of measurement, such as the position and momentum of a particle, cannot both be known exactly at the same instant of time. There is instead an *"intrinsic quantum fuzziness in the very nature of energy and matter."* If we attempt to precisely define the position of the particle, then uncertainty about its momentum becomes infinite; and if we attempt to exactly define its energy, then uncertainty about its position becomes infinite. *"Even at absolute zero temperature, a particle must still be jittering about: if it were at a complete standstill, its momentum and positions would both be known precisely and simultaneously, violating the uncertainty principle."* (1997, p. 83)

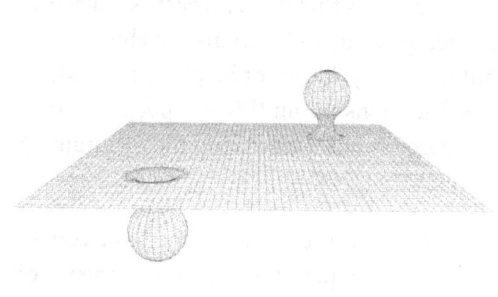

Electromagnetic radiation may be pictured as waves flowing through space at the speed of light. These waves carry energy and have specific directions, frequencies and polarizations. These states are referred to as the various *'propagating modes of the electromagnetic field.'* Since each of these modes is subject to the uncertainty principle, it must have a certain minimum energy (given by the formula hf/2). Although the modes carry minuscule amounts of energy, the number of modes is enormous. The product of the energy per mode and the huge number of modes yields a very high theoretical level of energy latent within every cubic centimeter of space. From this line of reasoning, quantum physics predicts that all of space must be filled with electromagnetic zero-point fluctuations (also called the zero-point field) creating a universal sea of zero-point energy. www.calphysics.org.

The Cal Tech group suggests that since space breaks down into a quantum foam at the tiny distance specified by the Planck scale (of 10^{-33} centimeters), the zero point fluctuations might cease at the related Planck frequency of 10^{43} Hertz. In this case, *"the zero-point energy density would be 110 orders of magnitude greater than the radiant energy at the center of the Sun."* www.calphysics.org.

The existence of the zero-point field has long lurked in the background of modern science and quantum theory in particular. Historically, scientists have dealt with the enigmas posed by the mathematics of quantum theory by a process of the "re-normalization" of quantum field equations. Thus, when the mathematics of quantum theory leads to infinite values, theorists eliminate the infinities through the "re-normalization" of quantum field theories. In this way, positive infinities are used to cancel out negative infinities yielding a sum of zero and other mathematical practices are used to leave a finite residue. In a *Scientific American* article, the infinities were described as being *"exorcized"* from nature through the tricks of re-normalization.

Nevertheless, to think of a vacuum as simply empty space is no longer valid. If all matter and radiation were extracted from a volume of space, this space is still permeated by the zero-point field with its ceaseless electromagnetic fluctuations. B. Haisch explains: *"if you add up all these ceaseless fluctuations, what you get is a background sea of light whose total energy is enormous: the zero-point field. The "zero-point" refers to the fact that even though this energy is huge, it is the lowest possible energy state. All other energy is over and above the zero-point state."* (www.science-spirit.org)

The universe exists within this vast sea of underlying light and electromagnetic activity—what Blavatsky described as the electric ocean of life. However, because this zero point energy permeates everything and is the lowest possible energy state, it is invisible and unobservable to us. It is completely uniform and pervades us from every direction. The world of light which we do see is over and above the zero-point field. Just how deep is this underlying quantum sea of light? McTaggart reports: *"It has been calculated that the total energy of the Zero Point Field exceeds all energy in matter by a factor of 10^{40}, or 1 followed by 40 zeros."* (2002)

In another *Scientific American* article (1997), P. Yam explores the controversial idea of extracting energy from the underlying zero-point field. The article *Exploiting the zero-point energy* has the caption: *"Energy fills empty space, but is there a lot to be tapped, as some propound? Probably not?"* The article notes that exactly how much zero point energy is within the vacuum is "unknown" and that the conventional view has been that there is very little. However, there is a core of researchers who *"think that the 21st century could be the zero-point energy age."* The implications of being able to tap the zero point fields would be utterly profound—in terms of alternate energy sources and possible means for space travel.[11] Of course, researchers in the zero point camp are criticized by more orthodox theorists for such speculative claims—pointing to the lack of scientific data and the absence of working prototypes or devices which tap this zero point energy.

The zero-point theory is also used to explain the concepts of mass and inertia in a novel way and to question the traditional understanding of the nature of gravity. In reference to inertia, which refers to a material object's resistance

---

11   One suggestion is that the zero point energy might act as a "negative mass" system for the propulsion of spacecraft; or that the Casimir effect might be used to create pressure differentials within the zero point fields.

to acceleration, the novel idea is that inertia is due to the *"drag effects of moving through the zero-point field."* Matter resists acceleration as it interacts with its surrounding fields of virtual particles. In this case, a zero point "wake" is left behind as an object moves through space, with virtual particles continuously popping in and out of existence, and moving in relation to the material particles. Both inertia and gravity could be due then to the interaction between the electromagnetic quantum vacuum and the fundamental charged particles (quarks and electrons) that compose matter.

In the case of gravity, an object fixed above the earth would experience the *"electromagnetic momentum flux"* created by the earth within the zero point field and this gives rise to its weight and acceleration towards the earth. Gravitational effects are thus produced by "asymmetry" within the electromagnetic zero point fields within the quantum vacuum. One futuristic idea is that the advanced forms of propulsion for space travel could involve modifying the electromagnetic quantum vacuum and/or its interaction with matter to nullify inertial and gravitational forces (Www.calphysics.org). The search for such mysteries of zero point energies and fields has long been explored as explanations for UFO propulsion, anti-gravity devices and spacecraft. [12]

McTaggart (2002) points out that since all subatomic matter is continually interacting with the zero point fields, this creates a record of everything that happens. She describes the Zero Point Field as *"a kind of shadow of the universe for all time, a mirror image and record of everything that ever was. In a sense, the vacuum is the beginning and the end of everything in the universe."* (p. 26) The zero point fields embody information about the whole—the Akashic record of Blavatsky and mystical sources.

Certainly, the newest concepts of zero point fields are quite startling. Space itself has a depth and is a plenum. The vast energies and information latent within the zero point fields permeate all of matter, sustaining the phenomena of the created world. Contemporary physics, far from arriving at "the end of science"—as some writers have speculated (c.f., John Horgan)—is encountering even stranger and more fantastic possibilities. B. Haisch and A. Rueda of the CalTech physics group comment: *"... we dare to predict that physics and astrophysics of the 21st century are going to love the quantum vacuum."* (2003)

The zero-point field concepts provide the basis for a new approach to the traditional idea of the "ether," although most scientists shy away from using the term ether because this was supposedly discredited when nineteenth century researchers were unable to demonstrate an "ether drift." However, space itself, at the level of the quantum vacuum, is a pleroma of energies, virtual particles, and information, which provides a medium for physical manifestation. Electromagnetic

---

12 Nick Cook, a journalist, explores the classified world of the aerospace industry and documents the secretive work carried out over the past fifty years in his book, The Hunt for Zero Point (2001).

fluxes within the underlying electromagnetic ocean could indeed constitute such 'ether drifts,' and even be responsible for gravitational effects. Physicist P. Davies comments: *"So clearly the quantum vacuum resembles the ether,"* which he refers to as the *"quantum ether."* (2001, p. 33)

H.P. Blavatsky describes exactly such an idea that Space itself—not the created space-time complex but the underlying "Eternal Parent Space" with its "Ceaseless Breath" or movement—is the foundation for all physical manifestation. Space is the Aether wherein there is a correlation of all forces and an Omniscience which thrills throughout every finite point of the universe. The zero point fields are latent within the Aether—the invisible foundation for physical manifestation.

4. The Mysteries of Matter

4a. Unifying the Laws of Nature into one God-Like Superforce

Scientists seek to establish unifying principles which explain the diverse phenomena of nature as being produced by the same underlying forces. Nowhere has this venture been as successful as in the area of physics. Physicists now regard the phenomena of life to be derived from four primary physical laws and *the holy grail* of physics is the task of unifying these four forces into one *"god-like Superforce"* —the term used by physicist Paul Davies.

Until the twentieth century, scientists were only aware of phenomena related to the gravitational and electromagnetic forces. Isaac Newton initially formulated the first law of nature—gravity— in 1687. Gravity describes terrestrial and celestial movement in terms of same principles and mathematical equations. The force of gravity is illustrated by the falling of an apple from a tree and by the movement of the planets and sun within the solar system. Gravity involves the mutual attraction of matter and its strength is reduced proportionately by distance. At the turn of the century, the brilliant physicist James C. Maxwell demonstrated that the phenomenon of electricity and magnetism were related and could be explained in terms of one underlying force—the electromagnetic force, which he described in terms of a set of differential equations. The electromagnetic force is responsible for such diverse phenomena as light radiating from a candle, the turning of a compass needle and why we bump into walls because of their and our electromagnetic structures.

In the last century, two additional quantum forces—the strong and weak forces—were discovered with the development of subatomic physics. The strong force binds protons and neutrons within atomic nuclei, and the three quarks within protons and neutrons. The weak force involves radioactivity and the spontaneous decay or transformation of particles. The weak force is particularly important in terms of the physics of the Sun. The range of influence of the strong and weak forces are approximately 10^{-13} centimeters and 10^{-15} centimeters respectfully. In contrast, the electromagnetic and gravitational forces are described as having infinite ranges.

The Four Fundamental Forces

Force	Strength (relative to the strong force)	Range
Strong Force	1	10^{-13} cm.
Electromagnetic	1/137	Infinite
Weak Force	10^{-5}	10^{-15} cm.
Gravity	6×10^{-39}	Infinite

The four fundamental forces have widely divergent strengths and ranges of influence and are related to very different phenomena in nature. However, all four are conceptualized in terms of 'quantum field theories,' a term reflecting the dualistic nature of quanta as point particles and as fields extended within space/time. All charged particles are supposed to radiate a field and the particles interact with the sum of all the fields rather than directly with other point particles.

Scientists' quest for unification requires that the four forces be mathematically translated into one another as expressions of a single force. Modern attempts to unify the laws of physics have been successful as far as the electromagnetic, weak and strong forces are concerned. The electromagnetic force and the weak force are described in the *electro-weak unification*, whereby the two forces are mathematically intertwined through the postulation of "gauge symmetries" and gauge fields. An electro-weak-strong synthesis is then described in *Grand Unification Theory* (G.U.T.), which is again based on the postulation of symmetries existing within underlying gauge fields (and the existence of the Higgs' field).

The fundamental problem in modern unification is to develop a model of quantum gravity—thereby bringing gravity into the fold. As it happens, there is a basic incompatibility between the general theory of relativity (describing space/time curvature in geometrical terms) and quantum theories. Three of the four fundamental forces of nature—the electromagnetic, strong and weak forces—act within a space/time setting, and are successfully described in the terms of *quantum field* (or particle/wave) theories. Each force has particles or quanta (with wave and field properties) which mediate that field or are influenced by it. In contrast, the force of gravity has a special status as it is not imposed on the passive background of space and time. Instead, the gravitational field *is* the "curvature of space/time" itself. This is Einstein's revolutionary insight as articulated in the general theory of relativity. The gravitational field is within the curvature of space and time—the container of all the quanta and their interactions.[13]

---

[13] In a universe governed by quantum gravity, the curvature of space-time and its structure should be subject to quantum fluctuations—as are the three other quantum field theories. However, as DeWitt explains: "any explicitly quantum-mechanical effects of gravitation would be confined to an exceedingly small scale"—indeed to the levels of

GOD, SCIENCE & THE SECRET DOCTRINE

The aim in science is to unify gravity with the other three quantum theories to identify the ultimate *Superforce* or *Theory of Everything* (T.O.E.). If scientists are to understand the origins of the cosmos, they have to unify the laws of physics into one superforce or unified field, which would have reigned supreme for the first instant of creation. This quest to develop a quantum theory of gravity is likened by Stephen Hawking to *"knowing the mind of God."*

The quest to unify the laws of physics has led scientists back to the origin of creation when the energy levels were so high that the one "god-like superforce" reigned supreme. In the beginning, before cosmic manifestation, the universe existed in a state of *perfect symmetry* and subsequent creation processes entailed *"a hierarchy of broken symmetries,"* whereby various forces/particles were differentiated out of the One. As the universe expanded and cooled, different forces broke off from the superforce in what are described alternatively as *phase transitions, successive unfreezing,* or *spontaneous symmetry breaking*. This scheme allows scientists to describe various eras in the early universe when different symmetries are broken. Symmetry breaking serves to differentiate various classes of elementary particles and forces out of the perfect symmetry of the void/plenum of the quantum vacuum.

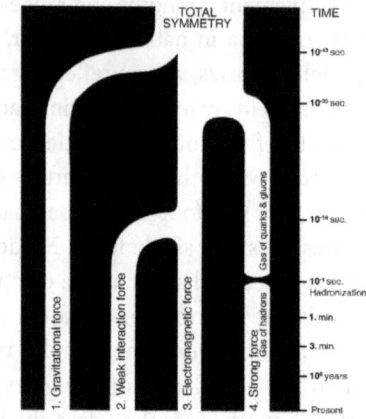

In *The Cosmic Code*, Pagels (1983a) provided a modern scientific account of the first moments of creation which illustrates these themes:

> At very high energy the distinction between the weak, electromagnetic, and strong interactions, does not exist—they are all unified and have the same strength. The interactions were all symmetrical and equal at the creation, but as the fireball expanded the temperature dropped and the exact symmetry of the interactions became spontaneously broken. With the breaking of the symmetry, the various different interactions became apparent... This symmetry breaking can be thought of as freezing out of the various interactions as the big bang explosion cooled. Our universe today is the frozen fossil of that remarkable event. (p. 275)

---

the Planck units—1.61 X 10⁻³³ centimeters, and 5.26 X 10⁻⁴⁴ seconds. The physicist cannot explore this order experimentally because it passes beyond our level of physical differentiation. DeWitt notes: "To probe these scales of distance and time experimentally, using instruments built with present technology, one would need a particle accelerator the size of the galaxy!" (Scientific American, Dec. 1983, p. 112)

The Cosmogenesis & Physics of Modern Science

The universe from its very beginning to the present may be viewed as a hierarchy of successively broken symmetries—a transition from a simple perfect symmetry at the beginning of time to the complex patterns of broken symmetries we see today. (p. 233)

Scientists maintain that at 10^{-43} seconds into creation, at Planck's time, the gravitational force was the first to be differentiated from the electro-weak-strong force. A second threshold is reached at 10^{-35} seconds when the strong force breaks off from the electro-weak force. Thirdly, at 10^{-10} seconds, the electromagnetic and weak forces differentiate, to complete the freezing out of the four fundamental forces. Subsequently, there are additional eras wherein different phase transitions give rise to successive sub-atomic and atomic processes (e.g., freezing of the quarks in the hadron era, then the lepton and photon eras, the nucleic era, the atomic era, etc.).

The study of the quantum vacuum is of primary importance within modern physics and cosmology. The existence of various kinds of vacuums states—as well as transitions between vacuum states, which occur as these abstract symmetries are broken—are now postulated. The classical vacuum was conceived of as being empty or void, as simply nothing, not even a thing in its nothingness. In contrast, modern views of the quantum vacuum suggest that it is *a plenum*, containing all particles, forces and energies in latent or virtual states. The vacuum before the inflationary period of creation is described as a *false vacuum* relative to the more stable vacuum state dominant after inflation. In fact, all the matter and energy of the Universe might have been created as the symmetries within the false vacuum were spontaneously broken by a random quantum fluctuation, which *"dumps"* immense amounts of energy in creating the Cosmos.

Scientists provide an awesome view of cosmic creation wherein all things manifest out of nothingness—as broken symmetries emerge from a state of perfect symmetry, where all quantities were set to zero. In this scenario, everything adds up to nothing. Manifestation of the cosmos then involves a hierarchy of broken symmetries, which precipitate levels and dimensions of being out of non-being. As this happens, three generations of three families of particles are produced, at widely different energetic levels.

Largely unbeknownst to modern scientists, mystical and spiritual descriptions of creation and metaphysics have long depicted similar processes of creation—in terms of a pre-existent state of perfect symmetry in NON-BEING and a hierarchy of broken symmetries in higher dimensional Space, which precipitate levels of being out of Non-Being. Mystical Kabbalah, Vedanta and *The Secret Doctrine* of H.P. Blavatsky are primary sources for such depictions of mystical creation through a hierarchy of broken symmetries out of the perfect symmetry of nothingness: Number issues from no number, as Blavatsky explains most simply. Nevertheless, modern scientists continue the struggle to understand creation and the "god-like superforce" that ruled in the beginning.

Illustration from Scientific American, 1985

4b. Sculpting the Void
Seven Hidden Compacted Dimensions in Hyperspace

> ... the broken symmetries of a higher dimensional space yield the four big dimensions ... Perhaps the real world with its four big dimensions corresponds to the broken but stable solutions to equations describing the symmetries of a multidimensional geometry. (Pagels, 1985b)
>
> Seven hidden dimensions of the universe ... have been proposed in a theory that seeks to unify the forces of nature. ... (the seven hidden dimensions) can be pictured as a small, compact structure such as a sphere that is associated with every point in space and every moment in time. (Freedman, Nieuwenhuizen, *Scientific American*, March 1985).
>
> There is no question of, say, an atom going off round the (7 hidden) dimensions. Rather, we should think of the extra dimensions as somehow inside the atom. (Davies, 1984, p. 160)

Profound new ideas have emerged in modern physics about the hidden dimensionality of existence. Traditionally, space has been regarded as three dimensional and time is considered as a fourth dimension. Thus, relativity theory describes the curvature of the four-dimensional space-time continuum. However, in the twentieth century, physicists suggested that the four ordinary dimensions are only the *"four large dimensions,"* because we experience our lives (seemingly) living within these dimensions. Physicists now describe the laws of nature evident within the four large dimensions as dependent upon processes occurring within underlying *"hidden compacted dimensions."* As physicists seek to integrate the four forces of physics into one fundamental force, additional higher dimensions of Space had to be postulated. One of the most advanced models of such "hidden dimensions," designed to explain the four laws of physics, in the 1980s, was the eleven dimensional Kaluza-Klein supergravity theory.

In 1921, Kaluza, a German physicist, had been inspired by Einstein's general theory of relativity, which explained gravity in terms of the 'geometry' of a four dimensional curved space-time continuum. Kaluza attempted to unify the electromagnetic force with gravity by postulating another fifth dimension of space. Kaluza demonstrated that Einstein's gravitational field equations, if written in a five dimensional form, could be arranged to yield the usual four dimensional equations plus the electromagnetic equations of Maxwell. Kaluza postulated that this extra dimension existed at every point underlying the four dimensional space-time as a "compacted" dimension; a tiny circle in the fifth dimension would allow an extra degree of freedom of motion to particles. Kaluza was the first to develop a unified field theory giving a geometric explanation of both the gravitational and electromagnetic forces.

In 1926, O. Klein, a Swedish physicist, noted that Kaluza's extra dimension would go unnoticed if it were "rolled up" very small or compacted. An example used to illustrate this is that of a garden hose as seen from a distance, where any point on the line of the hose as seen from a distance is actually a small circle extended around the circumference of the hose. Similarly, Klein suggested that perhaps Kaluza's extra dimension is so small that we cannot distinguish it from a point, but which is really a small circle extended into the fifth dimension. Klein computed the circumference of this fifth dimensional loop at about 10^{-30} centimeters, approximately 10 to 100 Planckian units.

B. Greene, *The Elegant Universe*, 1999

For years, Kaluza-Klein type theories postulating additional hidden dimensions fell out of favor as an approach to unifying the laws of physics. Instead, physicists attempted to unify gravity and the other quantum field theories using the concept of *gauge fields* and hidden symmetries. Gradually, physicists realized that the symmetries associated with K.K. hidden dimensions could be used to yield purely geometric interpretations of the Yang-Mills fields with their gauge symmetries. Pagels explained:

> ...the extra freedom of movement of a particle around a little circle in the fifth dimension, associated with a little circle symmetry at each point in space-time could be interpreted as the simply gauge symmetry of the electromagnetic field. This interpretation is not so surprising to us from a modern viewpoint if we realize that a symmetry (like the little-circle symmetry) automatically implies the existence of a gauge field. (1985, p. 312)

K.K. theory re-emerged when it was realized that it was compatible with approaches to unification based on the concepts of symmetry and gauge fields.

However, contemporary physicists want not only to unify gravity and the electromagnetic force but also to include the strong and weak forces. These additional forces require additional symmetries and gauge fields, or additional hidden dimensions. Thus, the new gauge theories came to be reformulated in terms of Kaluza-Klein theories with the addition of extra microscopic hidden dimensions. Pagels explains that:

> Theoretical physicists generalized the original five-dimensional theory to an arbitrary number of higher dimensions. All the higher dimensions are compact; they are curled up into a tiny multidimensional space that exists at each point of ordinary space and hence is unobservable. But the freedom of moving around these compact tiny spaces with symmetries more general that the simple symmetry of a circle corresponds exactly to the freedom of performing Yang-Mills gauge transformations. Remarkably, the local gauge symmetries are precisely the symmetries of the compact higher-dimensional space. Because of this mathematical fact, all the gauge theories of Yang-Mills fields can be interpreted purely geometrically in terms of such compact higher-dimensional spaces. (Pagels, 1985b, p. 313)

The term *Kaluza-Klein theory* is generally used to describe theories within a quantum mechanical framework which attempt to unify the fundamental forces of nature within a spacetime having more than the four large dimensions.

Paul Davies (1984) noted that the Grand Unification Theories required the existence of seven compacted dimensions:

> In the revitalized Kaluza-Klein theory, the gauge field symmetries become concrete; they are the geometric symmetries associated with the extra space dimensions. ...A simple count of the number of symmetry operations embodied in the grand unified force leads to a

theory in which there must be seven extra dimensions, making ten space dimensions in all, plus time; our theory postulates an eleven-dimensional universe. (pp. 160-1)

Paul Davies provides a valuable description of the dynamics and topology of these hidden dimensions:

> When it comes to seven dimensions the range of topologies is enormous. What shape is correct? One particularly attractive choice is the seven-dimensional analogue of the sphere, known simply as the seven-sphere. If the unseen space dimensions really do have this form it means that every point in three-dimensional space is in fact a minute seven-dimensional 'hyperball'. ... if nature had to find a closed geometrical structure that permits anything like the fundamental forces and fields that we perceive in the real world, then the seven-sphere would be the simplest choice. You couldn't get the sort of structures we see, from atoms to galaxies, out of some simpler mathematical arrangement. A sphere is a highly symmetrical shape, and a seven sphere contains many additional symmetries not found in an ordinary sphere. ... symmetry breaking is achieved by distorting the shape of the seven-dimensional structure somewhat away from exact sphericity. ... the structure of force fields depends on the geometrical symmetries of the compacted dimensions. (pp. 161-2)

Seven hidden dimensions are required to accommodate the three major quantum field theories (electromagnetism, the strong and weak forces) with their inherent symmetries and gauge fields. Geometrically broken symmetries within the seven hidden dimensions are then the 'nominal causes' of the phenomena of nature. Only gravity remained associated with the four large dimensions of space-time.

Modern physicists regard the creation of the matter and energies of the universe as resulting from "broken symmetries" within higher dimensional space. In the beginning, the quantum vacuum was in a state of *perfect symmetry* until a *random fluctuation* broke this symmetry leading to the differentiation of the forces of nature and the quantum particles, which mediate these forces. As Pagels explains in the opening quotation, *"the broken symmetries of a higher dimensional space yield the four big dimensions."* He then refers to *"the symmetries of multidimensional geometry"* as underlying *"the real world."*

Ideas concerning higher dimensional spaces, or hyperspace, have become a mainstay in the new physics. The quantum vacuum, on a very low level of differentiation at Planck's units, is a space-time foam having an inner hidden dimensional nature which scientists are seeking to grasp. Any particles or forces can be regarded as the result of broken geometric symmetries within the hyperspace of these compacted dimensions. These models of physics extend a geometric framework into understanding hyperspace dimensions.

In *Superforce: The Search for a Grand Unified Theory of Nature*, Paul Davies, provides an inspiring description of the universe as it appears in the newer models of the geometry of hidden higher dimensionality spaces:

> "All the forces of nature are revealed as nothing more than hidden geometry at work. ... There is a deep compulsion to believe in the idea that the entire universe, including all the apparently concrete matter that assails our senses, is in reality only a frolic of convoluted nothingness, that in the end the world will turn out to be a sculpture of pure emptiness, a self-organizing void. Geometry was the midwife of science (for early astronomers), and now, we have come full circle, and the forces and fields are themselves being explained in terms of geometry." (1984, p. 161-2)

Davies describes the universe as a *"sculpture of pure emptiness"* and as emerging out of a *"self-organizing void."* This is the direction in which science has moved—towards the study of the quantum vacuum and hidden dimensions. The void appears to have a dimensionality and organizing nature latent within its apparent nothingness. Creation involves the manifestation within/without of the principles latent within the hyperspace of the vacuum. Indeed *"all of physics is in the vacuum"* and the zero point fields.

When it comes to explaining why the universe might happen to be founded on such a seven dimensional hyperspace, Davies raises some interesting questions concerning the meaning of it all:

> "When numbers occur naturally in the world, it is tempting to search for meaning behind them. Sometimes they seem to be purely accidental, as with the number of planets in our solar system. Other naturally occurring numbers suggest a deeper significance. ... Is the dimensionality of spacetime merely an accident ... ? Or is it a pointer to a profound truth about the logical and mathematical structure of the physical world." (1984, p. 163)

Is there indeed some hidden seven dimensional layering within the root principles of creation—in the apparent void of hyperspace? Perhaps such patterns of existence are pre-existent in non-existence! Or perhaps this is just another random feature of the accidental universe? Scientists' search to unify the laws of physics has lead to seven hidden spatial dimensions, wherein all elements and forces are ultimately derivatives of one superparticle or superforce—a godlike superparticle, superforce or superstring.

4c. Superstrings & M-Theory as Ultimate Solutions

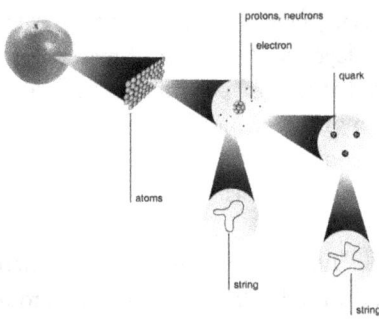

The search for a unified theory is a central activity in theoretical physics today, and just as Einstein foresaw, geometric concepts play a key role. The Kaluza-Klein idea has been resurrected and extended as a feature of string theory.... In both ... the laws of physics that we see are controlled by the shape and size of additional microscopic dimensions. (Bousso, Polchinsky, *Scientific American*, Sept. 2004)

As scientists peeled back the layers of material nature, they first developed an understanding of atoms. In the eighteenth century, John Newlands applied the 'law of the octave' to understanding the repetition of properties among the different atoms found in the first rows of the periodic table of elements. These elements appeared to fall naturally into an octave or eightfold pattern. Eventually, all of the elements composing material reality were arranged into seven rows of elements in the periodic tables, which embody different inner octaves patterns.

During the early part of the twentieth century, physicists came to understand that 'atoms' were not truly indivisible or atomic but composed of further three primary elements: protons, electrons and neutrons, embodying positive, negative and neutralizing forces. Subsequently, these elements were further divided into quarks—with protons composed of two 'up quarks' and one 'down quark,' and neutrons composed of one up quark and two down. Each has an inner triad of quarks which cannot be separated and which are bound together by their own messenger particles, *gluons*, which mediate the sub-atomic strong force.

The 11-dimensional K.K. theory regards any such quantum as the result of 'broken symmetries' in an underlying seven dimensional hyperspace. The more recent theories to be put forth as the ultimate theories concerning the nature of matter are superstring theory and its extension into M-Theory. These theories propose that point particles have extension as 'strings' and that different modes of vibration of these strings produce the varied quanta of nature. In this view, everything at the most microscopic level consists of combinations of vibrating strands or strings. The mass and force charges of the particles are due to the string's oscillatory pattern. Greene (1999) notes: *"... each particle contains a vibrating, oscillating, dancing filament what physicists... have named a string."* (p. 14) Once again, another layer of the onion of material nature is peeled away. What were once conceived of as point particles are now determined to constitute a whole inner world on a different inner order of scale. These strings exist at the level of the Planckian units and/or beyond—at many orders of magnitude greater than anything that can be measured or investigated directly with modern technology.

In string theory, the "ultimate building blocks of nature" are these small strings with diameters at the level of the Planck units—around 10^{-33} centimeters. This is inconceivably small. Each different mode of vibrations of these strings corresponds to different fundamental particles. These modes of vibration are referred to as the 'zero point vibrations' of the string.[14] Atkins (2003) provides this arresting analogy to describe these strings: *"Just think of the string as pulsing away quietly, like a human heart, each mode of its pulsing corresponding to a different particle."* (p. 197)

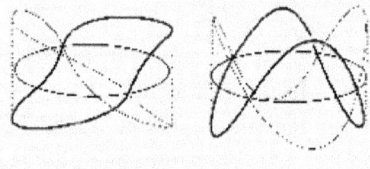

The word string implies 'elasticity' and string are both bendable and stretchable. They are also incredibly strong. Physicist L. Susskind notes:

> Indeed, despite the extreme thinness of fundamental strings, they are incredibly strong—vastly stronger than anything made of normal matter. The number of trucks that could be suspended from a fundamental string is about 10^{40}. That enormous tensile strength makes it extremely difficult to stretch a fundamental string to any appreciable length. As a result, the typically size of a fundamental string may be almost as small as the Planck length. (p. 336)

These strings can be open or closed, and can attach or not attach to various membranes-or *'branes.'* Photons are open strings, while gravitons are closed. Strings can also absorb or emit other strings. The ground states of these strings can also be energetically excited, although this takes massive energy expenditure. Susskind writes:

---

14 According to quantum theory, an 'oscillator' can never be still but always has some residual energy, referred to as its 'zero point energy.'

If you bombard a string with enough energy, it would spread out and become as big as a violently jittering, tangled ball of yarn. And there is no limit; even with more energy, the string could be excited to any size. ... black holes—even those giants at the centers of galaxies—are enormously large, tangled "monster strings." (pp. 337-8)

If point particles are replaced by vibrating strings, then this may resolve the inconsistencies between quantum theory and the general theory of relativity, and could ultimately provide that elusive 'theory of everything'—the holy grail of modern science. The string concept allows scientists to weld together an understanding of quanta with a new understanding of higher space dimensions. Although earlier versions of string theory predicted a twenty-six dimensional model of space-time and subsequently a ten dimensional model, the most advanced model posits eleven dimensions—with a seven dimensional hyperspace existing at every point underlying the four large spacetime dimensions of the everyday world. Atkins writes:

"... currently it looks as though the different theories can be united into one supertheory if the dimensionality is allowed to rise to eleven. ... string theory is all about strings vibrating in ten dimensions of space and one of time. ... In actuality, there are seven dimensions compactified in this way at each point, with the strings somehow wrapped round them, like a rubber band wrapped round a pipe. The compactified dimensions are thought to adopt a special shape at each point ... called *Calabi-Yau spaces* ... Shapes like these—in seven dimensions—are the hosepipes of string theory, for the strings wind round them and through their holes." (2003, pp. 197-9)

This image is a two-dimensional representation of a seven dimensional Calabi-Yau hyperspace! Closed strings can loop around the Calabi-Yau space many times, while not be extended at all within the ordinary directions of space.

Atkin says: *"Think of a structure like this (but in more dimensions) as attached to every point in space."* (p. 199) This illustration is then a revised version of the earlier *Scientific American* (1985) image of seven-spheres existing at each point. In a sense, we live in a 'pixilated universe,' as each Calabi-Yau space or manifold is like a pixel on a screen.

The latest version of string theory is called M-theory. The 'M' is related to 'membrane,' although Atkins suggests that it might be also in reference to *'the mother of all theories,'* or to *'matrix.'* Greene suggests that it might be related to *'mysterious.'* Regardless, M-theory describes two and other higher dimensional 'membranes' —instead of one-dimensional strings—wrapped up in these hyperspaces. It is the extra-dimensional geometry of these spaces which determines the fundamental physical properties of particles, such as the masses and charges observed within the four large dimensions of everyday experience.

The Calabi-Yau spaces or strings vibrate through all of the hidden dimensions and the manner in which these extra dimensions are twisted up and curled back upon each other determines the possible resonant vibration patterns. Hence, scientists are especially interested in exploring *"the dimensionality of the holes in these spaces... through which the stings are threaded."* (Atkins, p. 199) M-theory is trying to answer the question of why there are 'three families of particles' in nature. The answer, according to M-theory suggests that the number of particle families is related to how spacetime is compacted, all of which has to do with the higher-dimensional symmetries of the Calabi-Yau spaces and the dimensionality of their inner holes.

Calabi-Yau spaces contain a variety of *"multi-dimensional holes"* and different families of particles are a reflection of the *"number of holes in the geometrical shape comprising the extra dimensions."* (Greene, p. 217) Atkins notes, cryptically, that somehow *"the number three is emerging as possibly significant"* (p. 199), as there are three primary families of elementary particles, each of which exists at three distinct energetic levels (three generations). Perhaps the number three is inherent to the geometry of the world—as the number seven! Furthermore, if a string is wound around a compact dimension, it acquires an electrical charge. Each turn of the string gives a unit of charge, and these charges are positive or negative according to the directions of the turns. Such entities might be viewed as "a ball of electric charges," although it might appear from a four dimensional perspective, as electrically neutral.

Physicists are now exploring the extra-dimensional geometry of thousands of possible Calabi-Yau spaces—which vary according to how many of these holes they contain. Some have 3, 4, 5, 25, even 480 holes. Greene notes: *"The problem is that at present no one knows how to deduce from the equations of string theory which of the Calabi-Yau shapes constitutes the extra special dimensions."* Greene references the work of Strominger and Witten, which demonstrates that the masses of particles are dependent upon *"the way in which the boundaries of the various multidimensional holes in the Calabi-Yau space intersect and overlap with one another."* (p. 217) Since these strings vibrate through the curled up dimensions, the precise arrangements of the holes and the manner in which the Calabi-Yau shape "folds around them," have bearing upon which resonant patterns of vibration are possible.

Paul Davies described a model of 11 dimensional theory, with seven hidden compacted dimensions rolled up into elements at zero point levels. Davies explained: *"think of the extra dimensions as somehow inside the atom."* (p. 160) Remarkably, Blavatsky explained exactly such a peculiar inner dimensionality to 'atoms,' quanta, Monads and the Kosmos over a century ago. There is a complex metaphysics to reality at zero point levels. As Blavatsky explains, *"God 'geometrizes!"* and all living cosmoses differentiate from apparent point sources. (1877, I, p. 508)

Certainly, advances in modern physics as to the ultimate nature and constitution of quanta have lead to utterly awesome and inspired concepts related to what can be described as zero point dynamics and seven-skinned Eternal Parent Space of Blavatsky's Secret Doctrine. It seems that, as Blavatsky says, the Gods and other invisible bodies clothed themselves in bodies founded upon "material points without extension"—zero point laya centres. According to Blavatsky, such little 'holes dug in space' somehow form the basis for the manifestation of the laws of nature. Certainly, the Calabi-Yau spaces are such zero point structures embodying such inner multi-dimensional holes. The basic concepts of these modern theories are quite consistent with Blavatsky's description of a Kosmos as being founded upon seven such invisible points, *"holes dug in space,"* neutral laya centres, which patterns are reiterated through higher dimensions of Space. Science has certainly not rendered Blavatsky's views as incomprehensible or nonsense, but instead, it allows us to comprehend her archaic mystery teachings in a new way.

5. "The Baffling Holism" Quantum Interconnectedness & Non-Local Reality

5a. The Deterministic Paradigm of Physics

A French scientist, Pierre Laplace (1749-1827) expressed the ideal situation for the classic deterministic scientist:

> "An intelligence knowing, at any given instant of time, all forces acting in nature, as well as the momentary positions of all things of which the universe consists, would be able to comprehend the motion of the largest bodies of the world and those of the smallest atoms in one single formula, provided it were sufficiently powerful to subject all data to analysis; to it, nothing would be uncertain, both future and past would be present before its eyes."

Classical physics supported a deterministic view of creation, wherein it was believed that if we knew the laws of physics and the position and momentum of all the particles or atoms, then all future events would in principle be strictly causally determined and hence knowable. Laplace is infamous for his response to Napoleon's inquiry about the role of God in his mechanistic world, as he responded that he had no need for such 'a hypothesis.'

The ideal model of determinism was a clockwork universe of parts (particles and waves, or matter and energy) moving about and interacting within empty space and time. Atoms were pictured as discrete billiard balls imparting movement and other forces through local impacts and effects. Space itself was considered a void, a featureless nothing–a playground or backdrop for the transformations of matter and energy.

As it happens, there is something more at the heart of being than simply matter and energy within time and space. Quantum theory violated the deterministic ideal of a perfectly predictable universe by suggesting that at a quantum level, there would always remain an irreducible "uncertainty" or randomness within nature. This inherent randomness led Heisenberg to formulate the "uncertainty principle"—which Einstein rejected with the comment that he refused to believe that *"God played dice with the universe."* As a classic determinist, Einstein believed that the "uncertainty" Heisenberg was describing was not an inherent property of nature. Rather, he argued that the uncertainty reflected the failure of quantum theorists to formulate a comprehensive theoretical model of quantum processes. Einstein argued that quantum theory must be incomplete and that it was only out of ignorance that we cannot penetrate beyond a probabilistic model of quantum processes.

Einstein also believed in the objective nature of reality existing apart from and not dependent upon the existence of an observer. In contrast, quantum theory assigns the observer a fundamental role in *"collapsing the wave function"* of the particle/wave during measurement. In Einstein's view, the nature of a quantum should not depend upon whether we choose to measure one or another of its paired attributes (such as position and momentum). Surely, if we can measure either variable as we choose, then both must be defined in an objective way independently of our choice and the act of measurement. In contrast, quantum theory suggests that we can measure either variable, but then, we cannot know the other beyond the restriction imposed by the uncertainty principle. The inherent nature of the quantum world is that both attributes are not completely determined. The uncertainty principle sounded the death knoll for Laplace's deterministic view of the cosmos.

5b. The E. P. R. Paradox

Einstein argued that quantum theory must be incomplete and so he and his colleagues posed various *thought experiments* to demonstrate the illogical and seemingly impossible implications of quantum theory. The E.P.R. paradox in various forms is the most famous of these thought experiments. Einstein, Podolsky and Rosen posed the paradox in 1935 to illustrate the incompleteness of quantum theory and David Bohm and other experimental researchers later refined it. There are various editions of the EPR paradox, each of which poses enigmas concerning *'non-local effects.'*

Einstein et al. proposed the paradox by noting that quantum theory implied non-local effects existing between quanta which emerged from a singularity condition (sharing certain quantum properties). Suppose a scientist has a subatomic particle in a singlet state which then disintegrates into particles A and B. One element might fly off into the spaces of the universe while the other would be accessible to laboratory measurement. If an observer measured the position or momentum of the laboratory particle, then the position or momentum of the second particle could be determined through the equations of quantum theory. In effect, collapsing the wave function of particle A also collapses that of particle B–instantaneously. The question then arises as to how the particle traveling off into the universe could know whether it had a particular position or momentum, according to what attribute of its partner had been measured within the laboratory. Since the special theory of relativity does not allow for the transformation of information at a speed faster than the speed of light, this instantaneous collapse of the wave function of particle B should be impossible but it is predicted by quantum theory.

The thought experiment was designed to suggest that the free particle must have a specifiable position and momentum all the time, or else it would have to communicate instantaneously with the first particle in order to know what value to assume; i.e., whether it had a definite position or a definite momentum on any occasion according to the whims of the laboratory researcher. Einstein et al. were of the view that the quantum had both values and the thought experiment was to demonstrate the fallacies of the uncertainty principle–unless one accepted non-local effects and super-luminal transfer of information–which violated the principle of special relativity. However, the EPR experiment posed the possibility of elements actually having this kind of non-local quantum interrelationship, which Einstein considered impossible.

Bohr's reply to the E.P.R. paradox from the perspective of quantum theory was subtle and suggested that Einstein's argument was invalid since he assumed that the two particles could be considered as "separate." According to Bohr, both particles, like all quantum mechanical systems, are "undivided wholes"–single systems. In this case, a measurement of part of a system changes the whole system. Bohr maintained that no adequate picture of this wholeness could be obtained apart from the mathematical formalism of quantum theory and there was no room or necessity for hidden variables.

Einstein was not satisfied with Bohr's response, although it was consistent with quantum theory. Primarily, Einstein could not accept the *"baffling holism"* suggested by Bohr. Gleidman (1983) explains:

> Einstein preserved in his lonely combat against quantum theory. Increasingly he emphasized that quantum theory challenges another fundamental scientific belief about reality. It implies that you have to take virtually the whole universe into account when seeking the true causes of a physical event. Einstein said you didn't have to. ... In other words, if you believe that quantum theory is complete, you're stuck with its incredibly subversive holism. Even today the overwhelming majority of physicists don't concern themselves with the philosophical issues raised by quantum theory. Relatively few among the more philosophically inclined minority join Einstein in concluding that quantum theory is incomplete because of its baffling holism. (p. 109)

The implication of Bohr's view of quantum systems as undivided wholes is that separate quanta removed from each other in space are not independent of each other but have some non-local interrelationship. Non-local effects are part and parcel of the "subversive holism" of quantum theory, although most scientists do not address the staggering philosophical implications of this possibility.

5c. The Belief in Local Effects

The quantum field theories of the fundamental forces of nature are formulated in terms of *local effects* existing between elementary particles. In order for one particle to affect another, the interaction has to be mediated by messenger particles. Otherwise there is no *"action at a distance."* Wilkenson (1981) explains:

> "There is, among physicists, an abhorrence of "action at a distance" (or non-local effects). Crudely speaking, we have revulsion from any theory that speaks of an interaction–a force–between particle A and particle B without saying how particle A becomes aware of particle B's presence. In other words we demand (admittedly on philosophical or possibly even sentimental grounds) that interaction should depend on communication: A and B cannot know, cannot experience a mutual force, attractive or repulsive, unless they find out, via an appropriate messenger, about each other's existence. The messenger, of course, can only be some other particle which A emits and tosses across to B and vice versa." (pp. 18-19)

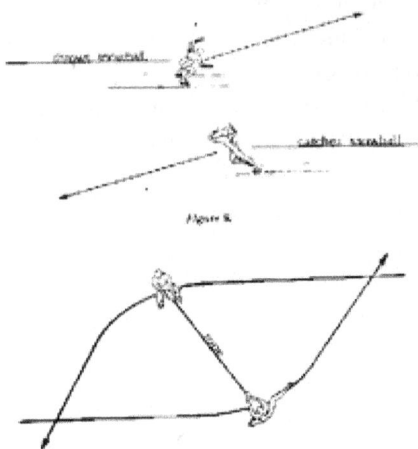

Modern physics describes the four fundamental laws of nature–electromagnetism, the strong and weak forces, and gravity–in the terms of "quantum field theories" in which the interaction of elementary quanta are mediated by "virtual particles." The messenger particles of the electromagnetic force are photons; gluons carry the strong force; and vector bosons convey the weak force. Popping out of the quantum vacuum for brief instances of time (as limited by the uncertainty principle), the virtual particles convey the influence of one quantum to another. That is, they provide the mechanism for the propagation of forces through "local effects." As noted by Wilkenson, physicists generally "abhor" action at a distance, or non-local effects, even though they are somehow inherent to quantum theory.

5d. Bell's Inequality & Non-Local Effects

Despite physicists' abhorrence of 'action at a distance,' A. Aspect (1982) and other researchers investigating *Bell's inequality* have experimentally established the existence of just such non-local effects. In 1964, physicist John Bell formulated the now famous 'Bell's inequality.' Bell was interested in the E. P. R. paradox and the fundamental questions it posed concerning the nature of reality. Bell's theorem is really quite simple. He began by assuming that reality is local and that measuring one particle could not affect its paired particle. In this case, there would be a maximum level of correlation found between the particles in an EPR type experimental arrangement. Bell thus formulated an inequality relationship, which should have held up if the locality assumption was valid. If quantum theory is correct, with its baffling holism, then the quanta would be more highly correlated than those levels specified by the inequality relationship. In actual fact, experimental tests of quantum inter-correlations were carried out and did indeed violate the inequality relationship. Thus, the assumption of locality was discovered to be incorrect. Instead, non-locality is a quantum fact.

To understand the nature of quantum interconnectedness, consider Bohr's response to the EPR paradox–which was that Einstein had erred in treating the two correlated particles *'as if'* they were separate particles, whereas quantum theory describes all quantum mechanical systems as undivided wholes. Bohr maintained that it was impossible to gain a commonsense image of this wholeness apart from the formalism of quantum theory.

In quantum theory, a quantum is represented by a wave function, *psi*. With ordinary waves, the square of wave amplitude measures the energy of the wave. However, in quantum theory, the square of the wave function at any point x is not a measure of its energy per se, but of the *mathematical probability* that a particle will be observed if a detector is located at point x. Quantum waves as such are never detected, only quantum particles, and the wave function is described as 'an empty wave.' Einstein called it a *Gespensterfeld*, or ghost field. Whenever two quanta interact, their wave functions merge. When these quanta separate, there is a separation of their wave amplitudes but not of their wave phases. The quanta become 'phase entangled.'[15]

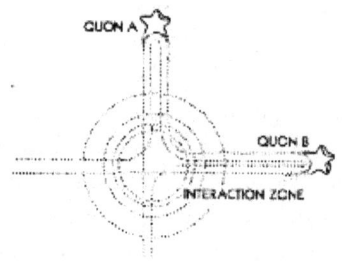

---

15 Physicist, Nick Herbert (1987) uses the term 'quon' instead of quantum in his discussions.

The Cosmogenesis & Physics of Modern Science

The reason that quantum waves become phase-entangled whereas ordinary waves do not is because quantum waves do not exist in ordinary three-dimensional space, but in what is called *configuration space*. In configuration space, each quantum is represented in three dimensions, and a two quanta system would be represented by 3+3, a 6 dimensional configuration space. In quantum theory, wave functions move around in these multidimensional configuration spaces (which are usually taken to be fictitious, *as if* they exist.)

This illustration (from Herbert) is a simplified representation of the differences between real and configuration spaces for a two quanta (or quon) system with phase entanglement. In ordinary or real space, represented on a one-dimensional string shown below, we appear to have two separate waves. In the configuration space depicted above, we have one wave in two dimensions, with waves A and B as different projections of a single waveform. The quantum proxy wave for the two quanta does not move in real space (Case II), but in configuration space (Case I). Quantum possibilities develop in a conceptual arena with more than three dimensions.

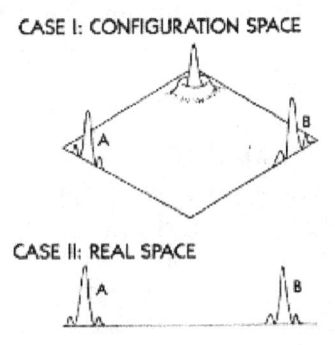

An analogy to this situation can be drawn from mystical teachings concerning higher dimensional spaces. Imagine, for instance, that we have a three-dimensional being which places its hand on a two-dimensional plane. In traveling around its plane, any two dimensional being would encounter five points (fingertips) apparently separated in both time and space from each other. In reality—in terms of the underlying higher dimensional structure—these five separate points are all aspects of one whole–a hand. The separate quanta are similarly interconnected in higher dimensional configuration spaces and only appear to be separate from a lower dimensional perspective.

The wholeness of quantum theory is suggested by the mathematical formalism which treats the configuration spaces as existent and the basis of quantum phase entanglement. Herbert (1987) explains:[16]

> A disturbing feature of phase-entangled quons (quanta), first emphasized by Erwin Schrodinger, is the strange action-at-a-distance such entangled systems seem to possess–at least on paper. Because of their phase-connectedness (or alternatively because they are represented by a *single wave* in multidimensional space) an action on quon A seems to have an instantaneous effect on the wave function of

---

16   Herbert's book *Quantum Reality: Beyond the New Physics* is highly recommended for its articulate presentation of basic quantum concepts, paradoxes and interpretations.

quon B even when the two quons are no longer capable of interacting via conventional forces. Schrodinger found this apparent instant communication so unusual that he called it not *one* but *the* chief feature of quantum theory.

However, the fact that such a tight connection between separated quons exists in the *formalism* of quantum theory is no guarantee that such connection exists *in reality*. (pp. 169-70)

When the EPR paradox was originally posed, the example used by Einstein et al. was of two momentum-correlated electrons. However, the same paradoxes can be explored using any "phase entangled quanta," and most of the research testing Bell's theorem has been done on photons with correlated polarizations. In a typical experiment, a pair of photons is produced by a light source in the state of parallel polarization, where the photons are phase entangled. Thus in (imaginary or real) configuration space, each photon's phase is dependent upon that of its counterpart even after being physically separated.

The work of A. Aspect (1982) and of other researchers has subsequently provided evidence that, in fact, quanta emerging from a singlet state (or phase entangled) are correlated to such an extent that the Bell inequality is violated–violating the locality assumption. (Shimony, 1988; d'Espagnat, 1984). This is the reason why Herbert, and other science writers maintain that, *"any complete theory of reality has to include non-local effects."* Further, this is described as quantum reality, not quantum science fiction. Despite the physicists' *"abhorrence of action at a distance,"* quantum theory, in its mathematical formalism and experimental research, establishes that any theory, which does not include non-local effects, is incomplete. Herbert notes: *"Because it's based on facts, Bell's theorem is here to stay."*

The implications of this research are obviously profound. Herbert sums up these startling quantum paradoxes:

Since there is nothing that is not ultimately a quantum system, if the quantum phase connection is 'real,' then it links *all systems that have once interacted at some time in the past*—not just twin-state photons—into a single waveform whose remotest parts are joined in a manner unmediated, unmitigated, and immediate. The mechanism for this instant connectedness is not some invisible field that stretches from one part to the next, but the fact that a bit of each part's "being" is lodged in the other. Each quon leaves some of its "phase" in the other's care, and this phase exchange connects them forever after. What phase entanglement really is we may never know, but Bell's theorem tells us that it is no limp mathematical fiction but a reality to be reckoned with. (pp. 222-3)

The Cosmogenesis & Physics of Modern Science

There are new age philosophers and science writers who do regard Bell's theorem as proof of the existence of *an invisible non-local reality*, which mystically or scientifically connects all things. One reason why all things would be so connected is that the whole Universe is a quantum system and it did indeed emerge from a singlet state–the singularity at the beginning of time. The formalism of quantum theory, Bell's inequality theory and Aspect's research all support Blavatsky's fundamental dogma of occultism, concerning the *undivided wholeness and Unity* within life. Blavatsky wrote: *"There is one indivisible and absolute Omniscience and Intelligence in the Universe, and this thrills throughout every atom and infinitesimal point of the whole finite Kosmos."* According to quantum theory, there is at least such an information field embodying the whole, entangling everything-everywhere, existing within multidimensional configuration space.

In 1989, Hollywood star and adventurer, Shirley MacLaine published *Going Within: A guide to personal transformation*, which work introduced some basic mystical ideas to the public and the New Age movement. MacLaine's books touched upon such diverse topics as reincarnation, out-of-body and extra-sensory experiences, body fields, patterns of synchronicity and even extra-terrestrials. All of these phenomena suggest that somehow human beings have a much deeper nature than they commonly understand. Somehow we are 'entangled' with the world and psychical and spiritual possibilities arise out of this entanglement. MacLaine summarizes eloquently what she labels as the *"New Age subatomic discoveries:"*

> Basic to New Age subatomic discoveries is the concept that in the subatomic world—the stuff of the universe—everything, every last thing, is linked. The universe is a gigantic multidimensional web of influences, or information, light particles, energy patterns, and electromagnetic "fields of reality." Everything it is, everything we are, everything we do, is linked to everything else. There is no separateness.

> This understanding brings us to the most controversial concept of the New Age philosophy: the belief that God lies within, and therefore *we* are each part of God. Since there is no separateness, we are each Godlike, and God is in each of us. We experience God and God experiences through us. We are literally made up of God energy.... (p. 100)

If we take seriously the baffling holism of quantum theory, then this type of spiritual view of life is not so incomprehensible. If everything comes from a unified life source and singularity condition, then THAT, or God, or whatever term one applies to the Absolute, must exist within all things. MacLaine proclaims the ancient axiom that *"God lies within"* and endorses Blavatsky's fundamental dogma of unity. Further, her descriptions of the "electromagnetic 'fields of reality'" are not far from the Blavatsky's Electric Ocean of Life and the Aethers. MacLaine mentions the multidimensional reality wherein we are all part of the Web, even living multiple lives—again quite consistent with Blavatsky and the occult teachings of reincarnation and hidden dimensions.

Of course, the implication that quantum theory has substantiated the idea of mystical unity or of any kind of psychical reality is a source of consternation and annoyance to scientists. Unfortunately, it does not lead to serious consideration of the occult and mystical sciences. Heinz Pagels (1983) writes:

> Some recent popularizers of Bell's work when confronted with this conclusion (of non-locality) have gone on to claim that telepathy is verified or the mystical notion that all parts of the universe are instantaneously interconnected is vindicated. Others assert that this implies communication faster than the speed of light. That is rubbish, the quantum theory and Bell's inequality imply nothing of this kind. Individuals who make such claims have substituted a wish-fulfilling fantasy for understanding. (p. 150) [17]

As it happens, Pagels' reasons for rejecting the mystical unity of quantum theory are really meager and simply based on a quantum leap of faith on Pagels' part, which matches that which he ascribes to the mystical wish-fulfillers. The main point of Pagels' critique is that since the polarizations of the photon pairs are random, then these non-local effects could never be used to transmit information; i.e., through one experimenter choosing polarized orientations to convey information to another. However, this misses the essential point that quantum elements maintain a non-local interconnectedness, whether or not this can intentionally be used to convey information. The configuration spaces are themselves rich information fields underlying and sustaining all quantum systems.

Certainly, we should not reflexively dismiss the baffling holism of quantum theory, because these ideas are supportive of mystical insights. Scientists can even indulge in self-deception and pretend that they discovered the concept of such unity—just as they claim that they discovered the singularity and the void/plenum of the quantum vacuum! Yet, this reflexive and uninformed dismissal of occult science is a common attitude among those physicists who so vehemently deny any mystical implications to quantum theory—as if they know themselves what all the quantum weirdness really means. They then offer their own opinions and prejudices as truths, instead of admitting that they are nothing more than personal viewpoints based on their assumptive framework of ideas and

---

17 It is ironic that in the preface to his work, F. Herbert writes: *"In the summer of 1970 my friend Heinz Pagels, a physicist at Rockefeller University, showed me a paper published in an obscure new journal. "Here's something strange that should interest you, Nick," he said. This strange new thing was Bell's theorem."* (p.xiii)

prejudices. At the very least, quantum interconnectedness does not disprove, but supports mystical doctrines, although the implications and applications of what this all means is not at all understood. Scientists' understanding of unity has not approached the elegance of Blavatsky's deeper wisdom teachings and her explanations of the Aether.

It seems most important to understand that skeptical physicists are conditioned by personal and scientific opinions just like everyone else. Herbert comments:

> It's difficult to convey to outsider the distaste which the majority of physicists feel when they hear the word 'non-locality.' ... these guys so treasure locality that they are willing to deny reality itself before accepting a world that's non-local. (p. 234)

The evidence for non-local effects has major implications for modern physics and for our understanding of the nature of reality.

In *Quantum Reality*, Herbert (1987) explains what an unusual reality follows from the non-local effects implied by quantum theory. He writes:

> Bell's theorem is easy to understand but hard to believe. This theorem says that *reality must be non-local*. "Non-local" means, that the atom's measured attributes are determined not just by events happening at the actual measurement site but by events arbitrarily distant, including events outside of the light cone–that is, events so far away that to reach the measurement site their influence must travel faster than light. In other words, when I probe an atom's momentum with a momentum meter, its true momentum is disturbed, according to Bell's theorem, not just by the momentum meter itself but by a vast array of distant events–events that are happening right now in other cities, in other countries, and possibly in other galaxies. According to John Bell, the act of measurement is not a private act, but a public event in whose details large portions of the universe instantly participate.
>
> Bell's theorem is a mathematical proof, not a conjecture or supposition." ... Thus Bell does not merely permit or suggest that reality is non-local; he actually proves it. (pp. xiii-xiv)

According to quantum theory, any particles, which have once interacted, continue to maintain a *"phase entanglement"* in *"configuration space."* Since all the matter and energy in the universe emerged from the singularity condition at the beginning of time, this would imply the ultimate unity and interrelatedness of all things within higher dimensional configuration space. Certainly, quantum theory provides mathematical formulas and experimental evidence which substantiate "the reality" of this 'baffling holism.'

However, to jump from such concepts as applies to elementary quanta, to the level of human beings on a completely different order of scale of being, as a massive quantum system composed of innumerable particles, leaves much to be filled in. Although quantum theory suggests the phase entanglement of elementary particles and such, how could this all apply on the level of an existent human being? Does it really imply, as Shirley MacLaine suggests, that we are all interrelated and that God lives through us all? There is certainly a quantum leap from the findings of quantum physics to the level of human beings and we need to bridge this quantum leap from ultra microscopic particles to living breathing human beings. The inspiration of Ms MacLaine is consistent with the teachings of *The Secret Doctrine* but it is only the latter which articulates the multidimensional nature of it all and the mechanisms and principles of life and creation.

In *The Secret Doctrine*, H. P. Blavatsky actually discusses the concept of 'action at a distance,' after a critique of the science of her day for its profound ignorance of the nature of the Aether. She writes: *"Official science knows nothing to this day of the constitution of the ether."* (S. D. I, p. 487) At least now modern science is focusing on those issues of the ether as raised by Blavatsky a century ago. The modern scientist declares: *"All of physics is in the vacuum."* This is a view quite in keeping with Blavatsky's arguments. In reference to 'action at a distance,' Blavatsky notes:

> in their efforts to support their individual hypotheses and systems, the majority of the eminent and learned materialists very often utter the greatest fallacies. Let us take the following case. Most of them reject *actio in distans* (one of the fundamental principles in the question of Aether or Akasa in Occultism) ... there is no physical action, "which, on close examination, does not resolve itself into *actio in distans*." (S. D. I, p. 487-8)

Whereas modern scientists have wanted to deny 'action at a distance,' Blavatsky maintains that there are actually no phenomena which on closer examination do not involve *'actio in distans.'* So the fundamental feature of quantum theory, the baffling holism, is quite in keeping with the wisdom of *The Secret Doctrine*. Even more enigmatic is the fact that Blavatsky explains that external objective space, as we ordinarily understand this concept, does not exist. Instead, it is an illusion produced by the limitations inherent to the finite mind and the state of subjective consciousness. In a very real sense, there is a fundamental unity to the whole of creation and this concept is inherent to quantum physics itself, although most small-minded materialists prefer their little bit science of local effects. We turn next to one prominent physicist who did venture into the unknown attempting to understand this concept of the fundamental unity of life and creation.

6. David Bohm on Wholeness & the Implicate Order

Ultimately, the entire universe (with all its 'particles,' including those constituting human beings, their laboratories, observing instruments, etc.) has to be understood as a single undivided whole, in which analysis into separately and independently existent parts has no fundamental status. (Bohm, 1980, p. 174)

6a. The Basic Paradigm

Dr. David Bohm was an associate of A. Einstein and author of the acclaimed *Wholeness and the Implicate Order* (1980). One of the world's foremost theoretical physicists, Bohm published classic works on quantum and relativity theory and was an important contributor to the debate concerning *hidden variables* in quantum theory. Because of his eminence as a physicist, David Bohm was in the privileged position of being able to espouse his radical theoretical model–one that postulated the undivided wholeness of reality. Dr. Bohm's ideas generated widespread interest not only amongst scientists but also within philosophical, religious and New Age circles. Bohm's work figured prominently in the holographic model of consciousness which arose during the 1980s. Bohm's conclusions about the unity and interrelatedness of all things have profound implications for the study of both physics and human consciousness.

Bohm's model of wholeness and the implicate orders arose from his attempt to reconcile relativity and quantum theory while accounting for non-local effects and other quantum paradoxes. He distinguished between the outward, manifest physical reality—the *"explicate order"*—and the underlying, un-manifest realm—the *"implicate order."* In the explicate order, we have separate little bits—the isolated quanta existing outside of each other in separate regions of spacetime and interacting only through local effects. However, Bohm suggests that beyond the explicate order, beyond the quantum level, are the implicate and super-implicate orders. Quanta which appear in the explicate order to be separate in space and time are interconnected within the underlying implicate and super-implicate orders. There is thus a deeper reality which plays a determining role in relationship to the manifestation of material particles or quanta within spacetime.

The implicate orders underlie the explicate orders and material reality in a sense *unfolds* from WITHIN/WITHOUT.

a new notion of order is involved here, which we called the *implicate order* (from a Latin root meaning 'to enfold' or 'to fold inward'). In terms of the implicate order one may say that everything is enfolded into everything. This contrasts with the *explicate order* now dominant in physics in which things are *unfolded* in the sense that each thing lies only in its own particular region of space (and time) and outside the regions belonging to other things. (Bohm, p. 177)

Within Bohm's framework, all manifest phenomena of the explicate order (the manifest physical world) must be understood as particular cases of the unfolding of a more general set of implicate orders (the unmanifest underlying realm). The fundamental relationships are between the implicated structures, which interpenetrate each other throughout the whole of space and time. The explicate order flows out of the laws and processes of a multi-dimensional implicate order—as apparent differentiations of an undivided whole! Bohm explains:

the central underlying theme (is) the unbroken wholeness of the totality of existence as an undivided flowing movement without borders. ... in the implicate order the totality of existence is enfolded within each region of space (and time). So, whatever part, element, or aspect we may abstract in thought, this still enfolds the whole and is therefore intrinsically related to the totality from which it has been abstracted. Thus, wholeness permeates all that is being discussed, from the very outset. (1980, p. 172)

Bohm's basic thesis is that even the whole of the Universe is implicated within any point. Such a view is remarkable–a profound revision of centuries of fragmentary little-bit scientific thought. Bohm turns everything upside down: whereas we had viewed causes as deriving from motion within the explicate order, now the causes are within the hidden implicate orders. Manifest reality is but a shadow of the deeper underlying realities.

Within Bohm's framework, there is a most unusual conception of time and space, matter and energy being *unfolded out* of the hidden implicate order. In Bohm's view, the fundamental reality is that of undivided wholeness and all quanta are interconnected within multidimensional implicate orders, instead of simply being isolated elements within spacetime.

6b. On Relativity & Quantum Theory

Bohm was led to the wholeness paradigm through his efforts to understand the paradoxes of modern relativity and quantum theory. These theories are the foundations of modern physics and yet have never been reconciled within a unifying theoretical framework. Bohm's major orientation in trying to unify these theories was to demonstrate how they both lead to a view of the fundamental unity of reality:

> science itself is demanding a new, non-fragmentary world view, in the sense that the present approach of analysis of the world into independently existent parts does not work very well in modern physics. It is shown that both in relativity theory and quantum theory, notions implying the undivided wholeness of the universe would provide a much more orderly way of considering the general nature of reality. (1980, pp. xi-xii)

In his attempt to integrate relativity theory and quantum mechanics within one framework, Bohm noted that despite their perceived differences, they shared the notion of wholeness:

> It is instructive to contrast the key features of relativistic and quantum theories. ... relativity theory requires continuity, strict causality (or determinism) and locality. On the other hand, quantum theory requires non-continuity, non-causality and non-locality. So the basic concepts of relativity and quantum theory directly contradict each other. It is therefore hardly surprising that these two theories have never been unified in a consistent way. ... What is very probably needed instead is a qualitatively new theory, from which both relativity and quantum theory are to be derived as abstractions, approximations and limiting cases.
>
> The basic notions of this new theory evidently cannot be found by beginning with those features in which relativity and quantum theory stand in direct contradiction. The best place to begin is with what they have basically in common. This is undivided wholeness. Though each comes to such wholeness in a different way, it is clear that it is this to which they are both fundamentally pointing.
>
> To begin with undivided wholeness means, however, that we must drop the mechanistic order. But this order has been, for many centuries, basic to all thinking on physics. (p. 176)

Einstein proposed that, instead of taking reality as composed of particles, we should take fields as the starting point. However, Bohm notes that Einstein's views of fields retained an essential feature of the mechanistic order—the belief in only 'local effects.' This is because:

> the field concept, which is his basic starting point, still retains the essential features of a mechanistic order, for the fundamental entities, the fields, are conceived as existing outside of each other, at separate points of space and time, and are assumed to be connected with

each other only through external relationships which indeed are also taken to be local, in the sense that only those field elements that are separated by 'infinitesimal' distances can affect each other. (p. 174)

Bohm notes that the unified field theory was not successful in the attempt to provide an ultimate mechanistic basis for physics in terms of the field concept, since it implied that *"no coherent concept of an independently existent particle"* is possible. However, unified field theory *"showed in a concrete way how consistency with the theory of relativity may be achieved by deriving the particle concept as an abstraction from an unbroken and undivided totality of existence."* (pp. 173-4)

In Bohm's analysis, a unified field theory of relativity leads to one view of wholeness. However, it is quantum theory, which Bohm describes as posing a second and *"much more serious challenge to this mechanistic order, going far beyond that provided by the theory of relativity."* (p. 175) According to Bohm, there are three features to quantum theory which challenge the mechanistic view within science.

> 1. Movement is in general *discontinuous*, in the sense that action is constituted of *indivisible quanta* (implying also that an electron, for example, can go from one state to another, without passing through any states in between).
>
> 2. Entities, such as electrons, can show different properties (e.g., particle-like, wavelike, or something in between), depending on the environmental context within which they exist and are subject to observation.
>
> 3. Two entities, such as electrons, which initially combine to form a molecule and then separate, show a peculiar non-local relationship, which can best be described as a non-causal connections of elements that are far apart (as demonstrated in the experiments of Einstein, Podolsky and Rosen). (Bohm, 1980, p. 175)

The first point concerns the quantized or discontinuous nature of movement. The fact that actions are in the form of discrete quanta suggests to Bohm that the interactions between different entities constitute *"a single structure of indivisible links, so that the entire universe has to be thought of as an unbroken whole."* (p.175) For example, in the explicate order, an electron will appear in one energy state one moment and then instantaneously appear in another–disappearing between states. This discontinuous (or quantized) jump of an electron from one orbit to another, with the particle leaving no traces of its path, points to underlying dimensions of existence which links the orbital arrangements into a larger whole. The implicate orders are beyond the level of the quantum. The discontinuous or quantized nature of movement, in the atom and more generally in quantum interactions, is one feature of quantum theory which suggests the underlying wholeness and the necessity for implicate orders to exist in relationship to the explicate orders.

The second point made by Bohm with respect to quantum theory concerns how entities, like electrons or photons, can exhibit the properties of waves or particles, or what he describes as *"something in between"*–depending on the environmental context within which they exist and are subject to observation. Einstein's view of an objective reality was of one that existed in a definite way independently of how it was being observed or known. The role of the observer in influencing the observed is a second aspect of quantum theory which challenges the mechanistic view of creation and which points towards an underlying wholeness—which includes even the consciousness and mind of the observer.

The third feature of quantum theory, which challenges the mechanistic order, has to do with non-local relationships and the E-P-R (Einstein, Podolsky and Rosen) paradox. In discussing the nature of the implicate order, Bohm uses the example of the EPR paradox and explains that the electrons which influence each other non-locally and instantaneously must both be regarded as *"projections of a higher dimensional reality:"* i.e., these particles do not simply interact between themselves but rather are projections of the same higher dimensions (infolded into each). The particles then refer to a single actuality, which is the common ground for both. A multidimensional implicate order thus projects into lower dimensional elements and is the basis for non-local relationships.

Bohm suggests that relativity and quantum theory, the two major foundations of modern physics, both ultimately lead to a view of wholeness. Bohm then argues that if we begin with this notion of wholeness as the fundamental reality, then both theories can be derived as abstractions or limiting cases explained from this starting point.

6c. Active Information, the Quantum Potential & Deep Reality

> ...the causal interpretation suggests that nature may be far more subtle and strange than was previously thought. (Bohm & Peat, 1987, p. 93)

In Bohm's view, there is a deep reality beyond the level of the quanta, which exerts determining, causal influences on the manifestations of the wave/particles in space/time. Thus, while the uncertainty principle is a limiting principle evident in the explicate order, there are hidden implicate orders beyond the physically observable realm.

Bohm emphasized that a quantum was indeed a real particle plus a real wave (Herbert, 1987), but it is linked to a new field composed of the *pilot wave* which guides the movement of the particle. Bohm viewed the electron or quantum as an ordinary particle but it is guided by a very non-ordinary wave. The 'pilot wave' was regarded as instantaneously affected whenever a change occurred within the whole environment and it communicates this change to the particle altering its position and momentum. Thus, Bohm put forth a non-local causal model accepting the implications of quantum theory's baffling holism and non-local effects.

Bohm uses various analogies to explain his non-ordinary waves—the *pilot waves* that carry the *quantum potential*. These pilot waves carry *information* rather than energy or mass and serve to guide the particle. The quantum potential is this information content. Thus, we have a triad of *matter, energy and information*—in contrast with the traditional matter-energy duality:

> By way of illustration, think of a ship that sails on automatic pilot, guided by radio waves. The overall effect of the radio waves is independent of their strength and depends only on their form. The essential point is that the ship moves with its own energy but that the *information* within the radio waves is taken up and used to direct the much greater energy of the ship. In the causal interpretation, the electron moves under its own energy, but the information in the *form* of the quantum wave directs the energy of the electron. (Bohm, Peat 1987, p. 90)

There are three elements: i) information in the pilot wave, ii) energy in the engines of the ship, and iii) the mass of the ship itself. The external direction of the matter of the ship is determined by the energy expenditure of the engines, which is informed by information content within the quantum potential.

The influence of the quantum potential does not depend on the energy of the field but on the *form* of the field, and the transfer of information is not limited by the speed of light. The quantum potential or pilot wave embodies "active information" and with little (if any) energy. Similarly, a quantum such as an electron moves under its own energy but the information in the "quantum potential" directs its energy expenditure.

The equation for the quantum potential is highly unusual in that its strength is independent of distance. This contrasts with the strength of other physical fields (e.g., electromagnetism or gravity) which depend upon distance; such that the further

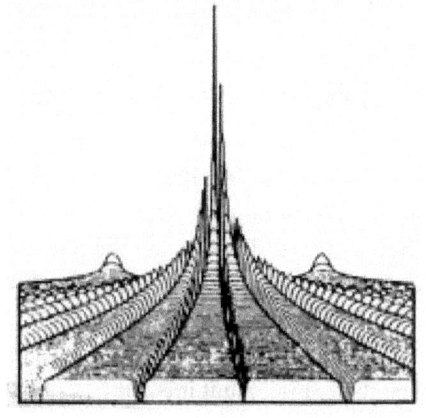

two quanta (or two cosmic bodies) are apart, then the weaker the force between them. Further, the quantum potential embodies information, not limited by the speed of light, but instantaneously present throughout the field. Time itself has a different meaning within this domain.

Bohm explains the profound implications of this view:

> The quantum field contains information about the whole environment and about the whole past, which regulates the present activity of the electron in much the same way that information about the whole past and our whole environment regulates our own activity as human beings, through consciousness. (p. 39)

> ...the higher level simply transcends the lower level altogether. It's immensely greater and has an entirely different set of relationships out of which the lower level is obtained as a very small part, in an abstraction. (p. 40)

> ...what is going on in the full depth of that one moment of time contains information about all of it.... In nonmanifest reality, it's all interpenetrating, interconnected, one. (In Weber, 1986, p. 41)[18]

According to this formulation, information about the whole informs any part and is more primary. Material reality is "unfolded" then from within/without: with the implicate orders "informing" the explicate order. Bohm takes quantum interconnectedness to the extreme by suggesting that any particular quanta (element, particle) is ultimately interconnected through the implicate and super-implicate orders to the whole of the universe![19] It is as if the universe somehow concentrates itself within every point.

All phenomena of the explicate order (the manifest physical world) involve the unfolding of a more general set of implicate orders (un-manifest, subtle dimensions). In Bohm's initial formulation, he posited the existence of only the implicate and explicate orders, but later added a third level of dimensions–the super-implicate orders beyond the implicate orders. He describes this higher order as:

---

18 This illustration depicts the invisible information field of the quantum potential for an electron in the two slit experimental situation widely used in physics to demonstrate quantum paradoxes. This complex information field serves to guide the electron's behaviour.

19 In terms of earlier discussion of quantum interconnectedness, the implicate orders are related to the configuration spaces wherein particles are phase entangled. Hence, what happens anywhere in the universe might instantaneously effect through *active information*, the manifestations of matter and energy within time and space. The configuration space contains information about the whole. Since all quanta emerged from a singularity condition at the beginning of time, all things are phase entangled in configuration space and are thus interrelated in the implicate order.

a super-information field of the whole universe, a super-implicate order which organizes the first level (of the implicate orders) into various structures and is capable of tremendous development of structure. The point about the super-implicate order is that if we take the holographic theory, though we have an implicate order, nothing organizes it. It is what's called "linear"... but it does not have an intrinsic capacity to unfold an order. The super-implicate order, which is the so-called higher field... makes the implicate order non-linear and organizes it into relatively stable forms with complex structures. (In Weber, 1986, p. 33)

According to this scheme, the physical world is the external manifestation of multidimensional hidden dimensions. The explicate order flows out of the laws and processes of multi-dimensional implicate and super-implicate orders–apparent differentiations of an undivided whole. According to Bohm, reality as it appears to our senses–the everyday world of matter and energy in time and space—is essentially a holographic image projected out of vast interconnected hidden dimensions. The separateness of quanta is an illusion produced by severing the relationship of the parts to the underlying whole.

Bohm's model of the implicate orders suggest that there is indeed a more fundamental hidden reality–inner worlds beyond the level of the quanta. Since all things are interconnected in informational fields that inform material/energetic processes, then there must be some inner dimensions of being capable of responding to this active information–some kind of receiver or resonator system. Bohm uses a radio analogy to explain this. The radio wave carries information or a signal which might be considered to be potentially available everywhere. However, for this potential information to have an active informational influence, there has to be a radio set with electrical energy capable of responding to this informational field. In this case, we might hear singing (molecular sound vibration) propagated from a radio. We require the harmonic resonator (the radio set), the information and the energy (electrical power) to produce a manifestation within the explicate order (sound). This analogy with a radio set has startling implications for the necessity of other deep levels of reality. Bohm and Peat note:

> The quantum wave carries "information" and is therefore *potentially* active everywhere, but it is *actually* active only when and where this energy enters into the energy of a particle. But this implies that an electron, or any other elementary particle, has a complex and subtle inner structure that is at least comparable with that of a radio. Clearly this notion goes against the whole tradition of modern physics, which assumes that as matter is analyzed into smaller and smaller parts, its behavior grows more elementary. By contrast, the causal

interpretation suggests that nature may be far more subtle and strange than was previously thought.

But this inner complexity of elementary matter is not as implausible as it may appear at first sight. For example, a large crowd of people can be treated by statistical laws, whereas individually their behavior is immensely subtler and more complex. Similarly, large masses of matter reduce to simple Newtonian behavior whereas atoms and molecules have a more complex inner structure. And what of the subatomic particles themselves? It is interesting to note that between the shortest distance now measurable in physics (10^{-16} cm) and the shortest distance in which current notions of space-time probably have meaning, (10^{-33} cm), there is a vast range of scale in which an immense amount of yet undiscovered structure could be contained. Indeed this range is roughly equal to that which exists between our own size and that of the elementary particles. (1987, pp. 93-4)

It seems that the world within is potentially as complex as the world without. Only such inner dimensions of being could allow for a quantum to be responsive to the active information of the quantum potential containing information about the larger whole.

Bohm in fact predicted new levels of complexity as suggested now within superstring and M-theories, and by the holographic paradigm, which provide such complex resonator systems with structures at least as complex as that of a radio. Such complex resonator systems are indeed now suggested by such concepts as that of the seven dimensional Calabi-Yau spaces, and in M-theory, by the concepts of multidimensional 'branes' extended within the hyperspace dimensions. Obviously there are complex implicate and super-implicate orders beyond the quantum for non-local effects to occur.

The whole argument of Bohm, as to the undivided wholeness of life, is certainly consistent with *The Secret Doctrine* of H. P. Blavatsky—who describes One Omniscience as thrilling throughout every finite point of the Kosmos—a view which is entirely consistent with Bohm's vast information fields underlying and sustaining all things from within without.

6d. Analogies: From Holographs to Atomic Memory

Bohm uses various analogies to illustrate the implicate and explicate orders. These analogies are limited in that they entail attempts to depict higher dimensional orders in terms of our common spacetime dimensionality. At the same time, they clarify features of the wholeness paradigm.

A first analogy contrasts the methods of photography and holography. In photography, a lens is used which focuses the image of the external object onto a photographic plate establishing a one-to-one correspondence between a point upon the plate and a point on the surface of the object. In this case, a photograph illustrates the explicate order of separate space/time objects. In contrast, the implicate order is demonstrated by the *lens-less* holographic methods–wherein light from the whole of the object impinges upon every point on the holographic film. In this case, any point on the hologram contains an image of the whole object 'enfolded' into it. Bohm states: *"... the form and structure of the entire object may be said to be enfolded within each region of the photographic record."* (p. 177) When a laser light is shone through the holographic plate to reconstruct the object image, the whole is *unfolded* out of the hidden implicate order and projected out into space within the explicate order. This is a basic analogy for Bohm's wholeness model, although it fails to portray the essential dynamic quality of the implicate orders–as actively organizing themselves and the explicate order.

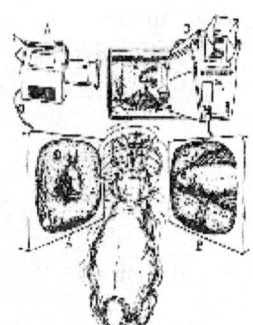

Image: The rabbit thinks that the two, fish A and B, are separate entities. He does not realize that they are actually projections of a three-dimensional world in which they are one.

A second analogy which Bohm cites to depict higher dimensional spaces and quantum interconnectedness involves a fish swimming in an aquarium. In this case, two video cameras record the fish's movement from different angles and the observer watches the recordings on monitors. Although it might appear to the observer rabbit that there are two separate fish, it is apparent that the two recordings are exactly correlated: The moment one image of the fish turns into a frontal view, the second turns into a side profile. The instantaneous correlation between the movements of the fish is really due to the fact that on a deeper level of reality the two fish are not separate entities at all but simply different projections of a single fish.

Similarly, in the E.P.R. type experiments with correlated quanta, the apparent separateness of the quanta in the explicate order is a lower dimensional projection of a higher dimensional reality: thus, the two quanta are projections of a single system. In this case, it is meaningless to talk of the quanta as isolated elements.

A third analogy used by Bohm to illustrate the wholeness paradigm involves a methodology which demonstrates *atomic memory* and the hidden order. In this case, a drop of colored dye is added to a vicious liquid enclosed between two glass cylinders. The outer cylinder is rotated slowly and the dye drop spreads out through the liquid until it completely disappears from view. At this point, the distribution of dye molecules within the liquid would appear to be *random* or *unordered*. However, if the outer cylinder is then moved in the opposing direction the same number of turns, then the dye drop reappears having been reconstituted out of the apparent randomness. When the dye drop was distributed in the fluid, it still maintains some form of order although hidden from observation. Its hidden order was "enfolded" or "implicated" in the larger body of liquid.

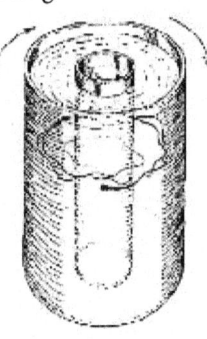

Bohm uses variations on this analogy to demonstrate the enfolding and unfolding of elements with respect to the implicate orders. In another case, a series of dye drops is added to the liquid as the outer cylinder is being turned–each drop at a slightly different position. The cylinder can then be rotated until the whole series of drops disappears and are apparently randomly distributed throughout the liquid. If we then reverse the turning, the last drop added will reappear first, then the second last, etc. Each drop will be reconstituted for a moment and the series of these drops will give the appearance of a single drop moving in space/time. Again, the analogy illustrates that the apparent movement of a drop in space/time might be an explicate manifestation of a series of hidden implicate orders.

All of these analogies are misleading in various respects—because they attempt to depict higher dimensional implicate orders using analogies based on explicate phenomena. Nevertheless, they do capture the idea of how an implicate order can be hidden and yet critical in accounting for observable phenomena. This suggests a different form of order than that usually considered in science. Normally, scientific laws are formulated in reference only to the explicate order– explaining phenomenon evident within the spacetime continuum as resulting from causes which also lie within the explicate order. Thus, two particles interact locally through the exchange of virtual particles—all occurring in the explicate order. In contrast, Bohm suggests that the laws of science need to be formulated to give a primary role to the hidden implicate orders, the root principles out of which explicate orders are manifest. The realm of true causes lies within these higher dimensional spaces and *movement*, wherein everything is interrelated to the larger whole. Manifest reality unfolds out the realm of the un-manifest.

6e. The Fullness of Emptiness

> That which is the abyss of nothingness to the physicist, who knows only the world of visible causes and effects, is the boundless Space of the Divine *Plenum* to the Occultist. (Blavatsky, S. D. I, p. 148)

> The physicist who regards Space merely as a representation of our mind, or extension unrelated to things in it ... who would have a void there, where he can see no matter, would reject with the utmost contempt the proposition that "Space is a substantial though (apparently) an absolutely unknowable living Entity." ... Such is ... that of Archaic philosophy. Space is the real world, while our world is an artificial one. It is the One Unity throughout its infinitude: in its bottomless depths as on its illusive surface a surface studded with countless phenomenal Universes, systems and mirage-like worlds. ... in the *real* world, which is a Unity of Forces, there is "a connection of all matter in the *plenum*," as Leibnitz would say. (S. D., p. 615)

H.P. Blavatsky regards Space as a living Unity–the plenum—the source of all things. Of course, when she talks of Space, she is referring to the *Eternal Parent Space* and not simply the manifest spacetime continuum of visible effects—the explicate order. In the terms of modern physics and cosmology, Blavatsky's Parent Space is a hyperspace or superspace, the container of the implicate and super-implicate orders–the root principles out of which the explicate order unfolds.

Bohm arrived at a similar view of the void of space as being full and a plenum. To explain the wholeness paradigm requires a cosmological and physical view of so-called empty space as being a vast underlying Sea of energy, information and potency. Emptiness—this apparent nothingness—constitutes a fundamental dimension which underlies and sustains the explicate order. Bohm arrives at the fullness of emptiness by adding up all the possible little bit wave-particle excitations present in empty space:

> if one considers the electromagnetic field in empty space, ... one finds from the quantum theory that each such 'wave-particle' mode of excitation of the field has what is called a 'zero-point' energy, below which it cannot go ... If one were to add up the energies of all the 'wave-particle' modes of excitation in any region of space, the

result would be infinite, because an infinite number of wavelengths is present. (1980, p. 190)

If the zero-point energies for the gravitational and electromagnetic forces are added up, the sum approaches infinity. Bohm suggests, however, that this may have a limit because we reach a point at which the measurement of time and space becomes undefined (at the level of Planck's unit of distance, 10^{-33} centimeters.)

The implication of Bohm's argument is that so-called empty space is pregnant with incredibly energies and potential:

> What is implied by this proposal is that what we call empty space contains an immense background of energy, and that matter as we know it is a small, 'quantized' wavelike excitation on top of this background, rather like a tiny ripple on a vast sea. In current physical theories, one avoids the explicit consideration of this background by calculating only the difference between the energy of empty space and that of space with matter in it. This difference is all that counts in the determination of the general properties of matter as they are presently accessible to observation. ... this vast sea of energy may play a key part in the understanding of the cosmos as a whole.
>
> In this connection it may be said that space, which has so much energy, is *full* rather than empty.... what we perceive through the senses as empty space is actually the plenum, which is the ground for the existence of everything, including ourselves. The things that appear to our senses are derivative forms and their true meaning can be seen only when we consider the plenum, in which they are generated and sustained, and into which they must ultimately vanish. (pp. 191-2)

All of creation is folded out of an immense underlying realm of the plenum and of Undivided Wholeness—as tiny ripples on a vast Sea. Bohm's model suggests that, ultimately, any quantum exists in relationship to information about the whole, even the past: *"... what is going on in the full depth of that one moment of time contains information about all of it.... In nonmanifest reality it's all interpenetrating, interconnected, one."* (Bohm, in Weber, 1986 p. 41) How similar this is to Blavatsky's explanation, that: *"There is but one indivisible and absolute Omniscience and Intelligence in the Universe, and this thrills throughout every atom and infinitesimal point of the whole finite Cosmos."* (1888, p. 277)

Summing up his views of nature and the holistic order, Bohm suggests a progression from the explicate order of manifest existence to multi-dimensional implicate and super-implicate orders—all of which are part of an immense sea of infinite information/energy sensed as empty space. The space *without* (the *explicate order*) is unfolded from the space *within* (the *implicate order* and plenum).

Bohm suggests that there might be various extension of the implicate order beyond the critical limit of 10^{-33} cm. into *"unknown depths of inwardness."*

6f. The Fundamental Holomovement

> Our basic proposal (is) that *what is* the holomovement, and that everything is to be explained in terms of forms derived from this holomovement. (Bohm, 1980, p. 178)

In Bohm's model, the idea of the whole is given primary importance and embodied in the idea of the fundamental *"holomovement."* Through the super-implicate and implicate orders, there are various modifications of this most fundamental holomovement and this produces—as a whole—everything manifest in form and structures within the explicate order. The holomovement ultimately produces all the phenomena evident within the explicate order. Bohm explains:

> order and measure can be 'enfolded' and 'carried' not only in electromagnetic waves but also in other ways (by electron beams, sound, and in other countless forms of movement). To generalize so as to emphasize undivided wholeness, we shall say that what 'carries' an implicate order is the *holomovement*, which is an unbroken and undivided totality.... all forms of the holomovement merge and are inseparable.... Thus, the *holomovement* is *indefinable* and *immeasurable*. (1980, pp. 150-1)

Bohm explains that different 'relatively' independent parts might be abstracted from the unity of the whole, but we must always remember that everything begins from the 'holomovement.' He elaborates upon the nature of a single particle:

> Thus, the word 'electron' should be regarded as no more than a name by which we call attention to a certain aspect of the holomovement, an aspect that can be discussed only by taking into account the entire experimental situation and that cannot be specified in terms of localized objects moving autonomously through space. And, of course, every kind of 'particle' which in current physics is said to be a basic constituent of matter will have to be discussed in the same sort of terms (so that such 'particles' are no longer considered as autonomous and separately existent). Thus, we come to a new general physical description in which 'everything implicates everything' in an order of undivided wholeness. (1980, p. 155)

Of course, the holomovement could never be completely defined nor put into words or measured. Bohm explains that analytic distinctions cease to be adequate. Instead, he introduces a special term—the *holonomy* or *"law of the whole."* This new order demands a new form of physics:

> Generally speaking, the laws of physics have thus far referred mainly to the explicate order. Indeed, it may be said that the principle function of Cartesian coordinates is just to give a clear and precise description of the explicate order. Now, we are proposing that in the formulation of the laws of physics, primary relevance is to be given to the implicate order, while the explicate order is to have a secondary kind of significance …. Cartesian coordinates can no longer be given a primary emphasis, and … a new kind of description will indeed have to be developed for discussing the laws of physics. (1980, p. 150)

In Bohm's view, the implicate orders involve processes of the unfoldment from within a "higher-dimensional space," all as derivatives of an underlying holomovement. The phenomena produced within the four large dimensions of the Cartesian coordinates are dependent upon motions proceeding within hidden interior realms of higher dimensions. The newer models of 11 dimensional K.K. theory, Superstring and M-theory, and the holographic model, that are now proposed in physics, all confirm Bohm's predictions about the existence of more complex levels of inner organization to life and the cosmos.

Most generally, Bohm's model of wholeness and the implicate orders is clearly supported by latter developments in modern physics. Scientists now conceive of levels of hidden dimensions beyond the level of the quanta, information as a third force in physics, and the quantum vacuum as being both a void and a plenum. The undivided wholeness of David Bohm is quite in accord with Blavatsky's fundamental dogma of occultism–that of the ultimate Unity of all things. Further, the fundamental holomovement is most similar to the *Eternal Ceaseless Breath* of *The Secret Doctrine*, the primordial motion out of which are derived all generations of causes and effects. For Blavatsky, the laws of nature are all modifications of the Ceaseless Breath.

7. The Universe as a Hologram

In August of 2003, *Scientific American* published an issue posing the question *"ARE YOU A HOLOGRAM? (Quantum physics says the entire universe might be)."* In a fascinating article, *Information in the Holographic Universe*, Dr. Jacob D. Bekenstein discusses some of the unusual features of modern information and holographic theory and the physics of black holes. The holographic principle is being proposed as the possible Holy Grail of physics—providing an approach to quantum gravity theory which reconciles quantum field theory and quantum loop theory, as well as string theory and M-theory. (Smolin, 2001)

7a. Information as Third Force

> "Ask anybody what the physical world is made of, and you are likely to be told "matter and energy." Yet if we have learned anything from engineering, biology and physics, information is just as crucial an ingredient.... a century of developments in physics has taught us that information is a crucial player in physical systems and processes. Indeed, a current trend, initiated by John A. Wheeler of Princeton University, is to regard the physical world as made of information, with energy and matter as incidentals. (Bekenstein, 2003, p. 59)

Professor Bekenstein regards "information" as a third force underlying the manifestations of matter and energy within time and space. This is similar to Bohm's 'pilot waves' and the 'quantum potential' permeating space, as information fields of the implicate orders that inform transformations of matter and energy.

In another *Scientific American* article, *Black Hole Computers*, Lloyd and Ng similarly emphasize the importance of 'information' as the third force in the new physics, noting:

> to a physicist, all physical systems are computers. Rocks, atomic bombs and galaxies may not run Linux, but they, too, register and process information. Every electron, photon and other elementary particle stores bits of data, and every time two such particles interact, those bits are transformed. Physical existence and information content are inextricably linked. As physicist John Wheeler of Princeton University says, "It from bit." (November 2004)

The statement *"it from bit,"* suggests that 'it,' meaning a material and energetic system, comes from 'bit,' meaning bits of information. In modern physics, information is now regarded as a primary element in nature. From this perspective, everything is a computer, as everything processes bits of information—whether an electron, a black hole, a cell or a human heart. Thus, a trinity of intelligence, energy and matter is basic to the new science—as it is to mystical orientations and *The Secret Doctrine*. According to Lloyd and Ng, the universe itself is a giant computer and not only that, but a quantum computer. They quote physicist Zizzi, *"It from qubit,"*—or quantum bit, as a variation on Wheeler's *"It from bit."*

7b. A Tale of Entropies and Black Holes

In *"Information in the Holographic Universe,"* Dr. Bekenstein explains aspects of information theory as apply to black holes and the emerging holographic theory. He suggests that: *"Theoretical results about black holes suggest that the universe could be like a gigantic hologram."*

In his analysis, Dr. Bekenstein explains that the *law of entropy* traditionally applied to material and thermal processes can also be applied to information processes. In 1877, physicist Ludwig Boltzmann defined *thermodynamic entropy* as the number of distinct microscopic states that particles in a body of matter could be in: For example, consider all the possible arrangements of the gas molecules in the room around you and their possible positions and momentum. It was in 1948, that Claude Shannon defined entropy in terms of information theory. The *Shannon entropy* is the number of binary bits needed to decode the information content within a message. The two measures and concepts of entropy are *"conceptually equivalent"* (under higher degrees of freedom), although they are expressed in different units—either 'units of energy divided by temperature' for thermal entropy, or as 'bits' which are *"essentially dimensionless"* for information entropy. The conservation of information is also demanded within quantum mechanics.

According to the *Generalized Second Law of Thermodynamics*, the loss or gain of entropy in a material/energetic system must be compensated for by changes in the entropy of information—as one balances the other in order to maintain an overall GSL. Bekenstein explains a consequence of this principle as it applied to the physics of black holes:

> when matter falls into a black hole, the increase in black hole entropy always compensates or overcompensates for the "lost" entropy of the matter. More generally, the sum of black hole entropies and the ordinary entropy outside the black holes cannot decrease. This is the generalized second law—GSL for short. (p. 62)

This implies that when the matter and energy of a quantum system are absorbed into a black hole, huge amounts of information should spew out or be made available within the deep substrates of space. *Scientific America* (November

2004) featured an article on *Black Hole Computers*, and states: *"Stephen Hawking was Wrong. Matter goes in. Answers come out."* The loss of entropy which occurs as matter and energy are absorbed into a black hole is compensated for by an increase of the entropy of the information—thus, answers come out—like the 0 and 1 sequences illustrated here as emerging from a mini black hole processor.

In an article on *Black Hole Computers*, Lloyd and Ng (November, 2004) explain that in the 1970s, Hawking proposed that when matter fell into a black hole, the radiation produced was simply random. However, the newer view now endorsed by Hawking is that the outgoing radiation is not simply random but *"a processed form of the matter that falls in."* The authors thus declare: *"Black holes, too compute."* (p. 54) Furthermore, the authors note: *"… a black hole is nothing more or less than a computer compressed to its smallest possible size."* Thus, when matter falls into a black hole past the event horizon, it cannot leave but the *"information content can."*

The total storage capacity of a black hole is proportional to its surface area. Susskind (2008) states the principle: *The entropy of a black hole, measured in bits, is proportional to the area of its horizon, measured in Planck units.* (p. 155) The illustration thus depicts the black hole as having its surface or horizon divided into bits, triangular sections containing 0's or 1's. This is counter-intuitive, as one might have expected that the information content of the black hole would be related to its interior volume. However, this is not so and instead the information is encoded on the surface of the black hole—on a two dimensional surface instead of in the 3 dimensional interior volume.

Paradoxically, this physics of black holes suggests that as a physical system of matter and energy collapses down to the level of Planck units at 10^{-33} cm and beyond, the amount of information potentially contained within a volume of space becomes huge—if there are indeed such mini-black hole dynamics. Bekenstein considers the amount of information contained within *'a Planck area'* which is the square of two Planck lengths of 10^{-33} cm—or 10^{-66} cm². At Planck's level, at zero point levels in the quantum vacuum or aether, the information content and capacity is potentially huge. Bekenstein states: *"The entropy of a black hole one centimetre in diameter would be about 10^{66} bits, roughly equal to the thermodynamic entropy of a cube of water 10 billion kilometres on a side."* (pp. 62-3)

The Cosmogenesis & Physics of Modern Science

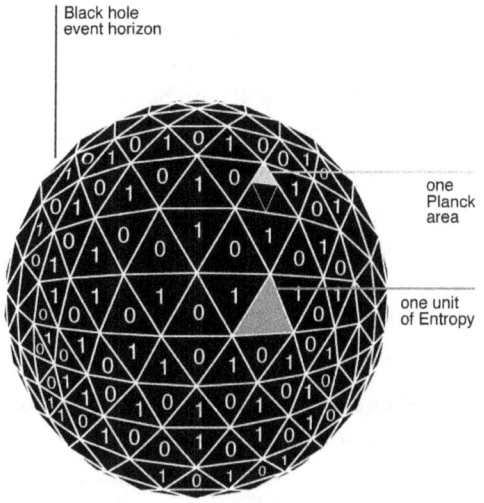

Dr. Bekenstein argues that there seems *"to be no limits to how densely information can be packed-and that our universe might be like a giant hologram."* In Bekenstein's model, the more we penetrate into the heart of being, vast amounts of information might be contained within the seeming emptiness and there might be such complex inner worlds and black hole dynamics. Black holes have both mass and rotational or spin properties, are capable of being electrically charged, and they could function as the ultimate mini-computers, processing immense amount of information at Planckian levels. Everything computes in the new science of information theory, including black holes.

Diverse new views of black holes suggest also that they are not such simple structures as once conceived. In string theory, they are regarded as:

> composite bodies made of multidimensional structures called branes, which arise in string theory. Information falling into the black hole is stored in waves in the branes and can eventually leak out.... Mathur... and his collaborators modelled a black hole as "a giant tangle of strings." This "fuzzyball" acts as a repository of the information carried by things that fall into the black hole. It emits radiation that reflects this information.

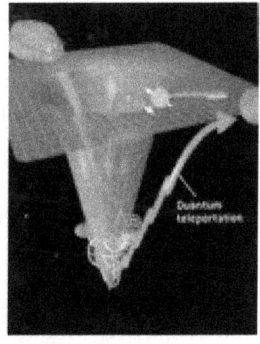

Lloyd and Ng report the work of Horowitz suggesting that this information has another "escape hatch" out of a black hole—that of 'entanglement,' whereby the properties of two systems inside and outside of the black hole remain correlated across spacetime:

> Entanglement enables teleportation, in which information is transferred from one particle to another with such fidelity that the particle has effectively been beamed from one location to another at up to the speed of light. ... The annihilation of the infalling photon acts as a measurement, transferring the information contained in the matter to the outgoing Hawking radiation. (p. 57)

Scientists are arriving at complex views of reality at zero point levels, looking at the information processor capacities of black holes and other structures at Planck's levels.

Lee Smolin, in *Three Roads to Quantum Gravity*. (2001) describes the world according to the holographic model emerging in physics:

> The world must be a network of holograms, each of which contains coded within it information about the relationships between the others. In short, the holographic principle is the ultimate realization of the notion that the world is a network of relationships. Those relationships are revealed by this new principle to involve nothing but information. Any element in this network is nothing but a partial realization of the relationships between the other elements. In the end, perhaps, the history of a universe is nothing but the flow of information. (Smolin, 2001, p. 178)

Smolin describes the atomic or quantized structure to space in terms of spin networks, information and relationships. Certainly, this is a profoundly alternative model of deep reality at zero point levels! It is almost as if an Omniscience might thrill throughout every finite point of the universe, if everything were parts of such larger holograms based on holes dug in higher dimensional space! Modern theoretical holographic physics certainly considers the most usual of ideas—quite relevant to Blavatsky's descriptions of seven invisible "holes dug in space," as the means by which higher dimensional intelligences inform material processes through the energetic activities of Fohat running circular motions. The zero point laya centres within the Stanzas of Dzyan might similarly follow such dynamics, spewing out information and radiation, and having mass, spin, magnetic and electric properties.

Dr. Bekenstein comments on the direction of modern physics towards finding deeper and deeper levels of structure at zero point levels:

> Many physicists today consider electrons and quarks to be excitations of superstrings, which they hypothesize to be the most fundamental entities. But the vicissitudes of a century of revelations in physics warn us not to be dogmatic. There could be more levels of structure in our universe than are dreamt of in today's physics. ... the deepest level of structure I shall refer to as level X. ... (p. 60)

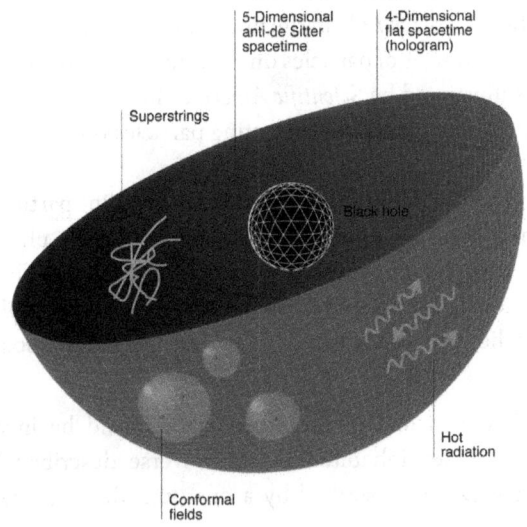

7c. Black Holes & Alternate Space Dimensions

This image is based upon that used within *Scientific American* to depict the most unusual ideas of the holographic model in physics. The interior of this sphere represents a *"5 dimensional anti-de Sitter spacetime"* and the circumference of the sphere, the shell, represents the *"four dimensional flat spacetime (hologram)."* Bekenstein explains that if the physics of the universe is holographic, then different sets of physical laws that apply in the de-Sitter spacetime (the shell surrounding the black hole) and the anti-de Sitter spacetime (within the sphere) are rendered equivalent. Thus, the *"conformal field theory of point particles"* applies on the two dimensional surface of the sphere (the holographic boundary or shell) and it is rendered equivalent to a physics of superstrings elements and black holes within the *"5 dimensional anti-de Sitter spacetime"* (within the interior of the sphere). Thus, what manifests in the physical realm is

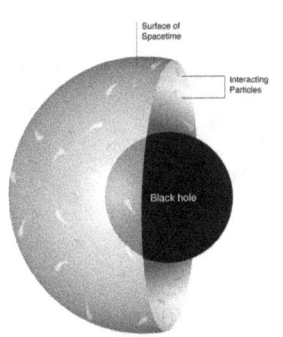

rendered equivalent to metaphysical processes in an alternative higher Space dimension (in this case the interior 5 dimensional anti-de Sitter spacetime).

The activities of a black hole in the interior of the anti-de Sitter space is rendered equivalent to swarms of particles on the boundary surface of the spacetime sphere. This was illustrated by *Scientific American* in 2005. The black hole at the centre is equivalent to a swarm as interacting particles on the boundary surface of spacetime.

Thus, quantum field theories and ideas about point particles might apply on the outer shell, but inside, superstrings and black hole physics apply. The holographic principle renders these two theories equivalent. The outer shell or surface of the sphere is compared to a two dimensional holographic plate which records or embodies processes occurring within the interior space. Bekenstein writes:

> Creatures living in one of these universes would be incapable of determining if they inhabited a 5-D universe described by string theory or a 4-D one described by a quantum field theory of point particles.

Bekenstein suggests that in this case, the three dimensional physical world is projected from a flat boundary or screen, the shell of the sphere, just like a holographic image is projected out into space from a flat two dimensional holographic plate. He notes:

> "... our universe, which we perceive to have three spatial dimensions, might instead be "written" on a two-dimensional surface, like a hologram. Our everyday perception of the world as three-dimensional would then be either a profound illusion or merely one of two alternative ways of viewing reality." (2003, p. 60)

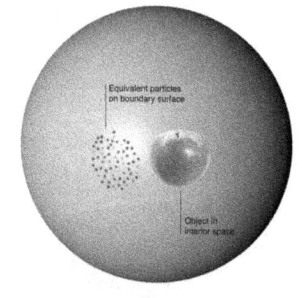

In this image, clouds of quarks and gluons on the boundary surface describe related complex objects such as an apple in the interior. The object in the interior experiences gravity even though such a gravitational attraction does not exist on the surface of the sphere. It turns out that the mathematics of particle physics are almost the same as the mathematics of string theory. What is so startling about this, is the fact that these phenomena are on such divergent orders of scale. The protons and neutrons can be 10^{20} times larger than the fundamental strings and they vibrate 10^{20} times more slowly.

Scientist L. Susskind similarly concludes:

the three-dimensional world of ordinary experience—the universe filled with galaxies, stars, planets, houses, boulders, and people—is a hologram, an image of reality coded on a distant two-dimensional surface. This new law of physics, known as the Holographic Principle, asserts that everything inside a region of space can be described by bits of information restricted to the boundary.... everything inside this giant shell is an image of microscopic bits spread over the shell.... everything taking place in the interior of the region is a holographic image of the pixelated boundary.... the world... is pixelated, and all information is stored on the boundary of space. (pp. 298-299)

Susskind comments upon this most peculiar holographic principle: *"Getting our collective head around the Holographic Principle is probably the biggest challenge that we physicists have had since the discovery of Quantum Mechanics."* (p. 305)

On the surface of the sphere, quantum theories and point particle analysis applies, but these reflect an even deeper metaphysics of membranes and strings, matrices and spin networks in higher dimensional space. Finally, at the centre of the holographic system is a black hole information processor in this alternate space dimension. This is analogous to how Blavatsky depicts material/energetic processes as based upon zero point foundations—*'holes dug in Space'*—established within an underlying seven skinned Eternal Parent Space.

Of course, Bekenstein and Susskind do not consider that such a model might be applicable to human beings—as their focus is on the black holes, information theory and the holographic principle within physics. It is not immediately evident how one might jump from the levels of Planckian units and elementary quanta in physics to the dimensions of human existence. However, the mystical idea—that the microcosm embodies the nature of the macrocosm—suggests the rationale for applying these concepts to the inner cosmos of consciousness. These concepts are all particularly significant in light of Blavatsky's description of seven such 'holes dug in space' as the means by which the Gods and other invisible powers 'clothe themselves in bodies.'

7d. The Illusion of Gravity

A holographic view of physics offers an alternative perspective on the nature of 'gravity.' In a *Scientific American* article on *The Illusion of Gravity*, J. Maldacena (November, 2005) explains:

the theories predict that the number of dimensions in reality could be a matter of perspective: physicists could choose to describe reality as obeying one set of laws (including gravity) in three dimensions or, equivalently, as obeying a different set of laws that operates in two dimensions (in the absence of gravity).... A hologram is a two-dimensional object, but when viewed under the correct lighting conditions it produces a fully three-dimensional image.

Gravity... would be part of the illusion: a force that is not present in the two-dimensional world but that materializes along with the emergence of the illusory third dimension. (p. 57)

Maldacena describes a quantum theory of gravity as the *"holy grail for a certain breed of physicist"* and explains that string theorists have developed such a *"complete, logically consistent, quantum description of gravity in what are called negatively curved spacetimes—the first such description ever developed. For these spacetimes, holographic theories appear to be true."* (p. 59)

The anti-de Sitter space is the simplest of such negatively curved spaces. They are neither expanding nor contracting, but look the same at all times. Maldacena explains the equivalency of the physics of these alternative dimensions in the interior of the sphere to those upon its boundary:

> the boundary of four-dimensional anti-de Sitter space at any moment in time is a sphere. This boundary is where the hologram of the holographic theory lies. Simply stated, the idea is as follows: a quantum gravity theory in the interior of an anti-de Sitter spacetime is completely equivalent to an ordinary quantum particle theory living on the boundary. If true, this equivalence means that we can use a quantum particle theory (which is relatively well understood) to define a quantum gravity theory (which is not). (2005, p. 61)

Thus, gravity, which can be accommodated within string/M-theory in the interior of the sphere, can be unified with the particle theories which apply on the holographic boundary on the circumference of the sphere.

In reference to the 'illusion of gravity,' Maldacena explains:

> gravity in four dimensions is an emergent phenomena arising from particle interactions in a gravityless, three dimensional world.... physicists have known since 1974 that string theory always gives rise to quantum gravity. The strings formed by gluons are no exception, but the gravity operates in the higher-dimensional space. (p. 62)

According to this formulation, *"gravity operates in the higher-dimensional space."* This is in accord with H.P. Blavatsky who argued that the underlying causes of gravity lay within the higher seven dimensional Eternal Parent Space and within the ethers of the Solar system—the electromagnetic ocean of life. The views of holographic physics and higher space dimensions illustrate the types of dynamics suggested by Blavatsky. Gravity is not simply due to non-sentient physical mass but has an underlying metaphysical nature, as all things adhere within the Aether of Spaces through zero point dynamics.

In physics, the holographic principle is a primary contender for the ultimate theory of everything—incorporating gravity with quantum theory. Gravity is incorporated within the alternate spacetime within superstring/M-theory (and black holes physics), while quantum theory (involving the triune electro-weak and strong forces) applies on the flat holographic boundary. Although there are many unresolved issues and problems to be faced in understanding this paradigm, it is a rich alternative model of how lower dimensional physics are an outward form or manifestation of a higher dimensional physics in an alternative Space dimension. This is the basic premise of *The Secret Doctrine* with its zero point 'holes dug in space' as being the foundations for the laws of nature.

The conjunction of an anti-de Sitter spacetime to accommodate string theory and black holes and produce the phenomena of gravity, and the de Sitter spacetime to accommodate the three other quantum forces of nature—produces a profound new model of higher dimensional physics.

It certainly seems that it is a strange universe we live in, wherein such vast amounts of information might be available at sub-atomic or zero point levels, which might surround a mini-black hole, or spinning *'holes dug in space.'* Further, there exists an alternative higher dimensional Space, whether or a 5-dimensional anti-de Sitter space—or some other formulation, such as a 7 dimensional Eternal Parent Space. This is exactly what Blavatsky was attempting to articulate, that the laws of physics evident within the material world, were really the end products of a higher dimensional physics in an underlying hyperspace and this includes gravity.

The holographic paradigm thus combines string theory and M-theory in higher dimensions which can incorporate gravity with quantum theory depicting particle interactions. Of course, there are many enigmas and uncertainties about these issues but scientists are certainly arriving at complex worlds underlying familiar reality. The authors of these articles do not really elaborate upon the implications and applications of their theories as they might apply to understanding our familiar reality—but illustrations using human examples are often used to depict the themes.

The physics within the interior of this realm of the anti-de Sitter space has other 'strange properties' according to Maldacena.

> Physics in anti-de Sitter space has some strange properties. If you were freely floating anywhere in anti-de Sitter space, you would feel as though you were at the bottom of a gravitational well. Any object that you threw out would come back like a boomerang. Surprisingly, the time required for an object to come back would be independent

of how hard you threw it. The difference would just be that the harder you threw it, the farther away it would get on its round-trip back to you. If you sent a flash of light, which consists of photons moving at the maximum possible speed (the speed of light), it would actually reach infinity and come back to you, all in a finite amount of time. This can happen because an object experiences a kind of time contraction of ever greater magnitude as it gets farther from you. (*Scientific American*, Nov. 2005, pp. 60-61)

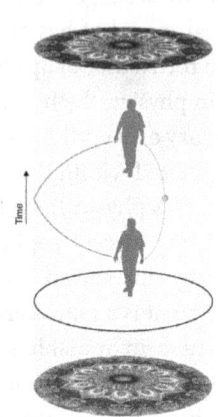

Within the anti-de Sitter space, the person is at the *centre of a gravitational well* and anything thrown out eventually returns to the source within a finite period of time. The negative space-time curvature in the anti-de Sitter space creates a gravitational field that pulls objects to the center, whether or not there is anything there. If a mass is displaced towards the boundary, it is then pulled back.

Certainly, if the outward physics on the holographic boundary reflects that of the hidden inner metaphysics, then we would predict that any effects produced in the physical world would similarly return to their source, just as must occur within the interior space. As above, so below: This might indeed lead us to hypothesize that the universe similarly will follow this boomerang principle and return to its source or gravitational well. This same logic might actually support another fundamental teaching of *The Secret Doctrine*, that of the law of Karma. Karma is just such an inevitable cosmic law, whereby the results of actions and inactions come back upon us. It is only a matter of time.

All of these concepts from modern holographic theory are helpful in trying to understand Blavatsky's archaic teachings about invisible zero point centres, circumgyrating holes dug in an Eternal Parent Space, information emerging from zero point levels and the principle of Karma as an intrinsic cosmic law, a metaphysical principle of higher dimensions.

8. The Akashic Field & Laszlo's Integrated Theory of Everything

According to Hindu teaching, Deity in the shape of Aether (Akasa) pervades all things.... The whole range of physical phenomena proceeds from the Primacy of Ether—Akasa .... (Blavatsky, S. D., pp. 343-4 & 536)

Scientist Ervin Laszlo, in the highly acclaimed *Science and the Akashic Field: An Integral Theory of Everything* (2007) and the *Science and the Reenchantment of the Cosmos* (2006), comes closest to the ideas of the aether as propounded by Blavatsky. Laszlo refers to Blavatsky in reference to the term *Akasha* in a chapter entitled *The Rediscovery of the Akashic Field*.

Laszlo explains that in the *"disenchanted world... inert matter moves impersonally against a backdrop of passive space"*—the familiar mechanist and materialist science. In contrast, in the *"enchanted world"* revealed by modern physics, biological science, paranormal and consciousness studies, *"the universe, with all things in it, is a quasi-living, coherent whole. All things in it are connected."* (p. 1) The medium for this interconnectedness is the Akashic field within the quantum vacuum which interpenetrates and sustains all physical manifestation.[20]

Laszlo provides a valuable conception of the nature of the Akasha, regarding it as a universally present field comparable to the universally present fields of the other forces of nature. He explains:

> what were initially seen as local force fields are later understood as universal fields, present at all points in space and time. Electric and magnetic phenomena are now ascribed to the universal EM-field; the mutual attraction of noncontiguous objects is ascribed to the universal G-field; and the presence of mass is ascribed to the universal Higgs field.
>
> The time has come to add another field to science's repertory of universal fields ... required to account for the special kind of coherence revealed at all scales and domains of nature, from the microdomain of quanta, through the mesodomain of life, to the macrodomain of the cosmos. This field is not the zero-point field, for its properties transcend those currently thought to be associated with that field. It is a different field, of which we know the effects but do not possess a mathematical description. It is nonetheless clear that this field exists,

---

20 Laszlo uses the spelling *Akasha*, which is generally more widely used than *Akasa*, as spelt by Blavatsky.

for it produces real effects. Just as electric and magnetic effects are conveyed by the EM-field, attraction among massive objects by the G-field, and the attraction and repulsion among the particles of the nucleus by quantum fields, so we must recognize that a universal in-formation field conveys the effects we described as "nonlocal coherence" throughout the many domains of science. ...

In the next development of science, the A-field will join the current known universal fields; the G-field, the EM field, the Higgs field, and the locally effective but universally present strong and weak nuclear fields. (2007, p. 75 & 77)

Laszlo concurs with Blavatsky on numerous points. Firstly, the Akasha is a field which interpenetrates the spacetime complex allowing for the correlation of all phenomena and non-local effects. There is nothing that is not 'action at a distance' for Blavatsky or Laszlo. Further, the Akasha is compared with the other fields of physics, as it should be. In fact, the Akasha is the original of the various fields and the fifth element, relative to those of fire, air, water and earth.

Laszlo points out that the standard *TOE's*, or theories of everything, within physics, are not truly theories of everything as they deal exclusively with the fundamental forces and quanta of nature, but not with a wide range of other phenomena which emerge in different departments of science and which must be accounted for. Laszlo discusses *'puzzles of coherence'* ranging across a wide range of disciplines—not only those of cosmology and physics, but also in biology, such as the instantaneous correlations of processes throughout living organisms regarded as *"macroscopic quantum systems,"* and in consciousness and paranormal studies.[21] In all of these areas, the new paradigm suggests an active role in nature of *"in-formation,"* which 'informs' or guides material and energetic processes. Laszlo defines information as *"a subtle, quasi-instant, non-evanescent and non-energetic connection between things at different locations in space and events at different points in time."* (2007, p. 6) This is the basis for *"non-local coherence"* throughout diverse realms of nature. The Akashic Field, in Laszlo's account, is a *"vacuum based holofield."*

Laszlo provides these descriptions of the Akasha:

In the new physics the unified, physically real vacuum is the equivalent of Akasha. It is the original field out of which emerged particles and atoms, stars and planets, human and animal bodies, all the things that can be seen and touched. It is a dynamic, energy–filled medium in ceaseless fluctuation. The vacuum is Akasha and Prana rolled into

---

21 We will consider Laszlo's views on the enigmas of coherence in consciousness and paranormal studies within our next sections of material. The focus at the moment is more on understanding the laws of physics and metaphysics within science.

one—the womb of all the "matter" and all the "force" in the universe. (2007, p. 77)

the unified vacuum fills all of space,... it is superdense and superfluid, ... it brings forth the particles that furnish local universes and receives them back at the end of their evolutionary cycle, and .. it generates the force-fields of gravitation, electromagnetism, and the strong and weak nuclear interactions, as well as the holographic field that instantly and enduringly interconnects particles and atoms, and all things built of them, in space and time. Science's emerging vision of reality is the vision of a reality that is interconnected and whole—it is an integral view of reality. (2006, p. 86)

Laszlo's enchanted world is congruent with Blavatsky's Secret Doctrine on numerous counts. In Laszlo's view of the *Metaverse*, particles and universes emerge out of and dissipate into a fundamental Akasha. Further, the Akasha is regarded as the source of the forces in nature and as embodying holographic field information—as a third force in relation to matter and energy. Information is holographically encoded within space itself. Further, Laszlo's description of the *"ceaseless fluctuations"* within space is analogous to Blavatsky *"ceaseless breath."* All of these concepts are consistent with Blavatsky's formulation of one Omniscience thrilling through every finite point of the Kosmos and a correlation of all forces within the plenum of Space, the Akasha.

Laszlo proposes a basic model of how information is holographically stored within the Akasha or space itself. He notes that particles have 'spin' properties associated with a specific 'magnetic momentums' and this is registered in the vacuum through *"particle-triggered secondary vortices"* which carry 'information'—just as do magnetic impulses on a computer disk. The interactions of particles create interference patterns which holographically carry information on the entire set of the particles that create them. Thus, *"interfering vacuum-vortices are nature's holograms."* Since the vacuum is superfluid, these interactions do not produce friction and information can propagate at speeds many multiples of c, the speed of light. This is why the enchanted world is essential 'non-local' and the Akashic Field is a *"cosmic holofield"* wherein even vast areas of the universe can be interconnected. Laszlo remarks: *"... the A-field of the vacuum records all things that happen in the universe."*

Laszlo provides this description of memory as inherent within all structures and latent within the Akasha (or the quantum vacuum):

The conclusion is evident. Vortices in the vacuum record information on the state of the particles that created them and their interference pattern records information on the ensemble of the particles whose vortices have interfered. In this way the vacuum records and carries information on atoms, molecules, organelles, cells, even on organisms and populations of organisms. There is no evident limit to the information that vacuum-waves could record and conserve. In the final count they can record information on the state of the whole universe. The interference patterns of propagating waves are holographic patterns in which the information conserved is in a distributed form: present throughout the patterns. ... Interfering vacuum-vortices are nature's holograms. ... the Akashic Field (is) a cosmic holofield.... (pp. 34-5)

In this view, the evolution of advanced forms of life on all its levels is due to *"vacuum-based information."* Laszlo maintains that *"life on Earth was not biologically, but informationally seeded."* (pp. 48-9) Edgar Mitchell, astronaut, consciousness researcher and commentator in Laszlo's book, similarly refers to *"the holographically information embedded in the quantum zero-point energy field."*

Although Laszlo's account of the Akashic Field, the A-Field, is excellent and similar to Blavatsky's descriptions of the Akasha on some essential points, there are additional dimensions to the Secret Doctrines still beyond the formulations emerging within the new paradigm of science. At a later point, we will reexamine some of the Secret Doctrine formulations in light of these newest ideas of holography, information theory and black hole microprocessors in higher dimensions.

However, firstly, we need to examine Blavatsky's descriptions of the *monads*, the divine sparks within living beings which are the life and consciousness principle within them. The plight of the monads needs also to be explored while drawing from the archaic *Stanzas of Dzyan*. We can then contrast the teachings of the wisdom traditions concerning human consciousness to the dogmas and theories of modern psychology, which deny the very existence of a spiritual or divine nature or element within human beings. After an overview of Theosophical teachings concerning the monads, we can return to the issues of holography and black hole physics—as all of these notions can be applied to human beings just as they can be applied to cosmological study.

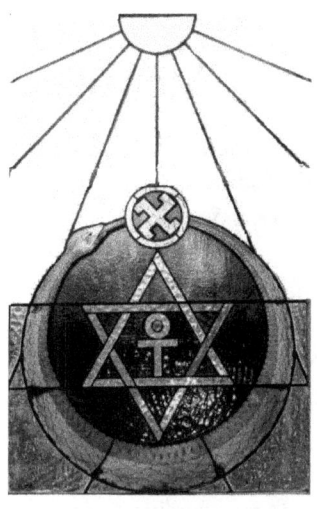

V
Pilgrimage of the Monads

THE SPARK HANGS FROM THE FLAME BY THE FINEST
THREAD OF FOHAT.
IT JOURNEYS THROUGH THE SEVEN WORLDS OF MAYA.
Stanza of Dzyan, 7, 5

*"The monad, then, viewed as ONE,
is above the seventh principle (in Kosmos and man) ... ."*
H.P. Blavatsky (S. D. I, p. 573)

"... a MONAD cannot either progress or develop, or even be affected by the changes of states it passes through. It is not of this world or plane, and may be compared only to an indestructible star of divine light and fire, thrown down on to our Earth as a plank of salvation for the personalities in which it indwells. It is for the latter to cling to it; and thus partaking of its divine nature, obtain immortality. ... a journey of the "pilgrim soul" through various states of not only matter but Self-consciousness and self-perception ... ." (S. D. I, pp. 174-5)

"... the monads are mere mathematical points and indivisible. ... Every monad is a living mirror of the Universe within its own sphere. ... in mirroring the world, the monads are not mere passive reflective agents, but spontaneously self-active; they produce the images spontaneously, as the soul does a dream." (S. D. I, p. 631)

1. Monads

Blavatsky uses the term "monad" in different contexts to refer to various entities on different orders of scale: a human monad, a Kosmos, a Son, an atom and even to *"a wink in the Eye of Self-Existence."* She wrote: *"... the term Monad being one which may apply equally to the vastest Solar System or the tiniest atom."* (S. D. I, p. 21)

Thus, although the *Stanzas of Dzyan* elaborate primarily upon the creation of the Cosmos, the verses also have a far broader significance and provide:

> an abstract formula which can be applied, *mutatis mutandis*, to all evolution; to that of our tiny earth, to that of the chain of planets of which that earth forms one, to the solar Universe to which that chain belongs, and so on, in an ascending scale, till the mind reels and is exhausted in the effort. The seven Stanzas... represent the seven terms of this abstract formula. (S. D. I, pp. 20-21)

Blavatsky regards the true elements or 'atoms' as existing prior to differentiation from a zero point centre. The laya state is the undifferentiated condition and the "eternal" and "normal" condition of the element. It only periodically that an element becomes manifest during cosmic differentiation, before eventually withdrawing again into its laya condition.

This primordial centre is the *"elemental atom"* or *"a jiva... a centre of POTENTIAL VITALITY, with latent intelligence in it."* (S. D. I, p. 566) Blavatsky explains: *"All those atom-Souls are differentiations from the ONE."* The differentiation from such a primordial centre initiates the 'pilgrimage' of the Son or monad through varied complex sevenfold dimensions of existence. Blavatsky wrote:

> "Pilgrim" is the appellation given to our *Monad* during its cycle of incarnations. It is the only immortal and eternal principle in us, being an indivisible part of the integral whole—the Universal Spirit, from which it emanates, and into which it is absorbed at the end of the cycle. When it is said to emanate from the one spirit, an awkward and incorrect expression has to be used, for lack of appropriate words in English. (S. D. I, pp. 16-7)

Blavatsky explains that the Monad is *"neither physical,"* nor is it composed of chemical elements, and yet it is a *"truly 'indivisible thing.'"* *"The Monads are not discrete principles, limited or conditioned, but rays from that one universal absolute Principle."* (II, p. 167) The Monads are not of this material plane and according to Blavatsky, *"can only be compared to an indestructible star of divine light and fire...."* (S. D. I, p. 174)

Pilgrimage of the Monads

Blavatsky explains that Stanza III, which describes the Re-awakening of the Universe to life after a *Prayalaya*, depicts *"the emergence of the "Monads" from their state of absorption within the ONE; the earliest and highest stage in the formation of "Worlds..."* In *The Secret Doctrine*, there is similarly such a Monad within a living human being and this element exists at zero point levels—within the higher dimensional metaphysics underlying the human heart. Within the higher dimensional Space of the heart, there is a Monadic Essence established within the seven-skinned Eternal Parent Space. This zero point centre is the foundation for the material bodies on different planes of existence. Recall Blavatsky's explanation that: *"... "material points without extension" are Leibnitz's monads, and at the same time the materials out of which the "Gods" and other invisible powers clothe themselves in bodies."* (S. D. I, p. 489)

The Monad in hyperspace differentiates from a Laya Centre and a web of spirit and matter are spun around it as it is embodied into the seven dimensions below. This metaphysical Heart centre is behind the electrodynamics of the material heart and the generation of the heartbeat, and the emergence of consciousness and life within a living breathing human being. Life and consciousness enters and exists a human being through the physics and metaphysics of the heart and the sevenfold *"holes dug in space,"* which underlie and sustain the material forms.

It is through the inner dynamics of zero point processes that Fohat, the cosmic electricity, conveys the influences of the Seven Sons above through seven invisible holes in space to inform the seven below—the material elements which form around the nucleus of the living being. Recall that whatever *"quits the Laya centre"* is drawn into the active vortex of life and the Sons embark on a grand pilgrimage in the worlds below. It is through such a higher dimensional magic that every monad *"is a living mirror of the Universe within its own sphere,"* as explained by H.P.B.

Blavatsky explains that each Monad is:

> an individual *Dhyan Chohan, distinct from others, a kind of spiritual individuality of its own*, during one special Manvantara. Its *Primary*, the Spirit (Atman) is one, of course with *Paramatma* (the one Universal Spirit), but the vehicle (Vahan) it is enshrined in, the *Buddhi*, is part and parcel of that Dhyan-Chohanic Essence .... (p. 265)

A human's divine nature is the Atma principle. Blavatsky explains that, *"the Self, is what we call Atma, and this constitutes the seventh principle, the synthesis of the "six."* These six are related to the elements of Ether, Air, Fire, Water and Earth and to the element of Manas. These seven principles are synthesized in the seventh element at the Heart of being. The Star of David with its central point illustrates the composition of the inner man or woman; just as it symbolizes the Dhyan-Chohans, the Lords of Light of the Invisible Sun, the Logos, and the actions of Fohat, the cosmic electricity differentiated into seven sons. The Atma is the central element and as Blavatsky explains: *"Parabrahman cannot be known except through the luminous Point (the LOGOS), which knows not Parabrahman but only Mulaprakriti."* (p. 432)

> Atma (our seventh principle) being identical with the universal Spirit, and man being one with it in his essence, what is then the Monad proper? It is the homogeneous spark which radiates in millions of rays from the primeval "Seven;"—of which seven further on. It is the Emanating *spark from the UNCREATED Ray*—a mystery. (pp. 570-571)

The point source Logos or Atma principle within the individual, the Monad, is not of this plane but established within a higher dimensional space, out of which it 'emanates.' The Monad is ultimately of a 'divine nature' and exists within a world of emanations, different from the world of radiations as related to the spiritual planes of existence. Sometimes the Atma is spoken of as the 7th element, although it is sometimes taken as the 8th, in its original abode within the Darkness.

> *Atma* alone is the one real and eternal substratum of all—the essence and absolute knowledge .... It is called in the Esoteric philosophy "the One Witness," and, while it rests in Devachan, is referred to as "the Three Witnesses to Karma." (pp. 570-571)

Buddhi is the primary vehicle for Atma, the spiritual nature or essence in contrast to the Divine nature. Blavatsky explains that humankind has the capacity to attain the triple Atma-Buddhi-Manas combination, the *three flamed fire,* which forms the upper triad relative to the four lower vehicles or bodies for the Jiva. Because of this triadic nature, as Blavatsky describes, *"... in man alone the Jiva is complete. As to his seventh principle, it is but one of the Beams of the Universal Sun."* (p. 224)

Blavatsky explains the role of Manas and what it adds to the dual Atmic-Buddhic nature:

> Cosmic Ideation focused in a principle or Upadhi (basis) results as the consciousness of the Individual Ego. Its manifestation varies with the degree of Upadhi ... through that known as *Manas* it wells up as Mind-Consciousness. (p. 329)

In contrast to the mind-consciousness of Manas, Blavatsky describes the *"stream of spiritual INTUITION"* associated with the Buddhi nature and the consciousness of the heart.

The four lower vehicles include the life prana, the *Kama* or passionate nature, the astral and physical bodies. Blavatsky presents this illustration in *The Secret Doctrine*. Thus a human being has an upper triadic nature as Atma-Buddhi-Manas and a lower four fold physical nature. Blavatsky explains the role of Manas

Pilgrimage of the Monads

in bridging between the four lower principles and the superior Atma-Buddhi nature:

> Manas, our *fifth* principle (the fifth, because the body was named the *first*, which is the reverse of the true philosophical order) is in affinity both with Atma-Buddhi and with the lower four principles. Hence our teaching: namely, that Manas follows Atma-Buddhi to Devachan, and that the lower (dregs, the residue of) Manas remain with Kama rupa, in Limbus, or Kama-loka, the abode of the "Shells." (p. 334)

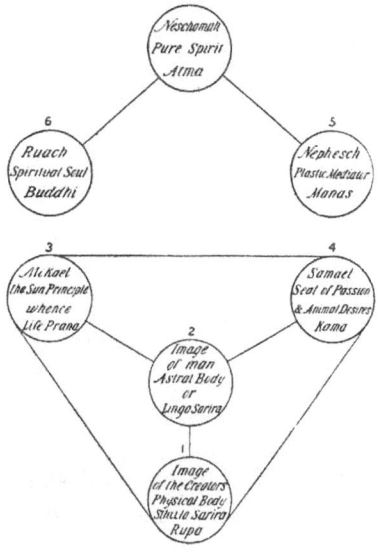

Blavatsky is describing the afterlife states and conditions as occur upon death. The higher *Atma-Buddhi-Manas* principles withdraw from the lower physical nature and pass into Devachan, the spiritual or heavenly realm. The lower manas remains attached to Kama, the passionate and desire nature (*Rupa* means *form*, in contrast to *arupa*, the formless) and is drawn into Limbus or Kama-loka, described as the *'abode of Shells.'* The Shells are soulless beings controlled by animal passions and the desire nature and haunting the 'loka' or sphere of such lower 'dregs.' The Oxford Dictionary defines *Limbus* as meaning *"edge, border; in Medieval Latin, a region on the border of Hell."* It seems that somehow the human soul can attain to either heaven or hell, and empty soulless creatures haunt the underworlds.

The seven principles in a human being correspond to the same principles of the seven planes of existence. Hence, Blavatsky describes seven possible levels of human consciousness:

> These seven *planes* correspond to the seven *states* of consciousness in man. It remains with him to attune the three higher states in himself to the three higher planes in Kosmos. But before he can attempt to attune, he must awaken the three "seats" to life and activity. And how many are capable of bringing themselves to even a superficial comprehension of Atma-Vidya (Spirit-Knowledge) ... ! (p. 199)

Certainly, the soul must cling to the thread that hangs from the Atma-Buddhi nature within oneself to attain more favourable afterlife conditions and to progress in the grand cosmic scheme of creation and evolution, ultimately allowing for the return of the Son into the ultimate states of Samadhi or Nirvana:

The "Monad," born of the nature and the very Essence of the "Seven" (its highest principle becoming immediately enshrined in the Seventh Cosmic Element), has to perform its septenary gyration throughout the Cycle of Being and forms, from the highest to the lowest; and then again from man to God. At the threshold of Paranirvana it reassumes its primeval Essence and becomes the Absolute once more. (p. 135)

The Monad is the Higher Self and as Blavatsky explains: *"It is the HIGHER-SELF, the real EGO who alone is divine and GOD."* (p. 445)

The monad... is here rendered as the *Atma* in conjunction with *Buddhi* and the higher Manas. This trinity is one and eternal, the latter being absorbed in the former at the termination of all conditioned and *illusive* life. The monad, then, can be traced through the course of its pilgrimage and its changes of transitory vehicles only from the incipient stage of the manifested Universe. In Pralaya, or the intermediate period between two manvantaras, it loses its name, as it loses it when the real ONE self of man merges *into Brahm* in cases of high Samadhi... or final Nirvana. (p. 570)

H.P. Blavatsky certainly provides a remarkable viewpoint on the higher dimensional origins and nature of human existence, life and consciousness. Just as cosmologists and physicists in modern times conceive of universes sprouting from singularities out of the nothingness of the quantum vacuum and possibly returning again at the end of time to such a final *omega point*, so also, *The Secret Doctrine* depicts such mystical dimensions to the lives of human beings! Such a conception of human existence makes modern thought and science philosophy seem puny indeed. Could human beings have their own white hole alpha points and black hole omega points, just as might the Macrocosm of the Kosmos? And could we live an afterlife, as before life, through a multidimensional universe of such unspeakable complexity and subtleness as Blavatsky describes?

Of course, the so-called real scientists all assure us that creation and life are accidental and random, and that a human being is simply a higher biological and material organism or animal, who lives and dies with the material body. Carl Sagan has declared that the cerebral cortex is where consciousness is manufactured out of matter according to fortunate circumstances and random mutations, and debunked the claims of such 'mystery mongers' as H.P. Blavatsky. Nobel Prize winner Frances Crick has declared that we are essentially nothing but *'a pack of neurons,'* and material scientist Isaac Asimov thinks that he would prefer his 'nothingness' at death instead of existence in some after-life state. Might Dr. Asimov have had the nothingness that he preferred, or gotten lost in limbo unsure of where to go? My God, life is such a mystery in light of *The Secret Doctrine*. In fact, the theories and ideas of modern science and psychology pale in comparison with the multidimensional holographic universe of H.P. Blavatsky.

Pilgrimage of the Monads

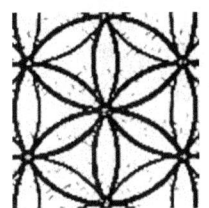

2. From the *Stanzas of Dzyan*

The third fundamental proposition of *The Secret Doctrine* declares:

"The fundamental identity of all Souls with the Universal Over-Soul... and the obligatory pilgrimage for every Soul—a spark of the former—through the Cycle of Incarnation (or "Necessity") in accordance with Cyclic and Karmic law, during the whole term. In other words, no purely spiritual Buddhi (divine Soul) can have independent (conscious) existence before the spark which issued from the pure Essence of the Universal Sixth principle,—or the OVER-SOUL,—has (a) passed through every elemental form of the phenomenal world of that Manvantara, and (b) acquired individuality, first by natural impulse, and then by self-induced and self-devised efforts (checked by its Karma), thus ascending through all the degrees of intelligence, from the lowest to the highest Manas, from mineral and plant, up to the highest archangel (Dhyani-Buddha). The pivotal doctrine of the Esoteric philosophy admits no privileges or special gifts in man, save those won by his own Ego through personal effort and merit throughout a long series of metempsychoses and reincarnations. This is why the Hindus say that the Universe is Brahma... for Brahma is in every atom of the universe, the six principles in Nature being all the outcome—the variously differentiated aspects of the SEVENTH and ONE. (S. D. I, p. 17)

Blavatsky postulates that the divine spark within a living human being derives from the Universal Over-Soul and acquires individuality through a series of incarnations and reincarnations in different realms of sevenfold Nature. Further, a distinction is made between the six differentiated elements and the SEVENTH, which contains them. This seventh element is represented by the centre point or ankh within the Star of David or by the central sphere of the 'seed of life' of Egyptian origin.

Stanza VII deals with the origins of life on the planet and the plight of the monads through the varied realms of nature.

1. BEHOLD THE BEGINNING OF SENTIENT FORMLESS LIFE.

FIRST THE DIVINE, THE ONE FROM THE MOTHER-SPIRIT; THEN THE SPIRITUAL; THE THREE FROM THE ONE, THE FOUR FROM THE ONE, AND THE FIVE FROM WHICH THE THREE, THE FIVE, AND THE SEVEN. THESE ARE THE THREE-FOLD, THE FOUR-FOLD DOWNWARD; THE "MIND-BORN" SONS OF THE FIRST LORD; THE SHINING SEVEN.

IT IS THEY WHO ARE THOU, ME, HIM, OH LANOO. THEY, WHO WATCH OVER THEE, AND THY MOTHER EARTH.

This verse suggests that initially there is the emergence of the Divine world and then the spiritual world. The "Mind Born Sons" refer to the seven Dhyan Chohans who are divided into three higher forces and four lower; just as these principles are divided withinin humans. Blavatsky comments on this verse: *"The hierarchy of Creative Powers is divided into seven (or 4 and 3) esoteric...."* (p. 213) The first generation of powers is then subdivided into *"numberless groups of divine Spiritual, semi-Spiritual, and ethereal Beings."*

2. THE ONE RAY MULTIPLIES THE SMALLER RAYS. LIFE PRECEDES FORM, AND LIFE SURVIVES THE LAST ATOM OF FORM. THROUGH THE COUNTLESS RAYS PROCEEDS THE LIFE-RAY, THE ONE, LIKE A THREAD THROUGH MANY JEWELS.

3. WHEN THE ONE BECOMES TWO, THE THREEFOLD APPEARS, AND THE THREE ARE ONE; AND IT IS OUR THREAD, OH LANOO, THE HEART OF THE MAN-PLANT CALLED SAPTASARMA.

This verse suggests that the One Atma becomes two in conjunction with Buddhi, and then the threefold appears as Manas is differentiated. These three, Atma-Buddhi-Manas are considered One and this is at the "HEART" of the man-plant call Saptasarma.[1] The term Saptasarma refers to a seven leafed plant sacred to the Buddhists and it represents the seven fold principles in humankind.

4. IT IS THE ROOT THAT NEVER DIES; THE THREE-TONGUED FLAME OF THE FOUR WICKS. THE WICKS ARE THE SPARKS, THAT DRAW FROM THE THREE-TONGUED

---

1   This representation of the Saptasarma is from G. Barborka's *The Divine Plan* based upon *The Secret Doctrine*. In *The Secret Doctrine*, different spellings of this term are used. In the opening listing of the Stanzas, the spelling is SAPTASARMA but in the body of the book, the spelling in the same stanza is SAPTAPARNA. (See pages 34 and 231.)

Pilgrimage of the Monads

FLAME SHOT OUT BY THE SEVEN—THEIR FLAME—THE BEAMS AND SPARKS OF ONE MOON REFLECTED IN THE RUNNING WAVES OF ALL THE RIVERS OF EARTH.

The three tongued flame refers to the Atma-Buddhi-Manas triad and these light (or bring life into) the 'four wicks' or the four lower principles.

The *Stanzas of Dzyan* next depict processes of metempsychosis and reincarnation as described in Blavatsky's third fundamental proposition:

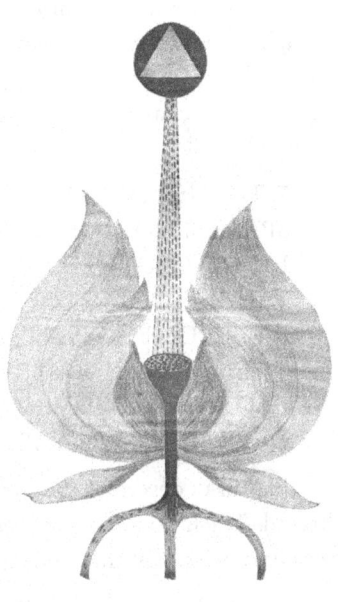

5. THE SPARK HANGS FROM THE FLAME BY THE FINEST THREAD OF FOHAT. IT JOURNEYS THROUGH THE SEVEN WORLDS OF MAYA. IT STOPS IN THE FIRST, AND IS A METAL AND A STONE; IT PASSES INTO THE SECOND AND BEHOLD—A PLANT; THE PLANT WHIRLS THROUGH SEVEN CHANGES AND BECOMES A SACRED ANIMAL. FROM THE COMBINED ATTRIBUTES OF THESE, MANU, THE THINKER IS FORMED. WHO FORMS HIM? THE SEVEN LIVES, AND THE ONE LIFE. WHO COMPLETES HIM? THE FIVE-FOLD LHA. AND WHO PERFECTS THE LAST BODY? FISH, SIN, AND SOMA....

Blavatsky explains that the seven Worlds of Maya refer to the *"seven globes of the planetary chain and the seven rounds, or the 49 stations of active existence that are before the "Spark" or Monad, at the beginning of every "Great Life-Cycle" or Manvantara. The "thread of Fohat" is the thread of life...."* (p. 238) Certainly, The Stanzas present a inspired view of the multidimensional nature of human existence as the Monad is embodied within different realms of nature working its way up to human form, which is informed by the SEVEN LIVES. Blavatsky asks, *"What is the Spark which "hangs from the flame?" It is the JIVA, the Monad in conjunction with MANAS... and hangs from Atma-Buddhi, the Flame, by the thread of life."* (p. 238)

6. FROM THE FIRST-BORN THE THREAD BETWEEN THE SILENT WATCHER AND HIS SHADOW BECOMES MORE STRONG AND RADIANT WITH EVERY CHANGE. THE MORNING SUN-LIGHT HAS CHANGED INTO NOON-DAY GLORY....

Blavatsky explains that the Silent Watcher is *"the Divine prototype... at the upper rung of the ladder of being"* while the shadow is at the lower rungs. With spiritual awakening and evolution, the morning sun light is progressively enhanced into a noon-day glory. However, Blavatsky explains also that Monads can through *"moral turpitude breaks the connection and runs loose and "astray into the lunar path...."* (p. 265) Individuals can be lead astray by the allurements of black magic, the lesser astral light realms and by their lower Kama nature (desires and passions).

7. THIS IS THY PRESENT WHEEL, SAID THE FLAME TO THE SPARK. THOU ARE MYSELF, MY IMAGE, AND MY SHADOW. I HAVE CLOTHED MYSELF IN THEE, AND THOU ART MY VAHAN TO THE DAY, "BE WITH US," WHEN THOU SHALT RE-BECOME MYSELF AND OTHERS, THYSELF AND ME. THEN THE BUILDERS, HAVING DONNED THEIR FIRST CLOTHING, DESCEND ON RADIANT EARTH AND REIGN OVER MEN—WHO ARE THEMSELVES....

Blavatsky describes the evolution of humanity as occurring through seven "Rounds," each of which is composed of seven periods with seven *root races*. Four races have passed in this fourth round and Blavatsky describes the situation of contemporary humankind with *"the middle point of the 5th being nearly reached."* (p. xliii)[2]

---

[2] Blavatsky portrays a grand evolutionary scheme—elaborated particularly in Volume II of *The Secret Doctrine*, entitled *Anthropogenesis*. Unfortunately, this is beyond the scope of the present analysis focusing primarily on the issues of cosmogenesis and metaphysics, but will hopefully be the subject of a second volume of *God, Science & The Secret Doctrine* exploring the issues of the origin, nature and evolution of human beings and the unknown history of humankind.

3. Evolution and Human Nature

No Occultist would deny that man—no less than the elephant and the microbe, the crocodile and the lizard, the blade of grass or the crystal—is, in his physical formation, the simple product of the evolutionary forces of nature through a numberless series of transformations; but he puts the case differently. (p. 636)

From an occult perspective, the modern tendency to dualistically contrast 'creationism' with 'evolution' is totally misleading, as occultism embraces both. However, from an esoteric view, there is both an involutionary process by which higher beings and powers produce materialized phenomena and living beings and there is an evolutionary stream involving the return movement from states of materiality to those of the spiritual and divine. *The Secret Doctrine* maintains that the astral body forms before the physical and both of these originate from forces on even more subtle planes of existence:

> In Esoteric Philosophy, every physical particle corresponds to and depends on its higher *noumenon*—the Being to whose essence it belongs; and above as below, the Spiritual evolves from the Divine, the psycho-mental from the Spiritual—tainted from its lower plane by the astral—the whole animate and (seemingly) inanimate Nature evolving on parallel lines, and drawing its attributes from above as well as from below. (p. 218)

Although one might consider evolution from above to below, in reality, the formative processes flow from 'within-without.' A commentary on the Stanzas of Dzyan thus notes: *"the form of man in the beginning evolves from within without."* (p. 184)

Furthermore, whereas modern so-called exact science considers evolution only from a physical or material perspective, Blavatsky explains that there are three simultaneous and interrelated evolutionary streams:

> there exists in Nature a triple evolutionary scheme, for the formation of the three *periodical Upadhis* (vehicles); or rather three separate schemes of evolution, which in our system are inextricably interwoven and interblended at every point. These are the Monadic (or spiritual), the intellectual, and the physical evolutions. These three are the finite aspects or the reflections on the field of Cosmic Illusion of ATMA, the seventh, the ONE REALITY.
>
> 1. The Monadic is... concerned with the growth and development into still higher phases of activity of the Monad in conjunction with:—

2. The Intellectual, represented by the Manasa—Dhyanis (the Solar Devas, or the Agnishwatta Pitris) the "givers of intelligence and consciousness" to man and:—

3. The Physical, represented by the Chhayas of the lunar Pitris, round which Nature has concreted the present physical body. This body serves as the vehicle for the "growth"... and the transformations through Manas and—owing to the accumulation of experiences—of the finite into the INFINITE, of the transient into the Eternal and Absolute.

Each of these three systems has its own laws, and is ruled and guided by different sets of the highest Dhyanis or "Logoi." Each is represented in the constitution of man, the Microcosm of the great Macrocosm; and it is the union of these three streams in him which makes him the complex being he now is. (p. 181)

This is a profound passage and depicts three evolutionary streams as reflections of the seventh Atmic principle, which is the Eternal principle or ONE REALITY.

Each of these evolutionary schemes is under the guidance of different Beings, Intelligences, Logoi or Dhyan Chohans. The Intellectual and Consciousness evolution are related to the *Solar Pitris*; while the *Lunar Pitris* are responsible for the formation of the astral body, which underlies the formation of the physical body (which also involves Pitris associated with the Earth.) Different cosmic forces are involved in the formation of the different vehicles, bodies or Upadhis, and man is indeed a microcosm of the larger macrocosm. Blavatsky explains that Nature on her own could not evolve intelligence unaided, and was only able to evolve *"senseless forms"* in earlier rounds. It is the Solar Pitris or Manasa-Dhyanis who fill this gap to link Spirit to Matter in this Round.

Of course, Blavatsky rejects completely the modern monkey to man business, noting: *"neither Occultism nor Theosophy has ever supported the wild theories of the present Darwinists—least of all the descent of man from an ape.* (p. 186) In fact, Blavatsky maintains that it was "men" from the Third Round (before ours) who had *"promiscuous connection with animal species lower than themselves, (which) created that missing link which became ages later the remote ancestor of the real ape as we find it now in the pithecoid family."* (p. 190) Blavatsky describes these as among the *"dumb races,"* the anthropoids and other apes which are half descended from man. Every Round brings about a new development and an entire change in the metal, psychic, spiritual and physical constitution of man, as these principles evolve on an ever ascending scale.

Blavatsky maintains that a Lunar Chain existed prior to our current Earth Chain and that humankind on our chain is the *"progeny of that of the Moon."* (p. 171) The moon is said to have played a role both in the formation of the Earth

Pilgrimage of the Monads

itself as well as in peopling it with human beings. Blavatsky states: *"The 'Lunar Monads' or Pitris, the ancestors of man, become in reality man himself."* These Lunar ancestors became man in order that the Monads might reach a higher plane of activity and self-consciousness. The Solar Pitris are then able to endow the "senseless shells" created by the Lunar Pitris with 'mind,' which occurred in the latter part of the Third Root Race.

The fourth member of any Round or Globe occupies a unique position, as it has no sister or companion globe on the same level or plane. It forms a fulcrum or balance with respect to the whole chain and a:

sphere of final evolutionary adjustments, the world of Karmic scales, the Hall of Justice, where the balance is struck which determines the future course of the Monad during the remainder of its incarnations in the cycle. And therefore it is, that, after this central turning point of the Fourth Race of the Fourth Round on our Globe—no more Monads can enter the human kingdom. The door is closed for this Cycle and the balance struck. (p. 182)

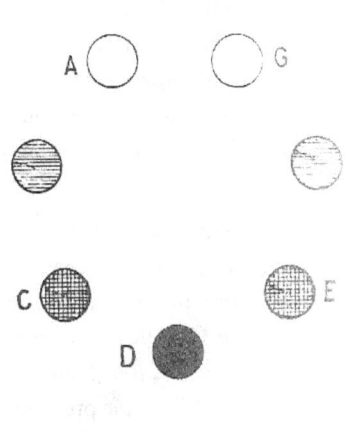

The cycle of metempsychosis for the human monad is now closed as we are in the Fourth Round and the Fifth Root Race.

The Secret Doctrine thus proposes a far more complex model of evolution than anything considered in modern science. Evolution is considered to occur within a multidimensional space and to involve simultaneous processes involving the monads, intelligence and consciousness, and the physical forms. The evolution of man's current physical body is the product of numerous intelligences and beings—Dhyan Chohans within different realms and is never simply a product of accidental and random forces even though Nature herself experiments and tries different avenues of creation. However, most importantly, The Secret Doctrine focuses on the evolution of the "inner, immortal man:"

It is the Spiritual evolution of the *inner*, immortal man that forms the fundamental tenet in the Occult Sciences. ... For, with every effort of will towards purification and unity with that "Self-god," one of the lower rays breaks and the spiritual entity of man is drawn higher and ever higher into the one and highest beam of the Parent- Sun. (pp. 634 & 638-9)

The Planetary origin of the Monad (Soul) and of its faculties was taught by the Gnostics. On its way back to the Earth, as on its way back from the Earth, each soul born in, and from, the "Boundless Light," had to pass through the seven planetary regions both ways. (p. 577)

How comes our physical body to the state of perfection it is found in now? Through millions of years of evolution, of course, yet never through, or from, animals, as taught by materialism. For, as Carlyle says:—"... The essence of our being, the mystery in us that calls itself 'I,'—what words have we for such things?—it is a breath of Heaven, the highest Being reveals himself in man. ... The *breath* of heaven, or rather the breath of life, called in the Bible *Nephesh*, is in every animal, in every animate speck as in every mineral atom. But none of these has, like man, the consciousness of the nature of that highest Being, as none has that divine harmony in its form which man possesses. (pp. 211-212)

All evolution is a product of intelligences and builders within varied realms and never simply a product of material forces, as indeed, nothing is simply 'material' in its nature. Ultimately, there is such a "breath of heaven" or a modification of the Ceaseless Breath within all living beings. *"Man proceeds from the Dhyan Chohan, and is a "Fallen Angel," a god in exile...."* (p. 450)

The Secret Doctrine proposes that there is a complex pilgrimage of souls occurring through the varied realms and seven dimensions of existence, and diverse builders and intelligences inform and sustain all cosmic phenomena. Blavatsky notes: *"the work of each Round is said to be apportioned to a different group of so-called "Creators" or "Architects," so is that of every globe; i.e., it is under the supervision and guidance of special "Builders" and "Watchers"—the various Dhyan-Chohans."* (pp. 232-233)

> while science speaks of its evolution through brute matter, blind force, and senseless motion, the Occultists point to *intelligent* LAW and *sentient* LIFE, and add that Fohat is the guiding Sprit of all this. Yet he is no personal god at all, but the emanation of those other Powers behind him who the Christians call the "Messengers" of their God.... Seven Creators called Elohim... the primordial Sons of Life and Light. (p. 139)

The role of the higher realms as underlying material processes is illustrated by Blavatsky's description of the 'germ' which is the spiritual potency which informs the physical cell or fertilised ovum. The "Imperishable Jivas" are "the germs that will fall into generation:"

> That germ will become the spiritual potency in the physical cell that guides the development of the embryo, and which is the cause of the

hereditary transmission of faculties and all the inherent qualities in man. The Darwinian theory, however, of the transmission of acquired faculties, is neither taught nor accepted in Occultism. Evolution, in it, proceeds on quite other lines; the physical, according to esoteric teaching, evolving gradually from the spiritual, mental, and psychic. This inner soul of the physical cell—this "spiritual plasm" that dominates the germinal plasm—is the key that must one day the gates of the terra incognita of the Biologist, now called the dark mystery of Embryology. (p. 219)

Certainly, Blavatsky offers a far broader view of evolutionary process than that offered within modern materialist science, which regards human consciousness and life as the fortunate and fortuitous by-products of simply material processes.[3] Further, living beings are regarded as having zero point or laya centres at the heart of being which allows the Gods and other invisible powers to well up from within without and to guide and inform all physical, psychical and spiritual evolution. There is a whole higher dimensional physical and metaphysics to the heart which allows for such a correlation of forces within the plenum.

---

3   Further, *The Secret Doctrine*, particularly in volume II *Anthropogenesis*, suggests a much longer unknown history to the solar system and the varied races and root races which have inhabited it through its varied rounds.

4. The Head Dogma & The Heart Doctrine

In this alone is contained the universal mystery, the doctrine of the identity of man's essence with god-essence, for him who understands the language of wisdom. (S. D. I, p. 78)

The Theosophists...are the first to recognize the intrinsic value of science. But when its high priests resolve consciousness into a secretion from the grey matter of the brain, and everything else in nature into a mode of motion, we protest against the doctrine as being unphilosophical, self-contradictory, and simply absurd, from a *scientific* point of view, as much and even more than from the occult aspect of the esoteric knowledge. (S. D. I, p. 296)

God, Science & The Secret Doctrine explores the zero point origins of three main phenomena—the Kosmos or Universe, atoms or quanta, and human consciousness. Blavatsky's zero point theses is supported by modern theories of the origin of the Universe and by physical theories depicting the mysterious nature of matter. Science regards the universe as having such zero point origins as a singularity and possibly returning again to such a *"naught point"* (Hawking's term) at the end of time. So also, theories about the nature of matter trace the atoms to quanta and then to superstring elements in a higher sevenfold space dimension—again, zero point sources as suggested by Blavatsky. And so, Blavatsky's thesis is supported and strengthened by scientific discoveries as to the ZERO POINT ORIGINS of both MATTER and the COSMOS. Scientists now believe that the Galaxy indeed might actually have such a black hole and singularity at its centre.

However, when it comes to modern consciousness studies, the idea of the zero point origin of human consciousness has never been considered. Instead, the 'scientists of new formation'—as Gurdjieff derisively calls them—have adopted *'the head dogma:'* the claim that material brain processes in the head somehow produce the inner consciousness, or awareness of being. Of course, no one knows where or how this is accomplished, or what this consciousness is. Nevertheless, researchers and theorists subscribe to this unsubstantiated assumption that the brain's neurological activities produce consciousness. Modern thought has also dismissed the study of the soul and of spirit as residues of religious and superstitious peoples, and assumes that we are simply material beings who live and die with the physical body. In the mainstream of modern psychology and science, there is no investigation of the soul, psychical phenomena or afterlife, nor higher states of consciousness and the like.

The contemporary scientific literature unequivocally demonstrates that scientists are in the dark about the mysteries of consciousness. This is exemplified by a recent *Scientific American* article—*"The Quest to find Consciousness"*—published in a special issue on *MIND* (2004). The most candid comments regarding consciousness offered by scientist G. Roth are that *"a true understanding of the phenomenon remains elusive,"* and further that, *"For now, no definitive explanations exist...."* When it comes to discussing 'states of consciousness,' Roth offers an extremely limited scheme of consideration:

> "Any effort to understand consciousness must begin by noting that it comprises various states.... At one end of the spectrum is the so-called alertness (or vigilance) state. States of lower consciousness include drowsiness, dozing, deep sleep and on down to coma." (p. 34)

A normal state of 'alertness' is put at one end of the continuum—as if this is the highest possible state of consciousness a human being can experience. All other levels are below this, down into coma and the extinction of consciousness. Roth assumes that there are no states of consciousness beyond basic vigilance. Hence there is no admission of any state of 'Self consciousness,' cosmic consciousness, spiritual or divine illumination, or God consciousness.

Unfortunately, according to the framework presented within *The Secret Doctrine*, the whole modern approach to consciousness is fundamentally flawed and misguided. The mysteries of consciousness are far deeper than imagined by Roth–who ends up associating the *"seat of consciousness"* with the association areas of the cerebral hemispheres in interaction with mid-brain structures. This is essentially the same view as criticized by Blavatsky in 1888: *"... its high priests resolve consciousness into a secretion from the grey matter of the brain."*

Current scientific thinking also regards consciousness as being *non-substantive*–that is, as being nothing in itself. According to this conception, there is no way for consciousness to exist separately from or beyond the mind and the body, because consciousness has literally no substance in itself–it is *no thing*. Psychologists and scientists further reject the existence of animistic or vital principles in the life of human beings and deny the existence of the soul. Ideas about the soul are regarded as having no scientific basis. Similarly, scientists have banished spirit from their considerations of the universe. The universe and life are regarded as having been created according to natural laws and principles, rather than being created by any kind of supernatural means or intelligences. Unfortunately, scientists generally have no idea of the profound alternative mystical and spiritual viewpoints on the issues of consciousness.

However, the mysteries of consciousness pose the most serious enigma for modern psychology and science. Scientists themselves recognize this. For example, science journalist John Horgan, in *The Undiscovered Mind* (1999), writes: *"Mind-scientists and philosophers cannot even agree on what consciousness is, let alone how it should be explained."* (p. 228) Horgan quotes Harvard psychologist Howard Gardner, who suggests that someone may find *"deep and fruitful commonalities between Western views of the mind and those incorporated into the philosophy and religion of the Far East."* Gardner suggests that a fundamentally new insight is necessary, although unfortunately, *"we can't anticipate the extraordinary mind because it comes from a funny place that puts things together in a funny kind of way."* (p. 260) These comments are ironic, as indeed, there is a fundamental difference between western views of the mind and the Eastern spiritual traditions and *The Secret Doctrine* with their emphasis upon the heart. Understanding this difference between the *head dogma* and the *heart doctrine* certainly does provide a novel perspective on the issues of consciousness—and put things together in a *"funny kind of way."*

While most people would regard the challenge of understanding human consciousness as being irrelevant to their life, this is simply not the case. In fact, if the strictly materialist conceptualization of consciousness is true, then this has profound implications for the nature and significance of human existence. Scientist Isaac Asimov identifies the most important of these implications:

> "The molecules of my body, after my conception, added other molecules and arranged the whole into more and more complex forms, and in a unique fashion, not quite like the arrangement in any other living thing that ever lived. In the process, I developed, little by little, into a conscious something I call "I" that exists only as the arrangement. When the arrangement is lost forever, as it will be when I die, the 'I' will be lost forever, too." (Asimov, 1981, p. 158)

This is the gist of the head doctrine. Human beings are purely material beings who live and die with their functioning brains. When the molecules or neurons are destroyed, consciousness is no more and so life ends at death and the "I" is lost forever.

The problem of consciousness has given rise to a diversity of ideas and theories, yet remains the most paradoxical, unexplained mystery within psychology and science today. Generally, theorists talk over consciousness, around it, under it, about it, but have few substantive ideas which do more than scratch the surface of this profound mystery. In this critical area, science is almost purely speculative. However, almost all recent theoretical perspectives subscribe to the common *assumption* that the brain produces consciousness and the mind–although the details of this magical transformation are completely lacking. When we look more closely at scientific explanations of what consciousness is, and *how* and *where* the brain produces it, we find that they are based on nothing more than speculation and hunches–a house of cards, as the eminent biologist and consciousness researcher Frances Crick admits.

If there is an immaterial mind, spirit and soul, or some form of irreducible consciousness, what are these things and how do they relate to the physically body and brain? There are many issues to be resolved and all the doors should be kept open in trying to understand these mysteries. The idea that a human being has a spirit or soul, or a zero point centre or divine spark, has not yet been disproved, because the nature and origins of human consciousness pose such profound mysteries. On the other hand, scientists' claim—that the brain's material produces consciousness—needs to be recognized as nothing more than an *assumption*. Scientists only *assume* that consciousness is produced by the neurology of brain processes and they gloss over the explanatory enormous gaps in their supposed explanation of this profound mystery. As Blavatsky simply notes: *"The Mind is the great Slayer of the Real...."* (1877)

Most science writers explaining physics and creation processes do not explore consciousness, except in a most cursory way. For the most part, they simply

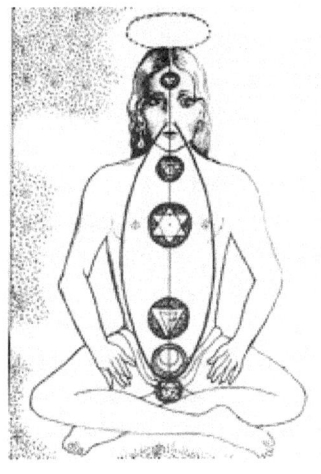

assume that the brain produces consciousness and that it arises at a certain level of biological complexity of brain function. Therefore, the theories and models of physics are not considered in relation to consciousness studies and consequently consciousness is generally left out of the equations. Similarly, psychologists do not even consider that there might be a physics or metaphysics to consciousness—or to the origin of the "I" experience. Scientists do not conceive that such an 'I' might exist. In contrast, Blavatsky (1891) comments: *"... every man as much as every God can boast of his existence, saying "I am that I am.""* (p. 17)

In contrast to the 'head doctrine,' the 'heart doctrine' regards the essential "I" as a point source Monadic essence established within the higher Space dimensions of the heart. The Monad, jiva-Atma or individual self, somehow infuses life and the light of consciousness into physical body through the initiating of the heartbeat, the circulation of the blood and the oxygenation of the body through the breath. Spiritual processes ensoul the material body through the heart, blood and breath—all through the electromagnetics of the living being. Consciousness thus enters through the heart in a newly conceived being and will withdraw into the Heart Space at moments of death–back into what the Dalai Lama calls the *'indestructible drop'* within the Heart.

Within the yogic literature, the indestructible drop within the heart is also called the *bliss sheath*. It is at the center of three major channels, (the Ida, pingala and sushumna), which circulate light through a system of seven chakras or wheels of energy within the subtle anatomy. Again, the circulation of light can be conceived of as embodying the number sequence 1-3-7. Blavatsky explains simply: *"From the one they become three; from the three, seven; from which seven primaries they fall into infinitude."* (1891, p. 26) Mystical teachings identify the 'Self' attained in 'self-realization' as involving the awakening of the Heart centre—depicted in the illustration by a Star of David with a central point—the seventh key. The realization of I within the Heart is the basis for Self-realization and for further states of samadhi, illumination and enlightenment as follows the awakening of the higher centres.

Most human beings—in the common sleepwalking condition—are controlled by the lowest three chakras (having only sounded the do, re and mi of their inner octave of being and evolution). Thus, the three lower centres control the common psyche and are related particularly to the pursuits of 'money, sex and power' within the tragic life of humankind. The awakening of the heart, the fourth wheel, can lend further to the awakening and realization of the three higher centres, each with latent psychical and spiritual faculties.

Mystical teachings regard consciousness as something different from thinking, feeling or sensation and action–the familiar 'psychological functions.' Consciousness is a more fundamental property and is identified most frequently with light and with Space. The Self within the heart is described as "self-luminous' like the Sun and the source of light rays of consciousness within the inner world. The light of consciousness can illuminate the realm of the mind and can be experienced throughout the whole body. This light originates within the higher Space dimensions of the heart and its influences circulate through the chakras, the subtle channels and bodies, and through the blood of the physical body. In this way, consciousness can exist throughout the physical body and is not simply produced within the head by neurological activity, nor is it confined there. Through the zero point physics of the human heart, a human being is ensouled by Fohat running circular errands and conveying the influences of Spiritual intelligences above. From one Monadic essence in the heart emerge seven invisible points, all part of that one, which form the centres of the seven chakras. There is a basic mathematics of light, of the 1-3-7, inherent to the metaphysical and physical structures of reality.

A human being can be regarded as a 'quantum system' and the material body does grow from a 'zero-point source'—a fertilized ovum, a barely visible point source—yet a whole inner world on another dimension of scale. From a point source, the body grows from within/without and the unfoldment of the biological growth is 'informed' by varied subtle fields of intelligence (energies and matters). The body is pervaded by such quantum information fields within fields. Certainly, considering a human being as a quantum system, the heart and not the head is the most dominant electromagnetic centre.

In *The Heart's Code*, psychologist Paul Pearsall (1998) maintains that, energetically speaking, the heart—rather than the brain—is clearly the centre of the psychological universe. Indeed:

> The heart's EMF (electro-magnetic field) is five thousand times more powerful than the electromagnetic field created by the brain and, in addition to its immense power, has subtle, non-local effects that travel within these forms of energy. ... the heart generates over fifty thousand femtoteslas (a measure of EMF) compared to less than ten femtoteslas recorded from the brain. (p. 55)

The profound significance of these facts leads Gary Schwartz and Linda Russe, in the forward of Pearsall's book, to comment:

> *The Heart's Code* points the way to a new revolution in our thinking. Metaphorically, the heart is the sun, the pulsing, energetic center of our biophysical "solar" system, and the brain is the earth, one of the most important planets in our biophysical system. One implication of the energy cardiology/cardio-energetic revolution is the radical (meaning "root") idea that energetically, the brain revolves around the heart, not the other way around. (1998, p. xii)

The heart is the largest source of biophysical energy in the body and within our psychological life. In Pearsall's view, the heart involves energy and information that comprises the essence or soul of who we are. Pearsall states that we have been too *"brain focussed"* in the search for mind and that instead of thinking in terms of a dual mind and body, a more rewarding and appropriate approach would be to adopt a triune model: of a thinking brain, the material body and the energetic and emotional heart. The heart is the primary energy centre within the individual and in Pearsall's terms *"conveys the code that represents the soul."* The heart's attributes and functions are much more mysterious and significant than conventional scientific thinking presupposes. Pearsall argues that through the psychology of the heart, modern psychology is *"beginning to make its first tentative contacts with the soul."* (p. 6)

The idea that the heart is the centre of the psychology of the individual instead of the brain would indeed revolutionize modern thinking about both normal and supernormal psychology. Adopting this view would be analogous to the Copernican revolution, wherein scientists realized that the Earth, rather than being the centre of the universe, circled around the sun within the solar system. With that radical re-conceptualization, human egocentrism was shattered. In the same way, a deeper conceptualization of the heart, consciousness and Self would constitute a revolutionary development in modern psychology, philosophy and the life sciences, and serve to further the understanding of the religious teachings of humanity. The esoteric side of all the world's primary religions elaborate such a heart doctrine.

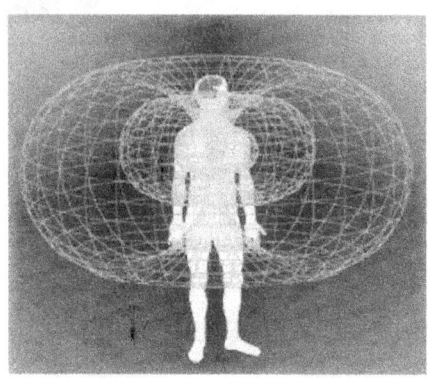

The Heart is the electromagnetic centre of a living being. The enigma of the inherent generation of the heartbeat is another of those unsolved gaps in the annals of science, which we would interpret differently within this perspective. There is indeed a higher dimensional physics and metaphysics to the heart producing such physical effects as the generation of life within the cardiac cells. Varied mystical teachings identify the Heart as the Sun of the body—not the brain or mind. Mystics compare the mind to the moon which only reflects the light of Sun, or of the Self. Further, the Mind can be enlightened expansively through the illumination of the Heart: as Manas is illumined by the Buddhic consciousness of the heart, in the terms of H.P.B.

In this mystical perspective, a human being does actually have a singular 'I,' not as a composite of cells or molecules, but a Monadic Essence at zero point depths in the deep Space in which we live and move and have our being. In terms of science, the monad might be depicted as such a seven dimensional Calabi Yau space, existing within the sevenfold Aether of hyperspace or the zero point fields of the quantum vacuum/plenum. There is some inner magic, a hidden physics and metaphysics to consciousness and the heart, beyond anything that modern scientists conceive with their 'brain secretions,' or their 'neurological correlates of consciousness,' as these are known.

According to *The Secret Doctrine*, a *divine spark* or Monadic essence is the essential zero point source of I. It is the source of individual light consciousness and of a life force within the living being. The Monad can be associated with the seven holes dug in Space within the higher dimensional Aether of the Heart. In a manner analogous to that of the Universe, seven invisible points or holes dug in space, real Space, are the means by which the Gods and other invisible powers clothe themselves in bodies. This is a "quantum Self," a real "I," a Monad, a jivatma, established as a metaphysical centre within the abode of the Divine Mother (the Parent Space). The influences of this 'God spark' or divine source emanation are clothed within the matters of the spiritual and psychical worlds and embodied within the physical heart. The presence of Self and this higher dimensional metaphysics initiates the heartbeat and distributes life energies and the light of consciousness through the blood and subtle matters to various levels of the body and psyche. The Self is a 'self-illuminating element'—the Sun of the body—and it illuminates inner psychological and psychic processes allowing consciousness and life within the inner world. This inner 'light' is intimately tied to the dynamics of a holographic universe.

In this view, there is an inner circulation of light, vitality and electromagnetic influences through the inner sevenfold constitution of an individual. The influence of Self within the heart centre is then distributed through a system of seven chakras, with the heart as the centre, three chakras above and three below. Each chakra has a zero point centre and a peripheral wheel of energy within a human being's subtle constitution. Thus, the Star of David with a seventh inner point is a perfect symbol for the heart centre and its positioning between heaven and earth.

The zero point *emanation* is from within divine and metaphysical dimensions of existence and is surrounded by a matrix—as it is clothed in different bodies in varied worlds spun out of a web of Spirit and Matter. Through the mechanisms and dynamics of such zero point centres, higher dimensional spiritual and divine intelligences do indeed *"micro-intervene"* within the laws of nature and all phenomena. A wide range of esoteric mystical and spiritual teachings suggests such an extremely peculiar perspective. It is quite astonishing then to discover that such a line of thought is consistent with contemporary scientific theories in physics—such as that which postulates seven dimensional Calabi-Yau Spaces underlying every point within the four dimensional space-time complex; or higher dimensional superstrings, Membranes and mini black holes in anti de-Sitter space. The ancient wisdom depicts such zero point sources, divine sparks or Monadic essences, with seven holes dug in space, at the heart of a human being or any Kosmos. The Sons expand and contract from such point sources through their own Selves and Hearts.

Each divine spark "reflects" the life of the "Self-Existing Lord," as a point source of supernal (or supernatural) light arising out of a sea of infinite light. Consciousness arises from the conjunction of divine sparks within the Divine Mother—the seven-fold Aether of Space. The Monad reflects the qualities of the Divine Father, the Self Existing Lord, the point source of supernal light, the lux. The sacred Aether of Space embodies the mysteries of the Divine Mother–

the Akasha, the Aether or ether–the medium of space itself, within which we live, move and have our being. Understanding the conjunction of the zero point Monadic essences within the holographic heart space is a key to unlocking the mystical origins of consciousness and self, as well as those of life and the universe. Mystical teachings depict a world of profoundly subtle dimensions interpenetrating and sustaining all of life.

The zero point is *a portal* by which influences of higher dimensions are channelled into physical manifestation. Below the zero point is the four-dimensional spacetime complex, while above it is rooted into a sevenfold higher dimensional space. The spiritual world 'ensouls' the material world through such peculiar zero point dynamics. Monads in Hyperspace exist within the innermost chamber of the Heart—with seven holes dug in space to enable the projection of a holographic universe surrounding a central laya condition. This is quite a remarkable view compared to that offered by the head doctrine!

VI
The Zero Point Metaphysics & Holographic Space of *The Secret Doctrine*

> *"Deity ... is in every point of the Universe."*
> (Blavatsky, S. D. I, p. 114)

> *"Occultism sees in all these Forces and manifestations a ladder, the lower rungs of which belong to exoteric physics, and the higher are traced to a living, intelligent, invisible Power, which is, as a rule, the unconcerned, and exceptionally, the conscious cause of the sense-born phenomenon designated as this or another natural law."*
> (S. D. I, p. 554)

> *"These abstractions become more and more concrete as they approach our plane of existence, until finally they phenomenalise in the form of the material Universe, by a process of conversion of metaphysics into physics, analogous to that by which steam can be condensed into water, and the water frozen into ice."*
> (S. D. I, p. 45)

1. The Basic Holographic Paradigm

There is but one indivisible and absolute Omniscience and Intelligence in the Universe, and this thrills throughout every atom and infinitesimal point of the whole finite Kosmos. (S. D. I, p. 277)

The term *holography* means literally *"to write the whole"* and suggests that any part or aspect somehow embodies the whole. Blavatsky articulated such a holographic model of creation—of physics and metaphysics, a century before science arrived at such concepts and possibilities. The modern ideas of holography and multi-dimensional physics now highlight the nature of the dynamics H.P. Blavatsky described. However, *The Secret Doctrine* suggested a more differentiated view of holographic dynamics than even that of contemporary science. Further, it applies the same perspective to understanding ourselves as holographic beings—microcosms of the macrocosm.

A holographic view is implicit in the *"fundamental dogma of Occultism:"*

The first and Fundamental dogma of Occultism is Universal Unity (or Homogeneity).... (S. D. I, p. 58)

no manifested thing can be thought of except as a part of a larger whole: the total aggregate being the One manifested Universe that issues from the unmanifested or Absolute—called Non-Being or "No-Number," to distinguish it from Being or "the One Number." (S. D. I, pp. 87-8)

The fundamental Law... the central point from which all emerged, around and toward which all gravitates, and upon which is hung the philosophy of the rest, is the One homogeneous divine SUBSTANCE-PRINCIPLE, the one radical cause.... It is latent in every atom in the Universe, and is the Universe itself. (S. D. I, pp. 272-3)

If there is *"one indivisible and absolute Omniscience and Intelligence in the Universe"* and this *"thrills throughout every atom and infinitesimal point of the whole finite Kosmos,"* then there are indeed vast information and zero point fields unseen within the fabric of space. Thus, any part is ultimately an expression of the whole.

In *Wholeness and the Implicate Order* (1980), David Bohm proposed such a model within physics. Although Bohm initially posited the existence of only the implicate and explicate orders, he later added a third level of dimensions—the super-implicate orders. He describes this hidden order as, *"a super-information field of the whole universe, a super-implicate order which organizes the first level (of the implicate orders) into various structures and is capable of tremendous development of structure."* (Weber, 1986, p. 33) The explicate order flows out of the laws and processes of these multi-dimensional implicate and super-implicate orders as apparent differentiations of an undivided whole:

> in the implicate order the totality of existence is enfolded within each region of space (and time). So, whatever part, element, or aspect we may abstract in thought, this still enfolds the whole and is therefore intrinsically related to the totality from which it has been abstracted. Thus, wholeness permeates all that is being discussed, from the very outset. (1980, p. 172)

According to Bohm, reality as it appears to our senses—the everyday world of matter and energy in time and space—is essentially a holographic image projected out of vast interconnected hidden dimensions. Bohm argued that there had to be deeper levels of structure within space which could respond to the quantum potential of the whole. He commented that an electron had to have at least as complex a structure as a radio receiver. Twenty years later, Dr. Bekenstein simply refers to an unknown *"level X"* and remains open as to what deeper levels there might be.

In the 1980's and 1990's, this concept of a part embodying the whole was the primary focus of the holographic paradigm. However, in newer formulation of the holographic model within physics, the notion of the part embodying the whole is secondary. Leonard Susskind (2008) provides these basic modern definitions:

> hologram—A two-dimensional representation of three-dimensional information. A type of photograph from which a three-dimensional image can be reconstructed.
>
> Holographic Principle—The principle that says that all information lies at the boundary of a region of space. (p. 453)

A hologram, as a two dimensional photograph, will appear to visual inspection as a jumble of light and dark areas. However, if a laser light is shone through the hologram, it projects a three dimensional image out into space. Similarly, the holographic principle suggests that information may be stored upon a two dimensional boundary or surface of a region of space, but that a three dimensional image (with gravity) is manifest within the interior volume of this surface. This suggests that a complex system of material-energetic processes might be informed by a inner complex of superstrings/membranes and black hole metaphysics within an alternative higher dimensional Space! Even such newer concepts of the holographic paradigm find support in the bizarre teachings of H.P. Blavatsky and *The Secret Doctrine*.

2. Gods, Monads & Atoms

"Whence the substance that clothes them—the apparent organism they evolve around their centres?" (Blavatsky, p. 632)

The *Secret Doctrine* maintains that the universe is founded upon an original zero point laya centre which differentiates into *seven zero point centres*. Whether a Universe, a quantum or an individual divine spark, the laws of nature manifest in the material worlds are due to Divine and spiritual forces and intelligences emerging within/without through seven dimensional zero point dynamics. Seven minute *'holes dug in space'* are the means by which higher dimensional forces sculpt the void through the process of creation and these form the metaphysical base of the laws of physical nature. Blavatsky offers this explanation of the *"Forces of Nature:"*

> all the so-called Forces of Nature... are *in esse*, i.e., in their ultimate constitution, the differentiated aspects of that Universal Motion.... Fohat is said to produce "Seven Laya Centres"... the GREAT LAW... modifies its perpetual motion on seven invisible points within the area of the manifested Universe. *"The great Breath digs through Space seven holes into Laya to cause them to circumgyrate during Manvantara."* (Occult Catechism).... "Seven Neutral Centres," then are produced by Fohat.... (S. D. I, pp. 147-8)

Blavatsky describes the great Breath or Law as *"digging holes in Space"* to channel intelligence and influences into the material realm. Any Cosmos, any Universe, any Monad (a divine or spiritual spark), any atom or quantum, is thus *"worked and guided from within outwards"* through the dynamics of such zero point centres. A *Stanza of Dzyan* reads: *"The Sons expand and contract through their own selves and hearts; they embrace infinitude.... Each is a part of the web. Reflecting the "Self-existing Lord" like a mirror, each becomes in turn a world."* (p. 489) The expansion and contraction of the Sons is through the zero point laya centre associated with the heart and each individual in turn becomes a world. At the heart of the universe, a galaxy, the sun, a quantum and a human being are such zero point laya centres, whereby the gods and other invisible powers clothe themselves in bodies. Thus, life within a living being originates within/without out of higher space dimensions through the dynamics of a multidimensional heart.

In elaborating upon the nature of Monads, Blavatsky distinguishes three distinct "Hosts" or classes, which:

> counted from the highest planes are, firstly, "gods," or conscious, spiritual *Egos*; the intelligent architects, who work after the plan in the *Divine Mind*. Then come the Elementals, or *Monads*, who form collectively and unconsciously the grand Universal Mirrors of everything connected with their respective realms. Lastly, the atoms, or material molecules, which are informed in their turn by their *apperceptive* monads, just as every cell in a human body is so informed. There are shoals of such *informed* atoms which, in their turn, inform the molecules.... (p. 632)

Gods, Monads and Atoms, form a hierarchy of dimensions of inner existence as propagated from within without, and which inform material and energetic processes manifested within a realm of existence. Each Monad is a Mirror of *"everything connected to their respective realms."* as information is holographically stored. These multidimensional zero point dynamics are propagated or reiterated through higher dimensional space.

Blavatsky then asks: *"Whence the substance that clothes them—the apparent organism they evolve around their centres?"* She then answers, explaining that:

> the *Formless* ("Arupa") Radiations...in harmony of Universal Will...unite together an infinitude of monads—each a mirror of its own Universe—and thus individualize for the time being an independent mind, omniscient and universal; and by the process of magnetic aggregation they create for themselves objective, visible bodies, out of the interstellar atoms. For atoms and Monads, associated or dissociated, simple or complex, are, from the moment of the first differentiation, but the *principles*, corporeal, psychic and Spiritual, of the "Gods,"—themselves the Radiations of primordial nature. (pp. 632-633)

Behind atoms are Monads, behind these are Gods and behind those, are the radiations of primordial nature. There is a whole hierarchy of inner metaphysical processes which inform and sustain living beings from within-without through zero point dynamics proceeding within higher dimensional Space—whether a molecule, a cell, a human being, a planet, a solar system, or a galaxy. These centres have magnetic properties and then serve to attract or draw upon matters produced by the ethers of space.

So, how are the centres "clothed"? The intelligences of a hierarchy of beings manifest through multidimensional zero-point dynamics, and Fohat conveys these influences through energetic dynamics. Further, these energetic centres, through magnetic aggregation, create bodies for themselves out of 'interstellar atoms' (in the case of a solar system or galaxy, or other 'foods' for other beings.) This is a remarkable conception of the inward structures and dynamics underlying existence.

Blavatsky describes such effects as propagated through different dimensions:

> The one Cosmic atom becomes seven atoms on the plane of matter, and each is transformed into a centre of energy; that same atom becomes seven rays on the plane of spirit, and the seven creative forces of nature, radiating from the root-essence… The atoms emanated from the Central Point emanate in their turn new centres of energy, which, under the potential breath of *Fohat*, begin their work from within without, and multiply other minor centres. These, in the course of evolution and involution, form in their turn the roots or developing causes of new effects, from worlds and "man-bearing" globes, down to the genera, species, and classes of all the *seven* kingdoms…. (p. 635)

The opening illustration depicts how a point within the central seed of life might multiply through a complex of higher dimensions through generations of causes and effects, as the same patterns of creation are re-iterated on successive planes of being. There are seven such centres depicted along the central axis of the figure.

In *The Secret Doctrine*, the Seven Sons of Fohat link Spirit above to Matter below and spin their magic through *seven holes dug in space*, the seven invisible centres within the Eternal Parent Space. The Universe, or any living Cosmos, is set upon such a foundation. These 'holes dug in space' might be regarded as seven mini white or black holes, according to whether we are speaking of the emergence or dissipation of a Cosmos. The seven holes 'dug in space' are 'whirlwinds' of activity—modifications of the Ceaseless Breath—which just like black holes, may have mass, rotational and spin properties, electric charge and magnetic moment.

Modern physics now actually supports such concepts and makes them more intelligible, rather than discrediting them as invented or exaggerated as H.P.B. describes. In fact, *The Secret Doctrine* postulates a holographic universe with a higher seven dimensional *Eternal Parent Space* underlying familiar reality, instead of the 5 *dimensional anti-de Sitter space* postulated within contemporary science. Further, instead of there being a singular black hole processor, there are seven interrelated processors, and seven surfaces or shells surrounding the central element—as layers of the Aether. Actually, we might consider there to be six surrounding surfaces while the seventh layer is the foundation of the central element. These dynamics are multiplied within without through various levels of higher dimensional space within the hierarchies of creation.

The Zero Point Metaphysics & Holographic Space

Thus, the metaphysics of a seven dimensional Monad in hyperspace or the Eternal Parent Space, with mass and spin properties of its seven holes dug in space, might be rendered equivalent to the physics of worlds spun out of spirit and matter which surround the central element—clothing it in different bodies. The six holographic shells surrounding the Monad are the basis for the physical bodies manifesting out of the ethers of Space. The metaphysics of the Monad in hyperspace with its seven holes dug in space could be rendered equivalence to the physics of the material and energetic processes made manifest in the seven bodies of the Kosmos or a human being. Blavatsky depicts a 'web' of spirit and matter spun around such central Laya Centres within holographic Space.[1]

Remarkably, modern physics is arriving at such zero point levels of creation and now posits just such a new 'metaphysics' to supplement the familiar physics of matter and energy within time and space. Of course, scientists would declare that there is nothing 'mystical' about holographic theory, information theory, black holes in alternative space dimensions, singularities, hyperspace or the quantum ether, or any of their theories and concepts, but that assessment is simply an expression of their prejudices and bias and not based upon any factual evidence and considered argument. There are many concepts from the Secret Doctrines illustrated by modern physical theories and speculations.

Another example concerns how physicists now consider that a string might be expanded from a essentially a point size at Planckian levels into any possible size according to the amount of energy added which expands the string structure. L. Susskind notes:

> Strings that are highly excited are bigger on average than their ground state counterparts; the additional energy whips them around and stretches them to a longer length. If you could bombard a string with enough energy, it would spread out and become as big as a violently jittering, tangled ball of yarn. And there is no limit; with even more energy, the string could be excited to any size. ... black holes—even those giants at the centres of galaxies—are enormously large, tangled "monster strings." (2008, pp. 337-8)

---

1   Blavatsky describes ordinary space and location as 'illusory' and suggests that there are innumerable worlds interpenetrating our own space, however invisible these are to us. This is similar to how different images can be projected from a hologram by simply shifting the angle of the laser light source.

Might dynamics occurring through the zero point centres similarly lead to expanding structures within both hyperspace and then physical space dimensions? Further, as black holes (or white holes) might be such tangled monster strings, we can conceive of how multidimensional holes dug in space could be the basis of such expanding structures through dimensions of hyperspace and then for these dynamics to produce an expanding Kosmos within different materialized dimensions of existence, due to the presence of the ethers of space—the holographic shells or boundaries, the veils of nature.

Spirit (Intelligence) ensouls matter through zero point dynamics and the *circumgyrating motions* of the seven Fohats—seven variants of Cosmic Electricity—within the seven ethers of Space. These metaphysical processes in a higher dimensional space are rendered equivalent to outward worlds of seemingly separate material particles moving about in external four-dimensional spacetime. The central point is thus 'clothed' in different bodies. In Blavatsky's view, there are varied external four-dimensional spacetime realms—physical, astral and mental worlds, each an illusory projection of dynamics founded upon another of the holographic boundaries or shells but created surrounding the central holes dug in space. Living beings have such LIFE Centres, as Monads existing within the Eternal Parent Space, and the outward physics of life is created as a great Chain of Being surrounding the higher dimensional metaphysics of a Monad in Hyperspace.

In terms of the holographic paradigm, a seven dimensional white hole—black hole zero point centre is established within a seven-dimensional Eternal Parent Space. The whirlwind activities emanating from this centre might appear as a radiant sun on the surfaces of the boundary spaces and give rise to material particles of different densities on different holographic shells. The modern physical concepts of mini-black holes as having mass and spin properties, and spewing out information, are all quite consistent with Blavatsky's archaic teachings. Divine Mind acts through such zero point centres and dynamics, which might manifest as hot radiations and materials on successive holographic shells, the seven ethers of space. A web of interrelationship is spun out of Spirit and Matter through levels of a multi-dimensional holographic universe. Each Star, each Universe, each Son or Monad, embodies such a higher dimensional geometry and metaphysics emerging within-without from zero point centres.

The newest models of the seven dimensional Calabi-Yau elements with multiple interior holes, of quantum information theory and the baffling holism of quantum theory, the manner in which *"It"* comes from *"Q-bit"* as material-energetic systems emerge from a quantized realm of information, the physics of black holes—all of these theories combined with explorations of singularities and vacuum genesis, serve to illustrate the profound secret doctrine explained by Blavatsky in 1888. While the scientists of her day conceived of solid material particles bouncing around in empty space and influencing each other through only local effects, Blavatsky was elaborating a holographic model of holes dug in higher dimensional Space as the basis for the manifestation of Kosmos, Atoms and Man. In Blavatsky's view, there are no phenomena due simply to 'local effects' because all manifest phenomena are produced by this inner hierarchy of effects reiterated through higher dimensions.

The history of the past century of physics and cosmology demonstrates major advances in substantiating concepts elaborated within *The Secret Doctrine*—in terms of understanding creation dynamics and the laws of physics and metaphysics. This is really quite astonishing. *The Secret Doctrine* presents a holographic model which reveals external reality to be ultimately, an illusory projection of metaphysical processes.

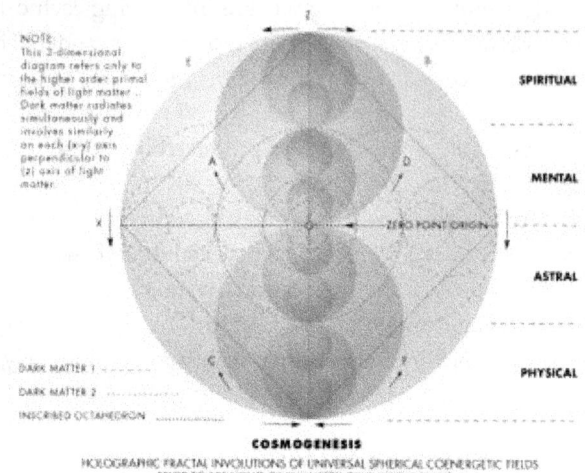

COSMOGENESIS
HOLOGRAPHIC FRACTAL INVOLUTIONS OF UNIVERSAL SPHERICAL COENERGETIC FIELDS
PRIOR TO BREAKING OF SYMMETRY ON PHYSICAL PLANE
ANALOGOUS TO HYPERSPACE FIELDS SURROUNDING EVERY MATERIAL FORM
AND TO ZPE FIELDS IN PLANCK VACUUM

3. Spinergy and G-Force

The 'spinergy' is the spin energy of the zero point sphere, and its sevenfold modification of the Eternal Ceaseless Breath, all around a point of 'absolute emptiness.' (Maurer, 2007)

Leon Maurer is an inventor, theorist and Theosophist, who has studied *The Secret Doctrine* as well as modern physics—including string/ M-theory and the holographic paradigm. My exposure to L. Maurer's work has been through Internet discussion groups at *theos-talk@yahoogroups.com*, *MindBrain@yahoogroups.com* and www.blavatsky.net. Mr. Maurer coins the word *'spinergy'* to depict the 'spin energy' of zero point dynamics and he conceives of dynamics similar to those being elaborated within *God, Science & The Secret Doctrine*. He writes:

> in my ABC theory, ... we start from the dimensionless zero-point and its abstract motion or "spinergy," and trace its essentially spherical expansion in a completely logical progression, through the transcendental hyperspace dimensions, as they fractally involve down and, after breaking their symmetry, finally evolve to the 4-D space (3 metric dimensions plus time) we experience. (Maurer, theos-talk@yahoogroups.com, Jan. 2004)

Maurer provides valuable descriptions of cosmic dynamics originating from *"the dimensionless zero point"* with its *'abstract motion'* or *'spinergy.'* He describes a spherical expansion from the zero point source through the "transcendental hyperspace dimensions'—the seven skinned *Eternal Parent Space* of *The Secret Doctrine*—which manifests eventually as our familiar 4-D spacetime. He depicts the 'fractal' involution from such zero point centres through symmetry breaking and re-iterations, generations of causes and effects, all from within-without.

> the Cosmos must begin at a truly zero (or non dimensional) point... infinitely energetic. And, therefore, it can expand fractally to an infinite series of such points to fill any dimension (or rather, frequency/energy phase order) of hyperspace.... Consider that the zero-point in any hyperspace field is the only non-dimensional (immeasurable) aspect of that particular field (that has its own particular frequency/energy-phase of vibratory motion).

Zero-points of infinite energy exist within absolute space, or hyperspace, with infinite axes of potential spinergy or 'G-force,' which we can identify as Mr. Maurer's God Force. He describes this as *"the primal COLOR=3D "G-force" or "spinergy" (infinite angular momentum) circling the zero-point of absolute ground SPACE."*

Maurer incorporates the ancient wisdom of the *Stanzas of Dzyan* into his modern theoretical explanation of the higher dimensional metaphysics. A series of quotes highlight zero point dynamics:

> An abstract sphere of spinning primal force (uninhibited angular momentum of absolute space I call "spinergy") in its pre cosmic state of perfect supersymmetry and super-spinergetic balance -- composed of infinite dimensionless lines of angular (circular) motion, spinning (both clockwise and counterclockwise on an infinite number of axes at infinite degrees of potential velocity-frequency) around a static zero-point of absolute emptiness... The "rootless root" or "causeless cause" of everything that is, was or ever will be ....

> ... there are an infinite number of such iterations possible starting from our cosmic zero-point and its abstract motion or *"spinergy."* This makes credible the theosophical view (based on fundamental laws of cycles, periodicity, harmony, electricity, etc., that imply super-symmetry and conservation of energy throughout all dimensions of cosmic and pre-cosmic space); that there are at least 49 stages within each evolution of fields within fields within fields, etc .... starting from the origin of the Cosmos, and extending down to the sub-microscopic particle/waves such as, photons, quarks, and finally, the physical "strings" that the scientific theory of Superstrings postulate—but can't directly observe or measure.

The G-force is the spinergy *"around a static zero-point of 'absolute emptiness."* There are various inner levels of such holes dug in space ultimately emerging from One primordial point. Such spinergy conveys the influence of the Divine

Builders or Divine Intelligences through Fohat running his circular errands and successive generations of causes and effects.

Maurer also discusses the triune nature of the creation:

> As this universe might reasonably be the result of the radiation on only three perpendicularly crossed axes of the primal "G-force" or "spinergy"* (infinite angular momentum) circling the zero-point of absolute ground SPACE.
>
> That triple axis "singularity" would necessarily be repeated infinite times as parts of the potentially infinite axes of that essentially spherical zero-point.
>
> Truly, the universe is like an infinitely complex hall of essentially simple mirrors who's smallest and largest dimensions would have to be in the shape of a triangle. Another example of this is the fractal division or multiplication of an octahedron or diamond shape (which can be perfectly inscribed in a sphere) into an infinite number of octahedrons that extend from zero to infinity.

Maurer's G-Force differentiates again and again through such inner triune and sevenfold (or octave) patterns. It is these metaphysical processes within hyperspace—the spinergy around and through the central points, which serve to cause symmetry breaking within the surrounding Aether of Space and the precipitation of quanta and matter upon different planes of being. The zero point is thus clothed in different bodies. The Seven inside give rise to the seven outside, connected together through seven holes dug in Space. This certainly does *"smack of divine microintervention"* and the divine mathematics of the lux. Echoing the Pythagorean axiom, Blavatsky declared that: *"God geometries,"* and further, that *"Deity ... is in every point of the Universe."*

An equivalence is established between *the spinergy of a Monad in hyperspace* with various levels of the physics of M-theory, (Matrix or Membrane), String theory and quantum field theory, on increasingly material dimensions of existence. The holographic boundaries are the seven fold ethers of an expanding or contracting 'spherical' spacetime. On these boundary conditions, the electroweak-strong forces are unified and can account for the material-energetic processes but 'without gravity.' Gravity, in this case, involves the inner dynamic of the zero point centres within the Eternal Parent Space, through which the inner influences and Fohat serve to bind it all together. The cosmos contracts when the Breath of the Mother, as a modification of the Ceaseless Breath, touches it. This suggests that a movement within hyperspace will bring about the eventual dissolution of the Cosmos and not simply gravity acting upon blind matter. Through generations of causes and effects, the Breath of the Mother, adheres in all things.

It is as if the love of the Divine Mother holds everything in Creation together as gravity and at the end of time, ingathers the Sons or Kosmos to her Bosom.

The mystical descriptions of zero point centres can be meaningfully related to the most advanced concepts of modern holographic theory. In both cases, metaphysical processes within higher dimensional space are rendered mathematically and holographically equivalent to matrices, superstring elements and quanta, which collectively manifest and take form on the varied physical planes of existence! A higher dimensional metaphysics of sevenfold invisible holes dug in Space, circumgyrating wheels and spinergy, is rendered equivalent to the physics of the webs of life. The webs of life, the matrix of spirit and matter, are spun surrounding such a primordial zero point conditions.

Maurer explains further that:

> there could be infinite potential universes that can spring out of that primal SPACE—as similar fractally involved, electrodynamically coenergetic fields within fields within fields, ad infinitum... Each at different triple axis spin angles. The apparent reason they are invisible to us is that, as two axis of this universe could be the root of invisible dark matter, each parallel universe of the multiverse spins on similarly different angles of primal SPACE than the single axis of spin of the "light" matter in this spacetime universe....

Different universes could manifest at different spin axes of the original triple axis. Thus, *"infinite potential universes ... can spring out of that primal SPACE."* This idea of different triple axis spin angles might explain how other dimensional spacetimes exist within our own Space although imperceptible to us—as described by H.P.B. Further, a slight shift of the three axes might enable the material, astral and mental worlds to be illuminated within our awareness and experience, manifesting as other holographic spacetimes.

Maurer describes the most mysterious aspect of the zero point condition, noting:

> the zero-point... contains the holographic information for the evolutionary construction of the entire Universe—empowered upon each awakening, by the intent (will) and consciousness (awareness) of the empty zero-point itself."

Maurer states that the *"essential circular spin momentum"* of the zero point *"contains the holographic information"* for the entire construction of the universe. There is indeed a deep frequency domain in this holographic model of existence and these holes dug in space might embody vast amounts of information and even Divine Intelligence.

Whereas physics has arrived at the holographic paradigm, models of higher dimensions, mini-black holes computers and holographic boundaries, they do not provide a philosophy or perspective on what such concepts might mean to us in regards to the phenomena of life and our own existence. In contrast, a mystical perspective on spinergy, 3-D axis and higher dimensions, allows us to understand that we are living in such a multiverse and that there are other worlds within worlds. Shift the angles of the 3-D axes and a different holographic shell provides the physics for another world—an astral world, a mental world, or higher worlds on super-symmetrical planes of being. Such ideas of higher dimensional metaphysics are not simply a matter of interest for the physicists but for us as beings living within a multidimensional universe.

Science has yet to even begin to explain the many states of afterlife existence, the mechanisms of coincidences, the vast evidences for paranormal phenomena, reincarnation, other worlds, and the like. Modern science has no model to allow us to understand any of the mysteries of such things. Modern soul-less psychology and spirit-less science will never understand the enigmas of the Ethers or Space, or the occult teachings of zero point dynamics.

Consider again, Blavatsky's description of space:

> The Secret Doctrine—postulating that conditioned or limited space (location) has no real being except in this world of illusion, or, in other words, in our perceptive faculties—teaches that every one of the higher, as of the lower worlds, is interblended with our own objective world; that millions of things and beings are, in point of localization, around and *in* us, as we are around, with, and in them; it is not metaphysical figure of speech, but a sober fact in Nature, however incomprehensible to our senses.

> "... such invisible worlds do exist. Inhabited as thickly as our own is, they are scattered throughout apparent Space in immense number; some far more material than our own world, others gradually etherealizing until they become formless and are as "Breaths." That our physical eye does not see them, is no reason to disbelieve in them; physicists can see neither their ether, atoms, nor "modes of motion," or Forces. Yet they accept and teach them." (S. D. I, pp 604-6)

This is a remarkable conception of the nature of holographic Space. Leon Maurer's ABC theory and the present work provide an actual model of what could underlie such dynamics, while integrating the ancient metaphysics with modern physics. The type of 'space' referred to by Blavatsky is a holographic Space and slight shifts of varied axes, might enable many worlds to exist within worlds at many levels of zero point dynamics and vibratory creation. The zero point fields of the aether allow for the correlation of all things and enable the universe and the gods to somehow concentrate within a point.

The ordinary four-dimensional spacetime is an outward projection from within higher dimensions of real Space from zero point levels, whereby the finite is rooted into the Infinite. Amazingly, all living beings have such deep roots in higher and real Space. Further, there are all kinds of worlds, dimensions and beings within the same space as us although they are invisible to our perceptive faculties.

Blavatsky explains that there is a correlation of all forces within the plenum and that anything is ultimately a part of the whole. A Divine Omniscience is an information field present throughout the whole at every point. Blavatsky has provided a remarkable description of the possibilities of life in the plenum of Deep Space and of how Deity does micro-intervene within a point. It is immensely difficult to fathom the depths of these unfamiliar and yet profound occult views.

4. The Physics of Anti-de Sitter Spacetime, the Law of Karma & the Dissolution of the Kosmos

As noted earlier, the physics within anti-de Sitter space has unusual properties. Firstly, if a person is freely floating in anti-de Sitter space, he or she would experience being at the bottom of a gravitational well. Thus, *"Any object that you threw out would come back like a boomerang."* (Maldacena. *Scientific American*, Nov. 2005, pp. 60-61) The time required for an object to return is independent of how hard it is thrown, although it travels farther away on its round-trip. Maldacena notes: *"If you sent a flash of light, which consists of photons moving at the maximum possible speed (the speed of light), it would actually reach infinity and come back to you, all in a finite amount of time. This can happen because an object experiences a kind of time contraction of ever greater magnitude as it gets farther from you."*

If this physics applies within anti-de Sitter spacetime—that *"any object that you threw out would come back like a boomerang"*—and further, that there is an equivalency between this physics and the familiar quantum theory on the holographic boundary, then we would predict the same conclusion to apply to the fate of the universe. We would predict that the Universe will eventually return to its source. This higher dimensional metaphysics in anti-de Sitter spacetime should bring about the closure of the universe projected out of this higher dimensional physics, if the equivalence holds. Any universe born from a dynamic centre would eventually return to such—like a boomerang. The point source is the initial point of emergence and ultimately the point of absorption—as determined by cycle of the *Breath of the Father* passing over to the *Breath of the Mother*. These modifications of the Ceaseless Eternal Breath, the fundamental Holomovement, determine the cycles of expanding and contracting universes. The zero point centre manifests as a gravitational well as the Breath of the Mother touches it. A variation of the fundamental movement in hyperspace, *a modification of the Ceaseless Eternal Breath* within the *Eternal Parent Space*, will serve to ingather the universe to the 'bosom' of the Divine Mother. It is also 'as if' the love of the Divine Mother gathers the universe or Kosmos back to her bosom or Heart at the end of time—back into its original undifferentiated laya centre.

Similarly, anything differentiating out of higher dimensional space eventually returns to its centre, its gravitational well at the heart of being in higher dimensions. Whereas scientists regard 'gravity' and 'anti-gravity,' or dark matter and dark energy, as the solutions to the problems of universal expansion or contraction (as well as to the issues of the formation of super-galactic structures, galaxies and solar systems), Blavatsky's *Secret Doctrine* allows for an alternate model and interpretation of the facts and enigmas of science. Blavatsky offers a radically different interpretation of "gravity." Rather than being the blind force of material mass/energy, she conceived of gravity as a variation of the electromagnetic force in relationship to the underlying *"universal Electric Ocean, which is Life."* The Solar System has a dynamic zero point centre and the influences of the metaphysics and spin properties of its higher dimensional holes rooted in real Space serve to bind the Solar System through the varied Ethers of spacetime. All of the effects that the astronomers ascribe to 'gravity' are regarded as variants of Fohat, the Divine or Cosmic Electric and Magnetic forces, operative within the Aether of Space.

Blavatsky's doctrines provide a legitimate scientific model and theory as regards to the existence of such LIFE centres and the mechanisms by which Universes might expand and contract through such zero point dynamics. She provides an alternative model of the fate of the universe, the mechanism of cosmic dissolution and a valuable perspective on the illusions of gravity, space and location. Further, in terms of a rebounding or oscillating universe, Blavatsky describes a sevenfold pattern to this process and states that humankind is currently on the fourth round of seven rounds in such an overall pattern of such oscillations. Between rounds, the LIFE principle may withdraw from without within from one body and re-emerge into another shell within another spacetime, again vivifying the ethers of another holographic shell and being clothed in new bodies.

In the Theosophical model of seven rounds of creation, the first cycles are actually within higher dimensional realms and not physical at all as we consider this. Early life is created within the sphere as a projection of the first holographic shell—the first of seven levels of the holographic shells or boundaries. The spin properties of forces emerging through the interior holes dug in space manifest in sequential symmetry breaking and the production of various intelligences, energies and matters upon seven successive planes of being, the ethers of Space. Blavatsky's ideas provide a provocative and detailed elaboration of a metaphysical model entirely compatible with modern holographic physics.

The 'boomerang physics' of anti-de Sitter space is also analogous to the law of Karma derived from Hinduism and elaborated by Blavatsky. The effects of our actions, the seeds we sow, will come back upon ourselves and we will ultimately, in a finite time, deal with reactions and retributions upon ourselves for our activities. The law of karma is built into the dynamics and structures of the universe.

Blavatsky was fundamentally opposed to the purely materialist view of the cosmos—which depicts non-sentient matter running down into states of increasing disorder or entropy in a mechanical soulless manner. Instead, she postulated a higher dimensional physics emerging from zero point levels which introduces life into the illusory worlds created surrounding such mysterious laya centres. Of course, modern science still has had no concept of Spiritual or Divine Intelligences operative within the Cosmos and the laws of nature, but instead regards everything in terms of blind and unconscious forces. Further, scientists have yet to conceive of how their holographic dynamics might apply to the multi-dimensional nature of their own human life.

In *The Secret Doctrine*, any cosmos is a "Son" with such a point source of unfoldment. Each Son is also described as a *"wink of the Eye of Self-Existence,"* and a *"spark of eternity."* Modern holographic physics, like *The Secret Doctrine*, certainly postulates the most unusual dynamics underlying the phenomena of life and make such ideas, as that of winks in the eye of self-existence, ever more conceivable.

5. The Holographic Mind/Brain in a Holographic Universe

...in some sense man is a microcosm of the universe; therefore, what man is, is a clue to the universe. We are enfolded in the universe. (Bohm, 1986)

Interfering vacuum-vortices are nature's holograms.... the Akashic Field (is) a cosmic holofield.... (Laszlo, 2006)

If there is truth to the possibilities of life after life, psychical phenomena, experiences of other worlds, disembodied mind, spirits and souls, and so on, then a fundamental revision is required in the modern understanding of the nature of reality. A human being is something completely different from what is currently imagined in modern psychology and science which regards man as simply a biological and material animal evolved through happenstance and random processes. The emergence of the holographic paradigm in modern psychology and science in the 1980s provided a basis for exploring hidden dimensions of consciousness, space and time—although once again, there were fundamental errors made in the approach. (These early explorations had of course no reference to the more modern holographic ideas in physics concerning alternate space dimensions, black hole physics and the like.)

In *The Doors of Perception*, Aldous Huxley described the possible relationship of individual mind to *"Mind at Large:"*

> each one of us is potentially Mind at Large. But insofar as we are animals our business at all costs is to survive. To make biological survival possible, Mind at Large has to be funnelled through the reducing valve of the brain and nervous system. What comes out at the other end is a measly trickle of the kind of consciousness, which will help us to stay alive on the surface of this particular planet.... The various "other worlds" with which human beings erratically make contact are so many elements in the totality of awareness belonging to Mind at Large. (1954)

Several philosophers have speculated upon this idea that the human brain acts as a reducing valve for *Mind at Large*.

The holographic paradigm emerged in modern psychology in the 1980s when Karl Pribram applied the principles of holography to the functioning of consciousness, the brain and mind. The holographic paradigm derived from the work of Pribram and Bohm suggested the plausibility of how a part of something might embody the whole, as an individual mind might embody the "Mind at Large." Essentially, the mind/brain is taken to exist in relationship to an underlying *"frequency domain,"* which consists of hidden dimensions containing information. The mind/brain then acts as a lens or filter, which focuses one particular space/time reality out of the underlying Mind at Large. A holographic mind/brain in a holographic universe might be rooted into deep hidden dimensions of being—given Bohm's model of wholeness and the implicate orders. As K. Wilber remarked:

> the brain is a hologram perceiving and participating in a holographic universe. ... the new science demands spirit; at least, it makes ample room for spirit. Either way, modern science is no longer *denying* spirit. (K. Wilber, 1982)

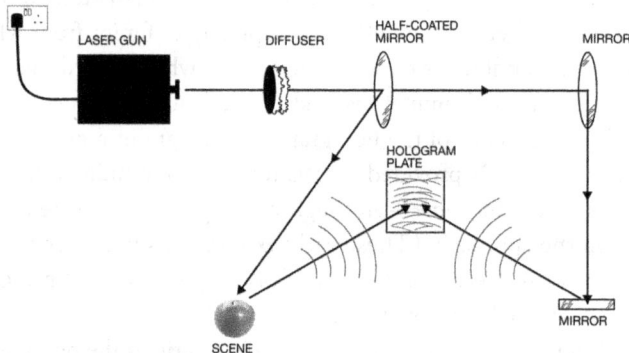

The principles of holography, a form of lens-less photography, were outlined in 1947 by Dennis Gabor. Holographs yield remarkable three-dimensional images of objects by using no lens, which contrasts with the usual flat two-dimensional photographs produced through the use of a lens. The creation of a holograph requires a source of coherent light derived from a point source, usually provided by a laser. In science, light is regarded as *coherent* if it has both temporal and spatial coherence. Temporal coherence means having one wavelength, or being monochromatic; and spatial coherence requires that the light issue from a point source, or be focused to a point. (Leith, 1976) In holographic photography, the coherent light beam issuing from the point source of a laser is split into two beams by a partially coated mirror. The *reference beam* impinges directly upon a holographic plate; while the *object beam* reflects off an object before impinging on the plate. The two light beams interact on the holographic plate to produce a wave interference pattern (determined by the phase shifts of the interacting waves and their mutual enhancement or reductive effects).

To visual inspection, a holographic plate bears no resemblance to the object 'holographed,' until the plate is again illuminated by a light source. In this event, a three dimensional image of the object is projected out from the holographic plate into space. In the reconstruction of the image, the interference pattern stored on the plate acts as a grating to bend the light by diffraction to re-establish the image projected. The holographic image produced with modern technology can be so similar to the original that it is impossible to tell the two apart. The projected image can be viewed from various angles and appears quite substantial and three dimensional—apparently real like our apparently real world. The holographic image is a *virtual image*, which possesses no substance or extension in space and is quite illusory and non-substantial.

The most unusual property of a holograph is that any portion of the holographic plate illuminated by a light source will recreate an image of the "whole" object: Any part embodies the whole within itself. The term holography means literally *"to write the whole."*

In order to understand how a holograph works, it is valuable to compare it with standard photography. A camera has a lens, which focuses the light from an outside source, so that a point-to-point correspondence is established between any part of the scene photographed and a portion of the recording film. By contrast, in holography, no lens is used and so light from the whole of the object impacts upon every point on the holographic film. Any point on the holographic film records interpenetrating wave patterns radiating from the whole object towards that point. The whole is thus *implicated* in any part, enfolded into each point. This unusual property of holographs suggests mechanisms for mystical states and knowledge, where the microcosm (the individual) embodies at some deep level the macrocosm (the larger world). A point implicates the whole, as individual mind might implicate Mind at Large.

This unusual property of holographs led a distinguished neuro-scientist, Dr. Karl Pribram, to apply this model to the study of the brain/mind. Initially, Pribram was attempting to explain why "memory engrams," the supposed site and substance of memory, did not appear to be localized within the brain. The traditional mechanistic model of memory predicted that memories are established by specific microcircuits or cell assembles (an atomistic approach) localized in particular areas of the brain. However, experimental evidence demonstrated that learning and memory were maintained in laboratory animals despite the removal or destruction of large brain areas. The expected one-to-one correspondence between brain sites and particular memories did not seem to exist. This fact has historically posed a fundamental enigma in the study of the brain: how and where are memories stored?

In *Languages of the Brain* (1971), Pribram explained how various psychological processes could be based on holographic principles. The neuro-circuitry of the brain, with its own standing wave patterns, could serve as a referent beam and interact with environmental stimuli (other wave patterns) to produce complex wave interference patterns spread over areas of the brain. Neurological processes store the resultant wave interference patterns holographically over both small and large volumes of the brain, with different interaction patterns superimposed upon one another. This might explain why attempts to isolate particular memory engrams have been unsuccessful.

A holographic model of memory and the brain would allow for the storage of immense amounts of information. Scientists have developed ways of taking "multiple holograms" which can record billions of bits of information within a cubic centimeter of a thick holographic plate. In multiple holograms, successive wave fronts are superimposed in infinitesimal layers upon each other by varying the angles of the projecting light beams. Layers of neurons provide the *holographic film* necessary to record successive interacting wave patterns. This would be a highly efficient way to encode, analyze and synthesize immense amounts of information.[2]

On one level, Pribram suggests that the whole brain might operate holographically, while at another level, this holograph would be composed of innumerable small *"patch holograms."* Pribram explains:

> The holograms within the visual system are patch holograms. The total image is composed much as it is in an insect's eye that has hundreds of little lenses instead of one big lens. ... In each patch, the activity of the cells creates a wave front; I believe that the interaction of these wave fronts is what you experience. You get the total picture all woven together as a unified piece by the time you experience it. (1979, p. 80)

An essential feature of Pribram's model was the proposal that the same mathematics used by Gabor to develop holography (Fourier transforms) are used within the brain to process and analyze sensory, perceptual, imaging and memory data. Fourier transforms provide methods of breaking any complex wave interference pattern into its component frequencies. Laboratory data confirmed Pribram's prediction: in effect, the brain/mind performs mathematical Fourier transforms on wave patterns established in the neuro-circuitry of the brain. This was a radically different perspective on the functioning of the mind.

Although Pribram regards the brain as operating holographically, he does not believe that there is any *"laser beam in the brain"*—that is, any source of co-

---

2   Pribram (1982) suggested that "local circuit neurons" might serve to establish the holographic interference patterns. These local circuit neurons have no long fibers to propagate discrete signals. However, they are responsive to the waxing and waning of neural potentials (waves) and are responsible for horizontal connections in sheets of neural tissue. The brain could be recording wave interference patterns in layers, like successive impositions on a holographic plate.

The Zero Point Metaphysics & Holographic Space

herent *inner light*, equivalent to the point source laser light used to produce an actual holograph. In an *Omni* interview, Pribram was asked about this:

> Omni: I'm a little puzzled by one thing. When I first read about the holographic brain, I thought of it as a metaphor. Then I began to think you meant it as an actual model. Which is correct?
>
> Pribram: Both. First it was a metaphor. Then... a model developed, because the mathematics fitted the data gathered in several laboratories around the world. *There are no laser beams in the brain.* I'm simply saying that the brain performs certain operations, which can be described by Gabor's mathematics, to code, decode, and recode sensory input. (1982)

Despite its revolutionary account of the dynamics of the brain, Dr. Pribram's theory remained in essence an *"under the hat theory"* of holographic mind. He assumed that the holographs are produced solely by the brain's physiological mechanisms and processes, and further, he did not believe that there is *an inner source of light* to illuminate the holographs of human experience. There is no laser beam, no inner coherent light source within the inner world. Most significantly, the heart is not recognized as the source of any 'standing wave patterns' or as the main source of electromagnetic influence within the human being. Instead, Dr. Pribram assumes that the brain produces consciousness and the holographs are within the head where the mind is assumed to be. Pribram never considered the idea that the whole human being—as a complex system—could be a microcosm of the macrocosm.

However, it was the combination of Pribram's model of the holographic mind/brain with David Bohm's model of wholeness and the implicate order which created the basis for the holographic paradigm. Indeed, Dr. Bohm suggested that there are incredible amounts of information present within the frequency domain which the mind/brain can access—because *"the entire Universe... (is)... a single undivided whole."* The holographic theory and Bohm's model suggest that a human being is a microcosm of the macrocosm rooted into interior dimensions of being and the plenum, and connected to the larger universe! Paranormal researcher, S. Grof noted: "*If this (holographic paradigm) is true, then we each hold the potential for having direct and immediate experiential access to virtually every aspect of the universe....*" (1993) Certainly, a holographic universe provides an unimaginable playground for a similarly holographic mind, consciousness and Self.

If the whole of the universe is implicated in any (apparently) localized region (or point) in space/time, then the brain/mind could potentially have unlimited access to this underlying storehouse of information in the implicate orders—the *Mind at Large*. Pribram viewed the brain as mathematically extracting information out of the underlying frequency domain. Now it seemed that this frequency domain could indeed contain vast amounts of the information potentially available for analysis by the mind and brain. In this view, the brain/mind operates mathematically to code and decode information (wave patterns) out of the underlying frequency domain. Pribram explained:

> The frequency domain deals with density of occurrences only; time and space are collapsed. Ordinary boundaries of space and time, such as locations of any sort, disappear.... in a sense, everything is happening all at once, synchronously. But one can read out what is happening into a variety of coordinates of which space and time are the most helpful in bringing us into the ordinary domain of appearances. (1979)

Dr. Pribram described the possibilities of a holographic mind/brain in a holographic universe:

> if you penetrate through and look at the universe with a nonlens system (holographically), you arrive at a different view, a different reality... that can explain things that have hitherto remained inexplicable scientifically.... the mystical experiences people have described for millennia begin to make some scientific sense. They bespeak the possibility of tapping into that order of reality that is behind the world of appearances.... I wonder if somehow (the mystics) haven't hit upon a mechanism that lets them tap into the implicate order.... In terms of holographic theory, all those events (paranormal and transcendental states) are plausible if the brain can somehow abrogate its ordinary constraints and gain access to the implicate order.
>
> Leibnitz talked about "monads," and... (an) indivisible entity that is the basic unit of the universe and a microcosm of it. God, said Leibnitz, was a monad.... In a monadic organization, the part contains the whole—as in a hologram. "Man was made in the image of God." Spiritual insights fit the descriptions of this domain. They are perfectly plausible by the invention of the hologram. (pp. 33-4)

Unfortunately, although Pribram speaks of Leibnitz's Monads, he does not consider such an idea seriously in his own holographic theorizing, to argue that an individual might have such a zero point Monadic essence or some inner point source of supernal light to illuminate the inner holographic world.

Of course, there are many unknowns existing between Pribram's small holograms of visual patches or the holographs of the brain's neuro-circuitry (of all the patch holograms woven together) and the holographic states of cosmic or spiritual consciousness. Nevertheless, the holographic paradigm provided a way of trying to understand the deeper relationship of mind to matter, or consciousness to the world.

Pribram (1982) contrasted two fundamentally different assumptions *'about the brain.'* The first traditional materialist viewpoint regards the brain as organizing input from the physical world and constructing mental properties. Scientists assumed that mental properties are derived from physical processes. The second viewpoint is that: *"Mental properties are the pervasive organizing principles of the universe, which includes the brain."* Many influential physicists and mathematicians have subscribed to the second viewpoint. Sir James Jeans, a prominent physicist of the early part of the twentieth century, famously asserted that the more we penetrate into the nature of matter, the more it appears as *"a great thought, rather than as a vast machine."*

A critical idea linking the holographic theory of consciousness to holographic views of the world is that the mind is *isomorphic* to the world. Isomorphism suggests *"a one-to-one correspondence between the form (morphology) of the world around us and the form in the brain representing that world."* (Pribram, p. 80) In this case, mind is not simply an emergent property of the brain's material organization, but instead, it *"reflects the basic organization of the Universe (including the organism's brain)."* (1984, p. 33) Similarly, Bohm explains:

> The mind may have a structure similar to the universe.... The particular forms which appear in the mind may be analogous to the particles, and getting to the ground of the mind might be felt as light.... (a) free, penetrating movement of the whole. (pp. 48-9)

Thus, man might be a microcosm of the macrocosm—having an inner form which isomorphically corresponds to the inner structures of the universe. This is exactly the type of model suggested by the study of Blavatsky's *Secret Doctrine* but which the modern holographic paradigm does not recognize.

The holographic paradigm attracted wide interest within the New Age movement and among those interested in the personal and scientific issues of consciousness. One New Age spokesperson, Shirley MacLaine (1989) gave this popular account of the emerging paradigm of wholeness:

> the seeds of all things, ourselves included, were present at the birth of creation, and every scrap of matter and energy and blood and bones and thought present in the cosmos today could be traced back to the origins of the universe from one small subatomic particle of light. That makes us each sparks of the same light. It also makes each of us a hologram of the entire event. The energies that fragmented and separated and multiplied as the young universe expanded and cooled continue to operate in the beating of our hearts and the movement of

our bodies, as well as in the alignment and behaviour of the stars. We and they—all things and everything are a connected whole. That is the meaning of "We are all one." The evolution of the Universe then is continuing not only around us but within us. Our thoughts, our dreams, and our awareness are part of that universe, the physical and the spiritual inextricably bound together. (p. 259)

Bohm's theory, the holographic paradigm and quantum theory (with its non-local effects and quantum interconnectedness) collectively paint a picture of the ultimate interconnectedness of things. Everything did originate from a singularity or zero point state: out of a state of perfect symmetry as an original point source of light. Further, quantum theory does suggests that all quanta are ultimately interrelated in higher dimensional spaces, the active information fields, the zero point fields or the frequency domain of holographic theory.

Unfortunately, the holographic paradigm has lacked *key elements*—which has meant that the full implications and applications of this model have not been substantiated as a model of consciousness and creation. In this regard, Pribram's comment — *"There are no laser beams in the brain"*—is most telling. Firstly, it indicates that the idea of a laser beam or of a "point source of coherent light" to light the inner world is not seriously considered. Secondly, his comment indicates that scientists have primarily looked for such holographic dynamics within *"the brain"*—that is, within the head. Once again, we encounter the limits of *the head doctrine* and the neglect of mystical, spiritual and occult views concerning the deepest levels of Self and the higher dimensional physics and metaphysics of the Heart.

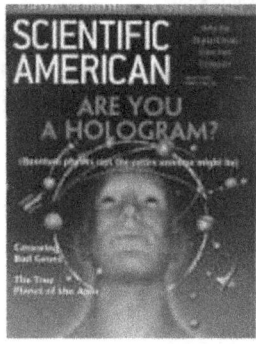

This *Scientific American* cover illustrates the assumptions of the modern high priests of modern psychology and science. They imagine that the head, a part of the whole of a human being, would be the basis for the human holographic system. Of course, the mind does function in terms of holographic principles, but it certainly is not the only basis of our experience of life. Of course, no one entertains such bizarre ideas of there being mini-black holes or white holes existing within the head, yet alone within the heart.

The mind might focus a particular reality out of the underlying frequency domain, acting as a lens to reduce Mind at Large to an ordinary world of objects and images manifest in space and time but this is not the complete basis of the human holograph. From the perspective offered by *The Secret Doctrine*, the holographic paradigm needs to be expanded to include the whole human being as a quantum system of electromagnetic influences, centered upon the higher dimensional metaphysics and physics of the heart. Further, mystics equate con-

The Zero Point Metaphysics & Holographic Space

sciousness with light and describe *a point source of supernal light* established within the higher dimensional Aether of the heart space. The addition of such elements to a holographic model would provide an alternative laser source of coherent light, even of the *divine lux*, to illuminate the holograms of our lives.

Mystics suggest that the isomorphism between the mind and the world does not simply happen somewhere up in the brain in the head. Instead, it involves the whole inner anatomy and the structures of being of the whole of the individual, centred in the mystical dimensions of the human heart and its laya centre dynamics. The individual microcosm reflects the same organizational and underlying principles as those that sustain the larger macrocosm. This certainly suggests vast possibilities for human consciousness and experience in a profoundly mysterious and enigmatic cosmos!

In *Science and the Reenchantment of Nature*, E. Laszlo (2006) provides valuable contemporary commentary on the possible holographic nature of a human being. As we live within the information fields of the Aether or Akasha, this could clearly be the basis of mystical states. Laszlo describes memory as inherent within all structures within the Akasha based upon interfering vacuum vortices. He states: *"the Akashic Field (is) a cosmic holofield ...."* (p. 35) Laszlo's answer to the neurological issues of where and how memories are stored, is that *"... long-term memory is not stored within the brain: it is extra-somatic."* (p. 57) Memories are available within the zero point fields and the Akasha and there are no discrete memory engrams within the brain.

Laszlo provides a curious case study which illustrates the potential information latent within the Akasha. He describes the talents of an *idiot savant*, an individual who is supposed to be below normal functioning in intelligence and adjustment, but who can speak seven languages, compute cube roots as fast as a calculator, and recall the constant *pi* to 22,514 decimal places! There is no known mechanism within a materialist and reductionist viewpoint to explain such unusual talents. How possibly could an idiot savant manifest such remarkable and complex talents—which are clearly not the result of education or the usual faculties of mind. Such case studies suggest that individual can indeed tap information fields latent within space or the Akasha itself.

Although at times, Laszlo tends to primarily relate consciousness and the mind to the brain, he holds a deeper understanding. Indeed, he notes: *"... the vacuum is ... the seat of the consciousness that infuses my body and brain the same as the rest of the universe ...."* (p. 88) Laszlo describes the experiences of seeker and mystics which illustrate his basic concepts:

> The field of cosmic consciousness they experience is a cosmic emptiness—a void. Yet, paradoxically, it is also an essential fullness. ... it contains all of existence in potential. The void they experience is a

fullness; the vacuum is a plenum. It is the ultimate source of existence, the cradle of all being. (p. 89)

Laszlo considers that human beings can so experience within various levels of the aether, as has been described for centuries through the mystical literature. Certainly, if there is one OMNISCIENCE which thrills throughout every finite point of the universe, as described by Blavatsky, then we indeed might live an enchanted life with access to such levels of the void, the plenum and many things in between.

6. Monads in Hyperspace

> Metaphysically and esoterically there is but One Element in nature, and at the root of it is the Deity; and the so-called seven elements ... are the garment, the veil, of that deity; direct from the essence whereof comes MAN, whether physically, psychically, mentally or spiritually considered. (S. D., p. 460)

A Monad exists at zero point levels and is established within an alternate seven dimensional Parent Space. The conjunction of a self-illuminating Monad within the Seven Skinned Eternal Parent Space, the Aether, is the ultimate bases for human consciousness. The light of consciousness is necessary for the creation of the human hologram. As Blavatsky explains: *"... it is only through a vehicle of matter that consciousness wells up as "I am I," a physical basis being necessary to focus a ray of the Universal Mind ...."* (S. D. I, p. 15)

In the modern physicists' description of holography, a black hole in a 5 dimensional anti-de Sitter space can manifest on the holographic boundary or shell as a radiant source or as a swarm of material particles. The physics of the black hole in the alternate space dimension is rendered equivalent to the energetic and material processes as produced on the holographic shell. This same line of reasoning can be applied to grasping how the metaphysics of a Monad within an alternate space dimensions, the Seven Skinned Eternal Parent Space, might be rendered equivalent to energetic and material processes upon seven dimensions or levels of the Aether. Thus, the Stanzas state: "SEVEN INSIDE; SEVEN OUTSIDE." Each of these holographic shells might provide the basis for experience of a four-dimensional spacetime world upon different planes of existence—a four-dimensional astral world, mental world and so on.

The Monad can also be compared to the little 7-dimensional Calabi-Yau Spaces depicted in modern physics as existent at every point. The idea is that the metaphysics of such a little Calabi Yau space with its interior holes might be the centre of a living being and produce surrounding effects within the ethers of Space through its whirlwind activities, serving to clothe it in different bodies. An equivalence is established between the activities proceeding within the Monad in hyperspace and the formation of various material bodies surrounding the central laya condition.

A human being in the material body is a quantum system based primarily upon the electrodynamics of the heart. The heart functions essentially as a quantum computer and exists within invisible quantized information and zero point fields. Ultimately, there is an underlying Unified Intelligence—or Omniscience which *"thrills throughout every atom and infinitesimal point of the whole finite Cosmos."* (p. 277) Human consciousness emerges through the dimensions of the Heart as the living entity is expanding and withdraws back into the heart at moments of death when it is contracting. Blavatsky explains that the 'Sons' or the *'Winks in the Eye of Self-Existence'* do so expand and contract through their own Selves and Hearts.[3]

The process of life review which can occur at death follows the same dynamic as that conceived in black-hole computer physics—wherein immense amounts of quantum field information is available within inconceivably small spaces—at zero point or Planckian levels. The human heart essentially functions as a mini-black hole computer at death and a white hole computer in its role in life generation. The lyrics from a rock song, *Between Angels and Insects* by the heavy metal group *Papa Roach*, illustrate these profound concepts about the nature of the heart and soul:

> "TELL 'EM WHAT YOU HEARD
> IT'S ABOUT A REVOLUTION IN YOUR HEART
> AND IN YOUR MIND

> CAUSE EVERYTHING IS NOTHING
> AND EMPTINESS IS IN EVERYTHING
> THIS REALITY IS JUST A FUCKED UP DREAM
> WITH THE FLESH AND THE BLOOD
> THAT YOU CALL YOUR SOUL FLIP IT INSIDE OUT,
> IT'S A BIG BLACK HOLE...."

Might such poets of the heart and soul really know something that the head scientists have not yet imagined? That within the heart, there might be some

---

3 The Dalai Lama describes life as entering and withdrawing from the planetary body through the *"indestructible drop within the heart."* From the Heart, according to Tibetan and yogic teachings, the vital and consciousness principles circulate through a system of three channels and seven centres or chakras—each with zero-point centres and dynamics. According to the Dalai Lama, as consciousness and the vital principle withdraw into the heart at death, this induces memories of all of the events of one's life, as if one's life is a unified quantum field at some lower level of articulation within the zero point fields.

big black hole or a sevenfold mini-black hole computer, with seven holes dug in Space, and that emptiness is in everything—especially at the Heart of Being.

The withdrawal of human consciousness into the mini black hole computer of the Heart at death is followed by the reawakening within further virtual realities, as the living entity is already clothed in other bodies within other projected virtual realms involving another holographic shell and a shift in the angle of the light. Alternatively, an individual might pass through a seeming tunnel and emerge into a super-symmetrical realm of being—a spiritual world within higher dimensions of space related to the Sun, the central quantum computer within the Solar system.

We can reconsider some of the unusual properties of the physics within the anti-de Sitter space, in view of these issues concerning human consciousness. Firstly, if a person is freely floating in anti-de Sitter space, they experience being at the bottom of a gravitational well. *The Secret Doctrine* similarly suggests such a gravitational well at the heart of a human being, as produced by variations of the Electric Ocean of life through Fohat and the Breath of the Mother, which adheres through the higher dimensions. Through death, the Sons 'contract through the heart' and the Mother 'ingathers' the Sons to her Bosom. Further, just as *"Any object that you threw out would come back like a boomerang,"* (Maldacena. Scientific American, Nov. 2005), moments of death and dissolution would involve a similar ingathering. This principle can also be applied to understanding the law of Karma. The effects of our actions create complex matrices throughout different holographic boundaries, which eventually have to be undone, resolved and balanced out, to release the soul. And so, the consequences of our actions and inactions eventually boomerang back upon us.

Another feature of the physics of hyperspace noted by Maldacena is that: *"If you sent a flash of light, which consists of photons moving at the maximum possible speed (the speed of light), it would actually reach infinity and come back to you, all in a finite amount of time. This can happen because an object experiences a kind of time contraction of ever greater magnitude as it gets farther from you."* Imagine such an emanation of primordial light, of the divine lux, initially emerging within the heart space of a human being. This primordial light is the light source for a holographic universe serving as a 'reference beam' and reflected also as an 'object beam'—illuminating the objects of our experiences—the apples of our eye and such. It is only because of the existence of the referent beam, that the object beams produce the phenomena of experience—the I and the It, or the I and the Qubit. However, the first illuminations radiating from the centre of the anti-de Sitter space will eventually return within a finite time to the higher dimensional laya centre of the heart. Similarly, might the return of the light of consciousness and vitality to the heart at death serve to illuminate the complex patterns and webs, plots and tales of one's life adventures, all maintaining some wholeness through the superstring and membrane structures of higher dimensional space? Perhaps all the details of one's life still adhere together within the vast zero point information realms of this holographic quantum system, and so can be reviewed and re-experienced through death and afterlife states by such a Mind of Clear Light—the Light returning to its gravitational well at the Heart of being with its seven hole mini-processor within the Parent Space.

Anything differentiating out of higher dimensional space eventually returns to its centre, its gravitational well at the heart of being in higher dimensions. Whereas scientists imagine that neurological brain activity and secretions produce consciousness, they do not imagine that the study of consciousness could require the examination of such a deep metaphysics of light and higher dimensions, and the mysteries of the heart. However, such an unusual perspective is suggested by H.P.B.'s archaic teachings.

Blavatsky's occult and mystical views of the zero point origin of human consciousness and her metaphysical model of the laws of nature provide profound insights into modern scientific theories. Cosmoses emerge from zero point sources out of a seven dimensional mystical void/plenum of the Eternal Parent Space, wherein the Ceaseless Eternal Breath modifies its motion on seven invisible points. All of these dynamics can be considered in relation to the newest ideas in modern physics and could bear upon understanding the multidimensional nature of a human being. These concepts provide the basis for a holographic model of human existence, not based upon neuro-networks in the brain but upon a physics and metaphysics of the heart and its zero point dynamics.

A human monad is like a pixel within this sevenfold higher dimensional space and it has sevenfold by sevenfold quantized spin states. The 'spinergy' of such is propagated through the surrounding space, breaking symmetries within the void, and precipitating the formation of energetic and material processes out of the varied levels of the Aether. In modern terms, virtual realities are created out of the zero point fields of the quantum vacuum, the Aether of Space, surrounding the Monadic essence. Virtual particles and realities, the webs of life, are created out of the vacuum surrounding the central zero point dynamics.

Modern neuroscientists and psychologists consider humans as only a *collection of neurons, molecules and particles*. None of them has been able to discover a human 'I,' although it is hard to know how one might discover a form of 'nothingness at the heart of being' or a Monad in hyperspace at Planckian depths! The newest theory in modern psychology and neuro-science is that a particular portion of the prefrontal cortex is the site where the experience of self arises. However, these huge errors have arisen because of the scientists searching for self primarily with the mind instead of awakening to Self within the lotus of the Heart. Blavatsky explains: *"The Mind is the Great Slayer of the Real,"* and further, she directs the Initiate to *"slay the slayer."* The Sons expand and contract through the higher dimensions of the human heart—as winks in the eye of self-existence.

The modern scientific view that *"All of physics is in the vacuum,"* confirms Blavatsky teachings of the mystical void/plenum wherein there is a correlation of all forces. Human consciousness needs to be understood in terms of the physics and metaphysics of the Heart and the nothingness at the heart of being—as a human being does live within the quantum vacuum and is one 'lens' within the holographic Space of the Universe. There can be no psychology of consciousness which does not consider the physics and metaphysics of the heart, the nature of consciousness as light, and the mysteries of Space. Somehow, the illusory virtual realities of the space-time continuum are produced out of an underlying sevenfold Parent Space through such an inner holographic magic.

The Dalai Lama describes human experience as involving the conjunction of *'minute space particles'* and the *'Mind of Clear Light.'* The sevenfold-quantized material creation is based upon such empty Space particles. These particles can be illumined by consciousness which reflects the deeper all-knowing Mind of clear light. So also, varied mystical writings depict point source emanations established within higher dimensional Space as the roots of human consciousness. A Sufi sage describes man as having such a 'divine spark' within and suggests that, "Not since God brought man out of nothingness has he ceased to be a traveller." God brought man out of nothingness and a web is spun of virtual realities through a hierarchy of broken symmetries within higher dimensions of Space. Further, eventually at death, the vital element of the human quantum system withdraws without-within, with consciousness and the life force resolving back into the nothingness at the heart of being, the laya centre, while the information of one's life might be illumined by the Mind of clear Light.

The advances and theories of modern physics make Blavatsky's mystical ideas about consciousness and light, higher dimensions and the dynamics of the Heart, ever more conceivable. Imagine the Self as a Star, a Monad, a point source of light consciousness and vitality within a dark nothingness of the void/plenum, a LIFE centre within the Heart. The Light of Self can illuminate the quantized realms of virtual and material realities spun out of the stuffs of the seven fold Aethers of Space. Consciousness as light does not '"create" the material realms as some new age scientists argue, but rather, consciousness illuminates them.

To create an actual holograph, a point source of coherent light is necessary, but of course, there are no laser beams within the brain, as Pribram notes. *The Secret Doctrine* suggests that such a supernal light *is* present within the depths of the heart in higher dimensions. Further, part of this light acts as a referent beam, while another portion as an object beam—illuminating the matters/energies of different planes or different aspects of the 'web' or 'matrix' surrounding the central point. The interaction of these two beams within the field of Infinite

Light produces the holograms of our multi-dimensional existence. It seems that Blavatsky's archaic teachings seem to provide various elements missing from the modern holographic paradigm in both psychology and physics.

Mystics maintain that an individual's 'I' is essentially a pixel in the field of the Supersoul, a jiva-Atma emerging out of the Paramatma, a divine spark emanating out of the mystical void/plenum—or a Monad established in hyperspace. The inner hidden dynamics operating within a microcosm are the same as those operative within the larger Macrocosm. Within a human being, the Monadic element is established in a seven fold higher dimensional Space with complex inner spin dynamics and holes dug in space. Complex virtual realities are spun around this central I creating the varied planes of being and life dramas, that the I pixel might experience as the Web or matrix of life. The Monad is more and more seemingly removed and obscured as consciousness is stepped down through interior dimensions of being and conditioned within varied subtle and material bodies. The metaphysical dynamics of the Monadic essence within hyperspace underlie the electrodynamics of the heart and the influx of the breath and the process of oxygenation, which ensoul the living being. There is a body, soul and spirit and even a divine element within the higher dimensional nature of Self.

Scientists *assume* that the material and energetic processes of the brain produce human consciousness, accidentally or randomly somehow, yet neuroscientists really do not understand any of this. Scientists generally do not even conceive that there might be a deep physics and metaphysics of consciousness, light and the heart. Are humans not simply a pack of atoms, molecules, neurons or organs? Thus, scientists do not even suspect that human beings might have a real I element under their noses the whole while.

The mystical literature leads us to the idea or formula, that: *God is first One, Three and then Seven.* Such a principle is somehow intrinsic to the nature of light on a mundane level and *Light* within the higher dimensional zero point fields. Further, the triune principles of matter, energy and intelligence exist upon seven quantized levels of vibratory existence. The sevenfold planes of existence interpenetrate and sustain one another and constitute a whole quantum system within the great chain of being. The principles of the laws of three and seven, as consistency mentioned or explicated throughout the mystical literature, have application in all areas of human inquiry. The significance of this mystical numerology completely escapes scientists and philosophers who unconsciously only construe reality in terms of contrasting dualities. They *'think in twos,'* with a psychology of the mind and body but no heart and soul, and an old physics of matter and energy but with no underlying intelligence to inform and sustain it—and further, no Aether.

"Seven inside, seven outside." If the Calabi-Yau Spaces spin away in seven dimensions, then it is certainly most likely that the virtual realities spun from

The Zero Point Metaphysics & Holographic Space

their activities would similarly have such a sevenfold nature. The common piano keyboard embodies the laws of three and seven, and the seven by seven planes of existence. Seven complete musical octaves are represented on the keyboard. Esoteric Buddhism similarly describes seven degrees of Maya or virtual realities, each of which is sevenfold again creating forty nine planes of being. If creation involves a supernal LUX, then what simpler mathematical principles might be applied to understanding its nature than this pattern of 1, 3 and 7 so intrinsically to light phenomena?

The human hologram somehow spins the realities of existence through a multidimensional universe, as a manifestation from within without through the Divine Principles of the Laws of Three and Seven inherent to the light phenomena and the quantized nature of creation. These principles in fact are even illustrated by modern concepts!

These teachings provide an esoteric holographic model of the Microcosm and Macrocosm, of consciousness and Zero point origins, and of the Laws of Three and Seven. Human beings have such higher dimensional origins emerging within/without from point sources, to eventually withdraw at the end of time without/within into other dimensions supported by hyperspace dynamics and zero point metaphysics. Human beings have white hole origins and black hole disappearances through varied realms of existence. The monadic essence spins another tale and the heart functions as a black hole computer remembering everything that happens since man emerged out of the nothingness at the Heart of Being.

The newest scientific ideas of the Universe as a hologram, the physics of black holes, quantum information theory and higher space dimensions, all help to illuminate the inner meanings of the mystical teachings about zero point sources, real Space and the possibilities for states of mystical consciousness through varied inner realms of existence. Human consciousness can be conceived of as having such a light and holographic nature and zero point metaphysics, and to exist within holographic Space wherein one Omniscience thrills throughout every finite point of existence. Each little 'wink in the eye of self-existence' is such a hologram.

Mystical concepts are profound when considered in relationship to the enigmas of physics and of human consciousness, and the holographic model. There is a physics and metaphysics to consciousness, the Heart and the deep substrates of a human being. The head doctrine is clearly inconsistent with the application of quantum theory itself to a human being as a whole, in which case the Heart would be regarded as the centre of a human being as an electromagnetic quantum system and quantum computer. The secret teachings of the mystics provide a new way of interpreting modern scientific theories and applying them to develop a physics and metaphysics of consciousness and the heart. Blavatsky's secret doctrine, the teachings of Kabbalah, Vedanta and Sufi sources, can all be used to illuminate such ideas concerning the nature of zero point centres, the triune and sevenfold laws which govern light phenomena, and the applications of holography and quantum theories. The profound new theories of science make mystical teachings ever more intelligible—as Blavatsky predicted over a century ago.

In his autobiographical writings, Adi Da describes an ultimate process of "Translation," whereby consciousness, polarized around the ego identity or personality, surrenders the position of Narcissus and experiences the prior condition of Self—related to the deepest Spaces of the Heart. Adi Da writes:

> In this Process of Translation, we pass as if through a point in space, at the root center of the heart. All awareness converges on that point in a kind of spiral or vortex. And that point is so small it is without dimensions, or any conceptions, or any objects. The independent self seems to dissolve in this narrow Passage. ... The Divine Translation is a matter of Transcendence of separate bodily, emotional, mental, astral, supermental, and egoic states of experience. It is a Transition through the infinitesimal space of the Heart. (1978, p. 83)

Clearly, Adi Da is describing the Zero Point condition: an infinitesimally small point source as the root principle of Self.

A study of ancient metaphysics allows a new way of interpreting scientific ideas and of trying to penetrate the nothingness at the Heart of Being. Certainly, this model of higher dimensions, Monads and such, provides an astonishing alternative view of the origins and nature of human consciousness.

7. Zero Point Origins of Consciousness

Since, all these fields must originate at a common zero-point, this is the basis of assuming that each individual human consciousness is simply a zero-point of awareness (at the source and center of its triune Monad) reflecting directly from, and entangled with the initial zero-point of initial Cosmic awareness.

This, of course, doesn't rule out the theosophical view that there are non-dimensional (from our point of view) "strings" (or rays of energy) that make up the composition of each hyperspace field .... (Maurer, 2007)

The Monad is established within a seven dimensional hyperspace. The spin energy or spinergy of this element—the 'G-force' within us—is a sevenfold modification of the Ceaseless Breath, reiterated fractally through hyperspace dimensions. This spinergy contains the holographic information underlying the manifest world orders established around the initial point.

In higher dimensions, membranes and strings (or rays) are the mechanisms of non-local influences through hyperspace dimensions and etheric fields. Ultimately, we have seemingly separate and isolated quanta moving about within seemingly empty space—material and energetic processes in 3-dimenional space; but these are all holographic projections out of a higher dimensional metaphysics. Maurer explains:

> Since, physically, we are all essentially, made up out of light, and each hyperspace field has its own limiting light velocity, it's perfectly natural that when we approach that limit, both sidereal time and 3-D space come to an end for us. But, since our center of consciousness is separate from this physicality, that doesn't preclude our continued conscious existence on any one or more of the higher levels of our being or, at least (as long as this universe exists) in our individual monad.

There are various bodies or vehicles surrounding the triune Monad established in a hyperspace, with seven interior holes dug in space, within a field of Omniscience. The sevenfold holographic boundaries—the aether of space—enable the Monad to experience life within seven quantized and distinct realms of vibratory existence. Thus, when we are separate from the physical body, we can still maintain conscious existence on more subtle levels of being, as there are different vehicles within different dimensions—an astral body in an astral world and a mental body in the mental worlds, and so on.

Maurer describes the Monad:

> Then, maybe, everyone will begin to understand the meaning of the Hermetic and Kabbalistic statements, "As above, so below." ... and give credence to the idea of the sevenfold division of primary fields within the human body that stems from the initial triune monadic fields centered in the Heart Chakra.

The Monad has an inherent G-force, the spinergy which unfolds within/without from the Holy Circumgyrating Breaths.

Of course, such a perspective on the fundamental nature of reality would explain why conventional reductive physics and psychology can never reach a physical explanation of any subjective conscious experience (awareness, will, qualia, etc.). Maurer notes:

> conventional science has no consistent idea or cogent explanation about the origin, nature or experience of consciousness; (i.e., awareness, will, perception, discernment, discrimination, determination, decision, etc.)—without which, all memory, mind, and brain would be useless. Nor does neuroscience, other than describing the neural correlates of consciousness, have any explanation about how the brain actually stores short term memory (let alone long term), what medium the memories are stored in or on, and in what form they are carried (either as sensory or memory information). Nor can it explain how the brain links to mind or memory, or how consciousness links to all of it? ... Science has never been able to understand the inner *consciousness* and *Self*--the nature of the observer, yet alone any of the mechanisms of mind and memory.

Maurer offers an alternate approach to the issues of the mind and brain, regarding them as dependent upon a much deeper physics and metaphysics—involving zero point dynamics and deep Space. He explains that the initial zero-point singularity is *"spread everywhere in the Planck vacuum between the particles of physical matter."* Maurer regards all the mechanisms of mind, memory and perception as involving complex holographic fields within fields. Consequently, nothing is explicable simply in terms of its component material processes. Instead, we have to grasp the ideas of the *"hyperspace metaphysics of fields within fields within fields."* Maurer notes that the universe itself is essentially an infinitely extended hologram.

This model of the G-force and a holographic Universe includes human beings in the equation. Maurer notes: *"the universe "lives" within each human being."* In Maurer's view, the subjective nature of human consciousness is ultimately related to *"the inherent subjective aspect of the immovable and empty zero-point of absolute space."* All living beings have such inner zero point Life centres.[4]

---

[4] Maurer explains qualia as holographic wave interference patterns modulated on the surfaces of the fractally involved electro-dynamic fields in the metaphysical Planck

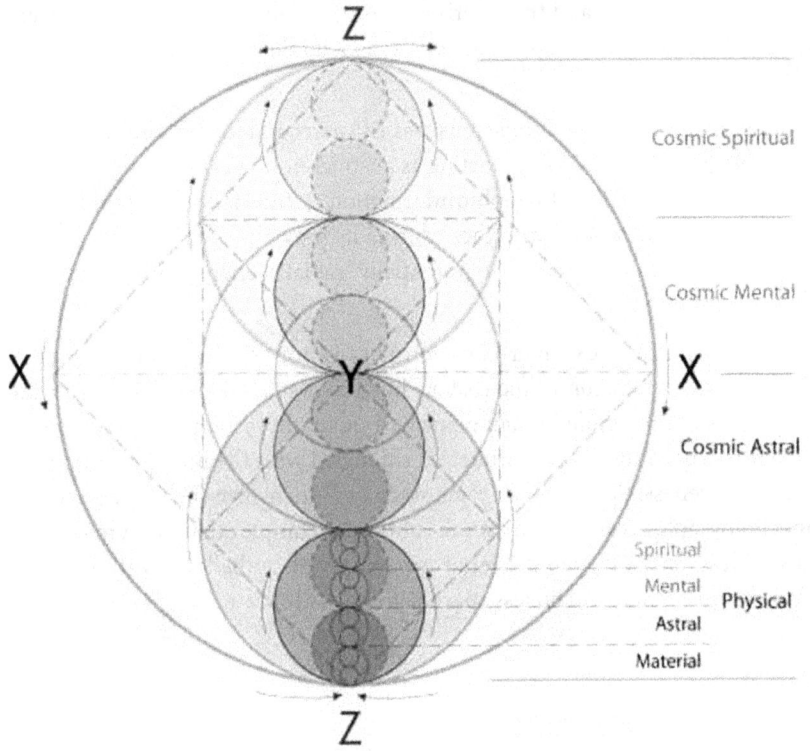

Modern psychology never advanced significantly in terms of the development of the holographic paradigm, because it assumed that there no *'laser beams in the mind'* as Pribram suggested, or any deeper physics of the multidimensional nature of consciousness and the heart. The idea that consciousness might be focused within varied hyperspace dimensions of the Heart is indeed most important for modern conceptions of the extended faculties of the heart, mind and spirit.

Maurer argues that "intelligent design" (not "creationism") is as real as the universal consciousness, *"that imagined this universe before it woke up its spinergy to form this material universe and all the beings in it."* The problem, Mr. Maurer explains, is how to interpret that mathematical knowledge in graphics, metaphors, word pictures or symbolic images, which the mind can visualize and truly comprehend. Maurer suggests that even most current scientific theories have been unable to accomplish this translation satisfactorily. Occult symbols and numerological principles embody such profound teachings most simply.

---

vacuum or hyperspace, and on the radiant physical matter fields of brain and body. This information is transformed from one field to the next by electro-dynamic inductive resonance processes.

Maurer provides an inspired description of the 'spinergy' of zero point dynamics, the G-force and the multi-dimensional nature of existence. In keeping with H.P. Blavatsky, Maurer provides a most intelligible model of Intelligent Design:

> the zero-point of pure consciousness (is) surrounded by its infinitely intelligent potential force existing as abstract non linear spin motion, containing infinite holographic information or knowledge (pertaining to its experiences and structures during its previous cyclic existence) as interference patterns of potentially radiant energy fields that fractally 'involve'....

The origin of one's inner consciousness is not as a by-product of material processes, *'a secretion of the cortex,'* but involves a far deeper physics and metaphysics of the whole human being as a quantum system with a zero point laya centre within the Heart, ultimately entangled with the initial zero-point of Cosmic awareness. Space and all phenomena of life involve such higher dimensional holographic realities—far more subtle and complex than what materialist and soul-less psychology and science has led people to believe, with their randomness and chance, and lifeless space with no Aether!

VII

The Secret Doctrine
A Final Word

"When the Theosophists and Occultists say that God is no BEING, for IT is nothing, NoThing, they are more reverential and religiously respectful to the Deity than those who call God a HE, thus make of Him a gigantic Male."
(Blavatsky, S. D. I, p. 352)

"Our Gods and Monads are not the Elements of extension itself, but only those of the invisible reality which is the basis of the manifested Kosmos.... The Monad ... the emanation and reflection of the Point (Logos) in the phenomenal World"... .
(S. D. I, p. 614)

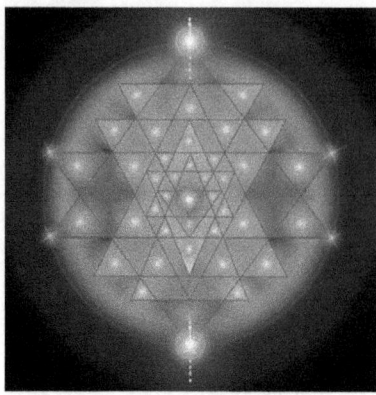

1. Intelligent Design: Deity in Every Point

> ...the design displayed in the mechanism,
> the order shown in the preservation, destruction
> and renewal of things forbid us to regard the world
> as the offspring of chance, and force us to
> recognize an intelligent design. (Blavatsky, 1954, p. 316)

There is something profoundly fraudulent and simplistic about modern science philosophy and the antiquated and pseudo-scientific worldview currently established in the mainstream of psychology, science and education. It is not that the *facts of science* that are wrong but rather, it is the interpretation of these facts and the underlying philosophical framework. It is a science philosophy of materialism, reductionism, neo-Darwinian evolution by randomness and happenstance, a soul-less psychology based on the head doctrine of consciousness studies, the study of little bits in isolation connected only through local effects, and with a pervasive denial of soul, spirit and higher intelligence within the phenomena of life. The facts of science can be interpreted in different ways and certainly already support important mystical claims about creation physics, metaphysics and cosmology as elaborated by Blavatsky over a century ago. Furthermore, the mainstream of science ignores the vast evidences for paranormal phenomena, mystical and spiritual experiences, and innumerable enigmas within the life sciences. Unfortunately, the masses of people lack any understanding of these issues and of their significance.

Hopefully, there will be significant insights from intelligent design advocates—as to the principles and applications of intelligent design theories. A model of intelligent design, such as that provided by Blavatsky and elaborated here, could be considered and applied within every department of knowledge, science and education. Unfortunately, the public advocates of intelligent design seem to be completely unaware and misinformed regarding even the esoteric

The Secret Doctrine: a Final Word

metaphysical teachings within their own religious traditions. It is a travesty that about the only consideration of intelligent design involves fundamentalist Christian views. Indeed, dogmatic Christian creationist views provide a straw man for pseudo-scientists posing as rational sceptics to attack, thereby illustrating the supposed formidable power of science over irrationality. Carl Sagan, the most fraudulent science philosopher of the past century, compared science to a *'candle in the dark,'* but really he only offered us a superficial pseudo-science masqueraded as truth.

The esoteric mystery teachings of religions are not understood nor investigated within the modern educational system and scientific community. In fact, they are not even mentioned in discussions of intelligent design! The sceptics and critics of intelligent design are generally correct in portraying Christian creationist views as simplistic and pseudo-scientific. In the form that such Intelligent Design models are generally offered, they are just as superficial as the materialist's own philosophy of a universe governed by chance and randomness. Both views are non-falsifiable in the terms of the philosopher of science Karl Popper, and outline no areas for significant scientific investigation.

However, if we consider the model of Intelligent Design suggested by *The Secret Doctrine*, then such a theory can be evaluated theoretically and experimentally. Blavatsky provides a complex model of *"divine micro-intervention,"* which we have applied to detailing the physics and metaphysics of life and creation. She did not intend that her teaching be simply accepted as dogma, but rather, it needed to be understood and investigated by comparing it with contemporary scientific understanding.

Since we live in a multi-religious and cultural society, humankind needs to seriously consider the esoteric creation teachings of different traditions--the Vedas, Kabbalah, mystical Christianity, Sufism and Islam, Tibetan Buddhism, native spirituality and the like. However, more than any other source, H. P. Blavatsky provided a profoundly unique synthesis of the perennial wisdom teachings and an alternative model of human existence and the metaphysics of the Kosmos. *The Secret Doctrine* has applications to every department of the physical and social sciences, arts, and philosophy; to understanding the enigmas of human consciousness, spirit and soul; and particularly to understanding the mysteries of cosmic creation—the physics and metaphysics of the holographic Universe. Unfortunately, intelligent design advocates seem to be aware of none of this. Educators must not simply add new dogmas to the rubbish already taught within science and philosophy and instead pursue serious investigations of intelligent design models—their implications and applications in all departments of knowledge. Surely, they will have to eventually stumble across the Sacred Laws of Three and Seven, if only by chance, and a new understanding of the multidimensional world and the nature of Space, and even of zero point dynamics.

Esoteric and religious metaphysical teachings as synthesized within Blavatsky's secret doctrines not only teach that there is a creative God principle within nature, but further, they articulate particular numerological and geometric principles of metaphysical and physical design. These are the Laws by which the One produces the Many—the diversity of creation. Creation embodies a triune and sevenfold nature in all things. Further, these patterns are repeated above and below, in metaphysical and physical reality, spirit and matter. Blavatsky offers a higher dimensional model of the Kosmos and of human consciousness, which compared with the scientists' *box* of matter and energy within time and space, makes the latter seem puny indeed. Only the holographic paradigm in modern science is beginning to arrive at concepts similar to those of H.P.B. and *The Secret Doctrine*.

Acknowledgement of esoteric teachings and claims is completely lacking within the public and scientific debates over the issues of Intelligent Design. People argue endlessly over the issues of science and religion, God versus chance, belief versus reason, creation versus evolution, and such dualistic non-sense. Unfortunately, religious believers do not grasp the basic esoteric principles underlying their own favourite dogmas. An understanding of sacred number study has been lost within the institutionalized churches and religions, as it has been within science and education. Numbers are mainly considered in a linear way, as on a number line, wherein each number is simply the number before plus one more. In contrast, the secret doctrines and mystical/occult literatures of the world are replete with symbols, glyphs, and formula, embodying sacred numerological principles. Blavatsky declares: *"God geometrises,"* (*Isis Unveiled*, 1877, p. 508)

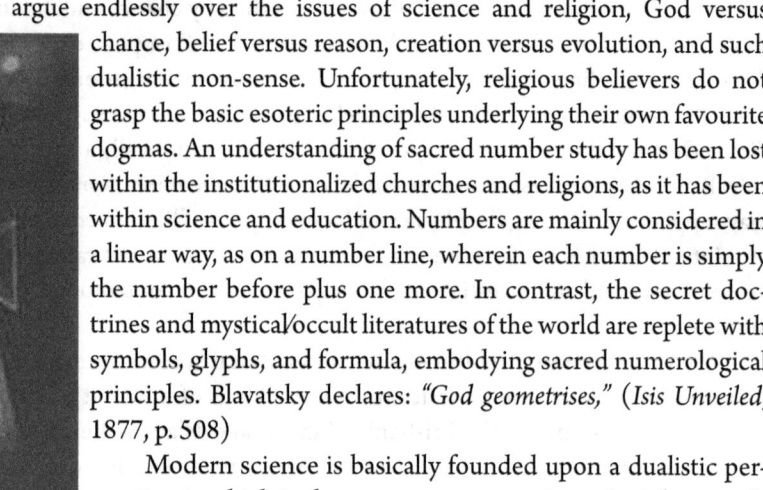

Modern science is basically founded upon a dualistic perspective in which it always contrasts opposing principles—such as matter and energy, waves and particles, observers and the observed, the mind and the body, conscious and unconscious, science and religion. In contrast, mystical and spiritual science suggests that the Divine Principles of a Triune and Sevenfold nature are embodied within all phenomena of nature. Thus, the One is divided by three and yields seven—just as white light divided by a prism creates a spectrum of colours. Similarly, the material world is composed of protons, electrons and neutrons constituting atoms, which are arranged in seven rows of elements of the periodic tables. These phenomena of nature embody the Sacred Principles. In modern physics, three main families of particles have now been identified, each of which has three generations of particles and all of which are equivalent to modes of motion on higher seven-dimensional superstrings or Calabi Yau spaces. 'Space'

The Secret Doctrine: a Final Word

can be considered as a unity, or as three-dimensional (x, y, z axes), or, as seven-dimensional—in which case, there is above and below, left and right, forward and backward, with a seventh central point—the origin point of the Cartesian co-ordinates. Time, can also be considered as a unity, or as having a triune nature of past, present and future, and as embodying a natural sevenfold cyclical unfoldment of rounds and races. Time, space, matter and energy—all of the four elements of modern science—can be regarded separately in such a 1-3-7 analysis, akin to the mathematical nature of light!

Whereas modern science has considered mainly matter and energy, within time and space, an occult perspective suggests a trinity of intelligence, energy and matter, or spirit, soul and body; upon seven planes or dimensions of being existence. An occult perspective offers a far more multidimensional model of human and cosmic existence, than does modern science. Scientists still think that there is only 'the material world' and deny the existence of the 'immaterial world,' in their typical dualistic philosophy of life.

Recall Margaret Wertheim's description of Grosseteste's metaphysics:

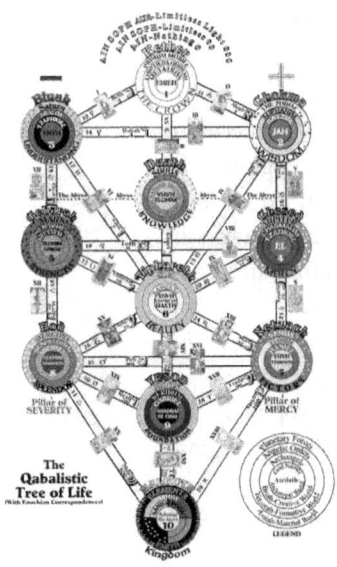

The Qabalistic Tree of Life

> In Grosseteste's metaphysics of light, we see the first full-blown expression of a mathematico-Christian cosmology, in which we may even recognize elements of the modern mathematical world picture.... the universe was generated from a point of primordial light–the divine illumination, or *lux*, of which visible light was said to be the physical manifestation.... Man could not study the divine *lux* directly, but he could study its physical manifestation in light.... a mathematical understanding of light would serve as the model for understanding all natural influence, or what we would now call force.... this is close to what mathematical men believe today. In contemporary physicists' quest to understand the forces of nature, it is light that has generally served as the model. (pp. 49-50)

Deity is a divine mathematician and geometry is inherent in nature as it reflects the same creative principles inherent in the Mind or Being of God. In this view, creation emerges from a point of primordial light, the divine lux, which is the ultimate basis for all manifestation—the Ray of Light that penetrates into the

Mother Deep. The dynamics and properties of light in the physical world reflect these same principles in keeping with the mystical axiom: *As above, so below.*

These principles of the Law of Three and the Law of Seven are found within Christianity, Judaism and Kabbalah, Islam and Sufism, Tibetan Buddhism and Hinduism, in the Fourth Way teachings of G. I. Gurdjieff, and elsewhere, but nowhere is their significance articulated as profoundly as within *The Secret Doctrine*, which provides the keys to unlocking wide areas of mystical and scientific study.

Writing about the Kabbalah, Blavatsky provides this succinct summary of these esoteric principles.

> The entire system of the Kabalistic numerals is based on the divine septenary hanging from the Triad (thus forming the *Decade*) ... which, finally, all merge into the ONE itself: an endless and boundless Circle.
> (S. D. I, p. 239)

Such esoteric number study pervades *The Secret Doctrine* but an understanding of its meaning is completely lacking within the mainstream literature or science, in new age philosophy and in popular discussions of the issues of intelligent design!

Nonetheless, the sacred numerology and goemetry articulated in *The Secret Doctrine* does provide *"a God Theory"* –not only claiming the existence of such invisible powers and forces but actually providing an intelligible explanation of metaphysical dynamics and the principles of creation. These teachings are absolutely worthy of scientific and scholarly examination, even if only to *"hone our minds for useful things,"* as Carl Sagan suggests. Blavatsky's masterpiece provides the keys to the study of the world's religions and mystical teachings and a complex metaphysical explanation of creation dynamics. She poses views on many issues still central within contemporary science, and in other areas, she offers ideas still in advance of the progress of mainstream science—particularly regarding zero point dynamics and the holographic nature of Space. An understanding of esotericism seems to have completely escaped modern philosophers, educators and scientists. They are instead dismissive of religion, spirituality, psychical phenomena and metaphysical study, and have no appreciation of the subtlety of esoteric number study, symbols and geometry.

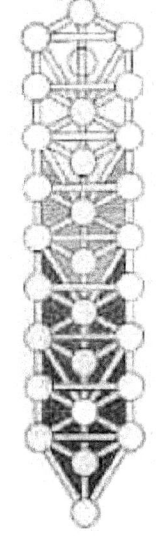

To compare an occult and mystical view of life with the traditional materialist scientific view, consider this Kabbalist glyph of the *Ladder of Jacob*. This symbol is based on four *Trees of Life*, representing the divine, spiritual, psychical and material worlds—the worlds of *emanation, creation, formation,* and the world *made;* and the elements of fire, air, water and earth. Each of these four worlds has a supernal triad and seven spheres below. The *Ladder of Jacob* actually depicts the creation of various world orders out of prime source substances through a hierarchy of broken symmetries in higher dimensional space. It is essentially a mathematical and geometric model of the inherent structure of the quantum vacuum—the zero point fields or ether. It also depicts the various metaphysical inward dimensions of human existence within Cosmic Space. The *Ladder of Jacob* is a model of intelligent design based upon four world orders created according to the laws of Three and Seven. The last sphere at the bottom of the Ladder is that which is finally made manifest physically, but the whole inner structure of the Ladder is inherent within the final sphere.

The modern materialist scientist simply takes the last Sphere or Sephiroh of this multi-dimensional *Ladder of Jacob* and would call it the material world. Imagining themselves to be uncommonly clever, these scientists are blind to the whole inner metaphysics of life, the heart and creation. Divine intelligences ensoul matter through zero point dynamics through varied planes of the Ethers of Space. Any material quantum is ultimately implicated in the whole through an inner multidimensional metaphysics.

Modern scientists automatically and unconsciously deny the existence of spirit, soul and intelligence within nature and the Ethers of Space. Now, they will simply extend their materialist science philosophy to their studies of holography and higher dimensions, and argue that there is certainly nothing 'mystical' about any of this, just as there is nothing mystical about singularities or the void/plenum of the quantum vacuum, or seven-dimensional hyperspace.

The *Tree of Life* is said to exist within the Garden of Eden, an indicator of its secret knowledge! The other Tree inside the Gates of Eden is the *Tree of Knowledge of Good and Evil*, suggesting a dualistic paradigm. Even the serpent, symbolizing the line of thinking that leads one astray, is double-tongued, saying one thing and doing another, like the madmen who deceived the masses of humanity. In Kabbalah, the *Tree of Life* is said to be hidden within the *Tree of Knowledge of Good and Evil*—and similarly, the study of dualistic science might eventually lead to an understanding of the higher laws and Divine Principles.

In the next illustration, the Zero Point centre is depicted as existing within the ethers of the void and plenum of the quantum vacuum. The dimensions of *Jacob's ladder* surround the central point. This simple Kabbalist diagram actually depicts a profound model of higher dimensional metaphysics. It represents zero point dynamics and the idea of how such points might be 'clothed in different bodies.'

In a scholarly study of Kabbalah and modern science, L. Leat (1999) provides another illustration of sacred geometry most relevant to our studies. In the following illus-

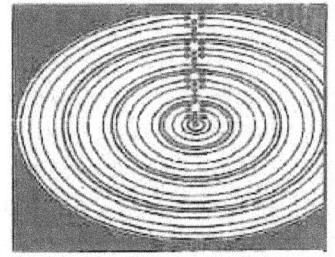

tration, Leat depicts the sphere *"Da'at,"* in the *Tree of Life,* surrounded by the *"matrix of creation."* Da'at is the eleventh hidden Sephira, represented within the abyss separating the three supernal spheres from the seven realms below. Just as Kether, the Crown Sphere, can be presented as an infinitesimal point source, a point within a circle, so also is Da'at—which embodies Kether and the supernal triad within the seven spheres below. The Supernal Triad give birth to a Son, as the *"Three fall into Four."* Da'at represents the emergence of the Son into the worlds below. In terms of modern science, Da'at is the singularity condition, the portal between the three realms of supernal Existence above into the seven lower dimensions of being existence below.

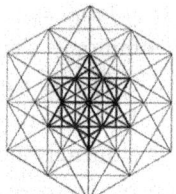

In an 'involving' *Tree of Life,* Da'at would appear as a white hole, a point source of Supernal Light. In an evolving *Tree of Life,* the dissolution of the world would be into a black hole. The creation and dissolution of the Cosmos occur within-without from such zero point sources. Da'at is a very special Sephira, which possesses properties and significance that are not easily discerned. Kabbalists state that as any living being emerges through the Abyss, it cries out 'I Am' (although this is also said of Kether.) The Universe is such a living being—a Son or *'a wink in the eye of self-existence.'*

In the *Ladder of Jacob* with four overlapping *Trees of Life,* this geometric image represents the *Da'at Sephira* in the *Tree of Creation*–the second realm of Beriah. Da'at is the final end product of the Divine World above and is the first appearance within the spiritual world. The *"matrix of creation"* surrounds Da'at and is represented by the complex geometric form surrounding the central point. This diagram essentially illustrates the dynamics governing the mystics' 'god-particle.' This could also represent Blavatsky's Monad, Shirley MacLaine's God Spark, the Sufis' divine spark, and the 'spark of holiness' of the Kabbalist. The 'matrix of creation' around the point depicts the metaphysical processes and forces that serve to embody this point source—to clothe it in different bodies.

In the illustration, the zero point source of 'creation' is established as the centre of a *Star of David,* or *Seal of Solomon.* This symbol is composed of two triangles turned up and down, representing the conjunction of Fire and Water, Spirit and Matter. The triangles depict the Law of Three as evident above and below. Blavatsky ascribed great significance to this symbol and especially to its lesser known form—with a seventh central element or point, which represents the laya centre. This form of the Star of David contrasts with that used by the

The Secret Doctrine: a Final Word

Rothschild as their red shield insignia, and as used on the flag of Israel—both of which are empty inside, or soulless. Blavatsky quotes another occultist from *Things Concealed*, depicting the Seal of Solomon with a central point: *"The seventh key is the hieroglyph of the sacred septenary, of royalty, of the priesthood (the Initiate), of triumph and true result by struggle. It is magic power in all its force, the true "Holy Kingdom." In the Hermetic Philosophy it is the quintessence resulting from the union of the two forces of the great Magic ... ."* Blavatsky then concludes: *"The force of this key is absolute in Magic. All religions have consecrated this sign in their rites."*

As it happens, the Kabbalist diagram of the first point of creation and the surrounding matrix of creation (a multidimensional Star of David with a central point) is most similar to that provided by scientists Greene and Atkins in their recent books on physics. In accord with the idea of placing ancient wisdom and axioms side by side with modern hypotheses, compare the following images depicting the scientists' seven-dimensional Calabi-Yau space—postulated to exist at every point within the universe—with the *Da'at of Creation*, the 'God particle' of the Kabbalist scholar. These Calabi-Yau Spaces are described as seven dimensional with varied inner holes in a manner most compatible with Blavatsky's description of the seven holes dug in space and the zero point foundations for the laws of nature. Physicists are trying to figure out exactly an interior mathematics and physics of such seven dimensional entities. The similarities between ancient esoteric teachings and contemporary physics are indeed profound.

 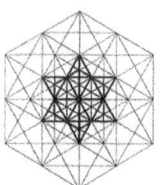

The teachings of the Kabbalah, like those of *The Secret Doctrine*, bear complex relationships to ideas in modern science. Further, they can be taken as providing a model of intelligent design—of the metaphysical and physical processes which underlie and sustain all things. The Kabbalist descriptions of negative existence, the void and plenum, the zero point source origins, the broken symmetries in higher dimensional space, the higher dimensional dynamics of light, and the descent from subtle into material planes of existence, are all ideas compatible with modern concepts in physics and cosmology, with Blavatsky's teachings and the mathematics of light. It seems that a singularity point of the Infinite might be embodied by such a complexity of inward dynamics.

In *Isis Unveiled*, Blavatsky (1877) provides a profound series of three geometric figures. She writes of these:

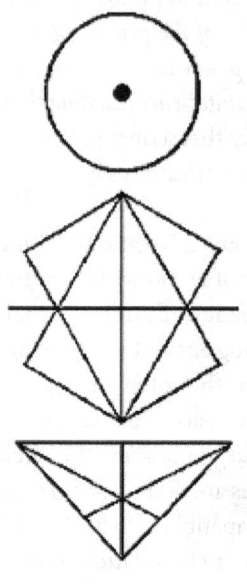

"Attach thyself," said the alchemist, "to the four letters of the tetragram disposed in the following manner: The letters of the ineffable name are there, although thou mayest not discern them at first. The incommunicable axiom is kabalistically contained therein, and this is what is called the magic arcanum by the masters." (p. 506)

The first circle with a central point represents the first point of cosmic differetiation or the zero point laya centre established within the *Eternal Parent Space*. The second figure has six vertices surrounding a central point—as if these were 'broken symmetries' relative to the symmetries inherent to the Star of David. The central figure also corresponds to the six upper sepheria of the *Tree of Life*, with the central point representing Da'at—the Son. Da'at represents the point from the upper circle as made manifest in the world below. The central figure portrays 'broken symmetries,' relative to the more perfect symmetry of the Star of David, thus representing the creative forces manifest with symmetry breaking.

The third figure represents a four-dimensional nature as the product of the seven forces in the realm underlying it. It represents the four laws of nature which hold it all together as a four-dimensional spacetime complex. The third figure also has seven points where lines interact.

These principles are similar to the *Stanzas of Dzyan* III:

3. DARKNESS RADIATES LIGHT, AND LIGHT DROPS ONE SOLITARY RAY INTO THE MOTHER DEEP. THE RAY SHOOTS THROUGH THE VIRGIN-EGG. THE RAY CAUSES THE ETERNAL EGG TO THRILL, AND DROP THE NON-ETERNAL GERM, WHICH CONDENSES INTO THE WORLD-EGG.

4. THEN THE THREE FALL INTO THE FOUR. THE RADIANT ESSENCE BECOMES SEVEN INSIDE, SEVEN OUTSIDE. ...

The first diagram in Blavatsky's sequence of the *magic arcanum* represents the 'non-eternal germ,' the first point of cosmic creation. The second figure represents the sevenfoldness of spiritual world or heaven worlds and the third figure represents the material world made. Blavatsky's geometric sequence portrays profound numerological principles.

The Secret Doctrine: a Final Word

Scientists have not begun to penetrate the hidden wisdom of *The Secret Doctrine* or Kabbalah, or to relate the ancient metaphysics to the concepts of modern physics and science. Ancient metaphysics, the study of light and divine principles, the concepts of zero point dynamics, the notion of a seven-skinned Eternal Parent Space, and many more concepts elucidated within *The Secret Doctrine* throw a most interesting light on the concepts and enigmas of modern science. Somehow, a manifest but essentially illusory four-dimensional space-time complex, with gravity to hold it all together, is produced out of a higher dimensional metaphysics within an underlying Eternal Parent Space.

H.P. Blavatsky's secret doctrines provide a multidimensional model of intelligent design and a subtle and complex explanation of how a higher dimensional metaphysics gives rise to a lower dimensional physics through zero point dynamics within holographic Space. Her work addresses the most significant failings in the modern formulation of these issues of intelligent design, evolution, consciousness and such. Blavatsky does not simply declare, *"God geometrises,"* but she provides a provocative model of the spiritual and metaphysical principles and forces that underlie the manifest material Universe. She explains how God does indeed *micro-intervene* in the laws of nature and how the universe does somehow concentrate itself in a point.

2. 1/137
Nature's Magical Constant

2a. David Peat on Synchronicity and the Plenum

> Synchronicities are the jokers in nature's pack of card, for they refuse to play by the rules and offer a hint that, in our quest for certainty about the universe, we may have ignored some vital clues. (Peat, 1987, p. 7)

> the seeds of synchronicity... will eventually flower into a unity of consciousness and the universe. (Peat, p. 57)

David Peat was born in Liverpool, England in 1938 and graduated with a Ph.D. in physics from Liverpool University, before moving to Ontario, Canada. Dr. Peat taught at Queen's University in Kingston and carried out research for the National Research Council of Canada. His work focused on quantum mechanical structures and the foundations of relativity and quantum theories. In 1971, Peat worked with David Bohm in London. He was also influenced by studies of Carl Jung, the first trans-personal psychiatrist who explored the realms of the 'collective unconscious,' and who had investigated 'synchronicities' with the famous physicist Wolfgang Pauli–known for formulating the *Pauli exclusion principle*. In 1987, Peat and Bohm together published *Science, Order, and Creativity*.

In *Synchronicity: The Bridge between matter and mind* (1987), Dr. Peat investigated synchronicity drawing from studies of Jung and Pauli, and with a background in Bohm's *Wholeness and the Implicate Orders* (1980). For Peat, *synchronicity* demonstrates the existence of 'a bridge' between mind and matter. Whereas science has tended to separate the study of mind and matter into separate sciences–of psychology and physics, synchronous events demonstrate instances where mind and material processes arise together or influence each other in mysterious ways inexplicable in terms of the "causality principle." Jung described 'meaningful coincidences' as demonstrating an *'acausal principle.'* In effect, meaningful coincidences and patterns of events demonstrate that there is a level of causality, which is 'non-local' as such events cannot simply be explained in terms of 'local effects.' Psychologists dismiss non-local effects, just as do most physicists–although the evidences for such effects are everywhere, with all kinds of scientific validation.

Peat is critical of the reductionist views, wherein *"consciousness (is assumed) to be an epiphenomena of the physical brain," "life is the product of random molecular*

The Secret Doctrine: a Final Word

processes" and *"the universe is an accident."* (pp. 2 & 4) Synchronicities are the jokers in Nature deck–events that demonstrate hidden orders of meaning and interrelationships existing beyond the purely physical world of matter. Peat explains:

> Synchronicities give us a glimpse beyond our conventional notions of time and causality into the immense patterns of nature, the underlying dance which connects all things and the mirror which is suspended between inner and outer universes. With synchronicity as our starting point, it becomes possible to begin the construction of a bridge that spans the worlds of mind and matter, physics and psyche. ... Synchronicity ... arises out of the underlying patterns of the universe rather than through a causality of pushes and pulls that we normally associate with events in nature. (pp. 2 & 16)

Causality involves visible and local pushes and pulls, whereas synchronicity demonstrates non-local psychological realities in addition to material realities. Mind and matter can have non-local effects upon each other—a sort of *acausal causal principle*. Everything in nature has such a local and non-local nature, at different levels of being.

Consider one example of a synchronous event used by Peat to demonstrate the enigmas poised by such fortuitous events or meaningful coincidences:

> One of the "classic" examples of synchronicity, told by Carl Jung himself, concerns a crisis that occurred during therapy. Jung's patient was a woman whose highly rational approach to life made any form of treatment particularly difficult. On one occasion the woman related a dream in which a golden scarab appeared. Jung knew that such a beetle was of great significance to the ancient Egyptians for it was taken as a symbol of rebirth. As the woman was talking, the psychiatrist in his darkened office heard a tapping at the window behind him. He drew the curtain, opened the window, and in flew a golden scarab ... Jung showed the woman "her" scarab and from that moment the patient's excessive rationality was pierced and their sessions together became more profitable. (pp. 6-7)

To skeptics or ultra-rational scientists, it is easy to simply declare that this is just a 'chance' or random happening that a scarab arrived at that moment as the woman was exploring her dream, and that such a chance event really requires no explanation. Alternatively, the skeptic could question the integrity of the report or reporters, or somehow or other dismiss the possibility of such events as being meaningfully interrelated. To consider seriously such 'jokers' in life experience points to profoundly complex interrelationships of events, people and psychological dynamics, and beetles, all in some deep patterns of 'meaning'–or information and intelligence, all non-locally present. The skeptic will find no causal explanations in local four-dimensional reality, but will dismiss the possibilities of non-local interrelationships to account for such happenings—such enigmatic bridges between mind and matter.

Peat, like Pauli and Jung, regards synchronous events as demonstrating how the physical world has to be linked in profound ways to the psychological world, in ways beyond local effects in our familiar four-dimensional space-time. Peat describes a necessary *"dynamism between the physical and the mental aspects of the universe."* Further:

> Such curious events may ... indicate that a mutual process is unfolding out of the same ground and that this ground must therefore lie beyond the individual consciousness that is located in space and time. ... evidence of some deeper, universal principle of hidden order. (p. 32)

Peat uses varied phrases to depict this deeper reality of hidden orders. He suggests *"everything causes everything else,"* and that *"the various phenomena of the universe arise out of the flux of the whole, and are best described as a 'law of the whole.'"* (p. 52) Further, *"within each element of matter and space-time is enfolded the entire universe."* (p. 67) And again, *"the operation of mind (has) resonances to the transformations of matter, and indeed, the two will be found to emerge from a deeper ground."* (p. 73) Peat elaborates further, that there is,

> an active field of information that unfolds in the various structures and processes of nature. ... matter has endless levels of subtlety ... (suggesting) that the whole order of nature may be more complex than was ever supposed." (p. 167)

Peat wrote this well before the advent of modern 11 dimensional Superstring theories, or holographic models of black holes and alternative space dimensions, and such–ascribing such inner complexities at zero point levels in hyperspace fields. The shocking ideas of superstring and holographic theory do suggest whole new orders of complexity beyond the level of the quanta.

Science has been *'third force blind'* as described by Gurdjieff, thinking that there is only matter and energy moving about within empty time and space. Third force is hidden within the medium–of Space itself–as the pleroma and akasa within which all manifestations are interrelated as aspects of one whole. Mystic Gurdjieff explains, *"Everything issues from everything, and again enters into everything."* How far is that expression from Peat's phrase, *"everything causes everything else,"* or from Blavatsky's dogma of One Unified Intelligence thrilling through every finite point of the Universe!

However, between a part and the Whole, there are many orders within space which are described by Peat as the 'generative orders,' as well as the implicate and super-implicate orders. Peat discusses the nature of the quantum vacuum as both pleroma and void, understanding nothingness as a state of perfect symmetry and of creation as a product of broken symmetries in higher dimensions, quantum inter-connectedness and the fundamental unity of life, and the nature of 'a zero point.' Peat writes:

> Like the vacuum state of physics, the pleroma is at once both empty and perfectly full, and as in Bohm's implicate order, a universe is enfolded within each of its points, for *"Even in the smallest point is the PLEROMA endless."* Out of this formless, infinite ground emerges the creatura, a world of order and distinctiveness. (p. 197)

All of reality has its ground in the pleroma, a state of perfect symmetry containing the completion of all possibilities. Similarly, the Kabbalist, Rabbi Yehuda Ashlag describes the matters contained within the "plenum" of the En Soph—unmanifest but latent within the fullness of emptiness:

> The matter is as follows: all the worlds, and all that is in this world, all the creatures of the universe, in whatever age they were to exist, before they ever entered into this world, with all the souls now on earth, and those that are destined still to be created, together with their complete curve of development until the final goal of completion and perfection–all these were previously included in the world which is called "Endless," "En Soph," along with their beauty and all their fulfillments. (1984, p. 57)

The En Soph includes all varied kinds of beings and their qualities and beauties, and all the laws and forces and particles of the universe. The ancient meta-physicist would certainly have predicted that the modern physicist would *"love the quantum vacuum."* The deepest substrates of being contain all things in all their possibilities for creation, involution and evolution, growth, change and perfection. The whole structure of the world orders on different dimensions and on different scales of existence, over all times, are all pre-existent in non-existence, latent within the Endlessness of the En Soph, the Eternal Parent Space.

Peat offers some profound descriptions of the origins of the universe and matter arising from the process of symmetry breaking out of the ground state of perfect symmetry. He notes also that 'consciousness' evolved out of this common ground state, and that *"'fundamental symmetries' play a role in the structure of consciousness as well."*

Peat's thinking and philosophizing tends at times to be dualistic, although his whole point is the nature of third force that underlies and sustains all things. Thus, there is a 'bridge' between mind and matter, as both are informed by a unified active field of intelligence and are ultimately parts of the whole. Further, *"... in unity, the dualities fall back into the nothingness and dissolution of the pleroma."* (p. 197) Peat does not consider the laws of three and seven in his arguments, as these occultists' principles might give even deeper insights into these mysteries of being.

2b. Enigmas of the Alpha Constant

However, there are some remarkable coincidences in life and Peat does mention another example concerning the life and death of physicist W. Pauli:

> One of the most curious of these stories about Pauli concerns the number 137. One of the great unsolved mysteries of modern physics is the value of the fine structure constant, for while the other fundamental constants of nature are all immensely small or enormously large, this fine structure constant 1/137 turns out to be a human-sized number. This number 137 and its place in the scale of the universe particularly puzzled Pauli and continues to challenge physicists today. It was a mystery that Pauli was to take to his death, for on being admitted into the hospital, the physicist was told that he was being put into room 137. According to one version of this story, on learning of his room number, Pauli said, "I will never get out of here." The physicist died shortly after." (p. 22)

Surely this is an unusual number–1/137. It is the first of the constants of nature, the 'fine structure constant' and it is represented by the first letter of the Greek alphabet a, 'alpha.' It is the only *"human sized number"* of the constants of Nature and it is also a prime number. We will consider the meaning and interpretation of alpha and then subsequently review some of the comments offered by modern physicists as to its enigmatic nature.

At a website dedicated to this number, www.137.com, C. Mann (2001) provides some basic definitions:

> Now, alpha is nothing more, nothing less than the square of the charge of the electron divided by the speed of light times Planck's constant. Thus this one number contains in itself the guts of electromagnetism (the electron charge), relativity (the speed of light), *and* quantum mechanics (Planck's constant). All in one number! Not only that, this number isn't like the gravitational constant or the universal gas constant, full of meters and kilograms and degrees Celsius. Alpha is a pure dimensionless number—little wonder that people have been fascinated.

Alpha is not expressed even in units but as a pure ratio of these three most fundamental quantities of nature: the charge on an electron, the speed of light and a measure of material discreteness, Planck's constant. These are fundamental measures of energy, intelligence and matter—the three modes of nature, in

Hindu terms. Alpha represents a ratio between the strengths of the three basic theories of modern physics—electromagnetism, relativity theory and quantum mechanics.

The simplest abbreviated formula for alpha is:

$$\alpha = e^2/\hbar c$$

In this equation, e is the elementary electrical charge, $\hbar$ is equal to $h/2\pi$, the reduced Planck's constant, and c is the speed of light in a vacuum. As a reciprocal, alpha is measured at 137.035999084.

It is not easy to understand or explain the meaning and interpretations of alpha, as it pops up in different contexts and different authors explain it somewhat differently. Mac Gregor (2007) in *The Power of Alpha*, notes in this regard:

> The mystery about α is actually a double mystery. The first mystery—the origin of its numerical value $\alpha \approx 1/137$ has been recognized and discussed for decades. The second mystery—the range of its domain—is generally unrecognized. (p. 69)

Different sources define or illustrate the fine structure constant in different terms. It is described as the 'coupling constant' or a *"measure of the strength of the electromagnetic force governs how electrically charged elementary particles (e.g., electron, muon) and light (photons) interact."* In physics, this number emerges in the table used earlier to illustrate the fundamental laws of nature and their relative strengths and ranges of influence.

The Four Fundamental Forces

Force	Strength (relative to the strong force)	Range
Strong Force	1	10^{-13} cm.
Electromagnetic	1/137	Infinite
Weak Force	10^{-5}	10^{-15} cm.
Gravity	6×10^{-39}	Infinite

The number 1/137 is the strength of the electromagnetic force relative to that of the strong force. The strong force binds particles within the nucleus of the atoms, and the three quarks in each of the protons and neutrons. This law applies on a micro-level with a range of .00000000000001 or 10^{-13} centimeters, in a different order of scale from that in which we live our lives (seemingly). In contrast, the electromagnetic force determines all the phenomena of our everyday world–our perceptions, thoughts, and the heartbeat, the structures of the body and of the world around us. In our everyday world, everything is due to the electromagnetic force in its various roles as the great protean magician. The number 1/137 thus represents in a way this bridge between worlds, on different orders of scale–as we pass form a higher to a lower dimension.

Another author describes it as "the probability that an electron will emit or absorb a photon," and another, "as the sq*uare of the completed screened charge, that is, the value observed at infinite distance or in the limit of zero momentum transfer."* L. Susskind (2006) explains:

> Roughly speaking the probability that any particular electron will radiate a quantum of light is given by the fine structure constant α. In other words, only one lucky electron out of 137 emits a photon. That is the meaning of α: it is the probability that an electron, as it moves along its trajectory, will capriciously emit a photon. (p. 49)

Susskind also describes α as controlling the strength of Feynman's exchange diagrams and how tightly the atomic nuclei pull the electrons towards it. The constant was initially introduced by Sommerfeld in 1916 to depict the size of the splitting or fine-structure of the hydrogen spectral lines. M. Born and A. Miller (2009), in *Deciphering the Cosmic Number: The Strange Friendship of Wolfgang Pauli and Carl Jung*, provide another perspective, noting:

> If alpha were bigger than it really is, we should not be able to distinguish matter form ether (the vacuum, nothingness), and our task to disentangle the natural laws would be hopeless difficult. The fact however that alpha has just its value 1/137 is certainly no chance but itself a law of nature. It is clear that the explanation of this number must be the central problem of natural philosophy. (p. 253)

Alpha shows up within different contexts and has long puzzled scientists. Mann notes: *"The great physicist Heisenberg told his friends that the problems of quantum theory would disappear only when 137 was explained, and spent years trying to explain it."* Similarly, one of the greatest physicists of the last century, R. Feynman is reported to have said that *"physicists ought to put a special sign in their offices to remind themselves of how much they don't know. The message on the sign would be very simple. It would consist entirely of one word, or, rather, number 137."* (www.137.com) Feynman himself penned these prophetic notes on the mysterious alpha constant.

> There is a most profound and beautiful question associated with the observed coupling constant, *a* the amplitude for a real electron to emit or absorb a real photon. ... Immediately you would like to know where this number for a coupling comes from: is it related to pi or perhaps to the base of natural logarithms? Nobody knows. It's one of the greatest damn mysteries of physics: a magic number that comes to us with no

understanding by man. You might say the "hand of God" wrote that number, and "we don't know how He pushed his pencil." ...we don't know what kind of dance to do on the computer to make this number come out, without putting it in secretly! (p. 129)

From a mystical perspective, it should be obvious from our preceding studies, that this expression 1/137 could be used to depict the basic metaphysical teaching of *The Secret Doctrine* and that it is intrinsic to the Kabbalah. From an occult perspective, 1/137 is clearly a magical number, secretly encoded into the Kosmos. Further, the number is not simply 137–but 1 divided by 137. Thus, we might take the 1 above, the numerator, as the Absolute undivided, as ultimately everything is of one undivided whole. The denominator represents the 'Son,' the created cosmos below, a divine fraction of the One. The Son as a point source, in its first point of differentiation from a laya centre, is a 1. This is then modified by the triune modes of nature (representing mind/intelligence, energy and matter) and manifests as Sevenfold–in all and everything, on different 'orders of scale.' Everything is some such Divine Fraction resultant from the operation of the sacred fundamental cosmic laws of 3 and 7. Certainly, this is an enigmatic number, which the scientists have found at the heart of being. Just as white light is divided by a three sided prism to yield a spectrum of seven colors, so also we can conceive of the Light of Brahman, the supernal lux of the Kabbalah and the Divine Light of Blavatsky, as entailing similar patterns of intelligent design–as above, so below. These are part of the basic teachings of the Stanzas of Dzyan, supposedly passed down to humankind at the beginning of the fifth round, to Lords of Light in central Asia! The expression 1/137 is a most apt depiction of the esoteric teaching of *The Secret Doctrine*, just as the Star of David with a central point, is the most apt geometric symbol of the archaic wisdom teachings.

Mann relates another paradoxical story:

The best explanation of the mystery ever given to Victor Weisskopf, another leading theorist from that time, was provided by Gershom Scholem, one of the most eminent scholars of Jewish mysticism. When Scholem met Weisskopf, he asked about the prominent unsolved problems in physics. Weisskopf said, "Well, there's this number, 137 ...." And Scholem's eyes lit up! He said, "Did you know that one hundred thirty-seven is the number associated with Cabala?"

1/137 is a very mysterious number indeed, basic to *The Secret Doctrine* as it is to Kabbalah. It certainly posses an enigma about the mysteries of science and why we no longer need God to explain anything, now that we have scientists who sit at their desks. Perhaps, the mysteries of alpha were written in from the beginning, "put in secretly" as a principle of intelligent design and a key to understanding the dynamics of light and creation?

2c. And so, How many Fundamental Laws?

Modern physics differentiates four fundamental forces of nature and is striving to unite these into one fundamental *"god-like Superforce,"* as described by Paul Davies. This contrasts with Blavatsky's explanation that there are seven fundamental modifications of Fohat responsible for the laws of nature. However, there are serious issues here concerning how we differentiate or enumerate these basic principles within nature.

Consider firstly that physicists have now arrived at a formulation of the electro-weak force, which synthesizes the principles of electromagnetism and the weak force. So should we subsequently now say that there are three fundamental principles instead of four? Further, the *Grand Unification Theories* can unify the electroweak and strong forces, so should we now state that there are only two fundamental forces? In spite of their unifying different fundamental forces into a unifying theory, physicists still generally count the fundamental forces of nature as four.

In terms of the history of science, it was centuries before an understanding of the electromagnetic force was articulated; as previously, the phenomena of electricity, magnetism and of light, were separately considered. Each of these phenomena manifested quite differently in nature. For example, electricity involves the flow of electrons carrying electrical charges and moving at speeds well below that of the speed of light. Magnetism is demonstrated by the sprinkling of iron filings onto a sheet of paper placed over a magnet, where there is no obvious electric current. Photons travel at 300,000 kilometers/second, have no inertial mass and do not carry electrical charge, as does an electron. The point to be made is although electrical, magnetic and light phenomena may be regarded as unified in terms of the electro-magnetic force, perhaps we should retain the distinctions between these forces. The electromagnetic force might then be represented as having a triune nature:

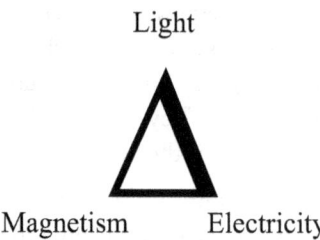

If we were also to represent the strong and weak forces, and gravity, on a second downward turned triangle, we could represent the laws of nature not as fourfold but actually as six-fold and embodied in the *Star of David*. In this case, the central point represents the seventh force, the synthesis of the other six—the god-like superforce described by physicist Paul Davies, or what Blavatsky describes as the *logos*, or the Lux—a point source of supernal or Divine light.

The *Star of David* with a central point might then be used to depict the sevenfold laws of nature, the seven variations of Fohat, the most basic cosmic electricity conveying the intelligence and will of the Spiritual or Divine Workman above. This enigma symbol also embodies the 137: with the one represented by the point, the three represented above and below, in spirit and matter, and the seven given by the addition of the point and the two triangles. There is a basic logic to retaining the distinctions between electric, magnetic and light phenomena, as variations of one underlying force. There is also a certain logic to the common nature of the strong, weak and gravity forces, as variations of material nature.

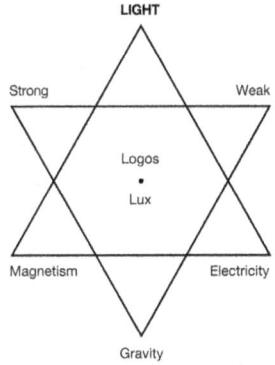

Perhaps, this is how we should consider the fundamental
laws of nature, not as fourfold but as sevenfold.

Certainly, we find profound enigmas and mysteries within science and mystical studies. Of course, to the materialist science philosopher, these enigmas of 1/137, the alpha constant, and the principles of mystical creation, are all only additional fortuitous coincidences in a universe devoid of spirit and soul, or cosmic design. As Blavatsky explains, the unholy trinity of modern science is that inert matter, senseless force and blind chance! And so the physicists can post the number 1/137 on their doors to remind themselves of how little they know, while failing to understand the truth under their noses all the while. At least our mystical studies and *The Secret Doctrine* provide some materials for what Carl Sagan has described as *"honing our minds for useful things."* If synchronicities show a link between mind and matter, then perhaps the formula of 1/137 is a clue to the nature of divine mind and the principles of mystical creation. My goodness, what an unusual synchronicity that the paradoxical alpha constant of science, which enables us *"to distinguish matter form ether (the vacuum, nothingness),"* takes on the numeric values of *The Secret Doctrine* and Kabbalah, and the principles of intelligent design.

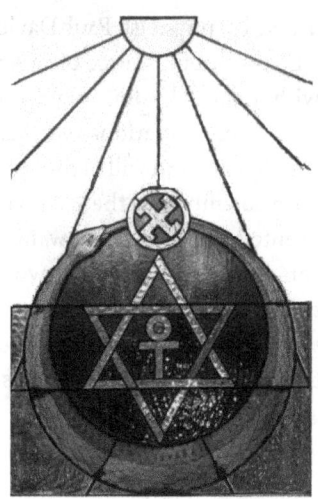

3. The Secret Doctrine: A Final Word

God, Science & The Secret Doctrine has explored the basic principles of cosmogenesis and metaphysics according to this *Magnus opus* of the literature of the modern world—*The Secret Doctrine*. As predicted by H.P. Blavatsky, the time has come to reconsider the profound ancient wisdom teaching which she articulated. I have assumed that role, as a fool at the *Zero Point Institute for Mystical and Spiritual Science,* to highlight the profound significance of Blavatsky's archaic teachings in light of modern concepts in physics, cosmology and psychology.

Most importantly, *The Secret Doctrine* depicts how God and other invisible powers do indeed *micro-intervene* throughout creation and through the laws of nature, even through the inward dimensions of zero point centres within ourselves. Blavatsky's writings offer a profound view of cosmic creation which anticipated modern views of vacuum genesis and singularities by over a century, as well as modern concepts of the void/plenum of the quantum vacuum with its zero point fields, seven-dimensional hyperspace, the enigmas of the uncertainty principle, the baffling holism of quantum theory, expanding and contracting spacetimes, the mysteries of light and most importantly, the holographic paradigm. *The Secret Doctrine* presented a holographic view of reality, a century before modern scientists arrived at similar concepts.

Whereas materialist science philosophers propound their puny dualities of matter and energy, in time and space, with a mind and a body, Blavatsky provides a shocking and profound alternative multidimensional model of cosmogenesis and metaphysics, as well as of the mysterious origins of human consciousness. Her teachings are consistent with and/or substantiated by many modern scientific findings and theories in physics and cosmology. *The Secret Doctrine* is truly a remarkable work come of Age—in the 21st century, providing a remarkable model of intelligent design based upon zero point dynamics, a holographic model of real Space and divine principles of mystical creation.

The Secret Doctrine—as the *Magnus opus* of the literature of the modern world, and the teachings of H.P. Blavatsky, the individual—a Holy World Star as I like to think of her, are really quite astonishing in light of the most advanced concepts, theories and enigmas in twenty-first century science. Further, these profound concepts and esoteric doctrines can be illustrated most simply by the image of a simple point within a circle—which is where Madame began as she sat with an archaic manuscript before her. The point represents the first point of differentiation and the last of dissolution, the Alpha and the Omega and the foundation upon which the various powers and Divine Workman spin their magic throughout all time between. It is the circle *"whose centre is everywhere and circumference nowhere...."* (S. D. I, p. 65) The circle represents the holographic sphere or real Space and the point represents the zero point foundation of any living Cosmos, Son or *"wink in the Eye of Self-Existence."*

The Secret Doctrine elaborated keys to understanding a profound model of *intelligent design* and *divine micro-intervention*—all through zero point metaphysics within holographic Space. The sciences of the new millennium must take up Blavatsky's challenges to place mystical axioms side by side with modern hypotheses: if only to hone our minds for useful things as Carl Sagan suggests or to provide a physics and metaphysics of the empty heart space for Stephen Hawking. All physics taken far enough must lead to the ancient metaphysics. *The Secret Doctrine* provides a comprehensive integrative perspective on the issues of God, science and religion, the mind and the heart, and incredibly, seems to have been neither *"invented nor exaggerated, but, on the contrary, simply outlined...."*

THE SECRET DOCTRINE

COSMIC EVOLUTION

In Seven Stanzas translated from the Book of Dzyan

STANZA I

1. THE ETERNAL PARENT WRAPPED IN HER EVER INVISIBLE ROBES HAD SLUMBERED ONCE AGAIN FOR SEVEN ETERNITIES.

2. TIME WAS NOT, FOR IT LAY ASLEEP IN THE INFINITE BOSOM OF DURATION.

3. UNIVERSAL MIND WAS NOT, FOR THERE WERE NO AH-HI TO CONTAIN IT.

4. THE SEVEN WAYS TO BLISS WERE NOT. THE GREAT CAUSES OF MISERY WERE NOT, FOR THERE WAS NO ONE TO PRODUCE AND GET ENSNARED BY THEM.

5. DARKNESS ALONE FILLED THE BOUNDLESS ALL, FOR FATHER, MOTHER AND SON WERE ONCE MORE ONE, AND THE SON HAD NOT AWAKENED YET FOR THE NEW WHEEL AND HIS PILGRIMAGE THEREON.

6. THE SEVEN SUBLIME LORDS AND THE SEVEN TRUTHS HAD CEASED TO BE, AND THE UNIVERSE, THE SON OF NECESSITY, WAS IMMERSED IN PARANISHPANNA, TO BE OUTBREATHED BY THAT WHICH IS AND YET IS NOT. NAUGHT WAS.

7. THE CAUSES OF EXISTENCE HAD BEEN DONE AWAY WITH; THE VISIBLE THAT WAS, AND THE INVISIBLE THAT IS, RESTED IN ETERNAL NON-BEING—THE ONE BEING.

8. ALONE, THE ONE FORM OF EXISTENCE STRETCHED BOUNDLESS, INFINITE, CAUSELESS, IN DREAMLESS SLEEP; AND LIFE PULSATED UNCONSCIOUS IN UNIVERSAL

SPACE, THROUGHOUT THAT ALL-PRESENCE WHICH IS SENSED BY THE OPENED EYE OF THE DANGMA.

9. BUT WHERE WAS THE DANGMA WHEN THE ALAYA OF THE UNIVERSE WAS IN PARAMARTHA AND THE GREAT WHEEL WAS ANUPADAKA?

STANZA II

1. ... WHERE WERE THE BUILDERS, THE LUMINOUS SONS OF MANVANTARIC DAWN? ... IN THE UNKNOWN DARKNESS IN THEIR AH-HI PARANISHPANNA, THE PRODUCERS OF FORM FROM NO-FORM—THE ROOT OF THE WORLD—THE DEVAMATRI AND SVÂBHÂVAT, RESTED IN THE BLISS OF NON-BEING.

2. ... WHERE WAS SILENCE? WHERE WERE THE EARS TO SENSE IT? NO, THERE WAS NEITHER SILENCE, NOR SOUND; NAUGHT SAVE CEASELESS, ETERNAL BREATH, WHICH KNOWS ITSELF NOT.

3. THE HOUR HAD NOT YET STRUCK; THE RAY HAD NOT YET FLASHED INTO THE GERM; THE MATRIPADMA HAD NOT YET SWOLLEN.

4. HER HEART HAD NOT YET OPENED FOR THE ONE RAY TO ENTER, THENCE TO FALL, AS THREE INTO FOUR, INTO THE LAP OF MAYA.

5. THE SEVEN SONS WERE NOT YET BORN FROM THE WEB OF LIGHT, DARKNESS ALONE WAS FATHER-MOTHER, SVÂBHÂVAT, AND SVÂBHÂVAT WAS IN DARKNESS.

6. THESE TWO ARE THE GERM, AND THE GERM IS ONE. THE UNIVERSE WAS STILL CONCEALED IN THE DIVINE THOUGHT AND THE DIVINE BOSOM....

STANZA III

1. ... THE LAST VIBRATION OF THE SEVENTH ETERNITY THRILLS THROUGH INFINITUDE. THE MOTHER SWELLS,

EXPANDING FROM WITHIN WITHOUT, LIKE THE BUD OF THE LOTUS.

2. THE VIBRATION SWEEPS ALONG, TOUCHING WITH ITS SWIFT WING THE WHOLE UNIVERSE, AND THE GERM THAT DWELLETH IN DARKNESS: THE DARKNESS THAT BREATHES OVER THE SLUMBERING WATERS OF LIFE…

3. DARKNESS RADIATES LIGHT, AND LIGHT DROPS ONE SOLITARY RAY INTO THE MOTHER DEEP. THE RAY SHOOTS THROUGH THE VIRGIN-EGG. THE RAY CAUSES THE ETERNAL EGG TO THRILL, AND DROP THE NON-ETERNAL GERM, WHICH CONDENSES INTO THE WORLD-EGG.

4. THEN THE THREE FALL INTO THE FOUR. THE RADIANT ESSENCE BECOMES SEVEN INSIDE, SEVEN OUTSIDE. THE LUMINOUS EGG, WHICH IN ITSELF IS THREE, CURDLES AND SPREADS IN MILK-WHITE CURDS THROUGHOUT THE DEPTHS OF MOTHER, THE ROOT THAT GROWS IN THE DEPTHS OF THE OCEAN OF LIFE.

5. THE ROOT REMAINS, THE LIGHT REMAINS, THE CURDS REMAIN, AND STILL OEAOHOO IS ONE.

6. THE ROOT OF LIFE WAS IN EVERY DROP OF THE OCEAN OF IMMORTALITY, AND THE OCEAN WAS RADIANT LIGHT, WHICH WAS FIRE, AND HEAT, AND MOTION. DARKNESS VANISHED AND WAS NO MORE; IT DISAPPEARED IN ITS OWN ESSENCE, THE BODY OF FIRE AND WATER, OR FATHER AND MOTHER.

7. BEHOLD, OH LANOO! THE RADIANT CHILD OF THE TWO, THE UNPARALLELED REFULGENT GLORY: BRIGHT SPACE SON OF DARK SPACE, WHICH EMERGES FROM THE DEPTHS OF THE GREAT DARK WATERS. IT IS OEAOHOO, THE YOUNGER, THE * * * HE SHINES FORTH AS THE SON; HE IS THE BLAZING DIVINE DRAGON OF WISDOM; THE ONE IS FOUR, AND FOUR TAKES TO ITSELF THREE, AND THE UNION PRODUCES THE SAPTA, IN WHOM ARE THE SEVEN WHICH BECOME THE TRIDASA (OR THE HOSTS AND THE MULTITUDES). BEHOLD HIM LIFTING THE VEIL AND UNFURLING IT FROM EAST TO WEST. HE SHUTS OUT THE ABOVE, AND LEAVES THE BELOW TO BE SEEN

AS THE GREAT ILLUSION. HE MARKS THE PLACES FOR THE SHINING ONES, AND TURNS THE UPPER INTO A SHORELESS SEA OF FIRE, AND THE ONE MANIFESTED INTO THE GREAT WATERS.

8. WHERE WAS THE GERM AND WHERE WAS NOW DARKNESS? WHERE IS THE SPIRIT OF THE FLAME THAT BURNS IN THY LAMP, OH LANOO? THE GERM IS THAT, AND THAT IS LIGHT, THE WHITE BRILLIANT SON OF THE DARK HIDDEN FATHER.

9. LIGHT IS COLD FLAME, AND FLAME IS FIRE, AND FIRE PRODUCES HEAT, WHICH YIELDS WATER: THE WATER OF LIFE IN THE GREAT MOTHER.

10. FATHER-MOTHER SPIN A WEB WHOSE UPPER END IS FASTENED TO SPIRIT—THE LIGHT OF THE ONE DARKNESS—AND THE LOWER ONE TO ITS SHADOWY END, MATTER; AND THIS WEB IS THE UNIVERSE SPUN OUT OF THE TWO SUBSTANCES MADE IN ONE, WHICH IS SWÂBHÂVAT.

11. IT EXPANDS WHEN THE BREATH OF FIRE IS UPON IT; IT CONTRACTS WHEN THE BREATH OF THE MOTHER TOUCHES IT. THEN THE SONS DISSOCIATE AND SCATTER, TO RETURN INTO THEIR MOTHER'S BOSOM AT THE END OF THE GREAT DAY, AND RE-BECOME ONE WITH HER; WHEN IT IS COOLING IT BECOMES RADIANT, AND THE SONS EXPAND AND CONTRACT THROUGH THEIR OWN SELVES AND HEARTS; THEY EMBRACE INFINITUDE.

12. THEN SVÂBHÂVAT SENDS FOHAT TO HARDEN THE ATOMS. EACH IS A PART OF THE WEB. REFLECTING THE "SELF-EXISTENT LORD" LIKE A MIRROR, EACH BECOMES IN TURN A WORLD.

STANZA I V

1. ... LISTEN, YE SONS OF THE EARTH, TO YOUR INSTRUCTORS—THE SONS OF THE FIRE. LEARN, THERE IS NEITHER FIRST NOR LAST, FOR ALL IS ONE: NUMBER ISSUED FROM NO NUMBER.

2. LEARN WHAT WE WHO DESCEND FROM THE PRIMORDIAL SEVEN, WE WHO ARE BORN FROM THE PRIMORDIAL FLAME, HAVE LEARNT FROM OUR FATHERS....

3. FROM THE EFFULGENCY OF LIGHT—THE RAY OF THE EVER-DARKNESS—SPRUNG IN SPACE THE RE-AWAKENED ENERGIES; THE ONE FROM THE EGG, THE SIX AND THE FIVE. THEN THE THREE, THE ONE, THE FOUR, THE ONE, THE FIVE—THE TWICE SEVEN THE SUM TOTAL. AND THESE ARE THE ESSENCES, THE FLAMES, THE ELEMENTS, THE BUILDERS, THE NUMBERS, THE ARUPA, THE RUPA, AND THE FORCE OF DIVINE MAN—THE SUM TOTAL. AND FROM THE DIVINE MAN EMANATED THE FORMS, THE SPARKS, THE SACRED ANIMALS, AND THE MESSENGERS OF THE SACRED FATHERS WITHIN THE HOLY FOUR.

4. THIS WAS THE ARMY OF THE VOICE—THE DIVINE MOTHER OF THE SEVEN. THE SPARKS OF THE SEVEN ARE SUBJECT TO, AND THE SERVANTS OF, THE FIRST, THE SECOND, THE THIRD, THE FOURTH, THE FIFTH, THE SIXTH, AND THE SEVENTH OF THE SEVEN. THESE "SPARKS" ARE CALLED SPHERES, TRIANGLES, CUBES, LINES, AND MODELLERS; FOR THUS STANDS THE ETERNAL NIDANA—THE OEAOHOO, WHICH IS:

5. "DARKNESS" THE BOUNDLESS, OR THE NO-NUMBER, ADI-NIDANA SVABHAVAT: --

I. THE ADI-SANAT, THE NUMBER, FOR HE IS ONE.

II. THE VOICE OF THE LORD SVABHAVAT, THE NUMBERS, FOR HE IS ONE AND NINE.

III. THE "FORMLESS SQUARE."

AND THESE THREE ENCLOSED WITHIN THE ARE THE SACRED FOUR; AND THE TEN ARE THE ARUPA UNIVERSE. THEN COME THE "SONS," THE SEVEN FIGHTERS, THE ONE, THE EIGHTH LEFT OUT, AND HIS BREATH WHICH IS THE LIGHT-MAKER.

6. THEN THE SECOND SEVEN, WHO ARE THE LIPIKA, PRODUCED BY THE THREE. THE REJECTED SON IS ONE. THE "SON-SUNS" ARE COUNTLESS.

STANZA V

1. THE PRIMORDIAL SEVEN, THE FIRST SEVEN BREATHS OF THE DRAGON OF WISDOM, PRODUCE IN THEIR TURN FROM THEIR HOLY CIRCUMGYRATING BREATHS THE FIERY WHIRLWIND.

2. THEY MAKE OF HIM THE MESSENGER OF THEIR WILL. THE DZYU BECOME FOHAT, THE SWIFT SON OF THE DIVINE SON WHOSE SONS ARE THE LIPIKA, RUNS CIRCULAR ERRANDS. FOHAT IS THE STEED AND THE THOUGHT IS THE RIDER. HE PASSES LIKE LIGHTNING THROUGHT THE FIERTY CLOUDS; TAKES THREE, AND FIVE, AND SEVEN STRIDES THROUGH THE SEVEN REGIONS ABOVE, AND THE SEVEN BELOW. HE LIFTS HIS VOICE, AND CALLS THE INNUMERABLE SPARKS, AND JOINS THEM.

3. HE IS THEIR GUIDING SPIRIT AND LEADER. WHEN HE COMMENCES WORK, HE SEPARATES THE SPARKS OF THE LOWER KINGDOM THAT FLOAT AND THRILL WITH JOY IN THEIR RADIANT DWELLINGS, AND FORMS THERE-WITH THE GERMS OF WHEELS. HE PLACES THEM IN THE SIX DIRECTIONS OF SPACE, AND ONE IN THE MIDDLE—THE CENTRAL WHEEL.

4. FOHAT TRACES SPIRAL LINES TO UNITE THE SIXTH TO THE SEVENTH—THE CROWN; AN ARMY OF THE SONS OF LIGHT STAND AT EACH ANGLE, AND THE LIPIKA IN THE MIDDLE WHEEL. THEY SAY: THIS IS GOOD, THE FIRST DIVINE WORLD IS READY, THE FIRST IS NOW THE SECOND. THEN THE "DIVINE ARUPA" REFLECTS ITSELF IN CHHAYA LOKA, THE FIRST GARMENT OF THE ANUPADAKA.

5. FOHAT TAKES FIVE STRIDES AND BUILDS A WINGED WHEEL AT EACH CORNER OF THE SQUARE, FOR THE FOUR HOLY ONES AND THEIR ARMIES.

6. THE LIPIKA CIRCUMSCRIBE THE TRIANGLE, THE FIRST ONE, THE CUBE, THE SECOND ONE, AND THE PENTACLE WITHIN THE EGG. IT IS THE RING CALLED "PASS NOT" FOR THOSE WHO DESCEND AND ASCEND. ALSO FOR THOSE WHO DURING THE KALPA ARE PROGRESSING TOWARDS THE GREAT DAY "BE WITH US." THUS WERE FORMED THE

RUPA AND THE ARUPA: FROM ONE LIGHT SEVEN LIGHTS; FROM EACH OF THE SEVEN, SEVEN TIMES SEVEN LIGHTS. THE WHEELS WATCH THE RING....

STANZA V I

1. BY THE POWER OF THE MOTHER OF MERCY AND KNOWLEDGE—KWAN-YIN—THE "TRIPLE" OF KWAN-SHAI-YIN, RESIDING IN KWAN-YIN-TIEN, FOHAT, THE BREATH OF THEIR PROGENY, THE SON OF THE SONS, HAVING CALLED FORTH, FROM THE LOWER ABYSS, THE ILLUSIVE FORM OF SIEN-TCHANG AND THE SEVEN ELEMENTS.

2. THE SWIFT AND RADIANT ONE PRODUCES THE SEVEN LAYA CENTRES, AGAINST WHICH NONE WILL PREVAIL TO THE GREAT DAY "BE-WITH-US," AND SEATS THE UNIVERSE ON THESE ETERNAL FOUNDATIONS SURROUNDING TSIEN-TCHAN WITH THE ELEMENTARY GERMS.

3. OF THE SEVEN—FIRST ONE MANIFESTED, SIX CONCEALED, TWO MANIFESTED, FIVE CONCEALED; THREE MANIFESTED, FOUR CONCEALED; FOUR PRODUCED, THREE HIDDEN; FOUR AND ONE TSAN REVEALED, TWO AND ONE HALF CONCEALED; SIX TO BE MANIFESTED, ONE LAID ASIDE. LASTLY, SEVEN SMALL WHEELS REVOLVING; ONE GIVING BIRTH TO THE OTHER.

4. HE BUILDS THEM IN THE LIKENESS OF OLDER WHEELS, PLACING THEM ON THE IMPERISHABLE CENTRES.

   HOW DOES FOHAT BUILD THEM? HE COLLECTS THE FIERY DUST. HE MAKES BALLS OF FIRE, RUNS THROUGH THEM, AND ROUND THEM, INFUSING LIFE THEREINTO, THEN SETS THEM INTO MOTION; SOME ONE WAY, SOME THE OTHER WAY. THEY ARE COLD, HE MAKES THEM HOT. THEY ARE DRY, HE MAKES THEM MOIST. THEY SHINE, HE FANS AND COOLS THEM. THUS ACTS FOHAT FROM ONE TWILIGHT TO THE OTHER, DURING SEVEN ETERNITIES.

5. AT THE FOURTH, THE SONS ARE TOLD TO CREATE THEIR IMAGES. ONE THIRD REFUSES—TWO OBEY.

THE CURSE IS PRONOUNCED; THEY WILL BE BORN ON THE FOURTH, SUFFER AND CAUSE SUFFERING; THIS IS THE FIRST WAR.

6. THE OLDER WHEELS ROTATED DOWNWARDS AND UPWARDS .... THE MOTHER'S SPAWN FILLED THE WHOLE. THERE WERE BATTLES FOUGHT BETWEEN THE CREATORS AND THE DESTROYERS, AND BATTLES FOUGHT FOR SPACE; THE SEED APPEARING AND RE-APPEARING CONTINUOUSLY.

7. MAKE THY CALCULATIONS, LANOO, IF THOU WOULDEST LEARN THE CORRECT AGE OF THY SMALL WHEEL. ITS FOURTH SPOKE IS OUR MOTHER. REACH THE FOURTH "FRUIT" OF THE FOURTH PATH OF KNOWLEDGE THAT LEADS TO NIRVANA, AND THOU SHALT COMPREHEND, FOR THOU SHALT SEE... .

STANZA VII

1. BEHOLD THE BEGINNING OF SENTIENT FORMLESS LIFE.

FIRST THE DIVINE, THE ONE FROM THE MOTHER-SPIRIT; THEN THE SPIRITUAL; THE THREE FROM THE ONE, THE FOUR FROM THE ONE, AND THE FIVE FROM WHICH THE THREE, THE FIVE, AND THE SEVEN. THESE ARE THE THREE-FOLD, THE FOUR-FOLD DOWNWARD; THE "MIND-BORN" SONS OF THE FIRST LORD; THE SHINING SEVEN.

IT IS THEY WHO ARE THOU, ME, HIM, OH LANOO. THEY, WHO WATCH OVER THEE, AND THY MOTHER EARTH.

2. THE ONE RAY MULTIPLIES THE SMALLER RAYS. LIFE PRECEDES FORM, AND LIFE SURVIVES THE LAST ATOM OF FORM. THROUGH THE COUNTLESS RAYS PROCEEDS THE LIFE-RAY, THE ONE, LIKE A THREAD THROUGH MANY JEWELS.

3. WHEN THE ONE BECOMES TWO, THE THREEFOLD APPEARS, AND THE THREE ARE ONE; AND IT IS OUR THREAD, OH LANOO, THE HEART OF THE MAN-PLANT CALLED SAPTASARMA.

4. IT IS THE ROOT THAT NEVER DIES; THE THREE-TONGUED FLAME OF THE FOUR WICKS. THE WICKS ARE THE SPARKS, THAT DRAW FROM THE THREE-TONGUED FLAME SHOT OUT BY THE SEVEN—THEIR FLAME—THE BEAMS AND SPARKS OF ONE MOON REFLECTED IN THE RUNNING WAVES OF ALL THE RIVERS OF EARTH.

5. THE SPARK HANGS FROM THE FLAME BY THE FINEST THREAD OF FOHAT. IT JOURNEYS THROUGH THE SEVEN WORLDS OF MAYA. IT STOPS IN THE FIRST, AND IS A METAL AND A STONE; IT PASSES INTO THE SECOND AND BEHOLD—A PLANT; THE PLANT WHIRLS THROUGH SEVEN CHANGES AND BECOMES A SACRED ANIMAL. FROM THE COMBINED ATTRIBUTES OF THESE, MANU, THE THINKER IS FORMED. WHO FORMS HIM? THE SEVEN LIVES, AND THE ONE LIFE. WHO COMPLETES HIM? THE FIVE-FOLD LHA. AND WHO PERFECTS THE LAST BODY? FISH, SIN, AND SOMA....

6. FROM THE FIRST-BORN THE THREAD BETWEEN THE SILENT WATCHER AND HIS SHADOW BECOMES MORE STRONG AND RADIANT WITH EVERY CHANGE. THE MORNING SUN-LIGHT HAS CHANGED INTO NOON-DAY GLORY....

7. THIS IS THY PRESENT WHEEL, SAID THE FLAME TO THE SPARK. THOU ARE MYSELF, MY IMAGE, AND MY SHADOW. I HAVE CLOTHED MYSELF IN THEE, AND THOU ART MY VAHAN TO THE DAY, "BE WITH US," WHEN THOU SHALT RE-BECOME MYSELF AND OTHERS, THYSELF AND ME. THEN THE BUILDERS, HAVING DONNED THEIR FIRST CLOTHING, DESCEND ON RADIANT EARTH AND REIGN OVER MEN—WHO ARE THEMSELVES....

***

Thus ends this portion of the archaic narrative, dark, confused, almost incomprehensive. An attempt will now be made to throw light into this darkness, to make sense out of this apparent NON-SENSE. (Blavatsky's 1888 note)

About the Author

Christopher Patrick Holmes was born in Sussex, England on October 7, 1949 and raised in Ontario, Canada. He graduated with a B.A. from Carleton University, Ottawa in 1971 and a Ph.D. in clinical psychology from the University of Waterloo in 1978. Christopher taught at York University, Downsview (Toronto) Ontario over an eleven-year period amidst controversy over his investigations of mystical and spiritual psychology, science and psychical phenomena. He co-founded three centers with Anita J. Mitra–the *Institute for Mystical and Spiritual Science*, Maple, Ontario, the *Rainbow Centre* in Toronto and *Zero Point* in the Ottawa valley. Christopher worked for twelve years as a forensic psychologist with young offenders and adults within the Ontario Ministry of Corrections. Since 2003, Christopher has dedicated himself to writing and furthering the aims of the *Zero Point* Institute for Mystical and Spiritual Science, while learning and working with Miss K. In 2010, the Zero Point Institute opened in Kemptville, Ontario. Christopher maintains a website at www.zeropoint.ca and hosts a bi-monthly radio show with co-host James A. Moffatt on www.bbsradio.com.

Christopher has studied the issues of consciousness, mystical and spiritual psychologies, modern physics and ancient metaphysics, for over thirty five years. In addition, he has experienced various paranormal phenomena, states of illumination and awakening.

Acknowledgements

I would like to acknowledge various individuals who have contributed in diverse ways to this publication.

Firstly, on a personal basis, I would like to acknowledge my five children, Alison, Matthew, Timothy, Peter and Daniel, who unfortunately lost their father too much to his life's work and concerns; my parents, for providing an early loving home life and Christian teaching, and support through lean years; Anita Mitra and Miss K, who have been such significant parts of my emotional and personal life. Lastly, I would like to thank James A. Moffatt, who has contributed over many years as an editor of my writings and shared in the adventures of esoteric studies.

Secondly, I would like to thank Odin Townley who encouraged me to attend the 2007 United Lodge of Theosophist's conference on *Theosophy & New Frontiers of Science* in Petaluma California, which led to the revision of my earlier book *Divine Mysteries* into an earlier edition of the current work. Odin emailed valuable and timely quotations and comments as I worked at these revisions, along with friends Helena Kerekhazi and Garrett Riegg. Odin has also made videos available to the public through the internet of my presentation on *The Secret Doctrine* at IONS, 2007. I would like further to thank Murray Stentiford and the New Zealand Theosophical Society for taking the chance of bringing me to New Zealand for a seminar on Theosophy and Science, and then facilitating my teaching and touring there.

Lastly, I would like to acknowledge various illustrators whose work has been included here; particularly Neel Sheerer for his cover illustration (originally published in professor Stephen Hawking's *The Universe in a Nutshell*) and Anita J. Mitra—for such prints as *"Hey, Flower, Open,"* Microcosm/Macrocosm, *A Fool at the Zero Point, The Heart Doctrine,* and *A Wink in the Eye of Self-Existence*, which illustrations have long been incorporated into my writings. In addition, I would like to thank a distant friend, Zeljka Zupanic from Croatia who came forward just at a time when I was facing the issues of copyrights for the pictures I had been using from *SciAm* and other sources, and she was able to provide illustrations even more attractive and useful than the originals. Thank you Zeljka.

BIBLIOGRAPHY

Adi Da. *The Enlightenment of the Whole Body.* Dawn Horse Press, California, 1978.

Ashlag, Y. In *Kabbalah: Ten Luminous Emanations.* Research Centre of Kabbalah Books, New York, N.Y., 1984.

Aspect, A. et al. Experimental Test of Bell's inequalities using time-varying analyzers. *Physical Review Letters* 49, 1982.

Atkins, P. *Galileo's Finger: The ten great ideas of science.* Oxford University Press, New York, 2003.

Barborka, G. *The Divine Plan.* Theosophical Publishing House, Adyar, India, 1980.

Bekenstein, J. Information in the Holographic Universe. *Scientific American.* August 2003.

Blavatsky, H. *The Secret Doctrine: The syntheses of science, religion and philosophy.* Theosophical University Press, Pasadena California, (1970) 1888.

———. *The Secret Doctrine.* Volume III and Indices. Theosophical Publishing House Ltd, London, England.

———. *Isis Unveiled. A Master Key to the Mysteries of Ancient and Modern Science and Theology.* Theosophical University Press. Pasadena, California, 1976 (1877).

———. *The Key to Theosophy.* Theosophical University Press, Pasadena, California. (1972) 1889.

———. *The Voice of the Silence.* Theosophical University Press, Pasadena, California, 1976/1889.

———. *Transactions of the Blavatsky Lodge.* The Theosophical Company, Los Angeles, (1987) 1891.

———. *Collected Writings*, Vol. VI, p. 316 "The Ten Sephiroth", 1st Ed, Blavatsky Writings Publication Fund, Los Angeles, California 1954.

Bohm, D. *Wholeness and the Implicate Order.* Routledge & Kegan, Paul, London, 1980.

———. Creativity: the signature of nature, interview in R. Weber, *Dialogues with Scientists and Sages: the search for unity.* Routledge & Kegan Paul, New York. 1986.

——— & Peat, D. *Science, Order, and Creativity.* Bantam Books, Toronto, 1987.

Born, M., Miller, A. *Deciphering the Cosmic Number: The Strange Friendship of Wolfgang Pauli and Carl Jung.* W.Norton & Co., New York, 2009.

Bousso, Polchinsky, *Scientific American*, September 2004.

Cole, K. *The Hole in the Universe: How scientists peered over the edge of emptiness and found everything.* Harcourt, New York, 2001.

———. Much ado about Nothing. *Discover*, June 1985.

Conselice, C. The Universe's Invisible Hand. *Scientific American*, February 2007.

Cook, N. *The Hunt for Zero Point: Inside the classified world of antigravity technology.* Broadway Books, New York, 2001.

Cowan, 2001, Pg 88

Cranston, S. *The Extraordinary Life & Influence of Helena Blavatsky, Founder of the modern theosophical movement.* Jeremy Tarcher, New York, 1994.

Davies, P. Liquid Space. *New Scientist.* November 3, 2001.

———. *The Mind of God: The Scientific Basis for a Rational World.* Touchstone Book, Simon & Schuster, New York, 1992.

———. *Superforce: The Search for a Grand Unified Theory of Nature.* Touchstone Book, New York, 1984.

———. *God and the New Physics.* Touchstone Book, New York, 1983.

Dea, J. Space, Time & Matter: Modern View Vs the Secret Doctrine. *Symposium on H. P. Blavatsky's Secret Doctrine.* Wizards Bookshelf, San Diego, 1981.

D'Espagnat, B. The Quantum Theory and Reality. Scientific American.

DeWitt, B. Quantum Gravity. *Scientific American*. December 1983.

Dicus et. al., The Future of the Universe. *Scientific American*, 1983.

Feynman, R. *QED: The Strange Theory of Light and Matter.* Princeton University Press, Princeton, New Jersey, 1985.

Freedman, D., van Nieuwenhuizen, P. The Hidden Dimensions of Spacetime. *Scientific American*, March 1985.

Genz, H. *Nothingness: The science of empty space.* Perseus Books, Reading, Massachusetts, 1994.

Gleidman, J. *Science Digest.* 1983.

Greene, B. *The Elegant Universe: Superstrings, hidden dimensions, and the quest for the ultimate theory.* Norton & Co., New York, 1999.

Grof, S. *The Holotropic Mind; The three levels of human consciousness and how they shape our lives.* Harper, San Francisco, 1993.

Haisch, B. *The God Theory: Universes, zero-point fields, and what's behind it all.* Red Wheel/Weiser, San Francisco, 2006.

Hall, M. *The Secret Teachings of All Ages: An encyclopedic outline of Masonic, Hermetic, Quabbalistic and Rosicrucian Symbolical Philosophy.* Philosophical Research Society, Los Angeles, 1978.

Hawking, S. *The Universe in a Nutshell.* Bantam Books, Toronto, 2001.

———. *A Brief History of Time.* Bantam Press, New York, 1988.

———. In Weber, R. *Dialogues with Scientists and Sages.* Routledge & Kegan Paul, New York, 1986.

Herbert, H. *Quantum Reality: Beyond the New Physics.* Anchor Books, New York, 1987.

Holmes, C. *Within-Without from Zero Points*: Book I: *The Heart Doctrine: Mystical views of the origin and nature of human consciousness.* Zero Point, Kemptville, Ontario, 2010.

———. *Within-Without from Zero Points*: Book II: *Microcosm-Macrocosm: Mystical Views on the origin of the universe, the nature of matter & human consciousness.* Zero Point Publications, Kemptville, Ontario, 2010.

Horgan, J. *The Undiscovered Mind: How the human brain defies replication, medication, and explanation.* Touchstone Books, New York, 1999.

———. Can Science explain Consciousness? *Scientific American.* July 1994.

Huxley, A. *The Doors of Perception.* Harper & Row, New York, 1954.

Jastrow, R. *Genesis Revealed.* Science Digest, Winter 1979/ Summer 1980.

———. *God and the Astronomers.* Warner Books, New York, 1978.

———. *Until the Sun Dies.* Warner Books, New York, 1977.

Jastrow, R. *Genesis Revealed.* Science Digest, Winter 1979/ Summer 1980.

———. *God and the Astronomers.* Warner Books, New York, 1978.

———. *Until the Sun Dies.* Warner Books, New York, 1977.

Jones, B. *The opposite of gravity is hate.* bjon@ix.netcom.com. 1996.

Kaku, M. *Beyond Einstein: The cosmic quest for the theory of the universe.* Bantam Doubleday Deli Publishing, New York, 1987.

———. *Hyperspace: A scientific odyssey through parallel universes, time warps, and the 10th dimension.* Oxford University Press, New York, 1994.

———. *Astronomy,* May 1996.

Kleczek, J., Jakes, P. *The Universe and Planet Earth*. Octopus Books, London, Great Britain, 1985.

Kramer, C. *Anatomy of the Soul*. Breslov Research Institute, Jerusalem, 1998.

Krauss, L. Cosmological Antigravity. *Scientific American*. January 1999.

Laszlo, E. Science and the Reenchantment of the Cosmos. Inner Traditions, Rochester, Vermont, 2006.

———. *Science and the Akashic Field: An Integral Theory of Everything*. Inner Traditions, Rochester, Vermont, 2007.

Leet, L. *The Secret Doctrine of the Kabbalah: Recovering the key to Hebraic Sacred Science*. Inner Traditions, Rochester, Vermont. 1999.

Lederman, L. *The God Particle: If the Universe is the Answer, what is the Question?* Houghton Mifflin Co., New York, 1993.

Leith, *Scientific American*, 1976.

Lloyd, S., NG, Y. Black Hole Computers. *Scientific American*, November 2004.

MacGregor, M. *The Power of Alpha*, World Scientific, 2007.

MacLaine, S. *Going Within*. Random House, New York, 1989.

Maldacena, J. The Illusion of Gravity. *Scientific American*, November 2005.

Mann, C., www.137.com, 2001.

McTaggart, L. *The Field: The quest for the secret force of the universe*. Harper/Collins, New York, 2002.

Morris, R. *The Nature of Reality*. McGraw-Hill Book Co., New York, 1987.

Origins: Higher Dimensions in Science. Bhaktivedanta Book Trust, Los Angeles, 1985.

Ostriker, J., Steinhardt, P. Quintessential Universe. *Scientific American*, January 2001.

Overbye. D. The Universe according to Guth, *Science Digest*. June 1983.

Pagels, H. *The Cosmic Code: Quantum Physics as the Language of Nature*. Bantam, New York, 1985a.

———. *Perfect Symmetry: The Search of the Beginning of Time*. Simon and Schuster, New York, 1985b.

Pearsall, P. *The Heart's Code: Tapping the Wisdom and Power of Our Heart Energy*. Broadway Books, New York, 1998.

Peat, D. *Syncronicity: The bridge between matter and mind*. Bantam Books, Toronto, 1987.

———. & D. Bohm. *Science, Order, and Creativity.* Bantam Books, Toronto, 1987.

Pribram, K. *Languages of the Brain.* Prentice-Hall, New Jersey, 1971.

———. *Psychology Today.* Interview, February 1979.

———. What the Fuss is all About. In. K. Wilber (ed.) *The Holographic Paradigm and other Paradoxes.* Shambahala, Boulder, 1982.

———. Holographic Brain. In *The Omni Interviews.* Ed. P. Weintraub,Ticknor & Fields, New York, 1982.

Roth, G. *The Quest to find Consciousness.* Scientific American, Special Edition, MIND. 2004.

Sagan, C. *Billions and Billions: Thoughts on life and death at the brink of the millennium.* Random House, New York, 1997.

———. *The Demon-Haunted World. Science as a candle in the Dark.* Random House, 1995.

———. *Cosmos.* Random House, New York, 1980.

———. *Broca's Brain: Reflections on the Romance of Science.* Random House, 1979.

———. *The Dragons of Eden: Speculations on the Evolution of Human Intelligence.* Random House, New York, 1977.

Sagan, C., Druyan, A. *Shadows of Forgotten Ancestors: A Search for who we are.* Random House, New York, 1992.

Shinmoy, A. The Reality of the Quantum World. *Scientific American,* January 1988.

Smolin, L. *Three Roads to Quantum Gravity.* Basic Books, Perseus, Great Britian, 2001.

———. *The Life of the Cosmos.* Oxford University Press, New York, 1997.

Strauss. Before the Bang. *Globe and Mail,* Toronto, January 21, 1985.

Susskind, L. *The Black Hole War: My battle with Stephen Hawking to make the world safe for quantum mechanics.* Little, Brown &Co., New York, 2008.

———. *The Cosmic Landscape: String theory and the illusion of intelligent design.* Back Bay Books, Little, Brown & Co., New York, 2006.

Talbot, M. *The Holographic Universe.* Harper Perennial, New York, 1991.

———. *Beyond the Quantum.* Bantam Books, New York, 1987.

———. *Mysticism and the New Physics.* Bantam, New York, 1981.

Trefil, J. *The Moment of Creation.* Collier Books, New York, 1983.

Tryon, E. In Strauss. Before the Big Bang. *Globe and Mail*. Toronto, January 21,1985.

Weber, R. *Dialogues with Scientists and Sages: The Search of Unity*. Routledge, Kegan & Paul, London, 1986.

Weinberg, S. *The First Three Minutes: A Modern View of the Origin of the Universe*. Bantam Books, New York, 1979.

Wertheim, M. *Pythagoras' Trousers: God, Physics, and the Gender Wars*. Norton & Co., New York,1997.

Wilber, K.(Ed.) *The Holographic Paradigm and other Paradoxes*. Shambhala, Boulder, 1982.

Wilkenson, D. In Mulvey, J. (Ed). *The Nature of Matter*. Oxford University Press, New York, 1981.

Www.calphysics.org

Yam, P. Exploiting Zero-Point Energy. *Scientific American*, December 1997.

Zero Point Publications

Box 700, Kemptville, Ontario, Canada K0G-1J0

WITHIN-WITHOUT from ZERO POINTS

I

THE HEART DOCTRINE

Mystical Views of the Origin
and Nature of Human Consciousness

Christopher P. Holmes

"... "material points without extension" are Leibnitz's monads, and at the same time the materials out of which the 'Gods' and other invisible powers clothe themselves in bodies ...."   H.P. Blavatsky, The Secret Doctrine, 1888

The Heart Doctrine explores the mysteries of human consciousness, the spiritual nature of the heart, and the question of the existence of an 'I' within the individual—a divine spark, a Monad, a jivatma, a quantum self or 'God spark!'

Modern psychology and science have been dominated by "the head doctrine"—the assumption that the material brain produces consciousness and that a human being does not have a true 'I,' except as an illusory by-product of neural events in the cerebral cortex. In contrast, mystics claim that the origins of consciousness and Self are related to the physical and spiritual dimensions of the Heart. A human being is ensouled through the heart. Further, consciousness and vitality are related to oxygenation and blood flow within the material body and to the subtle anatomy of the chakras. Mystical experiences involve penetrating veils of nature which allow for the awakening of consciousness and the Heart, the realization of higher Space dimensions and experiences of the unity of things with the inner life. We are individual "eyes" or "I"s of "THAT," the unity within which we live, move and have our being. Most importantly, human beings have a zero point centre and this is the means by which higher dimensional influences bring life and consciousness into the living being. There is a higher dimensional physics and metaphysics to the human heart and to the issues of consciousness.

"My mission is to help uncover the forgotten, deep heart teachings of Jesus.... The information you have gathered on the zero point has been a powerful validation of my own inner meditation practice and intuitions. Hence it has greatly enhanced my faith and the effectiveness of my meditation. Thank you so very much for your labors."
John Francis, The Mystic Way of Radiant Love: Alchemy for a New Creation. 1998

"... if Christopher Holmes' articulation of 'the heart doctrine' had been restricted to citing and commenting upon those awe-inspiring teachings, he would have accomplished a great deal by establishing the foundation of an alternative paradigm to that which dominates contemporary approaches to the study of consciousness. However, when he introduces the mysterious concept of "the zero point," his arguments take on a level of significance which is, in my opinion, unparalleled in modern consciousness research...." James A. Moffatt

ISBN 978-0-9689435-0-2 (0-9689435-0-0) $24.95

WITHIN-WITHOUT from ZERO POINTS

Book I I

MICROCOSM-MACROCOSM

Scientific and Mystical Views on the Origin of the Universe, the Nature of Matter & Human Consciousness

"... "material points without extension" are Leibnitz's monads, and at the same time the materials out of which the 'Gods' and other invisible powers clothe themselves in bodies. ... the entire universe concentrating itself, as it were, in a single point."

H. P. Blavatsky, *The Secret Doctrine, Cosmogenesis, 1888*

"... all the so-called Forces of Nature, Electricity, Magnetism, light, heat, etc., are in esse, i.e., in their ultimate constitution, the differentiated aspects of that Universal Motion. ... for formative or creative purposes, the Great Law modifies its perpetual motion on seven invisible points within the area of the manifest Universe."

H. P. Blavatsky, *The Secret Doctrine, 1888*

"It is necessary to notice that in the Great Universe all phenomena in general, without exception wherever they arise and manifest, are simply successively law-conformable 'Fractions' of some whole phenomenon which has its prime arising on the Most Holy Sun Absolute."

G. I. Gurdjieff, 1950

Microcosm-Macrocosm explores the newest theories in physics and creation science–including materials on superstrings, higher dimensions, singularities, the quantum vacuum and the holographic principle in science and in the psychology of consciousness. It draws from ancient metaphysics—particularly *The Secret Doctrine* of H.P. Blavatsky (1888), esoteric Judaism and Kabbalah, and the cosmology and metaphysics of G.I. Gurdjieff. This is a challenging and provocative work with deep insights into the Divine Mystery teachings and a unique critique of modern science philosophy. It provides a shocking alternative view of the zero point origins of human consciousness and cosmos.

ISBN 978-0-9689435-1-9 (0-9689435-1-9) $30

UPCOMING...
WITHIN-WITHOUT from ZERO POINTS

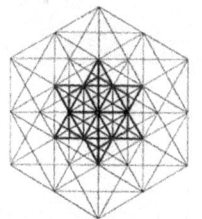

Book I I I
TRIUNE MONADS IN SEVEN DIMENSIONAL HYPERSPACE

Scientific and Mystical Studies of the
Multi-Dimensional Nature of Human Existence

Monads draws from the teachings of Madame Blavatsky, Kabbalah and Judaism, Gurdjieff and a wide range of mystical doctrine about the multidimensional nature of human existence. Esoteric teachings identify the abode of the 'I' as within the human heart, where a triune Monad element is established within a Seven Dimensional Eternal Parent Space which underlies and sustains our normal physical four-dimensional space-time complex. Such ideas from mystical sources bear profound relationships to theories in advanced physics as to the nature of Space itself, quantum interconnectedness and higher dimensional superstring elements at zero point levels. A triune and sevenfold Monadic Essence spins a Web of Spirit, Soul and Matter within a Seven Dimensional Virtual Reality out of the Aethers of the void and plenum, the quantum vacuum. In order to illustrate the necessity for such an alternative understanding of reality, this work examines evidences for out-of-body experiences, Sheldrake's fields of extended mind, enigmas posed by heart transplant patients and twin studies and an interpretation of other paranormal investigations.

Book I V
A FOOL AT THE ZERO POINT

An *Autobiographic* Tale about the Strange Case of Professor Z, the
Mysteries of Love and Ecstasies of the Heart & the Horror of It All

Christopher, by the grace of God, will provide an autobiographical account of his life experiences, his psychical and mystical experiences, his life struggles and relationships, and an account of awakening to the horror of it all. This work includes materials on Christopher's struggles for academic freedom at York University, his twelve years of work in correctional centres as a forensic psychologist, his life and loves, and his awakening to psychopathology of the world elites with their plans for committing genocide against the human race.

ZERO POINT TEACHINGS

Selected Articles and Writings
of Mystical Psychologist & Scientist

Christopher P. Holmes, Ph.D.

The zero point teachings are a portal of some sort to awaken you to a higher dimensional model of yourself and the structure of reality—to view the world in a magical and mystical way. The basic idea is that all living beings, including yourself, have a zero point centre within and this is the means by which *"the Gods and other invisible powers clothe themselves in bodies"*—as explained by mystic scholar Madame Blavatsky in *The Secret Doctrine* (1888). Just as the scientists conceive that the huge universe grew from an infinitesimal singularity out of the quantum vacuum, so also, I suggest that you also have such a hidden zero point or singularity source condition--a singular I within the Heart. Further, we ourselves emerge *"out of nothingness"* in some mysterious way unknown to modern science and contemporary understanding.

This selection of articles and writings is drawn from the *www.zeropoint.ca* web site and from Christopher's varied books, and includes original socio-political writings posted to the zero point website, but then withdrawn. This book includes materials on the origin and nature of human consciousness, the mystery teachings of the heart doctrine, Kabbalah and *The Secret Doctrine*, modern physics and quantum theory, a commentary on the psychopathology of humanity based on the teachings of G. I. Gurdjieff, book, movie and music critiques, and much more. It provides an overview of the mysteries of consciousness and the heart, and a view of the psychopathology of humankind upon planet earth.

ISBN 978-0-9689435-7-1 $30

PSYCHOLOGICAL ILLUSIONS

Explorations of the Gurdjieff
Fourth Way Teaching

Christopher P. Holmes, Ph.D.

The central illusion of humankind is that we *"know self."* The components of this illusion concern the different powers or capabilities which men and women think that they possess but which in reality they do not. Four primary illusions or misunderstandings concern the human faculties of consciousness, the unity of I, the possession of will (or the capacity to do) and the existence of the soul. The fourth way psychology begins with a study of humans as they are under the conditions of mechanical life and then describes the psychology of man's *possible evolution*. Humans can awaken and experience new states of consciousness, attain a unity of "I" and real will, and thus attain the soul. Unfortunately, wrong ideas and convictions about the nature of consciousness, unity, will and the soul are major obstacles to self knowledge. If we can begin to understand these illusions, then there is a chance of escape, of awakening and evolution.

According to Beelzebub, the central character in Gurdjieff's *Tales*, the three-brained beings on planet Earth are microcosmoses or *"similitudes of the Whole."* As such, they have the possibility of not only serving local cosmic purposes, feeding the earth and moon as part of organic life on earth, but also of experiencing sacred being-impulses—attaining varied levels of objective reason and individuality and even of *"blending again with the infinite."* (1950) As a microcosm of the macrocosm, a human being can potentially coat higher being-bodies for the life of the soul, instinctually sense cosmic truths and phenomena, and maintain existence within the subtle realms of being after death–achieving different levels of immortality. Unfortunately, humankind came to exist only in waking sleep states of automated consciousness, perceiving reality topsy-turvy, conditioned by pleasure and self love, and wasteful of their sacred sexual substances. Human beings no longer realize their deeper cosmic purposes and possibilities, or attain real "I."

Psychological Illusions explores the psychology, metaphysics and cosmology of the fourth way teaching. This includes material on the *Ray of Creation*, the fundamental cosmic laws, the alchemical crystallization of *higher being-bodies* for the life of the soul, and the miraculous possibilities existing for the evolution of the individual human being. The Gurdjieff fourth way teaching is a profound and coherent system of esoteric teaching about the horror of the situation for humanity asleep living under their psychological illusions.

ISBN 978-0-9689435-2-6 $30

"The Slugs"

On G. I. Gurdjieff's
Beelzebub's Tales to his Grandson

Christopher P. Holmes, Ph.D.

"This Most Great Foundation of the All-embracing of everything that exists constantly emanates throughout the whole of the Universe and coats itself from its particles upon planets–in certain three-brained beings who attain in their common presences the capacity to have their own functioning of both fundamental cosmic laws of the sacred Heptaparaparshinokh and the sacred Triamazikamno—into a definite unit in which alone 'Objective Divine Reason' acquires the possibility of becoming concentrated and fixed."—Beelzebub recounting the teachings of Lord Buddha (Gurdjieff, 1950, pp. 244-5)

Beelzebub's Tales to His Grandson is undoubtedly one of the most profound and mysterious books among the sacred literature of the world. The framework of ideas, claims and objective science offers a fundamentally alternative view of the miraculous nature of life–a perfectly coherent, intelligible and astounding account of "All and Everything." In the light of *The Tales*, all of modern thought and understanding is so much 'pouring-from-the-empty-into-the-void.' The 'sorry scientists' of 'new format' have no conception of the great inscrutable mysteries of Nature and the subtle inner dimensions of human beings. *Beelzebub's Tales* is a work not only of myth, allegory and fantasy, but also about the secrets of 'objective science' and the psychology of the soul.

Human beings are potentially similitudes of the whole–particles of the Great Universe. In this way, everything is some Divine Fraction-a law conformable portion of the whole. Behind essence is real I, behind real I is God, or at least the Most Most Holy Sun Absolute. Beelzebub provides strange and provocative tales for his grandson Hassein, about the hidden dimensions of those strange three-brained beings on planet Earth, the principles of esoteric science and the meaning and purpose of it all—for living, breathing creatures who might attain a "real I."

Zero Point Radio

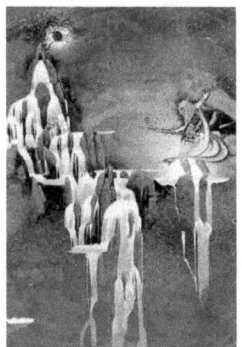

Live two-hour Internet Radio Broadcasts

every second Saturday

In North America: 4 to 6 p.m. Eastern Time, Every Second Saturday
1 to 3 p.m. Pacific, 10-12 pm GMT

Dr. Christopher P. Holmes hosts an online internet Radio Broadcast through www.bbsradio.com. Previous broadcasts are available for online listening at the Zero Point archive service. These include shows on the zero point hypotheses, the magical formula of 137, on consciousness and the heart doctrine, the metaphysics of *H. P. Blavatsky's The Secret Doctrine*, the insanity of humankind and the criminality of the elites. James A Moffatt serves as commentator and interviewer, with invited guests. Shows archived at www.bbsradio.com.

www.ingramcontent.com/pod-product-compliance
Lightning Source LLC
Chambersburg PA
CBHW071651160426
43195CB00012B/1426